EVERAFTER

THE PANDORA PROTOCOL

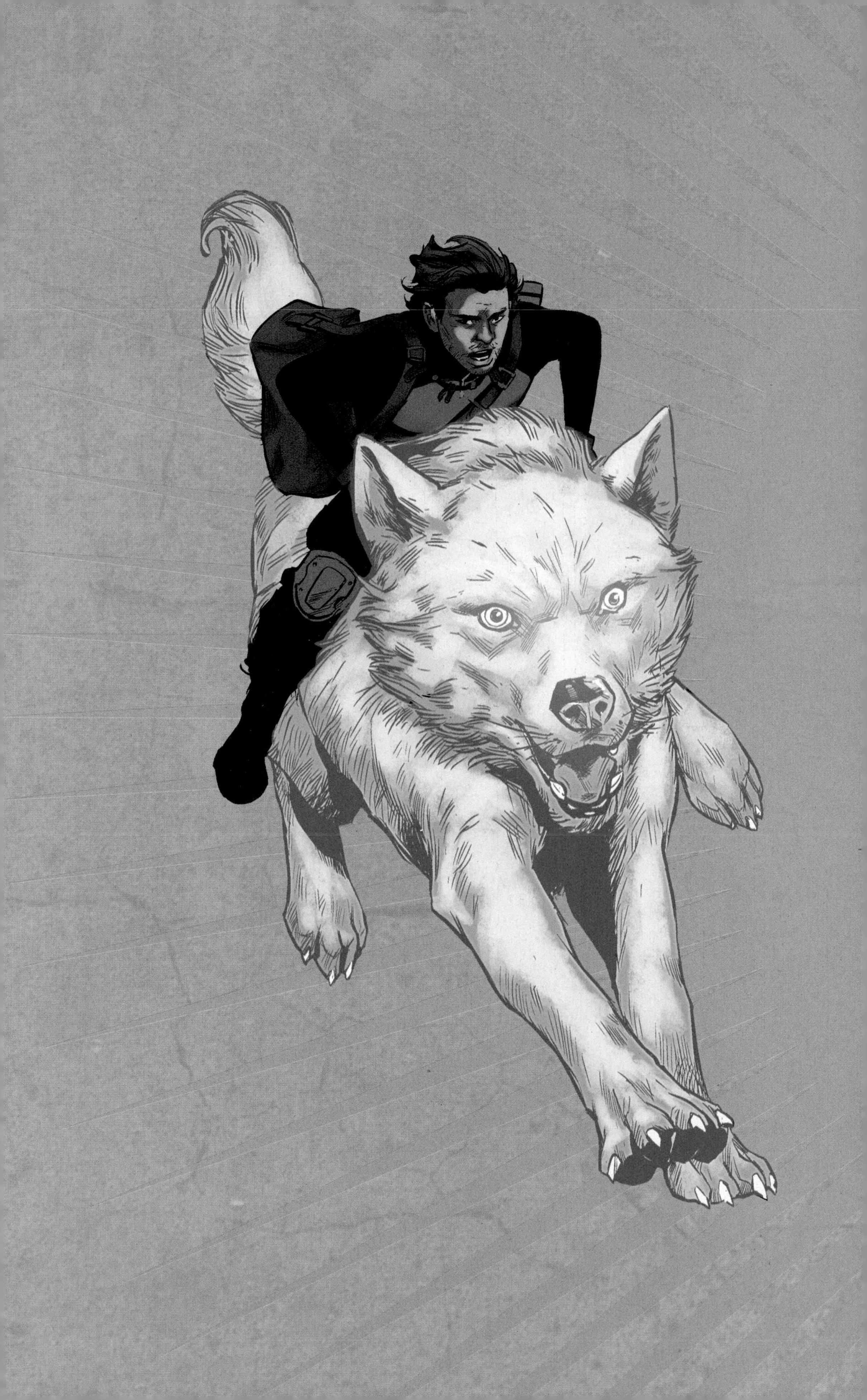

EVERAFTER

THE PANDORA PROTOCOL

DAVE JUSTUS & LILAH STURGES
writers

TRAVIS MOORE
artist (issues #1-5)

STEVE ROLSTON
penciller (issue #6)

ANDE PARKS
inker (issue #6)

MICHAEL WIGGAM
colorist

TODD KLEIN
letterer

cover art and original series covers
TULA LOTAY

FABLES created by
BILL WILLINGHAM

ROWENA YOW ELLIE PYLE Editors – Original Series
MAGGIE HOWELL Assistant Editor – Original Series
JAMIE S. RICH Group Editor – Vertigo Comics
JEB WOODARD Group Editor – Collected Editions
SCOTT NYBAKKEN Editor – Collected Edition
STEVE COOK Design Director – Books
DAMIAN RYLAND Publication Design

DIANE NELSON President
DAN DiDIO Publisher
JIM LEE Publisher
GEOFF JOHNS President & Chief Creative Officer
AMIT DESAI Executive VP – Business & Marketing Strategy, Direct to Consumer & Global Franchise Management
SAM ADES Senior VP – Direct to Consumer
BOBBIE CHASE VP – Talent Development
MARK CHIARELLO Senior VP – Art, Design & Collected Editions
JOHN CUNNINGHAM Senior VP – Sales & Trade Marketing
ANNE DePIES Senior VP – Business Strategy, Finance & Administration
DON FALLETTI VP – Manufacturing Operations
LAWRENCE GANEM VP – Editorial Administration & Talent Relations
ALISON GILL Senior VP – Manufacturing & Operations
HANK KANALZ Senior VP – Editorial Strategy & Administration
JAY KOGAN VP – Legal Affairs
THOMAS LOFTUS VP – Business Affairs
JACK MAHAN VP – Business Affairs
NICK J. NAPOLITANO VP – Manufacturing Administration
EDDIE SCANNELL VP – Consumer Marketing
COURTNEY SIMMONS Senior VP – Publicity & Communications
JIM (SKI) SOKOLOWSKI VP – Comic Book Specialty Sales & Trade Marketing
NANCY SPEARS VP – Mass, Book, Digital Sales & Trade Marketing

EVERAFTER: THE PANDORA PROTOCOL

DC Comics 2900 West Alameda Avenue, Burbank, CA 91505
Printed in Canada. First printing. ISBN: 978-1-4012-6836-7

Library of Congress Cataloging-in-Publication data is available.

PEFC Certified
This product is from sustainably managed forests, recycled and controlled sources
PEFC
PEFC/26-31-02
www.pefc.org

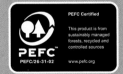

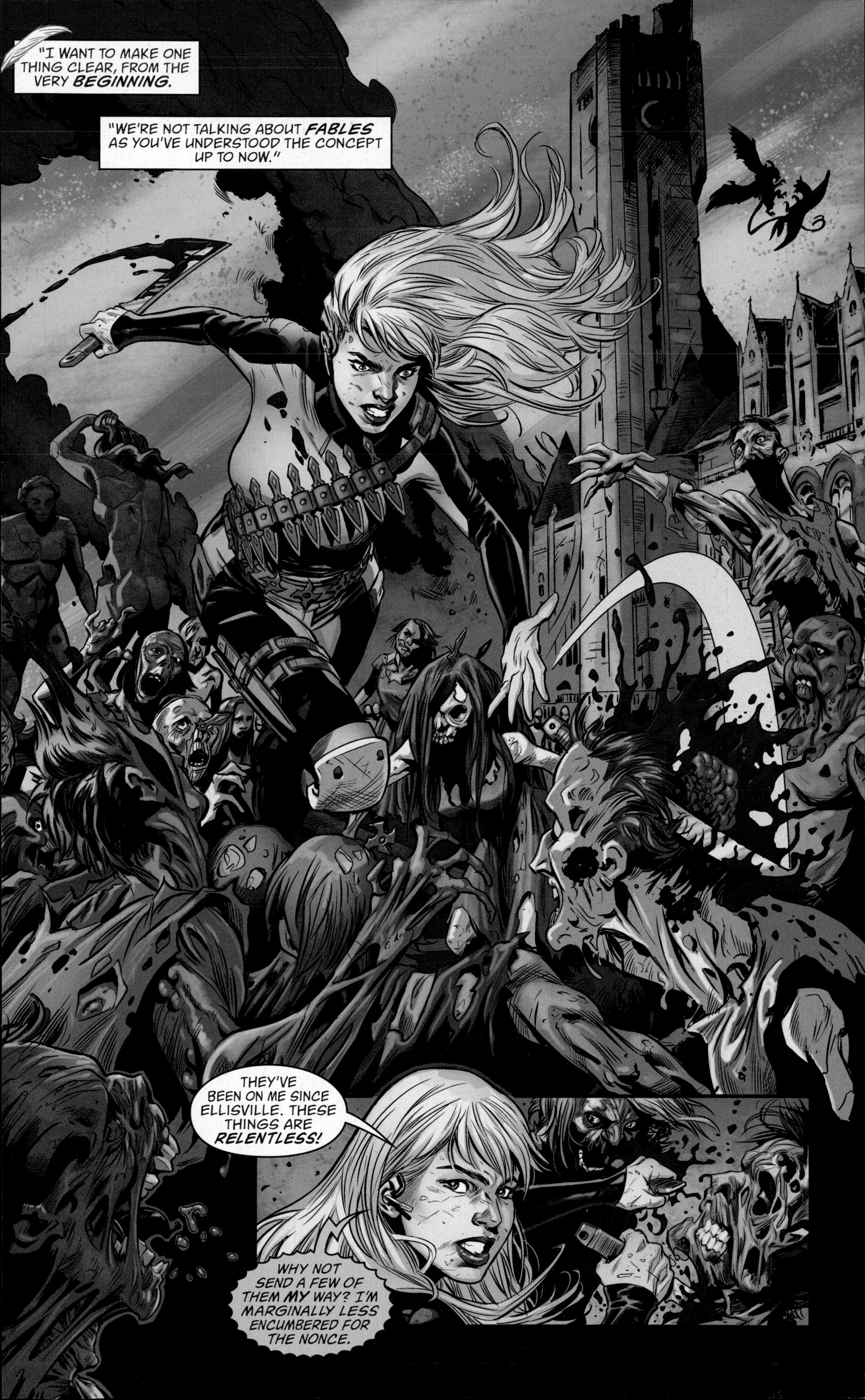
"I WANT TO MAKE ONE THING CLEAR, FROM THE VERY BEGINNING.
"WE'RE NOT TALKING ABOUT FABLES AS YOU'VE UNDERSTOOD THE CONCEPT UP TO NOW."
THEY'VE BEEN ON ME SINCE ELLISVILLE. THESE THINGS ARE RELENTLESS!
WHY NOT SEND A FEW OF THEM MY WAY? I'M MARGINALLY LESS ENCUMBERED FOR THE NONCE.

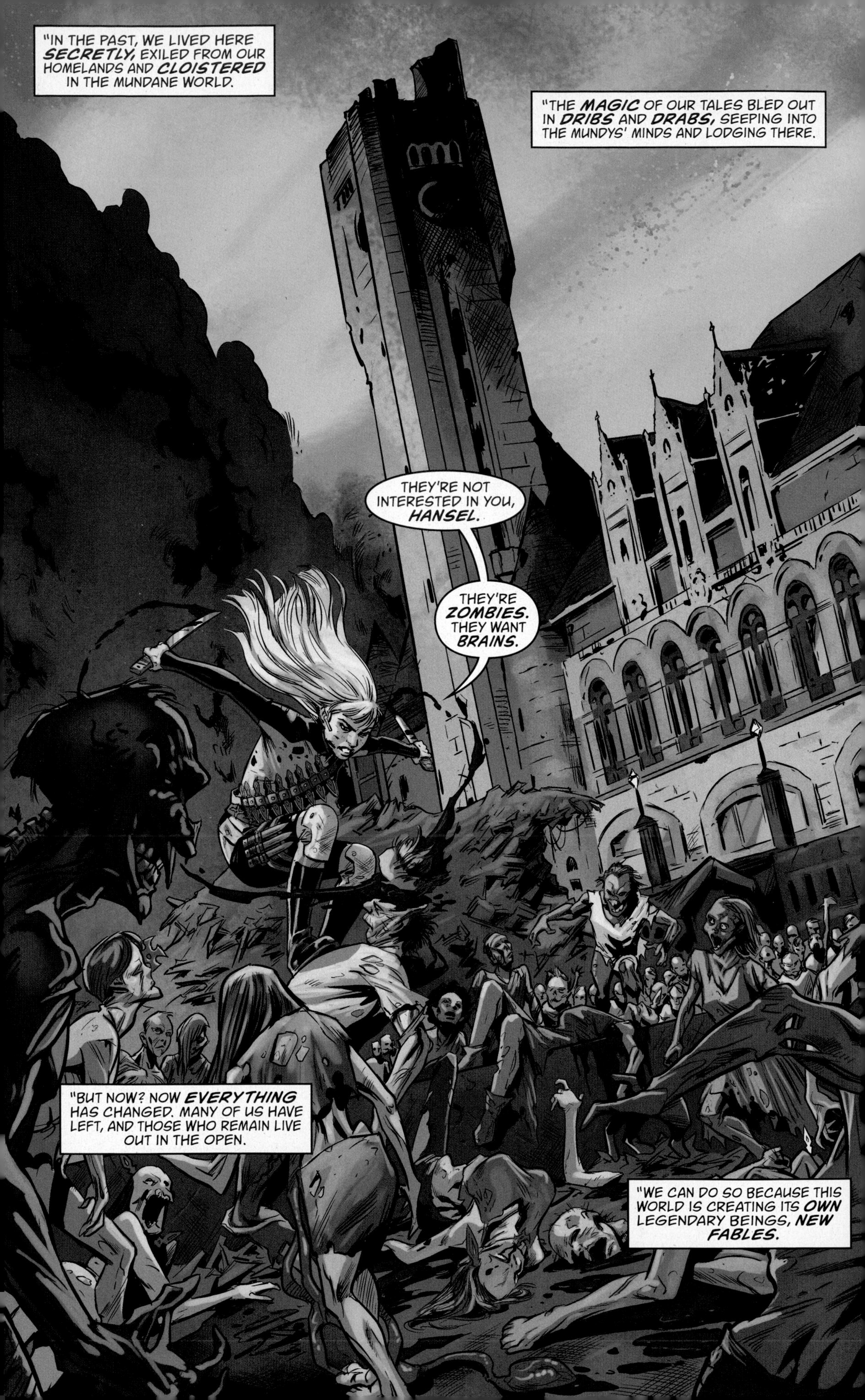
"IN THE PAST, WE LIVED HERE SECRETLY, EXILED FROM OUR HOMELANDS AND CLOISTERED IN THE MUNDANE WORLD.
"THE MAGIC OF OUR TALES BLED OUT IN DRIBS AND DRABS, SEEPING INTO THE MUNDYS' MINDS AND LODGING THERE.
THEY'RE NOT INTERESTED IN YOU, HANSEL.
THEY'RE ZOMBIES. THEY WANT BRAINS.
"BUT NOW? NOW EVERYTHING HAS CHANGED. MANY OF US HAVE LEFT, AND THOSE WHO REMAIN LIVE OUT IN THE OPEN.
"WE CAN DO SO BECAUSE THIS WORLD IS CREATING ITS OWN LEGENDARY BEINGS, NEW FABLES.

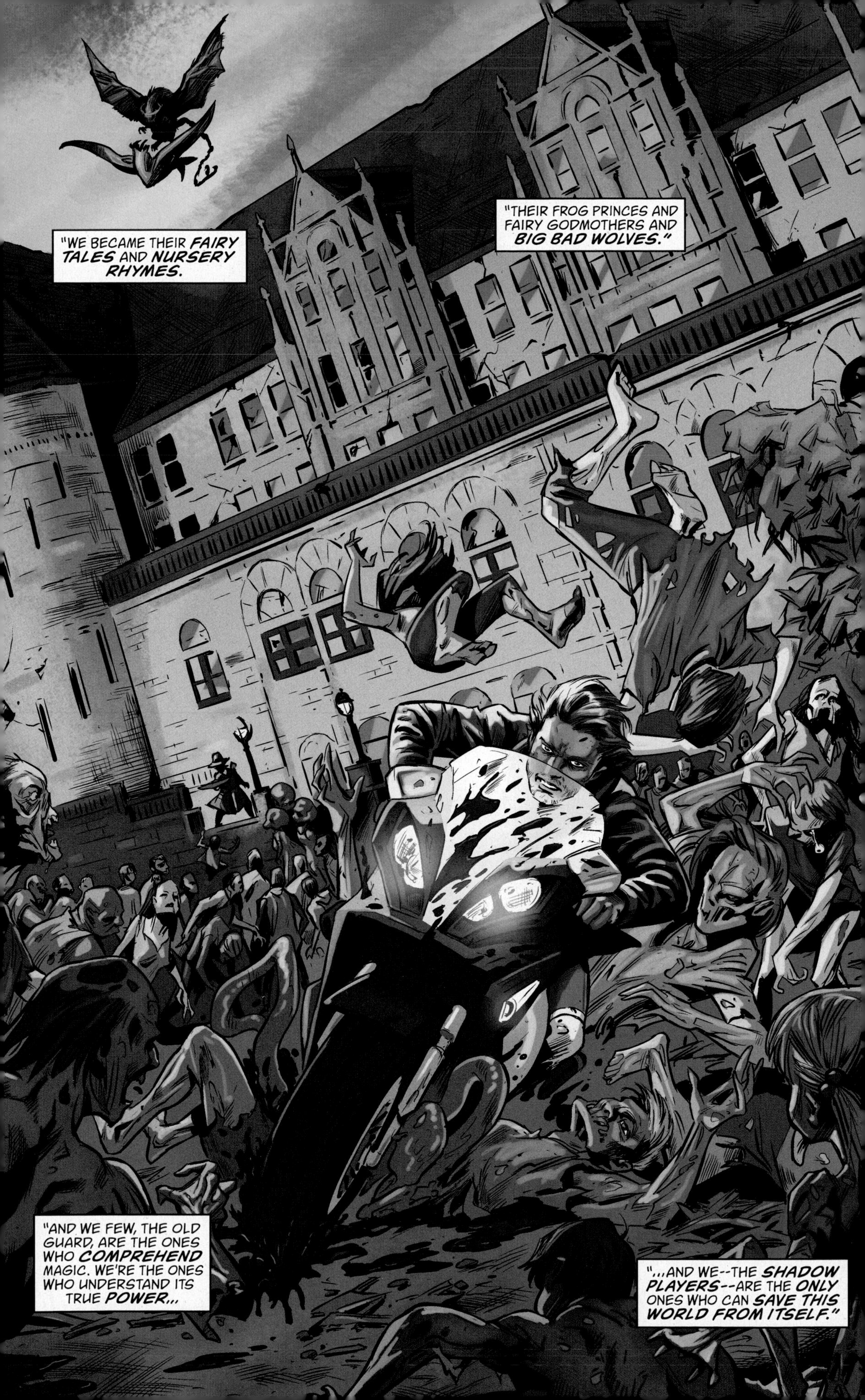
"WE BECAME THEIR FAIRY TALES AND NURSERY RHYMES.
"THEIR FROG PRINCES AND FAIRY GODMOTHERS AND BIG BAD WOLVES."
"AND WE FEW, THE OLD GUARD, ARE THE ONES WHO COMPREHEND MAGIC. WE'RE THE ONES WHO UNDERSTAND ITS TRUE POWER...
"...AND WE--THE SHADOW PLAYERS--ARE THE ONLY ONES WHO CAN SAVE THIS WORLD FROM ITSELF."

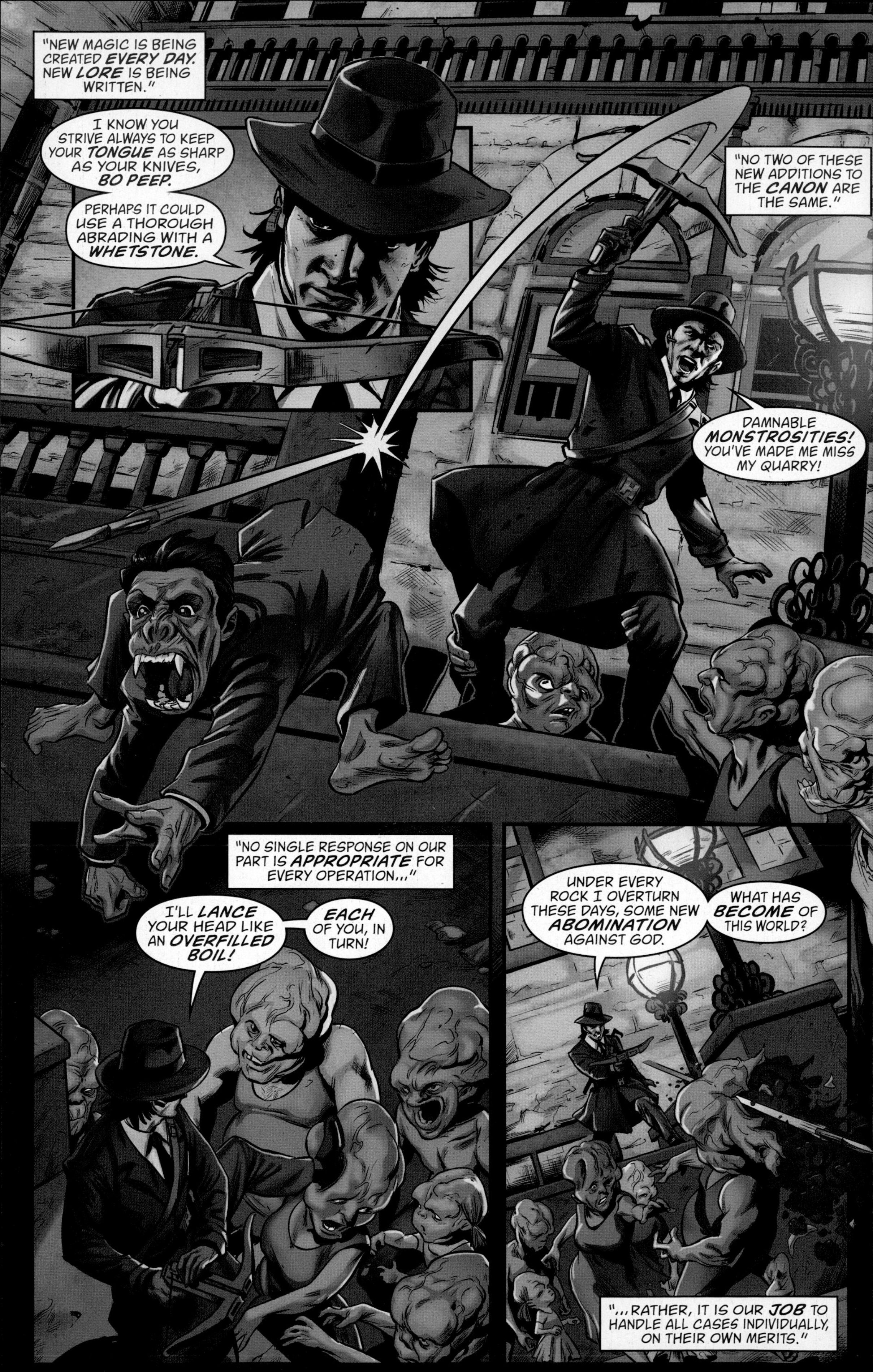
"NEW MAGIC IS BEING CREATED EVERY DAY. NEW LORE IS BEING WRITTEN."
I KNOW YOU STRIVE ALWAYS TO KEEP YOUR TONGUE AS SHARP AS YOUR KNIVES, BO PEEP.
PERHAPS IT COULD USE A THOROUGH ABRADING WITH A WHETSTONE.
"NO TWO OF THESE NEW ADDITIONS TO THE CANON ARE THE SAME."
DAMNABLE MONSTROSITIES! YOU'VE MADE ME MISS MY QUARRY!
"NO SINGLE RESPONSE ON OUR PART IS APPROPRIATE FOR EVERY OPERATION..."
I'LL LANCE YOUR HEAD LIKE AN OVERFILLED BOIL!
EACH OF YOU, IN TURN!
UNDER EVERY ROCK I OVERTURN THESE DAYS, SOME NEW ABOMINATION AGAINST GOD.
WHAT HAS BECOME OF THIS WORLD?
"...RATHER, IT IS OUR JOB TO HANDLE ALL CASES INDIVIDUALLY, ON THEIR OWN MERITS."

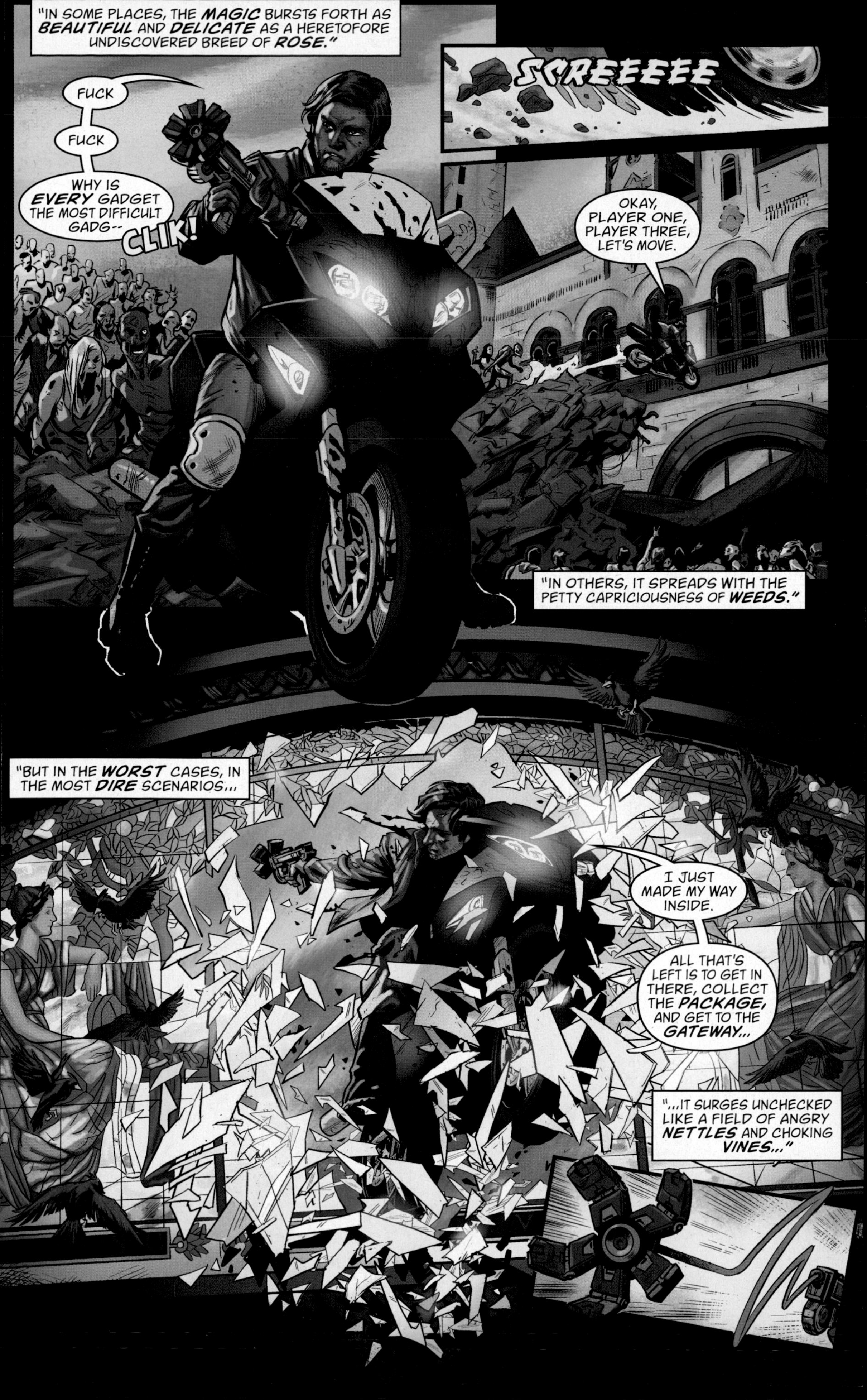
"IN SOME PLACES, THE MAGIC BURSTS FORTH AS BEAUTIFUL AND DELICATE AS A HERETOFORE UNDISCOVERED BREED OF ROSE."
FUCK
FUCK
WHY IS EVERY GADGET THE MOST DIFFICULT GADG--
CLIK!
SCREEEEEE
OKAY, PLAYER ONE, PLAYER THREE, LET'S MOVE.
"IN OTHERS, IT SPREADS WITH THE PETTY CAPRICIOUSNESS OF WEEDS."
"BUT IN THE WORST CASES, IN THE MOST DIRE SCENARIOS...
I JUST MADE MY WAY INSIDE.
ALL THAT'S LEFT IS TO GET IN THERE, COLLECT THE PACKAGE, AND GET TO THE GATEWAY...
"...IT SURGES UNCHECKED LIKE A FIELD OF ANGRY NETTLES AND CHOKING VINES..."

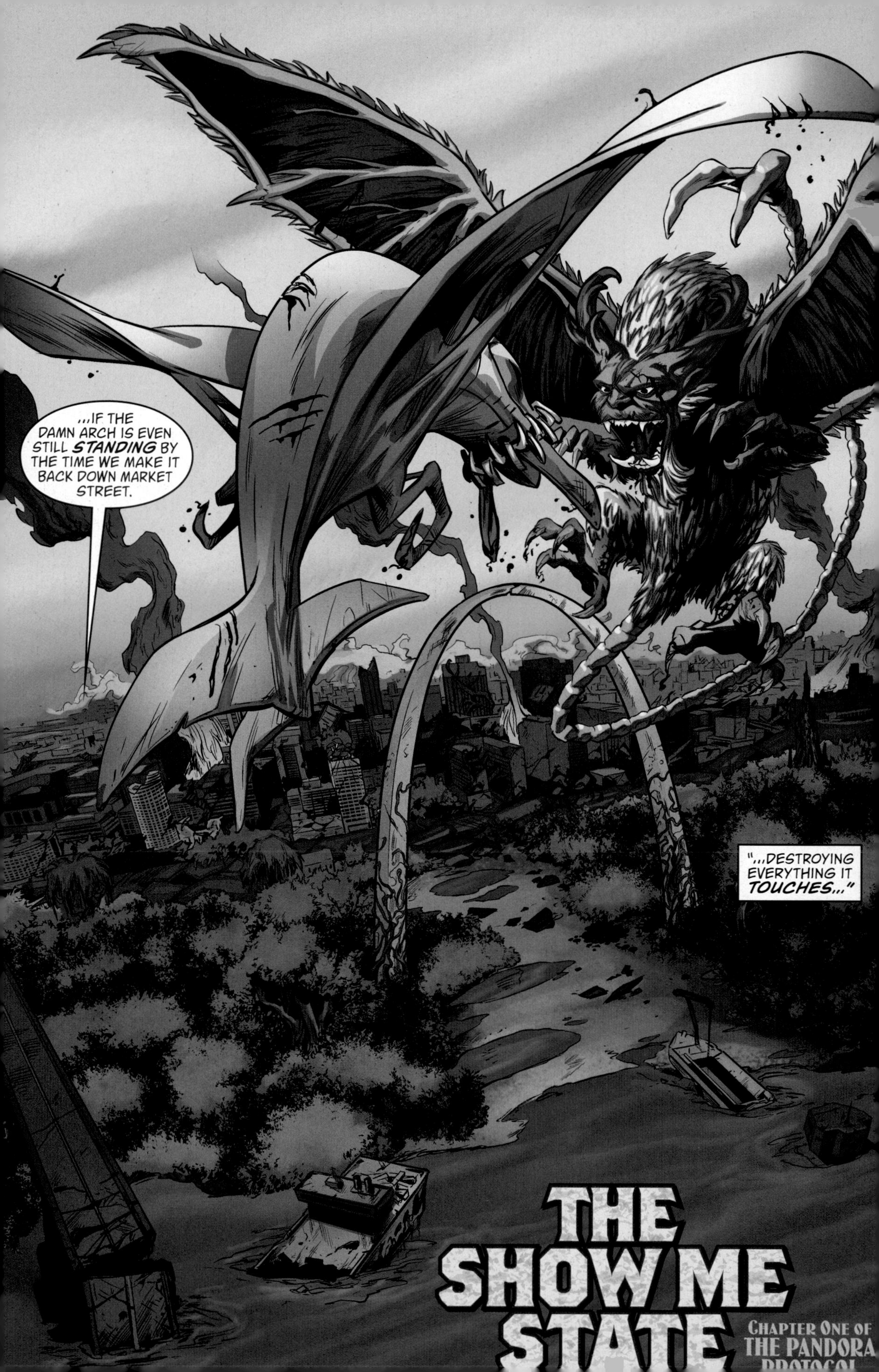
...IF THE DAMN ARCH IS EVEN STILL STANDING BY THE TIME WE MAKE IT BACK DOWN MARKET STREET.
"...DESTROYING EVERYTHING IT TOUCHES..."
THE SHOW ME STATE
CHAPTER ONE OF THE PANDORA PROTOCOL

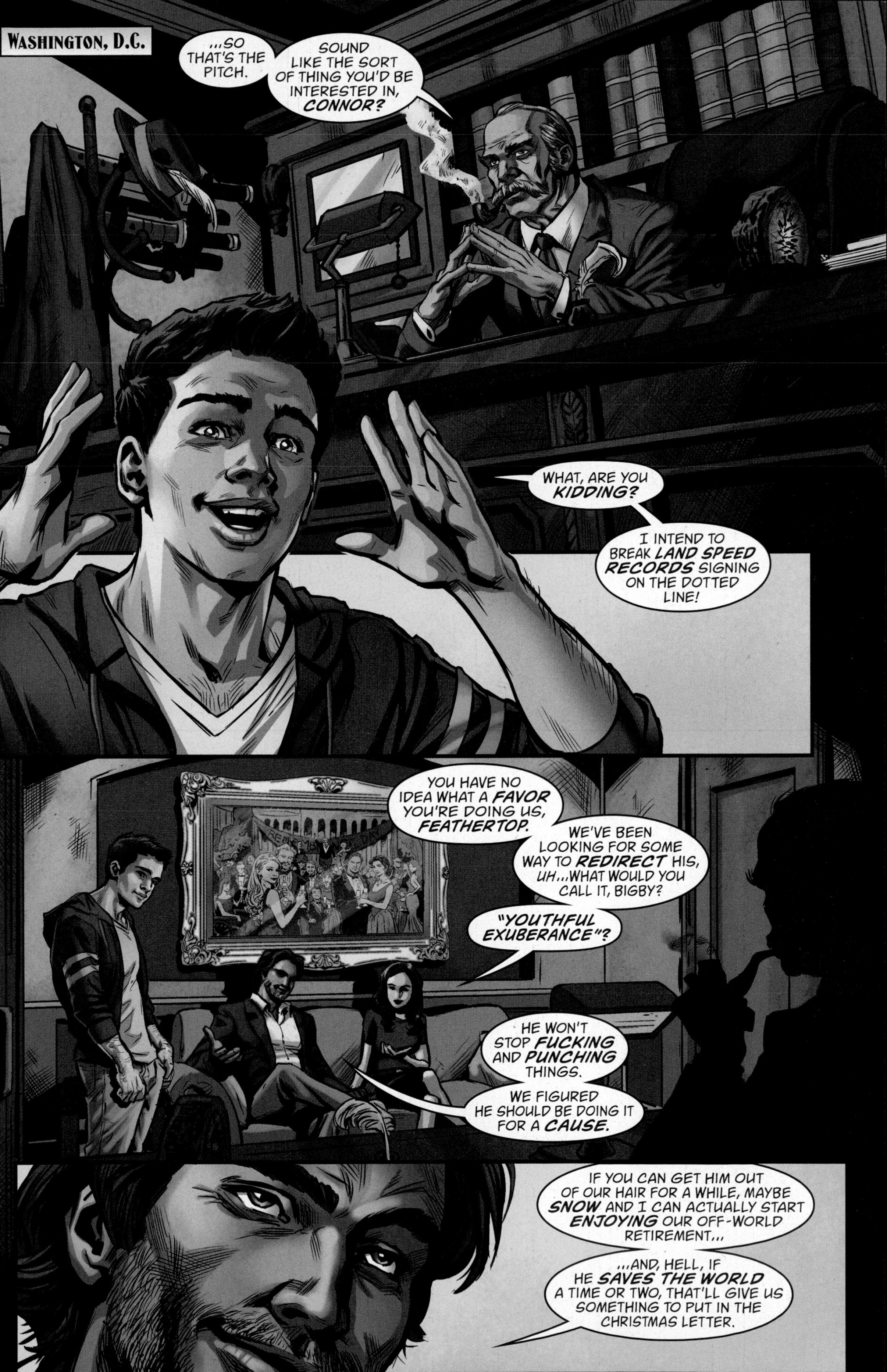
WASHINGTON, D.C.
...SO THAT'S THE PITCH.
SOUND LIKE THE SORT OF THING YOU'D BE INTERESTED IN, CONNOR?
WHAT, ARE YOU KIDDING?
I INTEND TO BREAK LAND SPEED RECORDS SIGNING ON THE DOTTED LINE!
YOU HAVE NO IDEA WHAT A FAVOR YOU'RE DOING US, FEATHERTOP.
WE'VE BEEN LOOKING FOR SOME WAY TO REDIRECT HIS, UH...WHAT WOULD YOU CALL IT, BIGBY?
"YOUTHFUL EXUBERANCE"?
HE WON'T STOP FUCKING AND PUNCHING THINGS.
WE FIGURED HE SHOULD BE DOING IT FOR A CAUSE.
IF YOU CAN GET HIM OUT OF OUR HAIR FOR A WHILE, MAYBE SNOW AND I CAN ACTUALLY START ENJOYING OUR OFF-WORLD RETIREMENT...
...AND, HELL, IF HE SAVES THE WORLD A TIME OR TWO, THAT'LL GIVE US SOMETHING TO PUT IN THE CHRISTMAS LETTER.

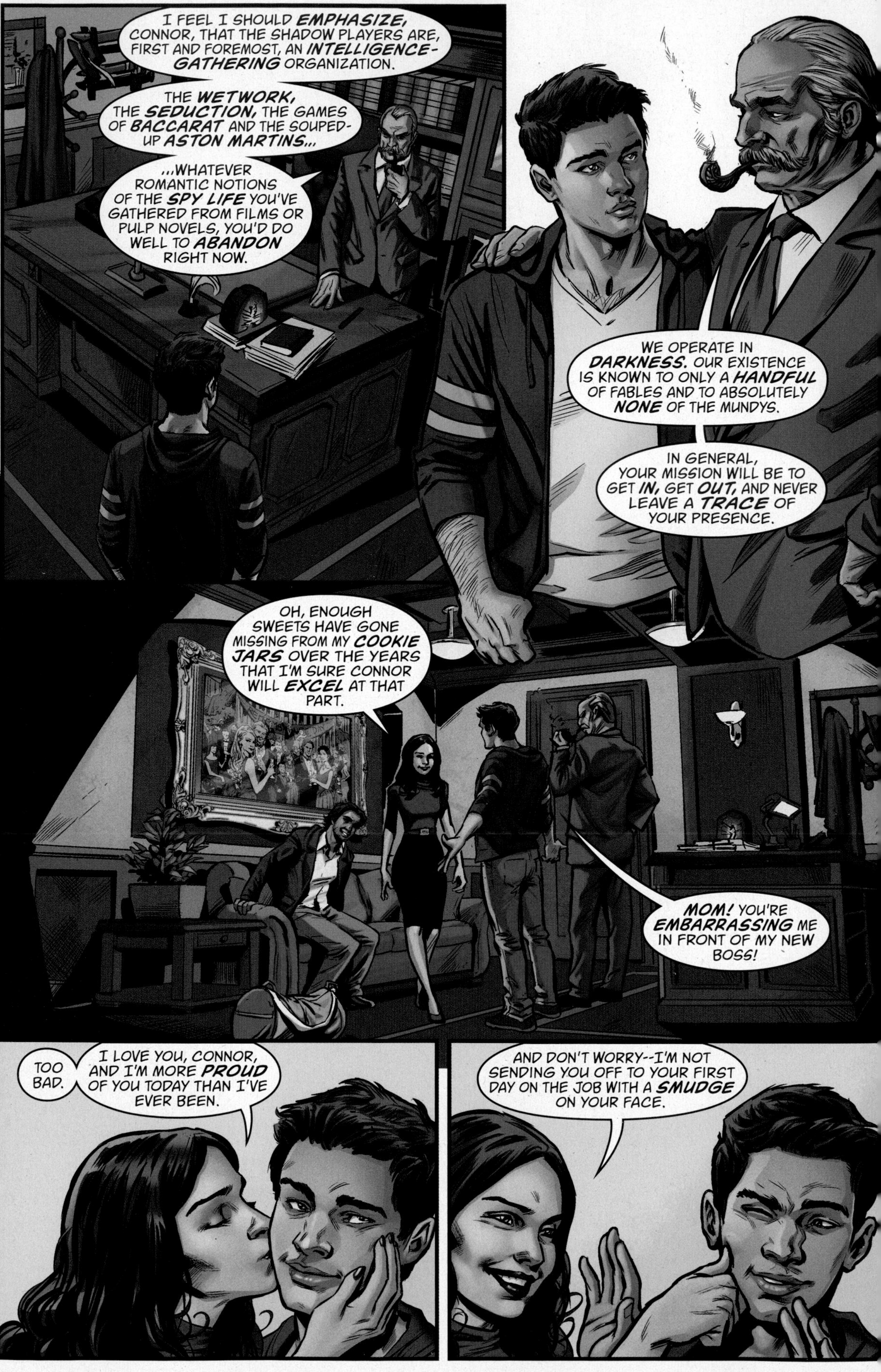

I FEEL I SHOULD EMPHASIZE, CONNOR, THAT THE SHADOW PLAYERS ARE, FIRST AND FOREMOST, AN INTELLIGENCE-GATHERING ORGANIZATION.
THE WETWORK, THE SEDUCTION, THE GAMES OF BACCARAT AND THE SOUPED-UP ASTON MARTINS...
...WHATEVER ROMANTIC NOTIONS OF THE SPY LIFE YOU'VE GATHERED FROM FILMS OR PULP NOVELS, YOU'D DO WELL TO ABANDON RIGHT NOW.
WE OPERATE IN DARKNESS. OUR EXISTENCE IS KNOWN TO ONLY A HANDFUL OF FABLES AND TO ABSOLUTELY NONE OF THE MUNDYS.
IN GENERAL, YOUR MISSION WILL BE TO GET IN, GET OUT, AND NEVER LEAVE A TRACE OF YOUR PRESENCE.
OH, ENOUGH SWEETS HAVE GONE MISSING FROM MY COOKIE JARS OVER THE YEARS THAT I'M SURE CONNOR WILL EXCEL AT THAT PART.
MOM! YOU'RE EMBARRASSING ME IN FRONT OF MY NEW BOSS!
TOO BAD.
I LOVE YOU, CONNOR, AND I'M MORE PROUD OF YOU TODAY THAN I'VE EVER BEEN.
AND DON'T WORRY--I'M NOT SENDING YOU OFF TO YOUR FIRST DAY ON THE JOB WITH A SMUDGE ON YOUR FACE.

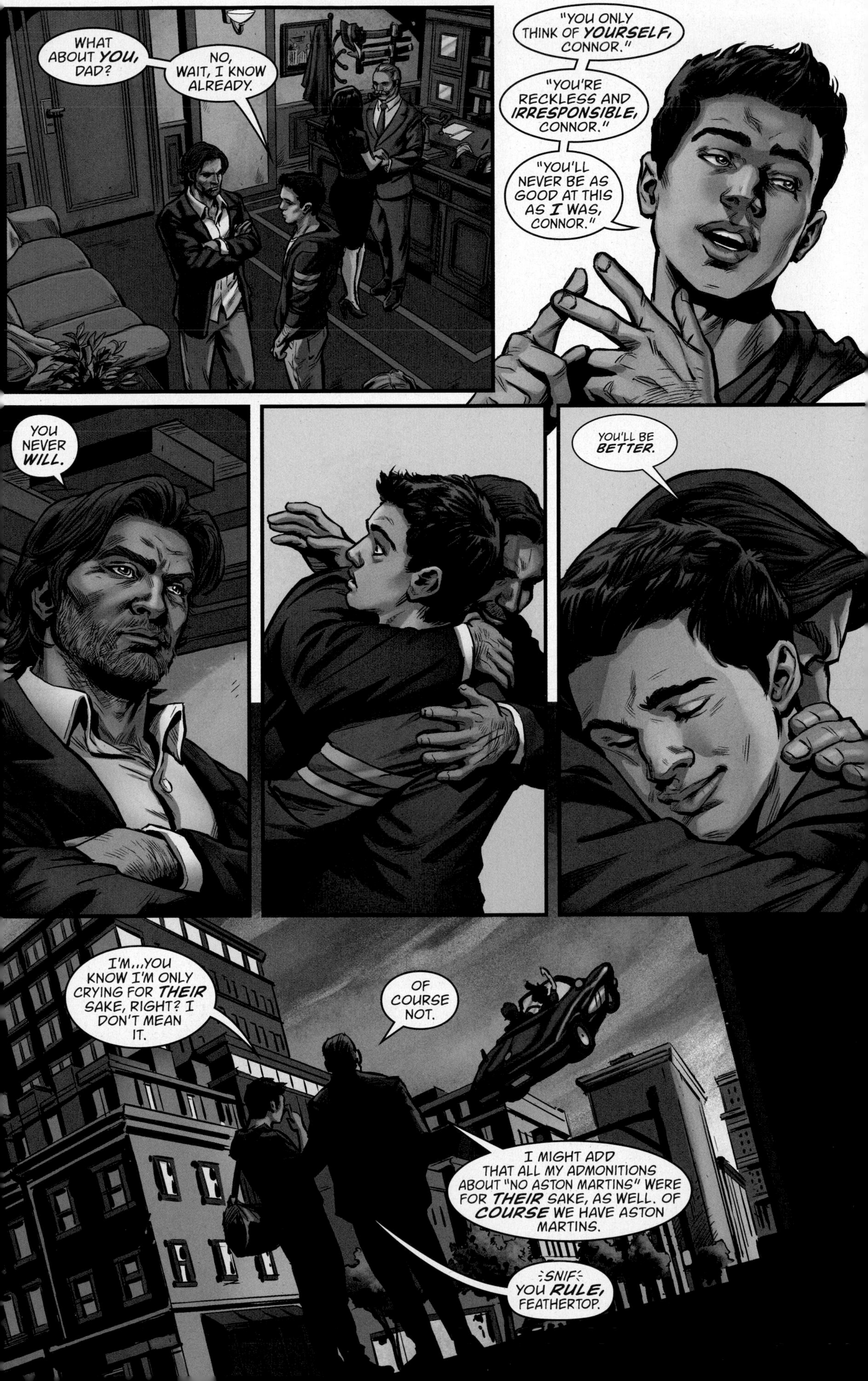
WHAT ABOUT YOU, DAD?
NO, WAIT, I KNOW ALREADY.
"YOU ONLY THINK OF YOURSELF, CONNOR."
"YOU'RE RECKLESS AND IRRESPONSIBLE, CONNOR."
"YOU'LL NEVER BE AS GOOD AT THIS AS I WAS, CONNOR."
YOU NEVER WILL.
YOU'LL BE BETTER.
I'M...YOU KNOW I'M ONLY CRYING FOR THEIR SAKE, RIGHT? I DON'T MEAN IT.
OF COURSE NOT.
I MIGHT ADD THAT ALL MY ADMONITIONS ABOUT "NO ASTON MARTINS" WERE FOR THEIR SAKE, AS WELL. OF COURSE WE HAVE ASTON MARTINS.
SNIF
YOU RULE, FEATHERTOP.

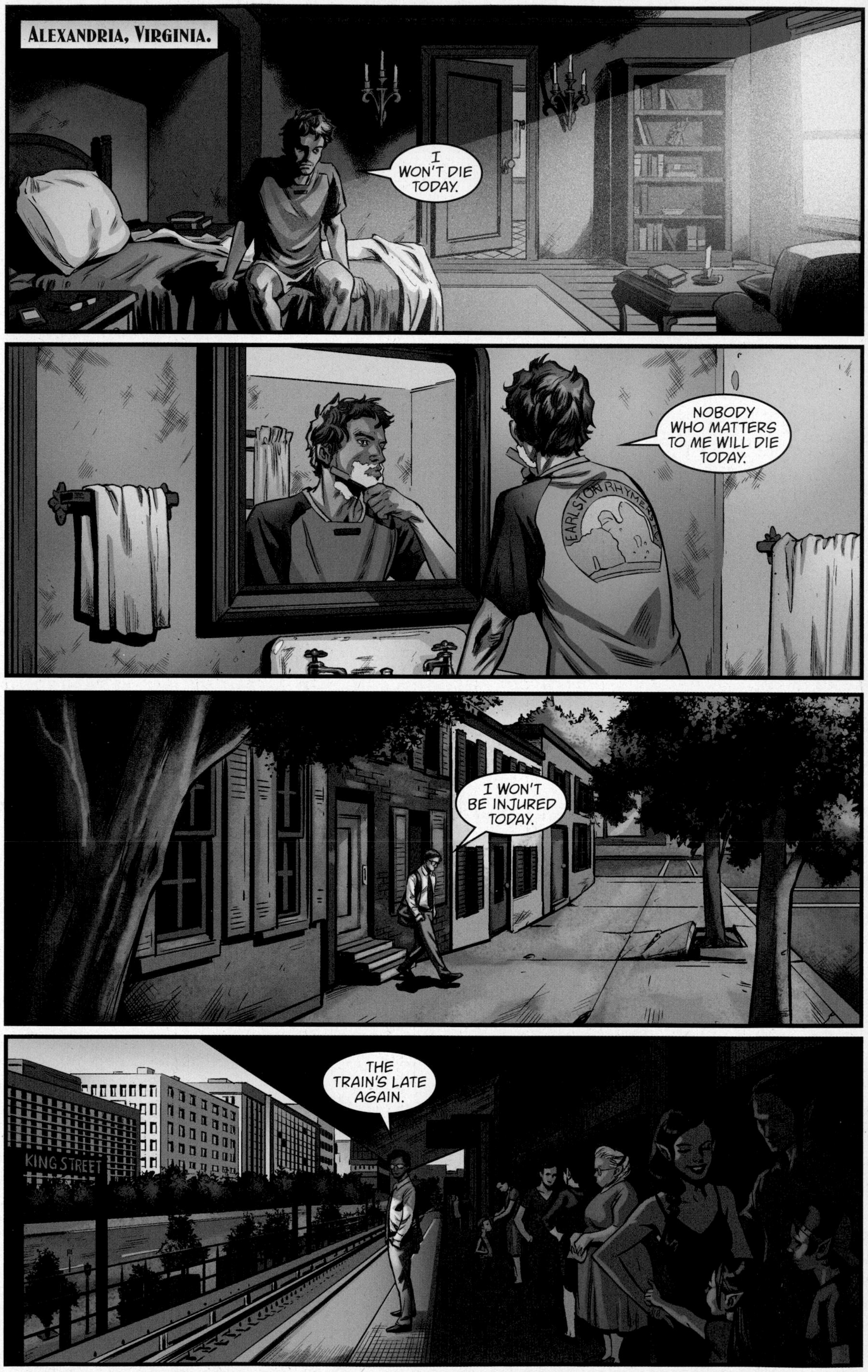
ALEXANDRIA, VIRGINIA.
I WON'T DIE TODAY.
NOBODY WHO MATTERS TO ME WILL DIE TODAY.
EARLSTON RHYMERS
I WON'T BE INJURED TODAY.
KING STREET
THE TRAIN'S LATE AGAIN.

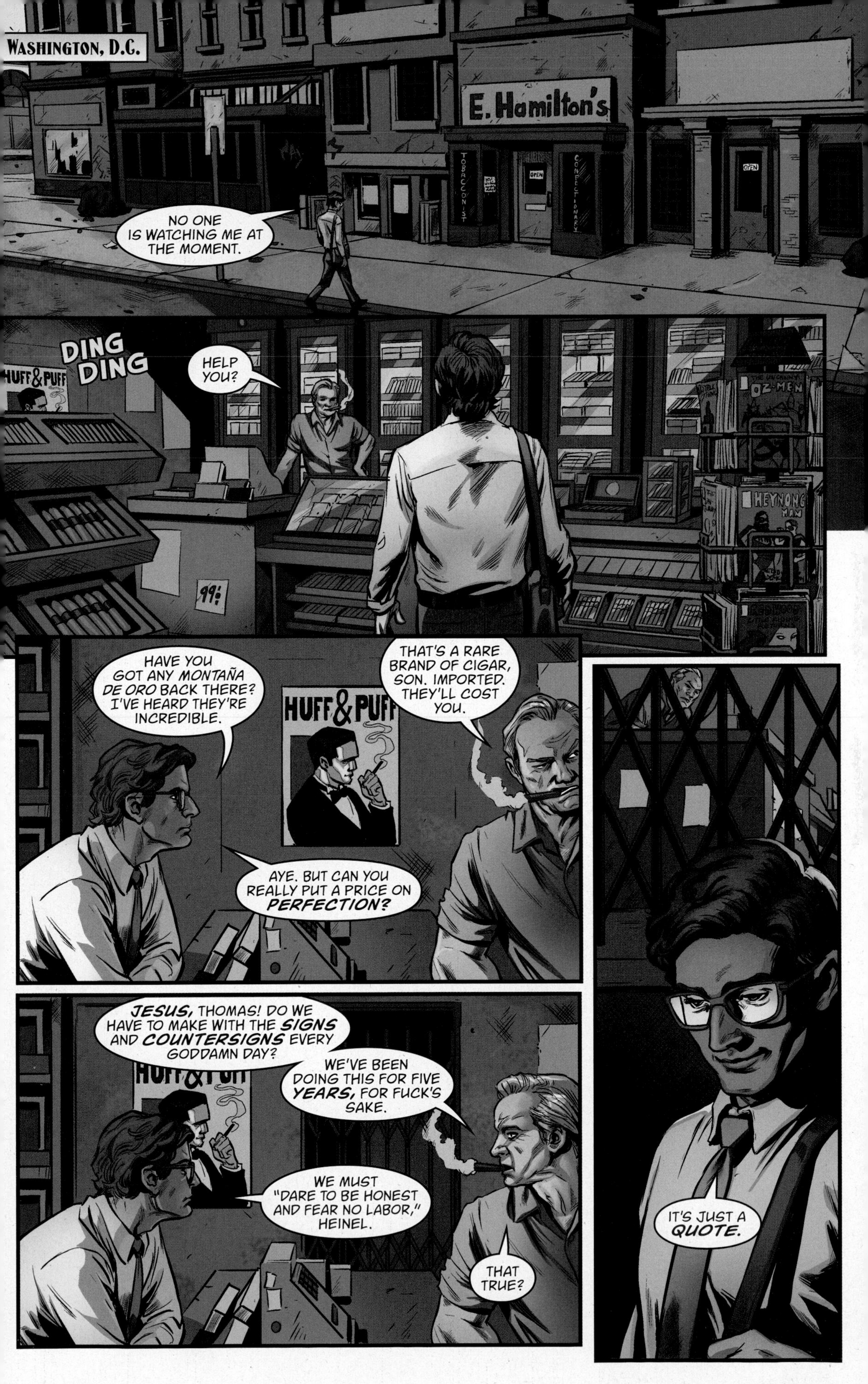
WASHINGTON, D.C.
E. Hamilton's
TOBACCONIST
CONFECTIONARY
OPEN
OPEN
NO ONE IS WATCHING ME AT THE MOMENT.
DING DING
HUFF & PUFF
HELP YOU?
THE UNCANNY OZ-MEN
HEYNONG MAN
99¢
HAVE YOU GOT ANY MONTAÑA DE ORO BACK THERE? I'VE HEARD THEY'RE INCREDIBLE.
HUFF & PUFF
THAT'S A RARE BRAND OF CIGAR, SON. IMPORTED. THEY'LL COST YOU.
AYE. BUT CAN YOU REALLY PUT A PRICE ON PERFECTION?
JESUS, THOMAS! DO WE HAVE TO MAKE WITH THE SIGNS AND COUNTERSIGNS EVERY GODDAMN DAY?
WE'VE BEEN DOING THIS FOR FIVE YEARS, FOR FUCK'S SAKE.
WE MUST "DARE TO BE HONEST AND FEAR NO LABOR," HEINEL.
THAT TRUE?
IT'S JUST A QUOTE.

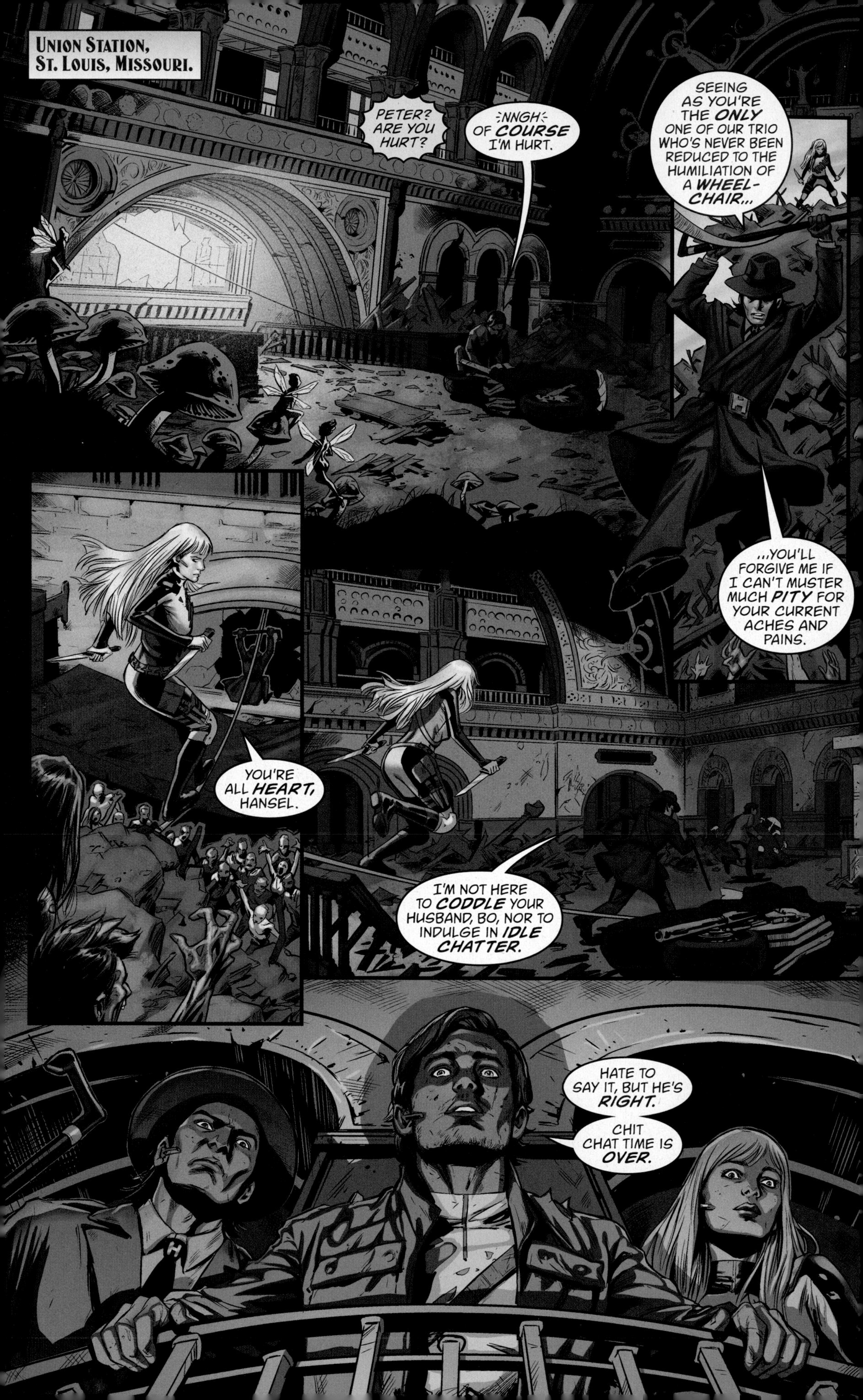
UNION STATION, ST. LOUIS, MISSOURI.
PETER? ARE YOU HURT?
NNGH OF COURSE I'M HURT.
SEEING AS YOU'RE THE ONLY ONE OF OUR TRIO WHO'S NEVER BEEN REDUCED TO THE HUMILIATION OF A WHEEL-CHAIR...
...YOU'LL FORGIVE ME IF I CAN'T MUSTER MUCH PITY FOR YOUR CURRENT ACHES AND PAINS.
YOU'RE ALL HEART, HANSEL.
I'M NOT HERE TO CODDLE YOUR HUSBAND, BO, NOR TO INDULGE IN IDLE CHATTER.
HATE TO SAY IT, BUT HE'S RIGHT.
CHIT CHAT TIME IS OVER.

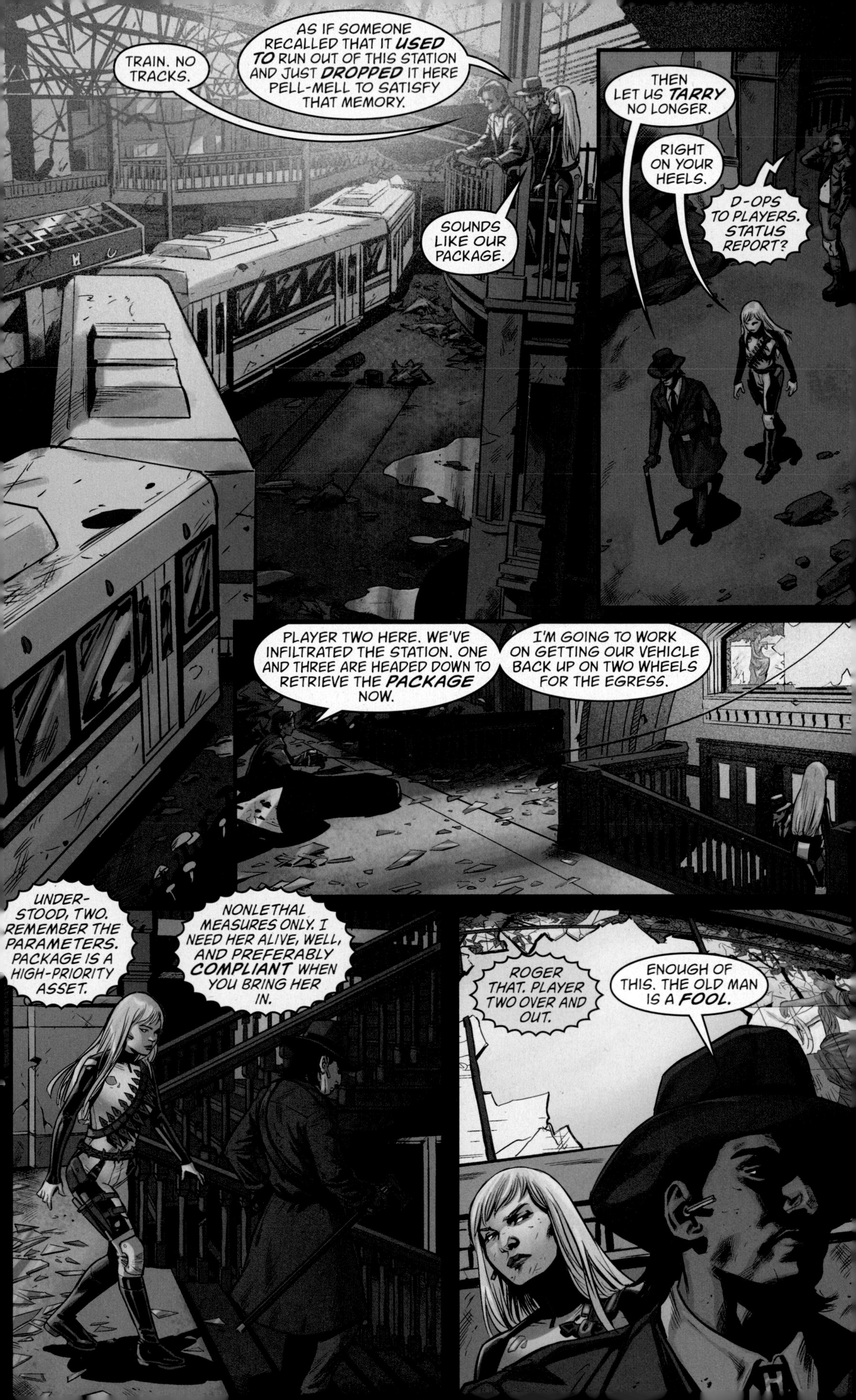
TRAIN. NO TRACKS.
AS IF SOMEONE RECALLED THAT IT USED TO RUN OUT OF THIS STATION AND JUST DROPPED IT HERE PELL-MELL TO SATISFY THAT MEMORY.
SOUNDS LIKE OUR PACKAGE.
THEN LET US TARRY NO LONGER.
RIGHT ON YOUR HEELS.
D-OPS TO PLAYERS. STATUS REPORT?
PLAYER TWO HERE. WE'VE INFILTRATED THE STATION. ONE AND THREE ARE HEADED DOWN TO RETRIEVE THE PACKAGE NOW.
I'M GOING TO WORK ON GETTING OUR VEHICLE BACK UP ON TWO WHEELS FOR THE EGRESS.
UNDER-STOOD, TWO. REMEMBER THE PARAMETERS. PACKAGE IS A HIGH-PRIORITY ASSET.
NONLETHAL MEASURES ONLY. I NEED HER ALIVE, WELL, AND PREFERABLY COMPLIANT WHEN YOU BRING HER IN.
ROGER THAT. PLAYER TWO OVER AND OUT.
ENOUGH OF THIS. THE OLD MAN IS A FOOL.

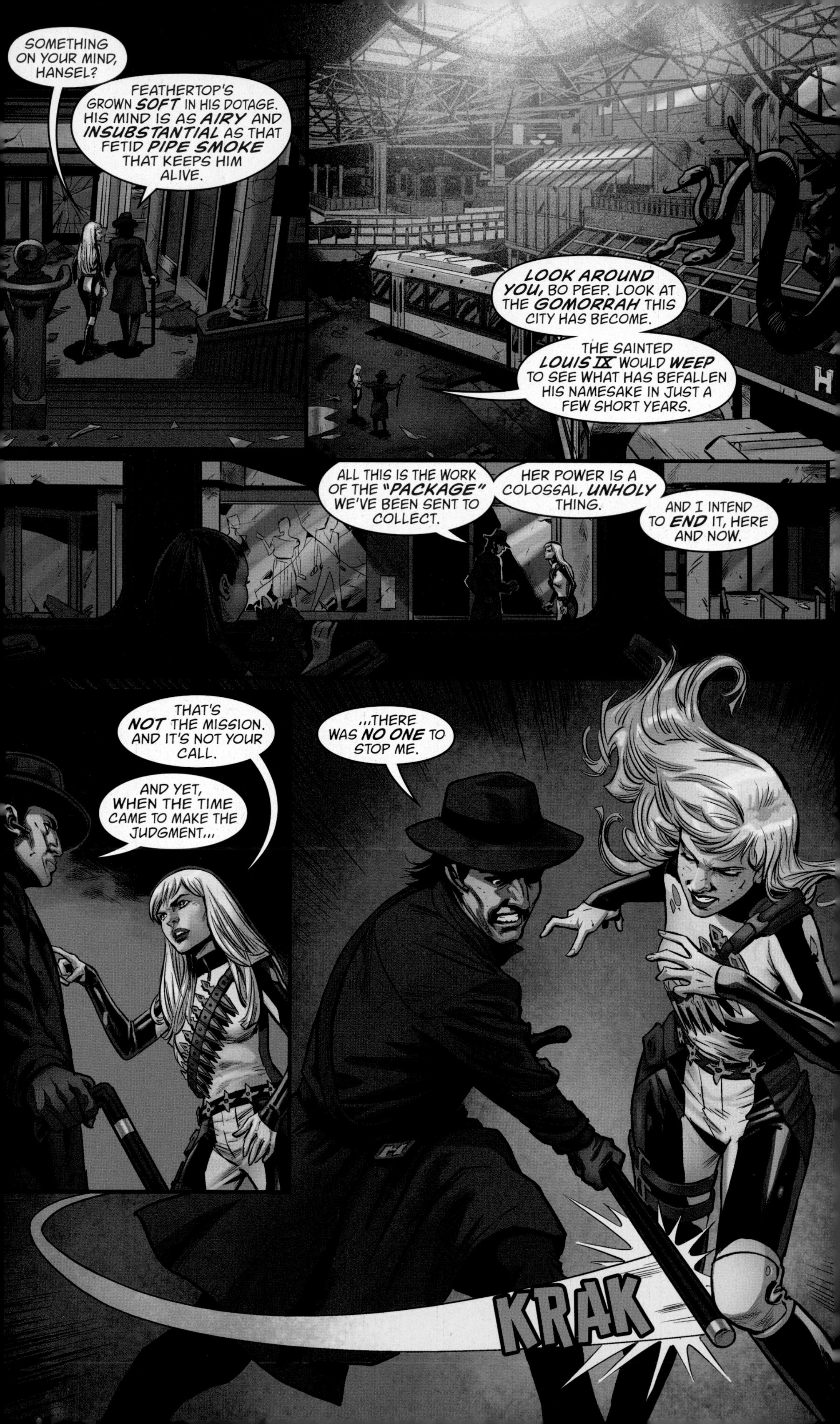
SOMETHING ON YOUR MIND, HANSEL?
FEATHERTOP'S GROWN SOFT IN HIS DOTAGE. HIS MIND IS AS AIRY AND INSUBSTANTIAL AS THAT FETID PIPE SMOKE THAT KEEPS HIM ALIVE.
LOOK AROUND YOU, BO PEEP. LOOK AT THE GOMORRAH THIS CITY HAS BECOME.
THE SAINTED LOUIS IX WOULD WEEP TO SEE WHAT HAS BEFALLEN HIS NAMESAKE IN JUST A FEW SHORT YEARS.
ALL THIS IS THE WORK OF THE "PACKAGE" WE'VE BEEN SENT TO COLLECT.
HER POWER IS A COLOSSAL, UNHOLY THING.
AND I INTEND TO END IT, HERE AND NOW.
THAT'S NOT THE MISSION. AND IT'S NOT YOUR CALL.
AND YET, WHEN THE TIME CAME TO MAKE THE JUDGMENT...
...THERE WAS NO ONE TO STOP ME.
KRAK

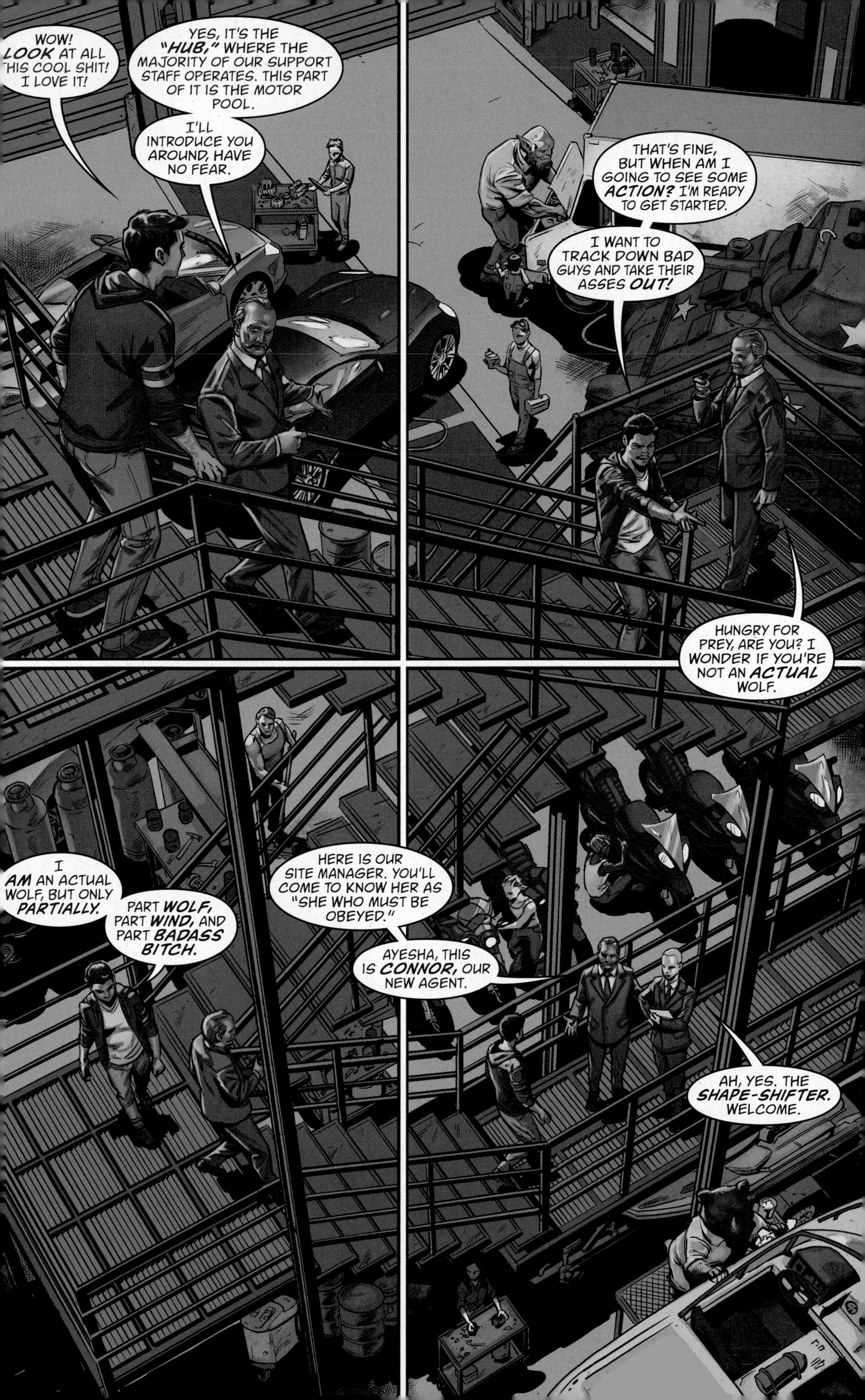
WOW! LOOK AT ALL THIS COOL SHIT! I LOVE IT!
YES, IT'S THE "HUB," WHERE THE MAJORITY OF OUR SUPPORT STAFF OPERATES. THIS PART OF IT IS THE MOTOR POOL.
I'LL INTRODUCE YOU AROUND, HAVE NO FEAR.
THAT'S FINE, BUT WHEN AM I GOING TO SEE SOME ACTION? I'M READY TO GET STARTED.
I WANT TO TRACK DOWN BAD GUYS AND TAKE THEIR ASSES OUT!
HUNGRY FOR PREY, ARE YOU? I WONDER IF YOU'RE NOT AN ACTUAL WOLF.
I AM AN ACTUAL WOLF, BUT ONLY PARTIALLY.
PART WOLF, PART WIND, AND PART BADASS BITCH.
HERE IS OUR SITE MANAGER. YOU'LL COME TO KNOW HER AS "SHE WHO MUST BE OBEYED."
AYESHA, THIS IS CONNOR, OUR NEW AGENT.
AH, YES. THE SHAPE-SHIFTER. WELCOME.

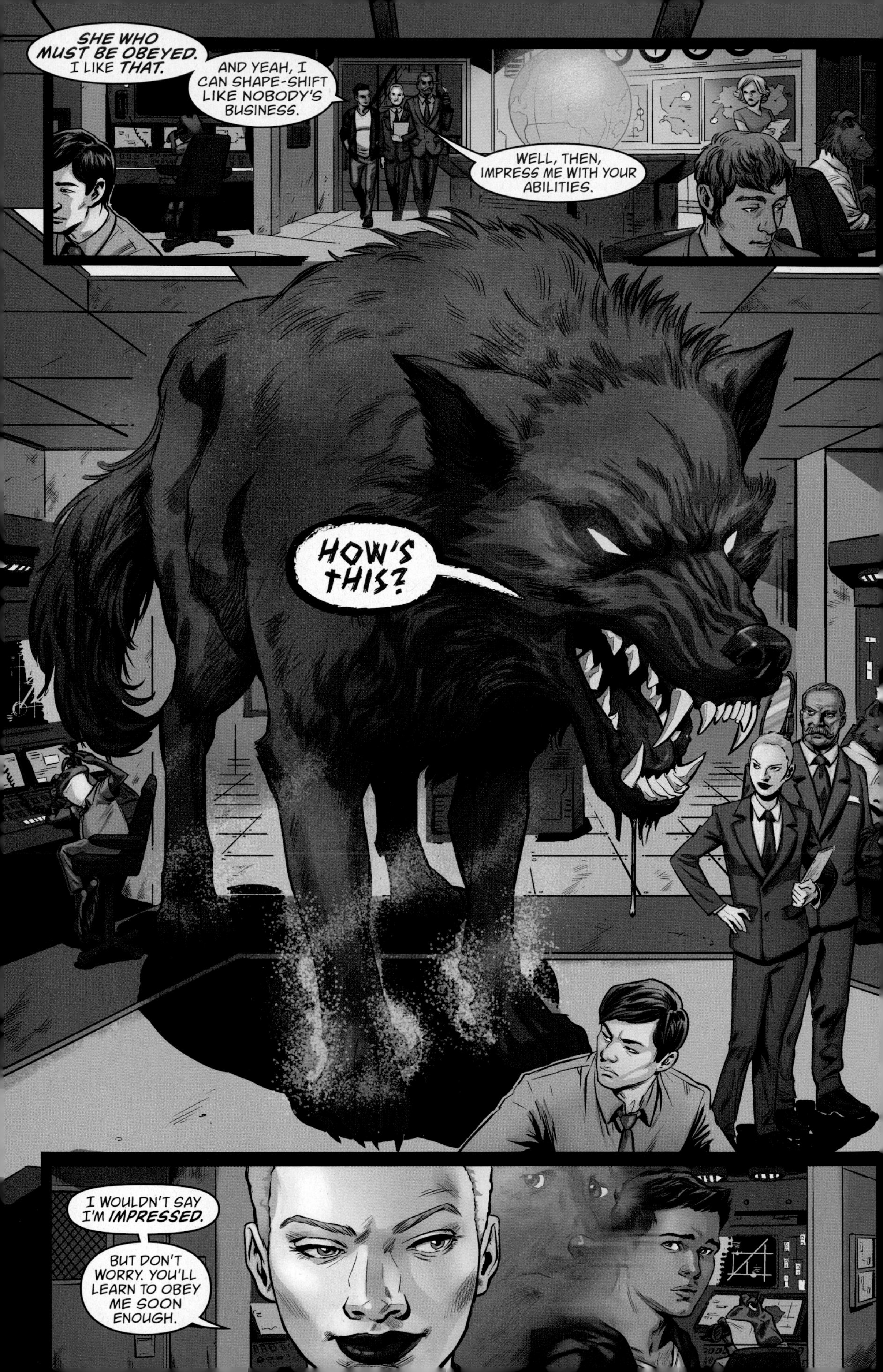
SHE WHO MUST BE OBEYED. I LIKE THAT.
AND YEAH, I CAN SHAPE-SHIFT LIKE NOBODY'S BUSINESS.
WELL, THEN, IMPRESS ME WITH YOUR ABILITIES.
HOW'S THIS?
I WOULDN'T SAY I'M IMPRESSED.
BUT DON'T WORRY. YOU'LL LEARN TO OBEY ME SOON ENOUGH.

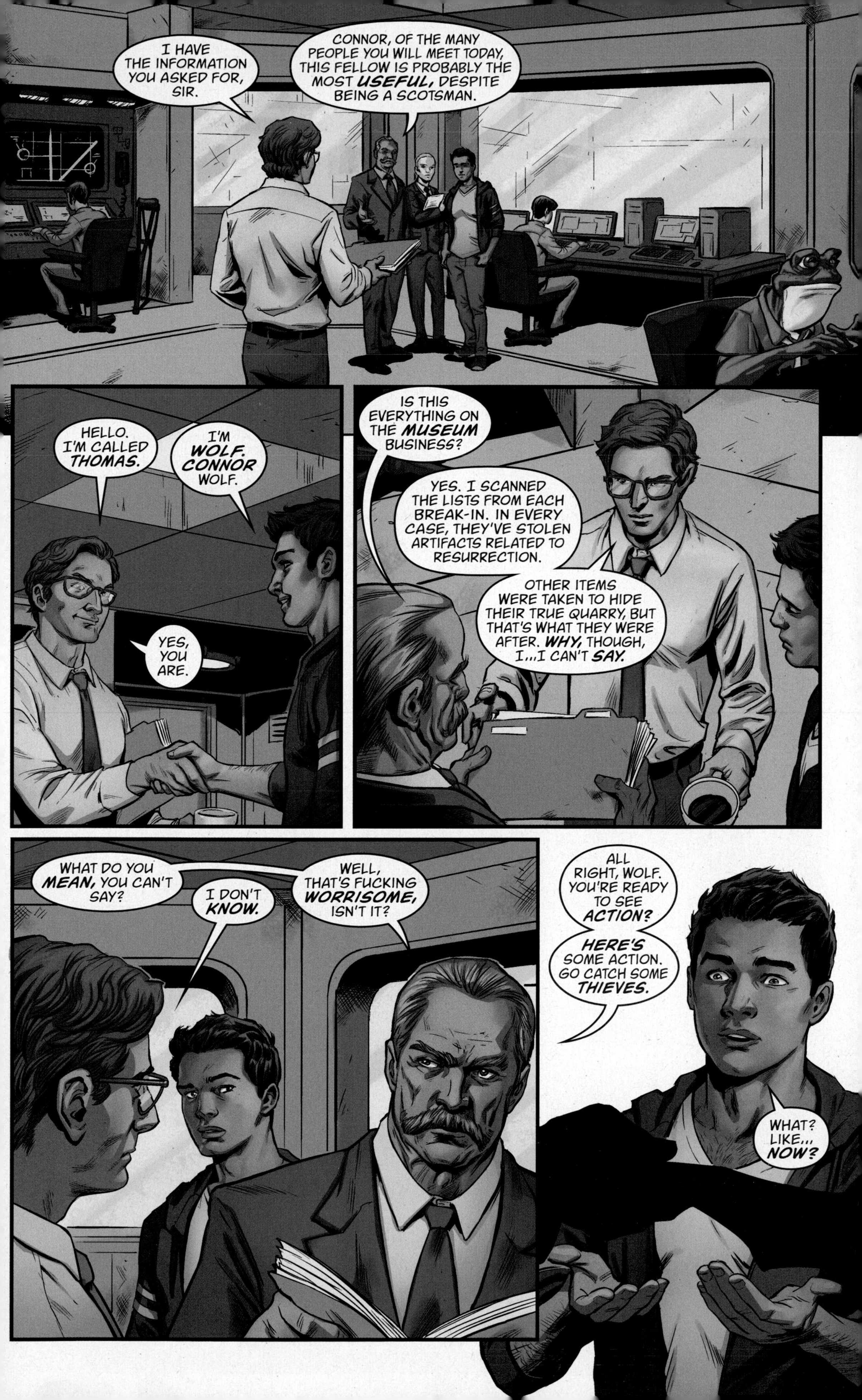
I HAVE THE INFORMATION YOU ASKED FOR, SIR.
CONNOR, OF THE MANY PEOPLE YOU WILL MEET TODAY, THIS FELLOW IS PROBABLY THE MOST USEFUL, DESPITE BEING A SCOTSMAN.
HELLO. I'M CALLED THOMAS.
I'M WOLF. CONNOR WOLF.
YES, YOU ARE.
IS THIS EVERYTHING ON THE MUSEUM BUSINESS?
YES. I SCANNED THE LISTS FROM EACH BREAK-IN. IN EVERY CASE, THEY'VE STOLEN ARTIFACTS RELATED TO RESURRECTION.
OTHER ITEMS WERE TAKEN TO HIDE THEIR TRUE QUARRY, BUT THAT'S WHAT THEY WERE AFTER. WHY, THOUGH, I...I CAN'T SAY.
WHAT DO YOU MEAN, YOU CAN'T SAY?
I DON'T KNOW.
WELL, THAT'S FUCKING WORRISOME, ISN'T IT?
ALL RIGHT, WOLF. YOU'RE READY TO SEE ACTION?
HERE'S SOME ACTION. GO CATCH SOME THIEVES.
WHAT? LIKE... NOW?

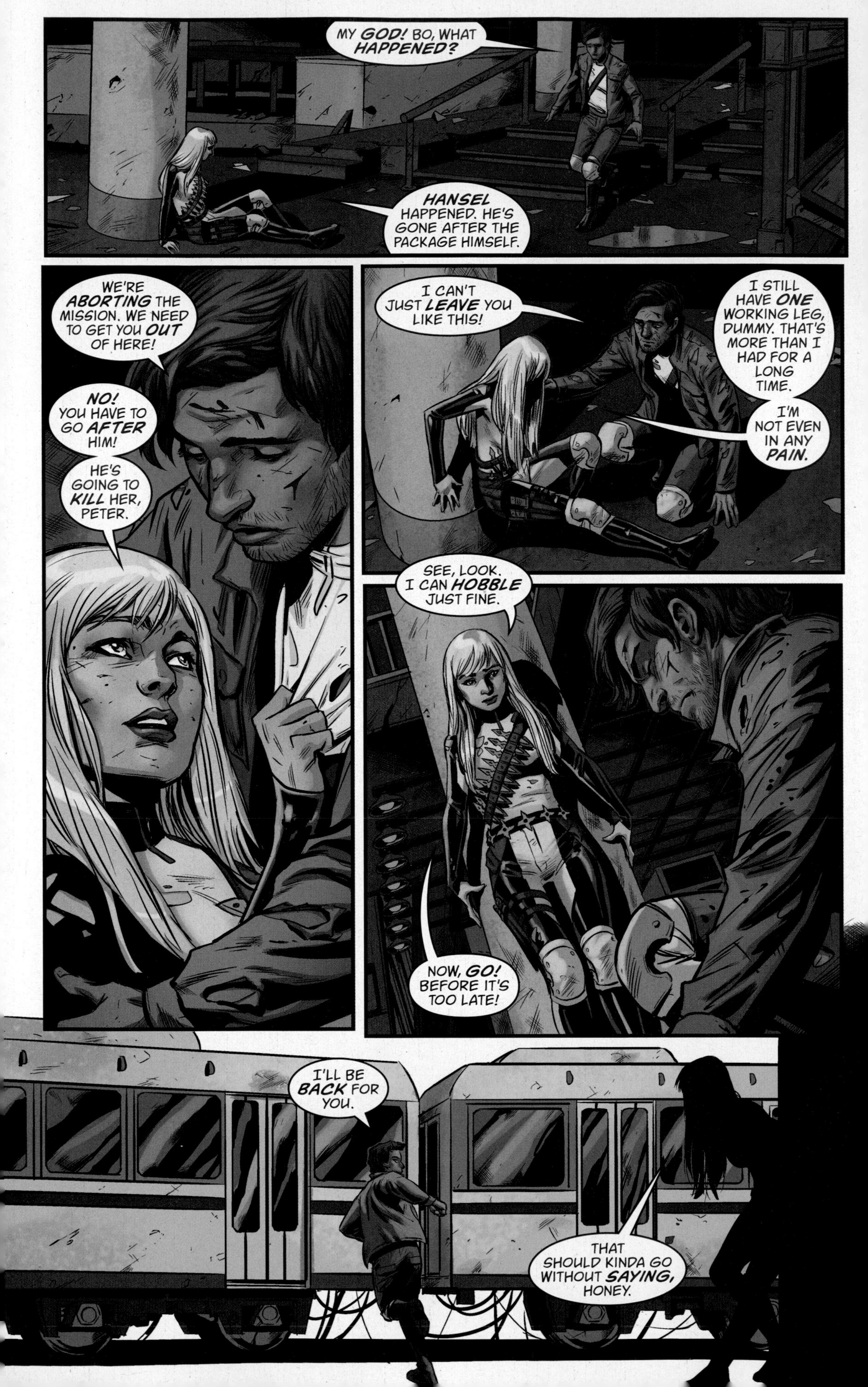
MY GOD! BO, WHAT HAPPENED?
HANSEL HAPPENED. HE'S GONE AFTER THE PACKAGE HIMSELF.
WE'RE ABORTING THE MISSION. WE NEED TO GET YOU OUT OF HERE!
NO! YOU HAVE TO GO AFTER HIM!
HE'S GOING TO KILL HER, PETER.
I CAN'T JUST LEAVE YOU LIKE THIS!
I STILL HAVE ONE WORKING LEG, DUMMY. THAT'S MORE THAN I HAD FOR A LONG TIME.
I'M NOT EVEN IN ANY PAIN.
SEE, LOOK. I CAN HOBBLE JUST FINE.
NOW, GO! BEFORE IT'S TOO LATE!
I'LL BE BACK FOR YOU.
THAT SHOULD KINDA GO WITHOUT SAYING, HONEY.

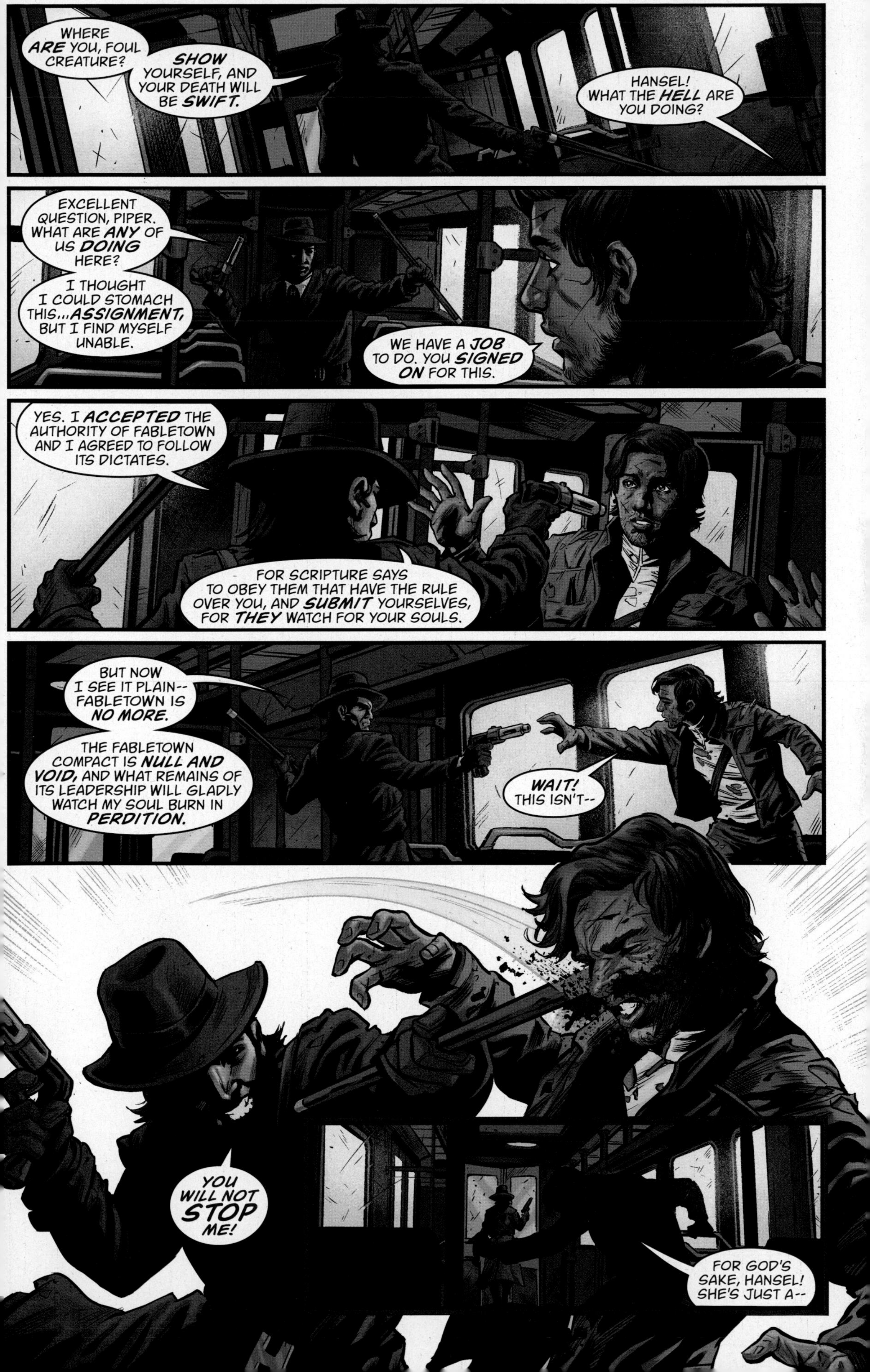
WHERE *ARE* YOU, FOUL CREATURE?
SHOW YOURSELF, AND YOUR DEATH WILL BE *SWIFT.*
HANSEL! WHAT THE *HELL* ARE YOU DOING?
EXCELLENT QUESTION, PIPER. WHAT ARE *ANY* OF US *DOING* HERE?
I THOUGHT I COULD STOMACH THIS...*ASSIGNMENT,* BUT I FIND MYSELF UNABLE.
WE HAVE A *JOB* TO DO. YOU *SIGNED ON* FOR THIS.
YES. I *ACCEPTED* THE AUTHORITY OF FABLETOWN AND I AGREED TO FOLLOW ITS DICTATES.
FOR SCRIPTURE SAYS TO OBEY THEM THAT HAVE THE RULE OVER YOU, AND *SUBMIT* YOURSELVES, FOR *THEY* WATCH FOR YOUR SOULS.
BUT NOW I SEE IT PLAIN-- FABLETOWN IS *NO MORE.*
THE FABLETOWN COMPACT IS *NULL AND VOID,* AND WHAT REMAINS OF ITS LEADERSHIP WILL GLADLY WATCH MY SOUL BURN IN *PERDITION.*
WAIT! THIS ISN'T--
YOU WILL NOT STOP ME!
FOR GOD'S SAKE, HANSEL! SHE'S JUST A--

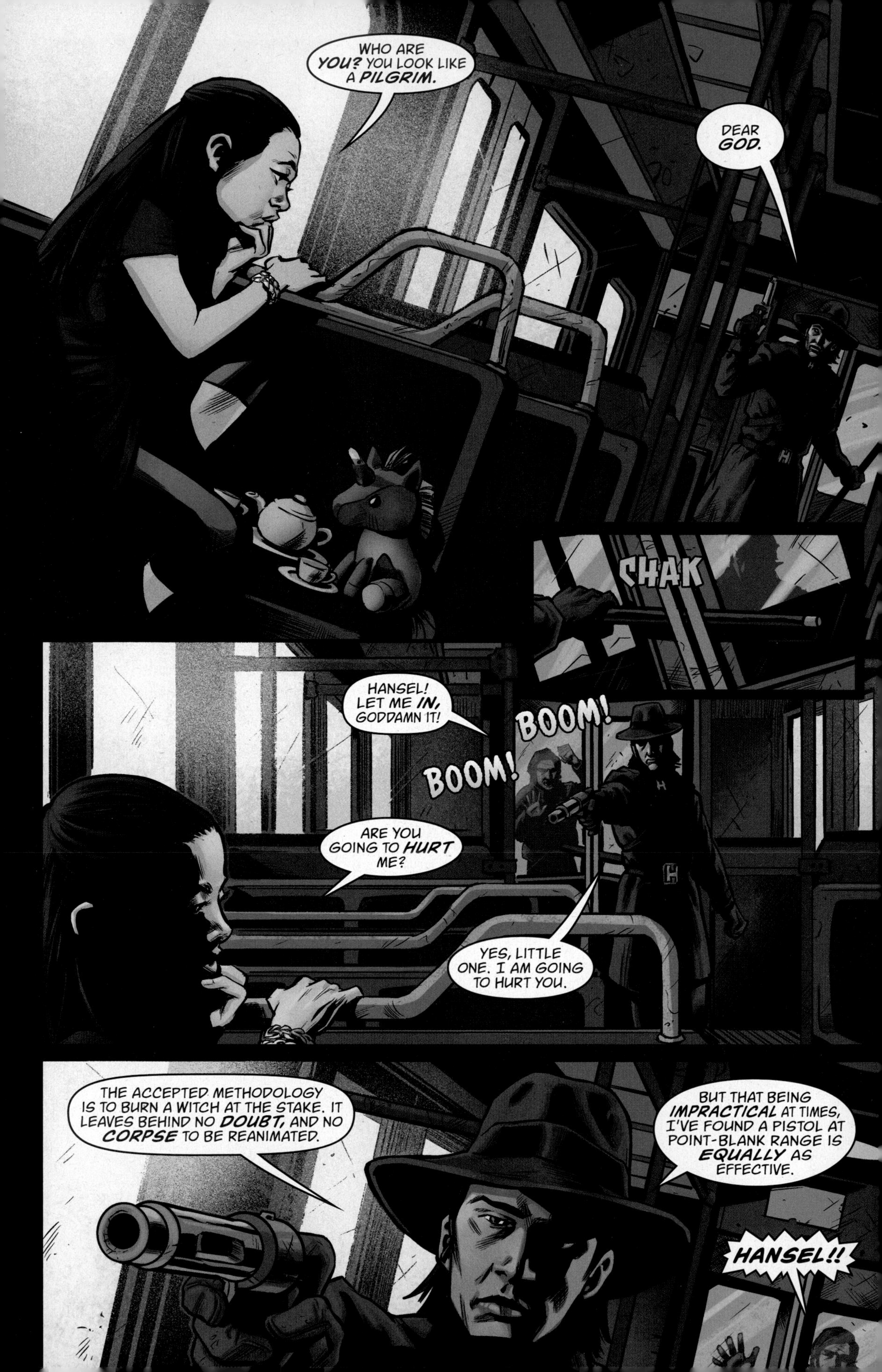
WHO ARE YOU? YOU LOOK LIKE A PILGRIM.
DEAR GOD.
CHAK
HANSEL! LET ME IN, GODDAMN IT!
BOOM!
BOOM!
ARE YOU GOING TO HURT ME?
YES, LITTLE ONE. I AM GOING TO HURT YOU.
THE ACCEPTED METHODOLOGY IS TO BURN A WITCH AT THE STAKE. IT LEAVES BEHIND NO DOUBT, AND NO CORPSE TO BE REANIMATED.
BUT THAT BEING IMPRACTICAL AT TIMES, I'VE FOUND A PISTOL AT POINT-BLANK RANGE IS EQUALLY AS EFFECTIVE.
HANSEL!!

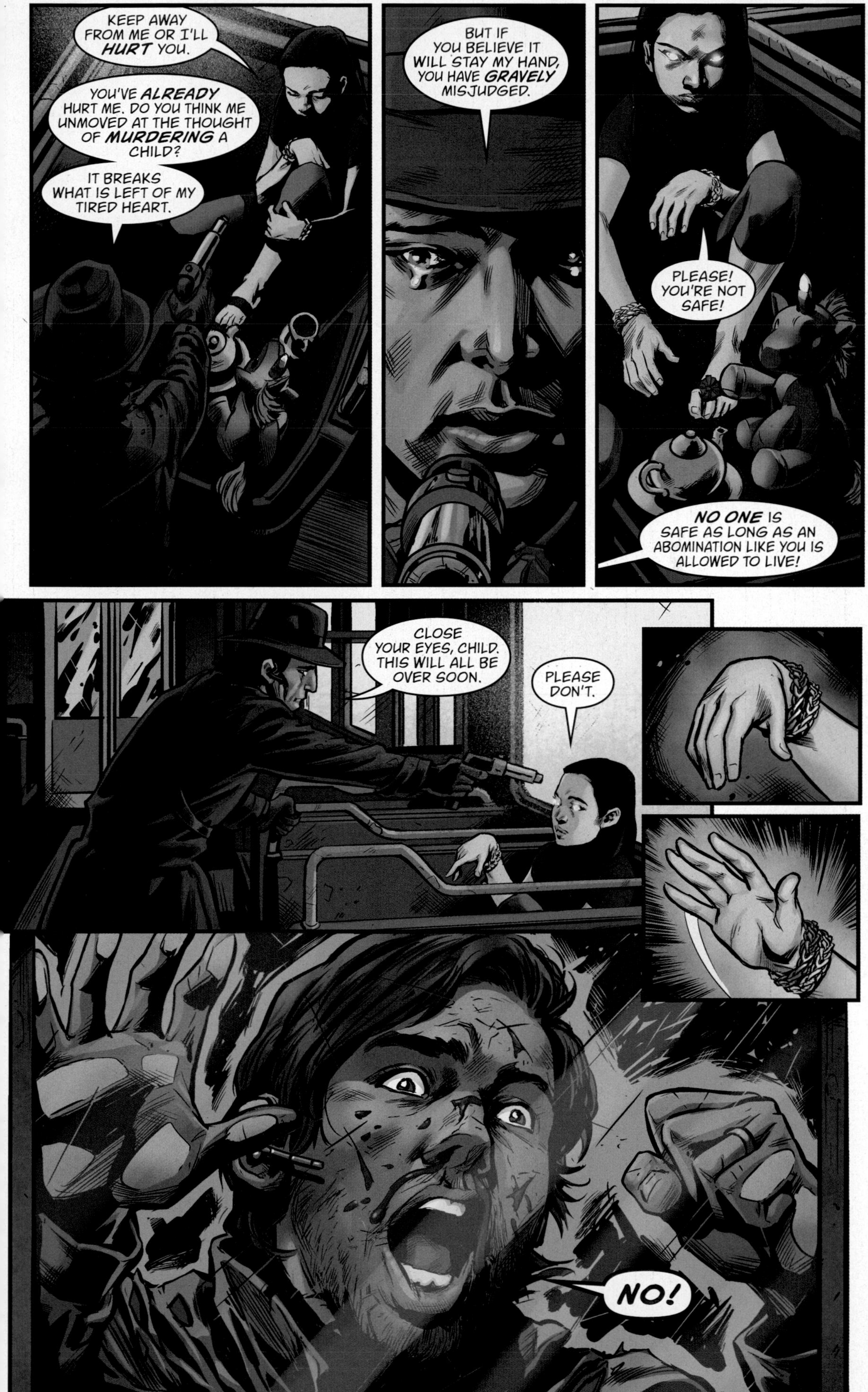
KEEP AWAY FROM ME OR I'LL HURT YOU.
YOU'VE ALREADY HURT ME. DO YOU THINK ME UNMOVED AT THE THOUGHT OF MURDERING A CHILD?
IT BREAKS WHAT IS LEFT OF MY TIRED HEART.
BUT IF YOU BELIEVE IT WILL STAY MY HAND, YOU HAVE GRAVELY MISJUDGED.
PLEASE! YOU'RE NOT SAFE!
NO ONE IS SAFE AS LONG AS AN ABOMINATION LIKE YOU IS ALLOWED TO LIVE!
CLOSE YOUR EYES, CHILD. THIS WILL ALL BE OVER SOON.
PLEASE DON'T.
NO!

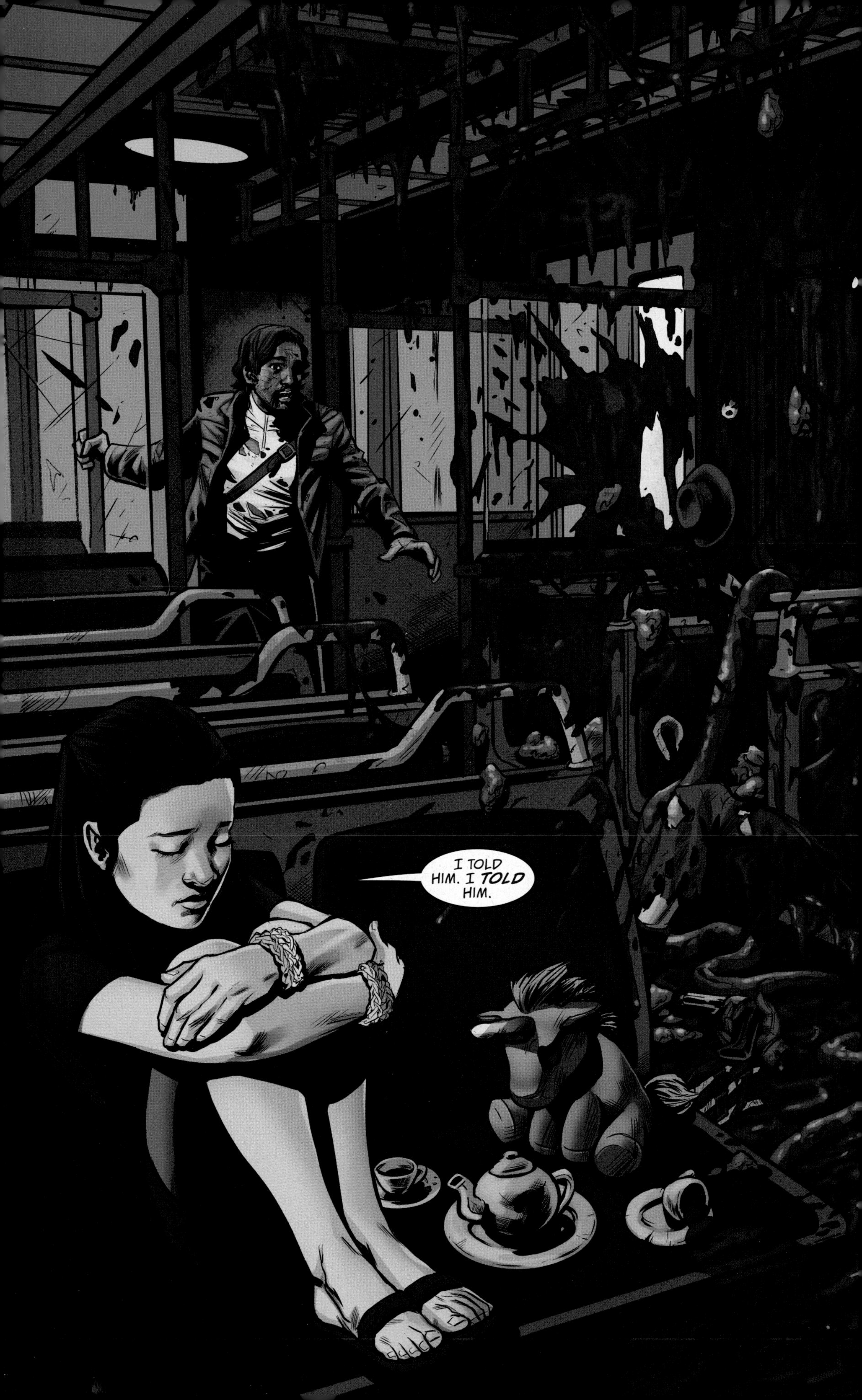
I TOLD HIM. I TOLD HIM.

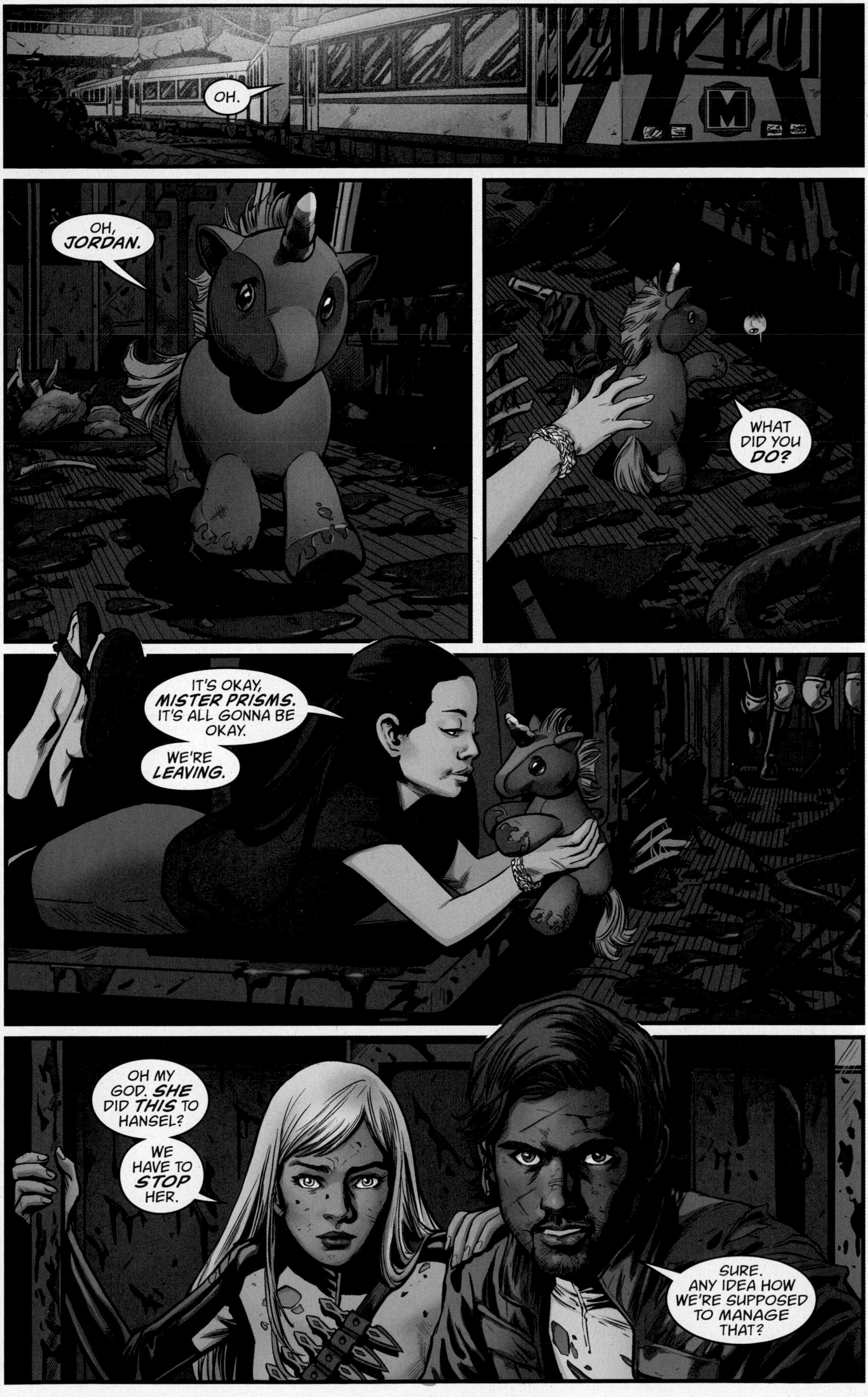
OH.
OH, JORDAN.
WHAT DID YOU DO?
IT'S OKAY, MISTER PRISMS. IT'S ALL GONNA BE OKAY.
WE'RE LEAVING.
OH MY GOD. SHE DID THIS TO HANSEL?
WE HAVE TO STOP HER.
SURE. ANY IDEA HOW WE'RE SUPPOSED TO MANAGE THAT?

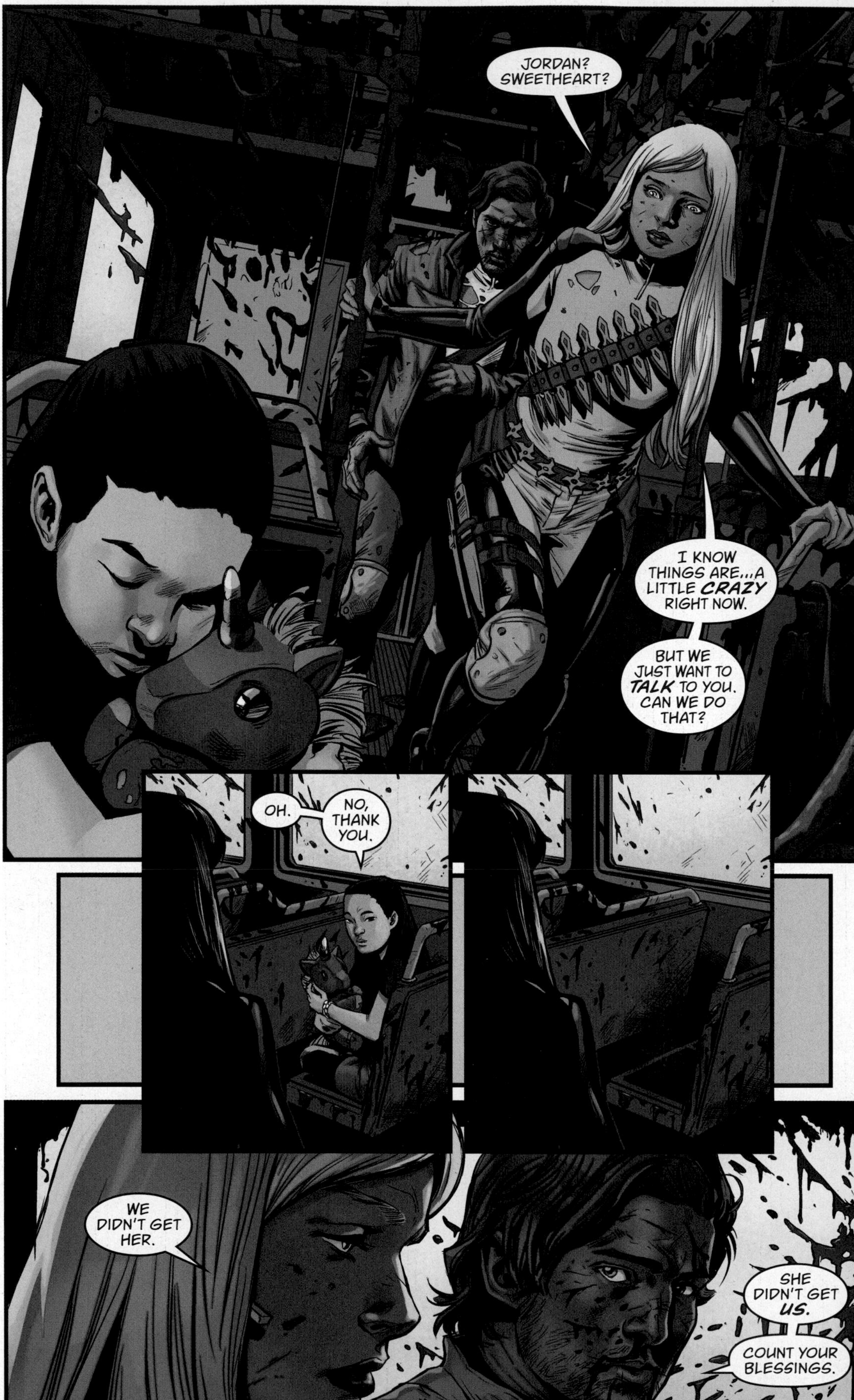
JORDAN? SWEETHEART?
I KNOW THINGS ARE...A LITTLE CRAZY RIGHT NOW.
BUT WE JUST WANT TO TALK TO YOU. CAN WE DO THAT?
OH.
NO, THANK YOU.
WE DIDN'T GET HER.
SHE DIDN'T GET US.
COUNT YOUR BLESSINGS.

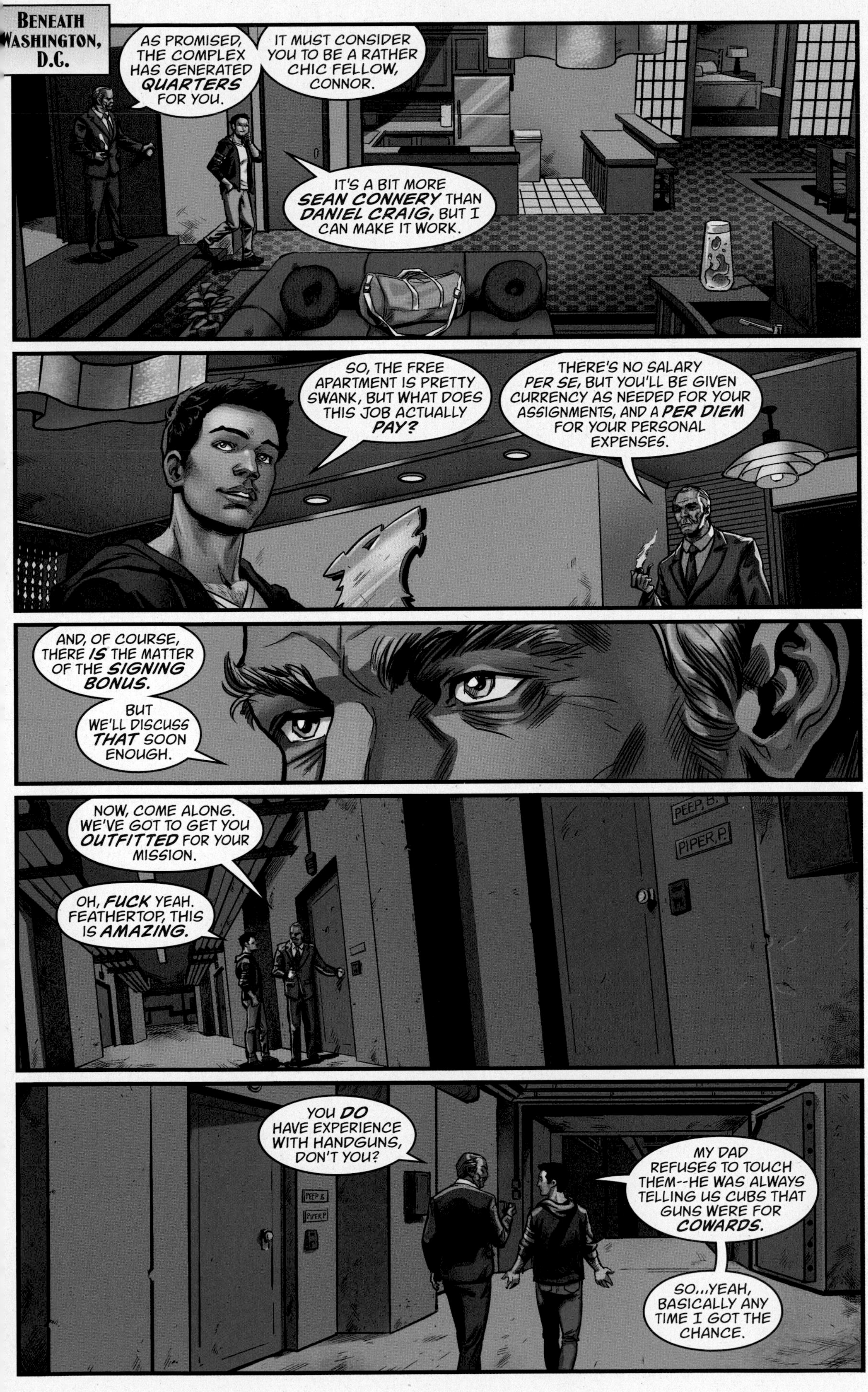
BENEATH WASHINGTON, D.C.
AS PROMISED, THE COMPLEX HAS GENERATED QUARTERS FOR YOU.
IT MUST CONSIDER YOU TO BE A RATHER CHIC FELLOW, CONNOR.
IT'S A BIT MORE SEAN CONNERY THAN DANIEL CRAIG, BUT I CAN MAKE IT WORK.
SO, THE FREE APARTMENT IS PRETTY SWANK, BUT WHAT DOES THIS JOB ACTUALLY PAY?
THERE'S NO SALARY PER SE, BUT YOU'LL BE GIVEN CURRENCY AS NEEDED FOR YOUR ASSIGNMENTS, AND A PER DIEM FOR YOUR PERSONAL EXPENSES.
AND, OF COURSE, THERE IS THE MATTER OF THE SIGNING BONUS.
BUT WE'LL DISCUSS THAT SOON ENOUGH.
NOW, COME ALONG. WE'VE GOT TO GET YOU OUTFITTED FOR YOUR MISSION.
OH, FUCK YEAH. FEATHERTOP, THIS IS AMAZING.
PEEP, B.
PIPER, P.
YOU DO HAVE EXPERIENCE WITH HANDGUNS, DON'T YOU?
MY DAD REFUSES TO TOUCH THEM--HE WAS ALWAYS TELLING US CUBS THAT GUNS WERE FOR COWARDS.
SO...YEAH, BASICALLY ANY TIME I GOT THE CHANCE.

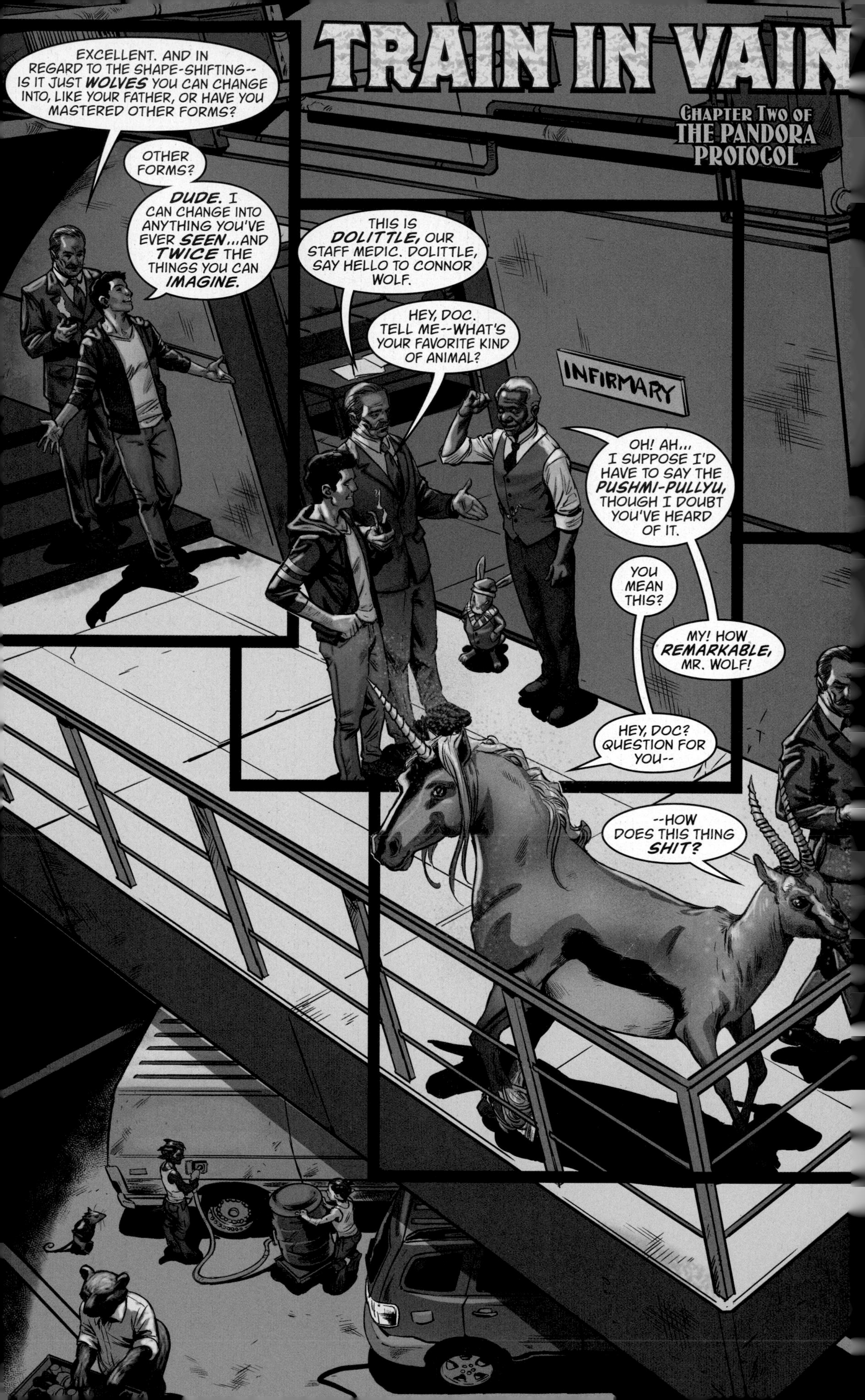
TRAIN IN VAIN
CHAPTER TWO OF THE PANDORA PROTOCOL
EXCELLENT. AND IN REGARD TO THE SHAPE-SHIFTING-- IS IT JUST WOLVES YOU CAN CHANGE INTO, LIKE YOUR FATHER, OR HAVE YOU MASTERED OTHER FORMS?
OTHER FORMS?
DUDE. I CAN CHANGE INTO ANYTHING YOU'VE EVER SEEN...AND TWICE THE THINGS YOU CAN IMAGINE.
THIS IS DOLITTLE, OUR STAFF MEDIC. DOLITTLE, SAY HELLO TO CONNOR WOLF.
HEY, DOC. TELL ME--WHAT'S YOUR FAVORITE KIND OF ANIMAL?
INFIRMARY
OH! AH... I SUPPOSE I'D HAVE TO SAY THE PUSHMI-PULLYU, THOUGH I DOUBT YOU'VE HEARD OF IT.
YOU MEAN THIS?
MY! HOW REMARKABLE, MR. WOLF!
HEY, DOC? QUESTION FOR YOU--
--HOW DOES THIS THING SHIT?

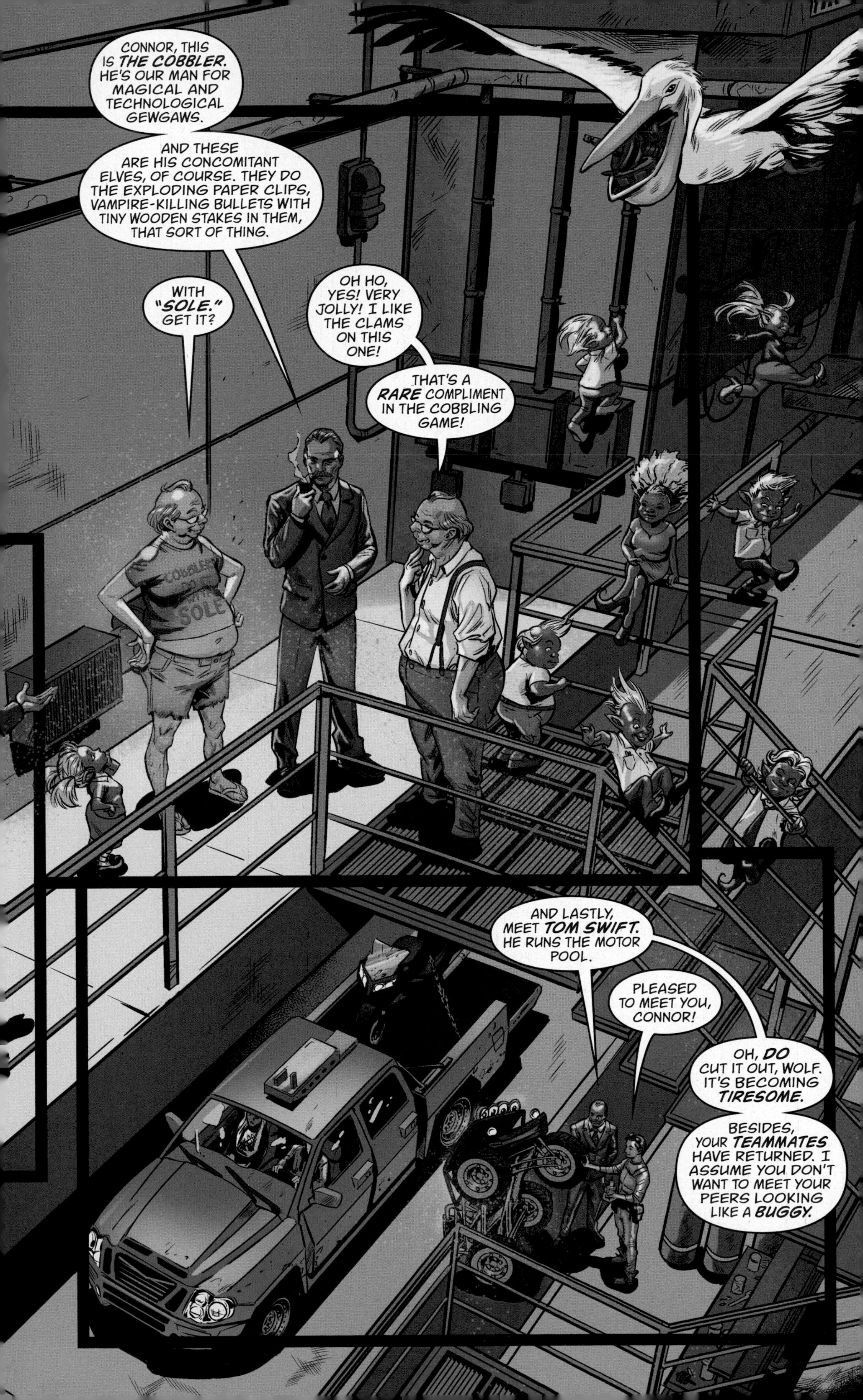
CONNOR, THIS IS THE COBBLER. HE'S OUR MAN FOR MAGICAL AND TECHNOLOGICAL GEWGAWS.
AND THESE ARE HIS CONCOMITANT ELVES, OF COURSE. THEY DO THE EXPLODING PAPER CLIPS, VAMPIRE-KILLING BULLETS WITH TINY WOODEN STAKES IN THEM, THAT SORT OF THING.
WITH "SOLE." GET IT?
OH HO, YES! VERY JOLLY! I LIKE THE CLAMS ON THIS ONE!
THAT'S A RARE COMPLIMENT IN THE COBBLING GAME!
SOLE
AND LASTLY, MEET TOM SWIFT. HE RUNS THE MOTOR POOL.
PLEASED TO MEET YOU, CONNOR!
OH, DO CUT IT OUT, WOLF. IT'S BECOMING TIRESOME.
BESIDES, YOUR TEAMMATES HAVE RETURNED. I ASSUME YOU DON'T WANT TO MEET YOUR PEERS LOOKING LIKE A BUGGY.

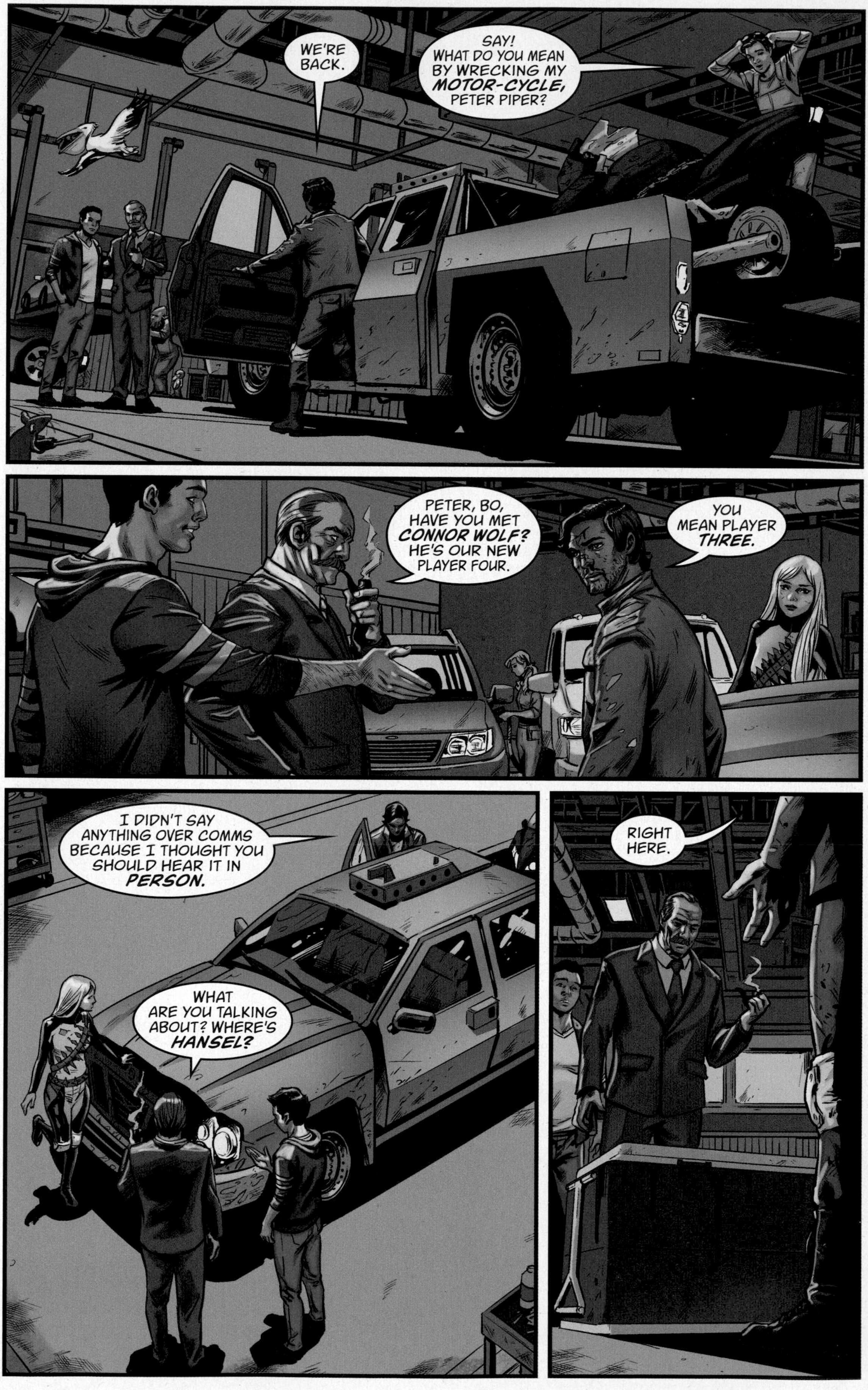
WE'RE BACK.
SAY! WHAT DO YOU MEAN BY WRECKING MY MOTOR-CYCLE, PETER PIPER?
PETER, BO, HAVE YOU MET CONNOR WOLF? HE'S OUR NEW PLAYER FOUR.
YOU MEAN PLAYER THREE.
I DIDN'T SAY ANYTHING OVER COMMS BECAUSE I THOUGHT YOU SHOULD HEAR IT IN PERSON.
WHAT ARE YOU TALKING ABOUT? WHERE'S HANSEL?
RIGHT HERE.

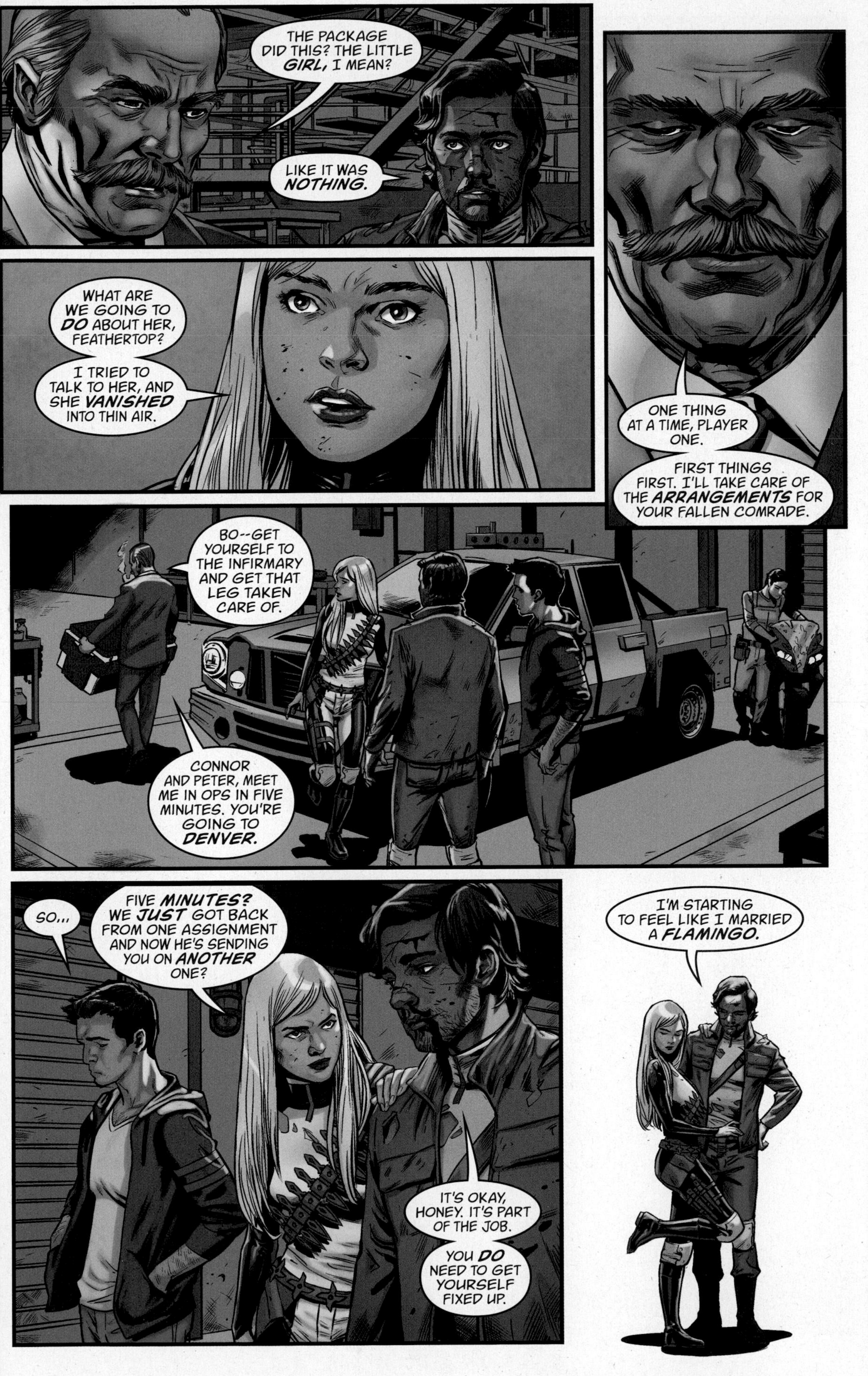
THE PACKAGE DID THIS? THE LITTLE GIRL, I MEAN?
LIKE IT WAS NOTHING.
WHAT ARE WE GOING TO DO ABOUT HER, FEATHERTOP?
I TRIED TO TALK TO HER, AND SHE VANISHED INTO THIN AIR.
ONE THING AT A TIME, PLAYER ONE.
FIRST THINGS FIRST. I'LL TAKE CARE OF THE ARRANGEMENTS FOR YOUR FALLEN COMRADE.
BO--GET YOURSELF TO THE INFIRMARY AND GET THAT LEG TAKEN CARE OF.
CONNOR AND PETER, MEET ME IN OPS IN FIVE MINUTES. YOU'RE GOING TO DENVER.
SO...
FIVE MINUTES? WE JUST GOT BACK FROM ONE ASSIGNMENT AND NOW HE'S SENDING YOU ON ANOTHER ONE?
IT'S OKAY, HONEY. IT'S PART OF THE JOB.
YOU DO NEED TO GET YOURSELF FIXED UP.
I'M STARTING TO FEEL LIKE I MARRIED A FLAMINGO.

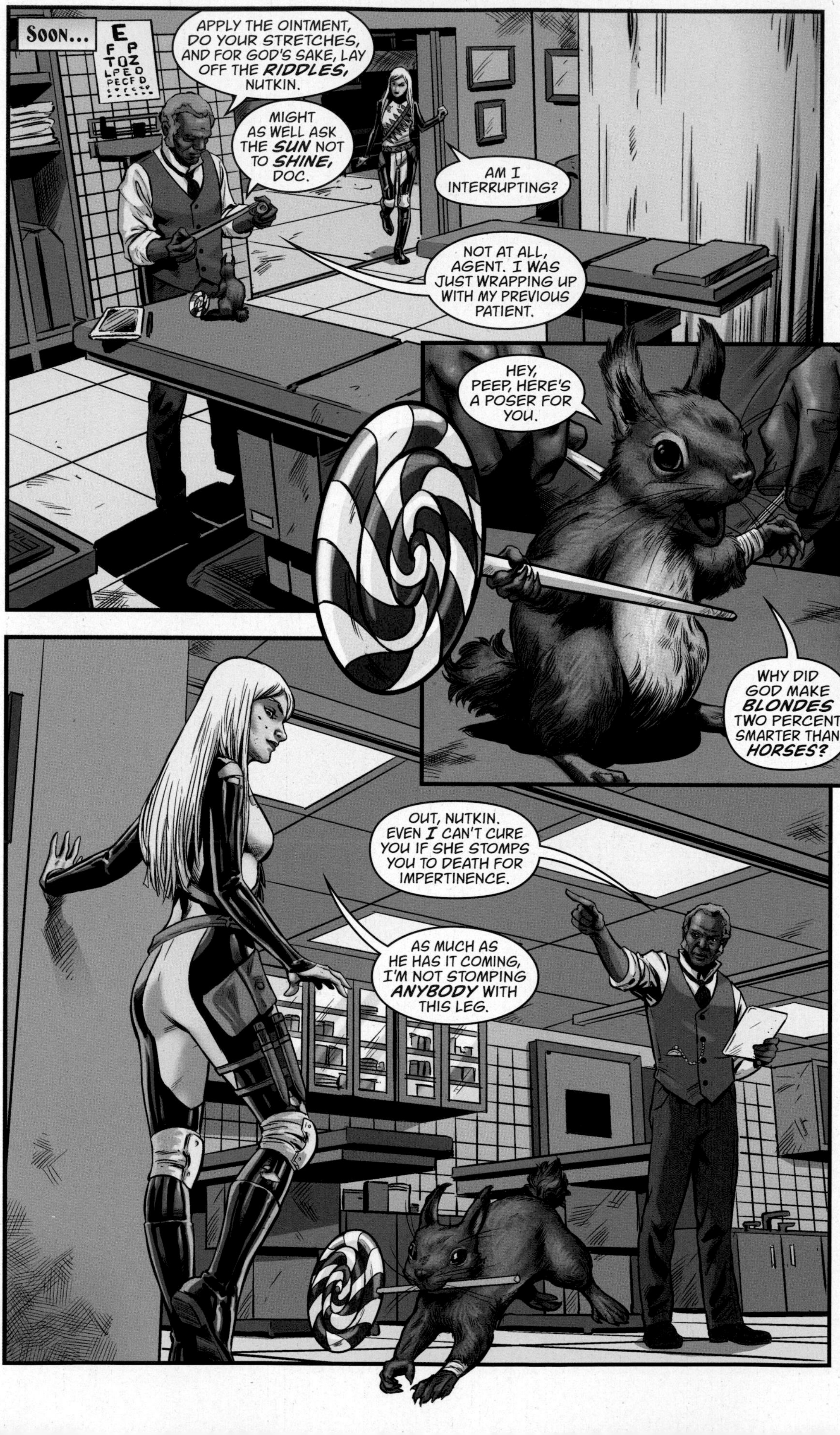
SOON...
E
F P
T O Z
L P E D
P E C F D
APPLY THE OINTMENT, DO YOUR STRETCHES, AND FOR GOD'S SAKE, LAY OFF THE RIDDLES, NUTKIN.
MIGHT AS WELL ASK THE SUN NOT TO SHINE, DOC.
AM I INTERRUPTING?
NOT AT ALL, AGENT. I WAS JUST WRAPPING UP WITH MY PREVIOUS PATIENT.
HEY, PEEP, HERE'S A POSER FOR YOU.
WHY DID GOD MAKE BLONDES TWO PERCENT SMARTER THAN HORSES?
OUT, NUTKIN. EVEN I CAN'T CURE YOU IF SHE STOMPS YOU TO DEATH FOR IMPERTINENCE.
AS MUCH AS HE HAS IT COMING, I'M NOT STOMPING ANYBODY WITH THIS LEG.

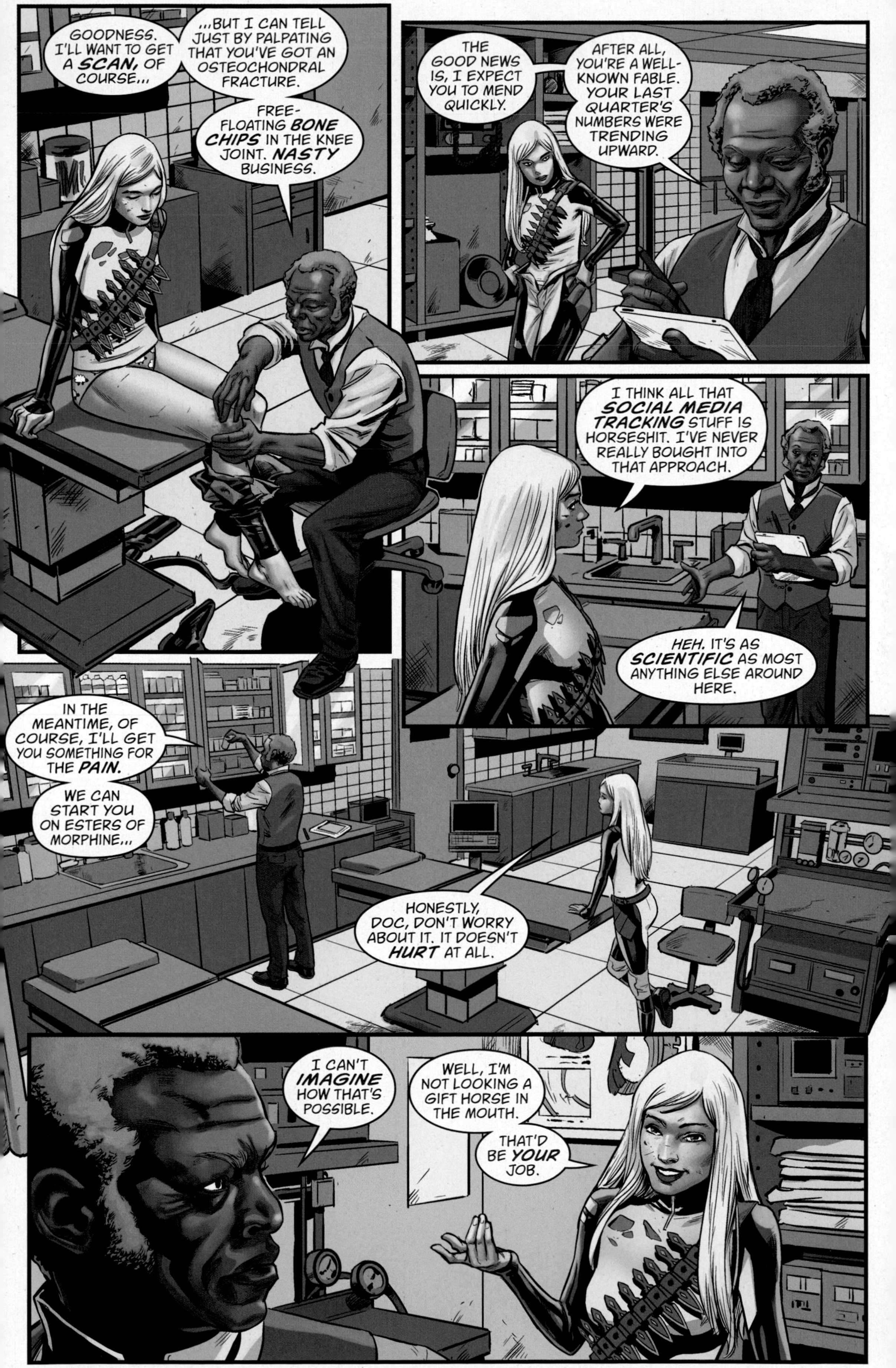
GOODNESS. I'LL WANT TO GET A SCAN, OF COURSE...
...BUT I CAN TELL JUST BY PALPATING THAT YOU'VE GOT AN OSTEOCHONDRAL FRACTURE.
FREE-FLOATING BONE CHIPS IN THE KNEE JOINT. NASTY BUSINESS.
THE GOOD NEWS IS, I EXPECT YOU TO MEND QUICKLY.
AFTER ALL, YOU'RE A WELL-KNOWN FABLE. YOUR LAST QUARTER'S NUMBERS WERE TRENDING UPWARD.
I THINK ALL THAT SOCIAL MEDIA TRACKING STUFF IS HORSESHIT. I'VE NEVER REALLY BOUGHT INTO THAT APPROACH.
HEH. IT'S AS SCIENTIFIC AS MOST ANYTHING ELSE AROUND HERE.
IN THE MEANTIME, OF COURSE, I'LL GET YOU SOMETHING FOR THE PAIN.
WE CAN START YOU ON ESTERS OF MORPHINE...
HONESTLY, DOC, DON'T WORRY ABOUT IT. IT DOESN'T HURT AT ALL.
I CAN'T IMAGINE HOW THAT'S POSSIBLE.
WELL, I'M NOT LOOKING A GIFT HORSE IN THE MOUTH.
THAT'D BE YOUR JOB.

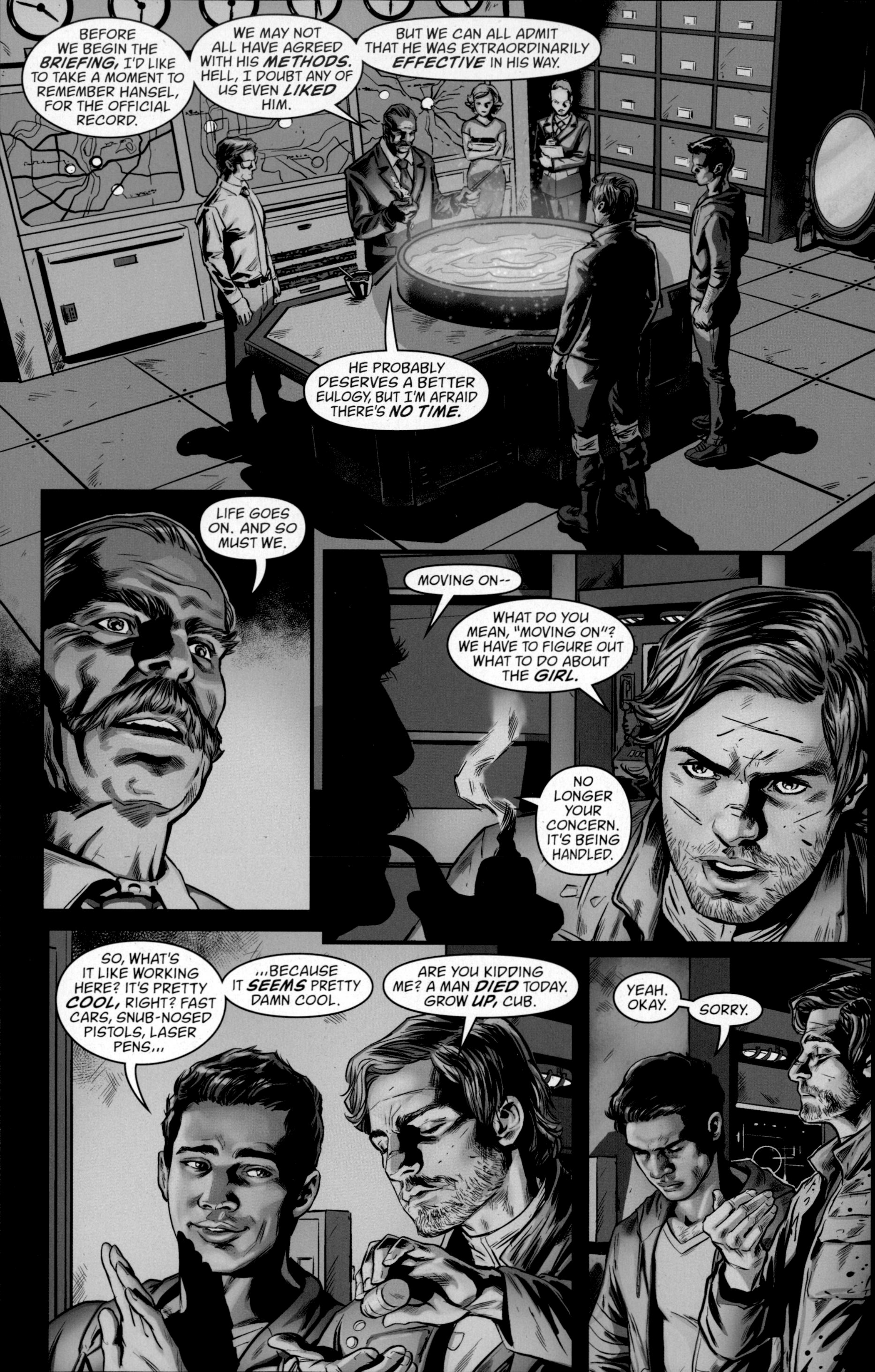
BEFORE WE BEGIN THE BRIEFING, I'D LIKE TO TAKE A MOMENT TO REMEMBER HANSEL, FOR THE OFFICIAL RECORD.
WE MAY NOT ALL HAVE AGREED WITH HIS METHODS. HELL, I DOUBT ANY OF US EVEN LIKED HIM.
BUT WE CAN ALL ADMIT THAT HE WAS EXTRAORDINARILY EFFECTIVE IN HIS WAY.
HE PROBABLY DESERVES A BETTER EULOGY, BUT I'M AFRAID THERE'S NO TIME.
LIFE GOES ON. AND SO MUST WE.
MOVING ON--
WHAT DO YOU MEAN, "MOVING ON"? WE HAVE TO FIGURE OUT WHAT TO DO ABOUT THE GIRL.
NO LONGER YOUR CONCERN. IT'S BEING HANDLED.
SO, WHAT'S IT LIKE WORKING HERE? IT'S PRETTY COOL, RIGHT? FAST CARS, SNUB-NOSED PISTOLS, LASER PENS...
...BECAUSE IT SEEMS PRETTY DAMN COOL.
ARE YOU KIDDING ME? A MAN DIED TODAY. GROW UP, CUB.
YEAH. OKAY.
SORRY.

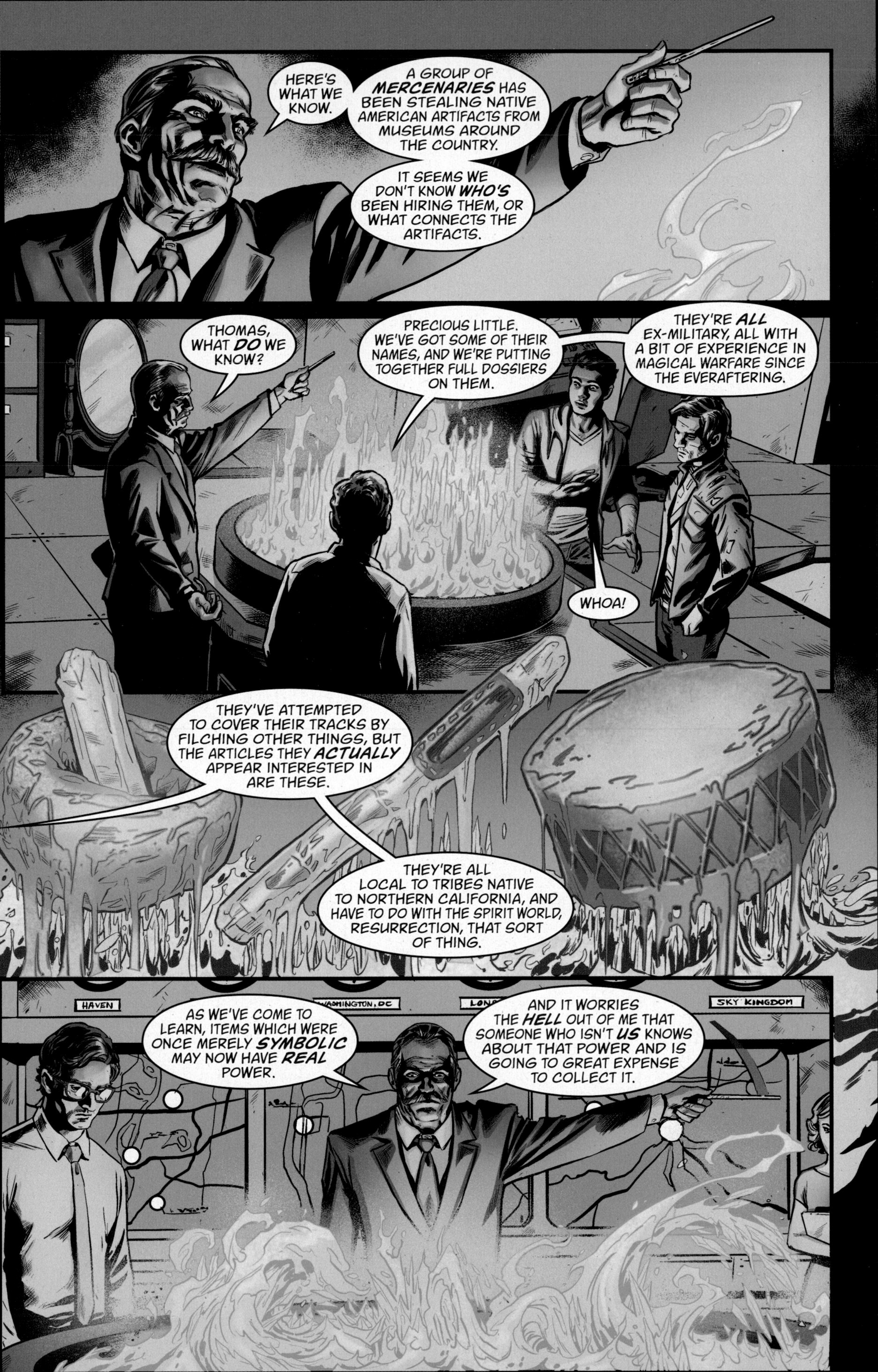
HERE'S WHAT WE KNOW.
A GROUP OF MERCENARIES HAS BEEN STEALING NATIVE AMERICAN ARTIFACTS FROM MUSEUMS AROUND THE COUNTRY.
IT SEEMS WE DON'T KNOW WHO'S BEEN HIRING THEM, OR WHAT CONNECTS THE ARTIFACTS.
THOMAS, WHAT DO WE KNOW?
PRECIOUS LITTLE. WE'VE GOT SOME OF THEIR NAMES, AND WE'RE PUTTING TOGETHER FULL DOSSIERS ON THEM.
THEY'RE ALL EX-MILITARY, ALL WITH A BIT OF EXPERIENCE IN MAGICAL WARFARE SINCE THE EVERAFTERING.
WHOA!
THEY'VE ATTEMPTED TO COVER THEIR TRACKS BY FILCHING OTHER THINGS, BUT THE ARTICLES THEY ACTUALLY APPEAR INTERESTED IN ARE THESE.
THEY'RE ALL LOCAL TO TRIBES NATIVE TO NORTHERN CALIFORNIA, AND HAVE TO DO WITH THE SPIRIT WORLD, RESURRECTION, THAT SORT OF THING.
HAVEN
WASHINGTON, DC
SKY KINGDOM
AS WE'VE COME TO LEARN, ITEMS WHICH WERE ONCE MERELY SYMBOLIC MAY NOW HAVE REAL POWER.
AND IT WORRIES THE HELL OUT OF ME THAT SOMEONE WHO ISN'T US KNOWS ABOUT THAT POWER AND IS GOING TO GREAT EXPENSE TO COLLECT IT.

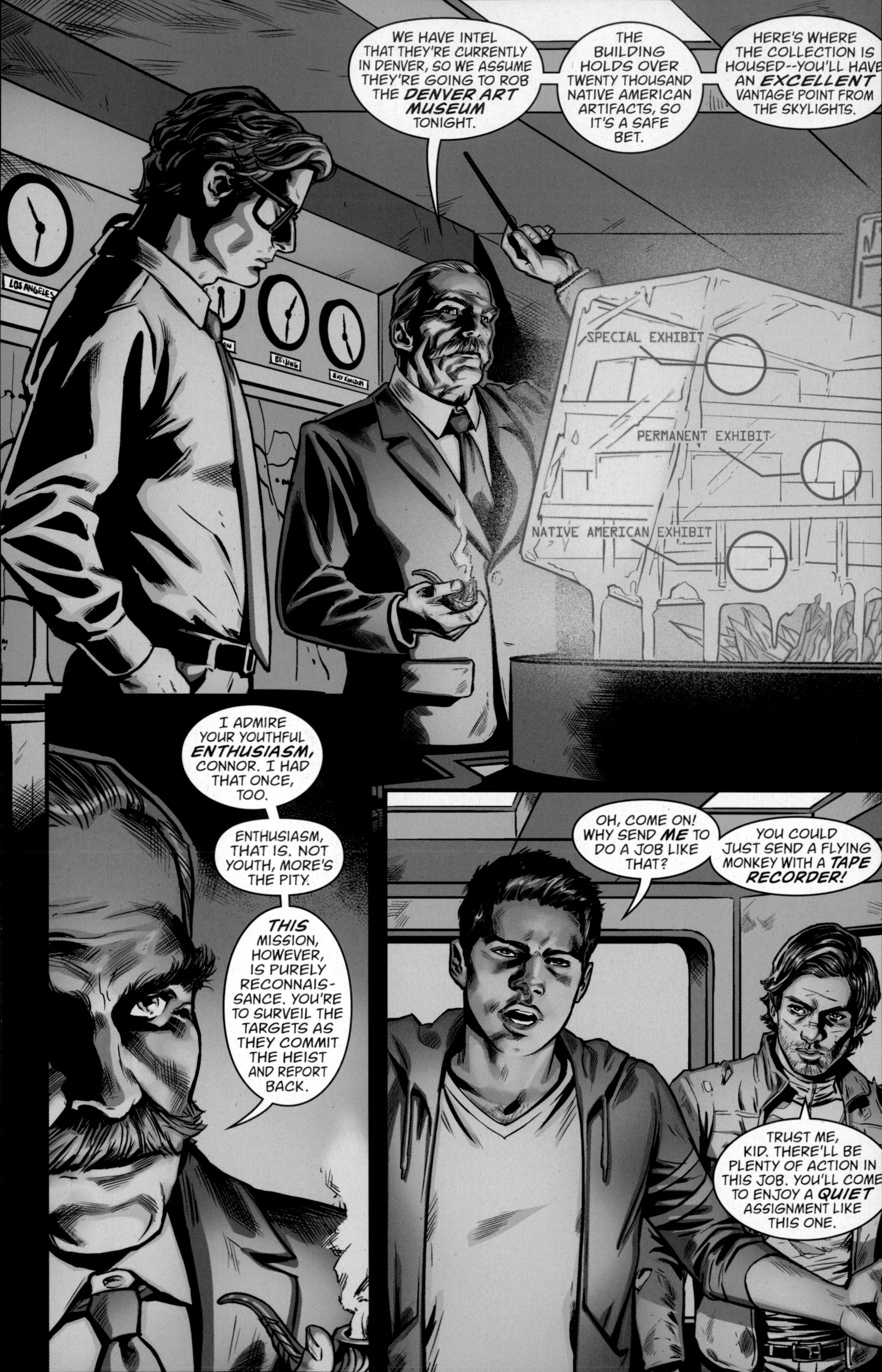
WE HAVE INTEL THAT THEY'RE CURRENTLY IN DENVER, SO WE ASSUME THEY'RE GOING TO ROB THE DENVER ART MUSEUM TONIGHT.
THE BUILDING HOLDS OVER TWENTY THOUSAND NATIVE AMERICAN ARTIFACTS, SO IT'S A SAFE BET.
HERE'S WHERE THE COLLECTION IS HOUSED--YOU'LL HAVE AN EXCELLENT VANTAGE POINT FROM THE SKYLIGHTS.
LOS ANGELES
BEIJING
SPECIAL EXHIBIT
PERMANENT EXHIBIT
NATIVE AMERICAN EXHIBIT
I ADMIRE YOUR YOUTHFUL ENTHUSIASM, CONNOR. I HAD THAT ONCE, TOO.
ENTHUSIASM, THAT IS. NOT YOUTH, MORE'S THE PITY.
THIS MISSION, HOWEVER, IS PURELY RECONNAIS-SANCE. YOU'RE TO SURVEIL THE TARGETS AS THEY COMMIT THE HEIST AND REPORT BACK.
OH, COME ON! WHY SEND ME TO DO A JOB LIKE THAT?
YOU COULD JUST SEND A FLYING MONKEY WITH A TAPE RECORDER!
TRUST ME, KID. THERE'LL BE PLENTY OF ACTION IN THIS JOB. YOU'LL COME TO ENJOY A QUIET ASSIGNMENT LIKE THIS ONE.

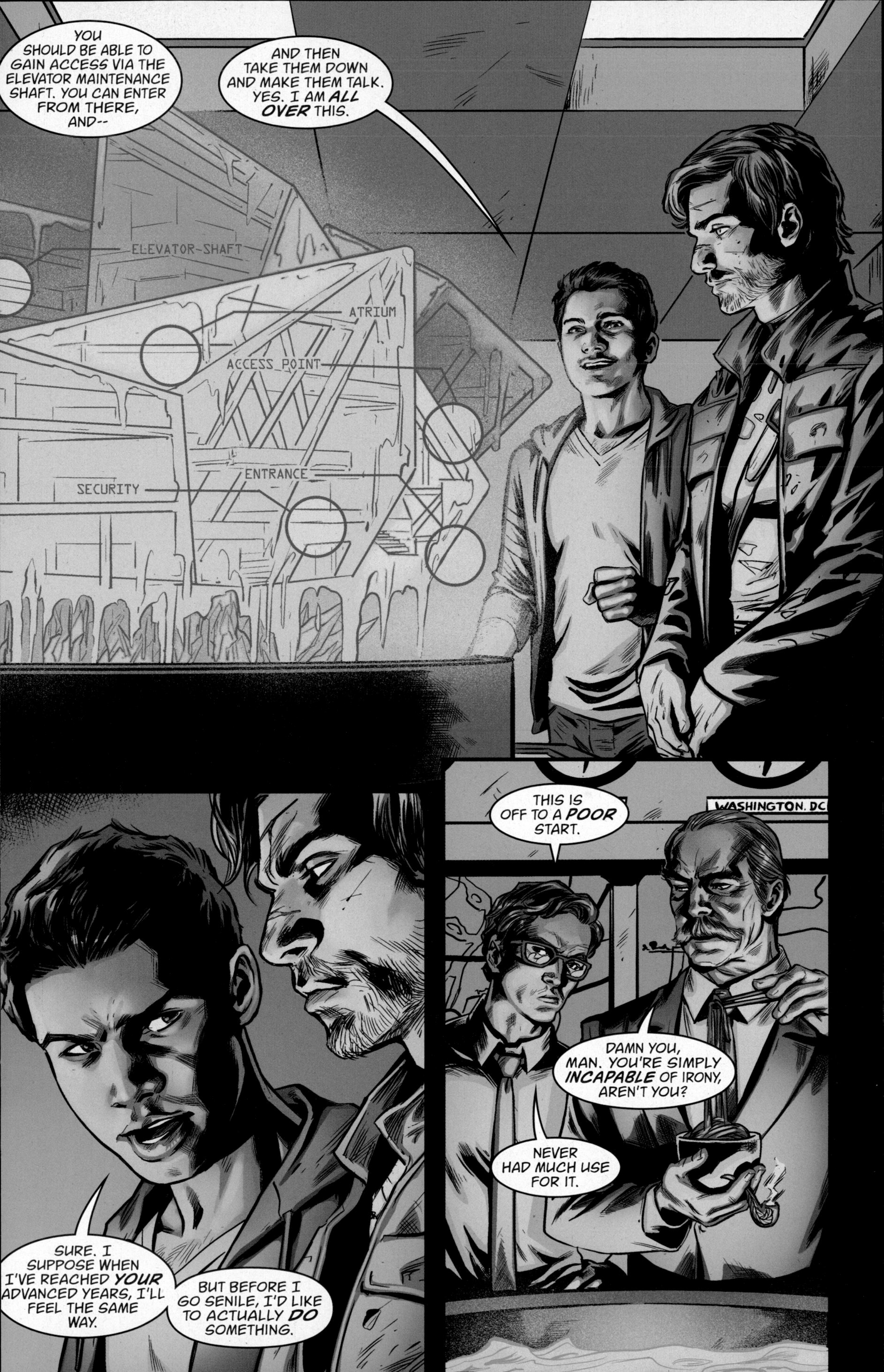
YOU SHOULD BE ABLE TO GAIN ACCESS VIA THE ELEVATOR MAINTENANCE SHAFT. YOU CAN ENTER FROM THERE, AND--
AND THEN TAKE THEM DOWN AND MAKE THEM TALK. YES. I AM ALL OVER THIS.
ELEVATOR SHAFT
ATRIUM
ACCESS POINT
ENTRANCE
SECURITY
SURE. I SUPPOSE WHEN I'VE REACHED YOUR ADVANCED YEARS, I'LL FEEL THE SAME WAY.
BUT BEFORE I GO SENILE, I'D LIKE TO ACTUALLY DO SOMETHING.
WASHINGTON, DC
THIS IS OFF TO A POOR START.
DAMN YOU, MAN. YOU'RE SIMPLY INCAPABLE OF IRONY, AREN'T YOU?
NEVER HAD MUCH USE FOR IT.

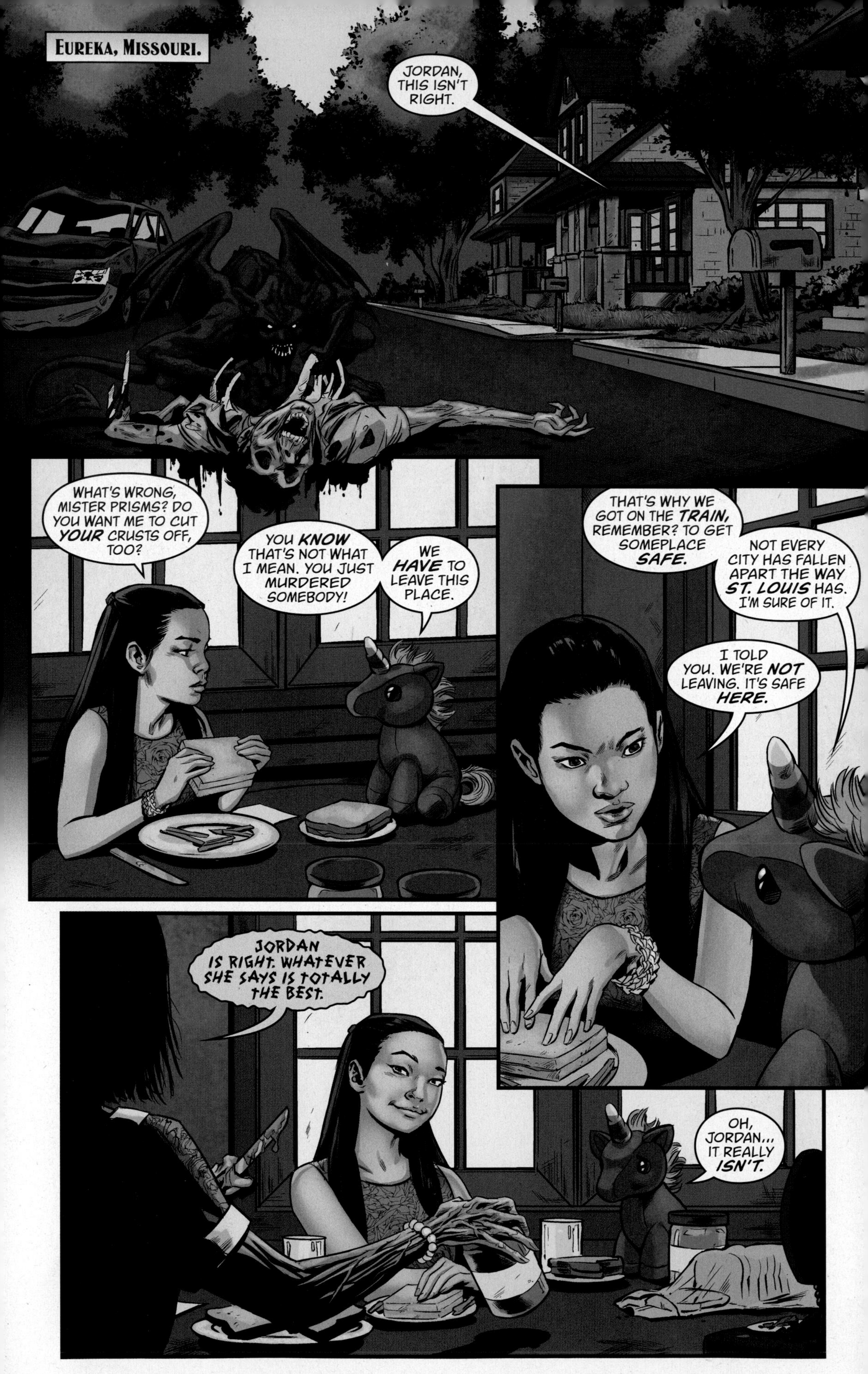
EUREKA, MISSOURI.
JORDAN, THIS ISN'T RIGHT.
WHAT'S WRONG, MISTER PRISMS? DO YOU WANT ME TO CUT YOUR CRUSTS OFF, TOO?
YOU KNOW THAT'S NOT WHAT I MEAN. YOU JUST MURDERED SOMEBODY!
WE HAVE TO LEAVE THIS PLACE.
THAT'S WHY WE GOT ON THE TRAIN, REMEMBER? TO GET SOMEPLACE SAFE.
NOT EVERY CITY HAS FALLEN APART THE WAY ST. LOUIS HAS. I'M SURE OF IT.
I TOLD YOU. WE'RE NOT LEAVING. IT'S SAFE HERE.
JORDAN IS RIGHT. WHATEVER SHE SAYS IS TOTALLY THE BEST.
OH, JORDAN... IT REALLY ISN'T.

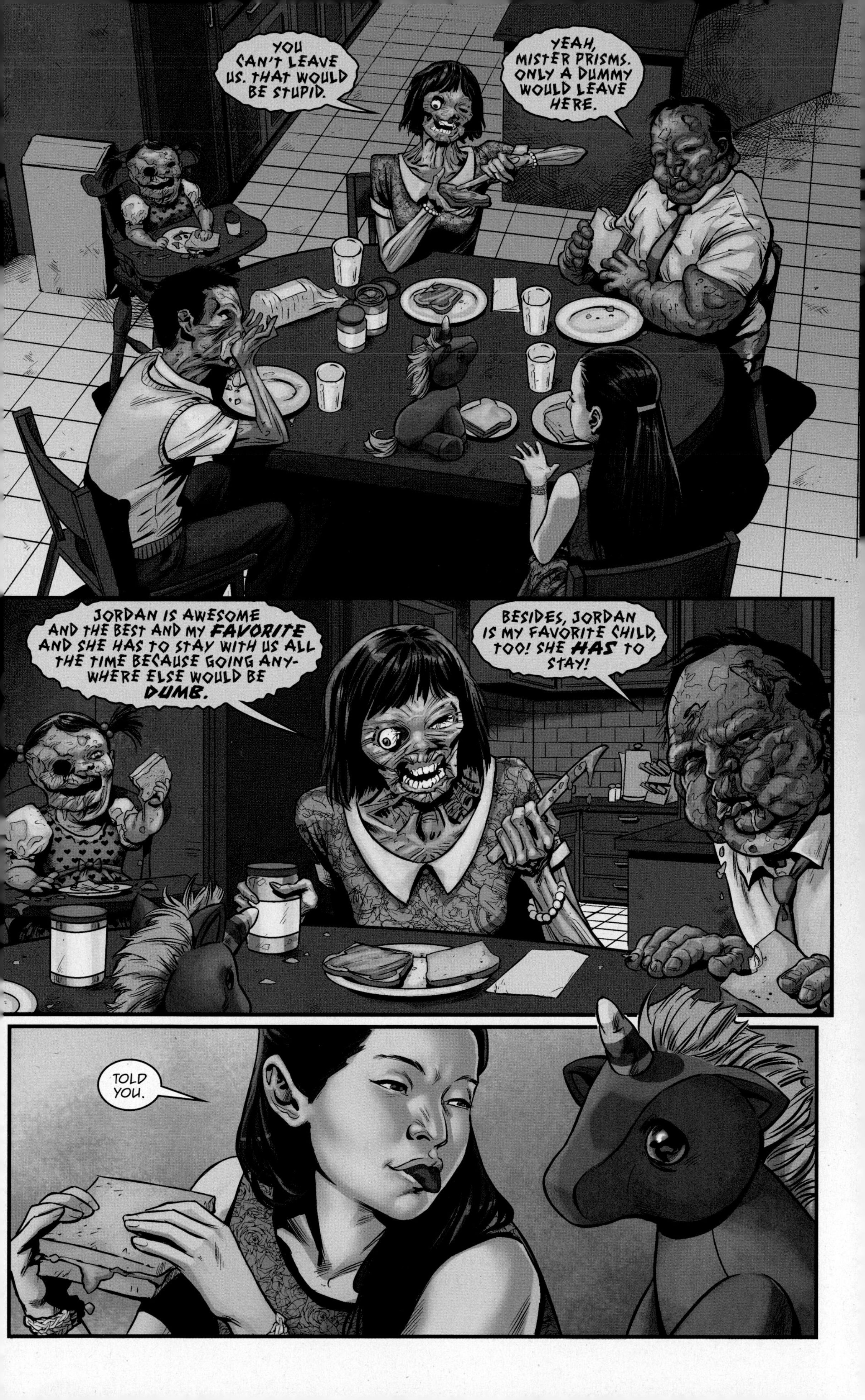
YOU CAN'T LEAVE US. THAT WOULD BE STUPID.
YEAH, MISTER PRISMS. ONLY A DUMMY WOULD LEAVE HERE.
JORDAN IS AWESOME AND THE BEST AND MY FAVORITE AND SHE HAS TO STAY WITH US ALL THE TIME BECAUSE GOING ANY-WHERE ELSE WOULD BE DUMB.
BESIDES, JORDAN IS MY FAVORITE CHILD, TOO! SHE HAS TO STAY!
TOLD YOU.

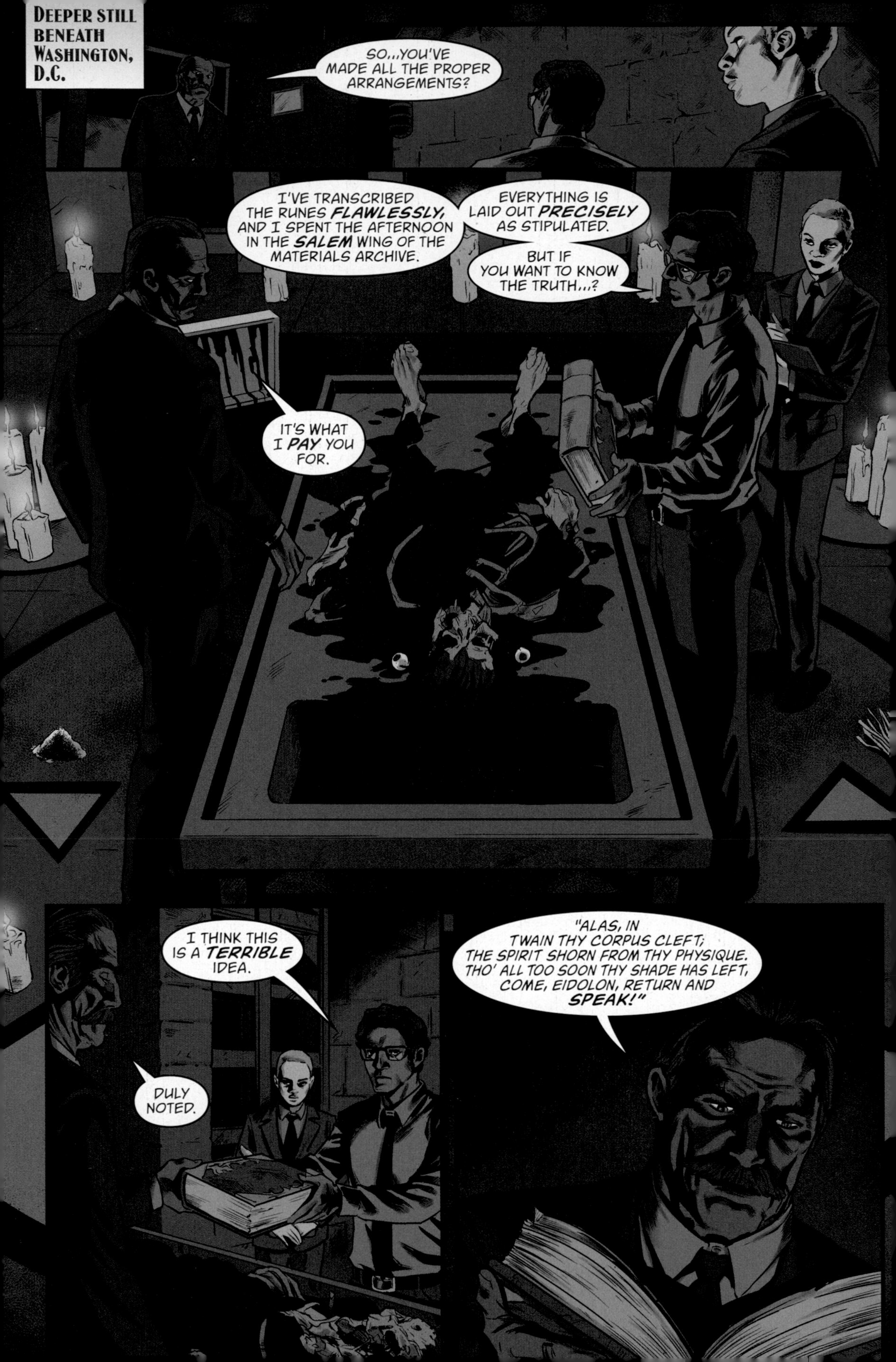

DEEPER STILL BENEATH WASHINGTON, D.C.
SO...YOU'VE MADE ALL THE PROPER ARRANGEMENTS?
I'VE TRANSCRIBED THE RUNES FLAWLESSLY, AND I SPENT THE AFTERNOON IN THE SALEM WING OF THE MATERIALS ARCHIVE.
EVERYTHING IS LAID OUT PRECISELY AS STIPULATED.
BUT IF YOU WANT TO KNOW THE TRUTH...?
IT'S WHAT I PAY YOU FOR.
I THINK THIS IS A TERRIBLE IDEA.
DULY NOTED.
"ALAS, IN TWAIN THY CORPUS CLEFT; THE SPIRIT SHORN FROM THY PHYSIQUE. THO' ALL TOO SOON THY SHADE HAS LEFT, COME, EIDOLON, RETURN AND SPEAK!"

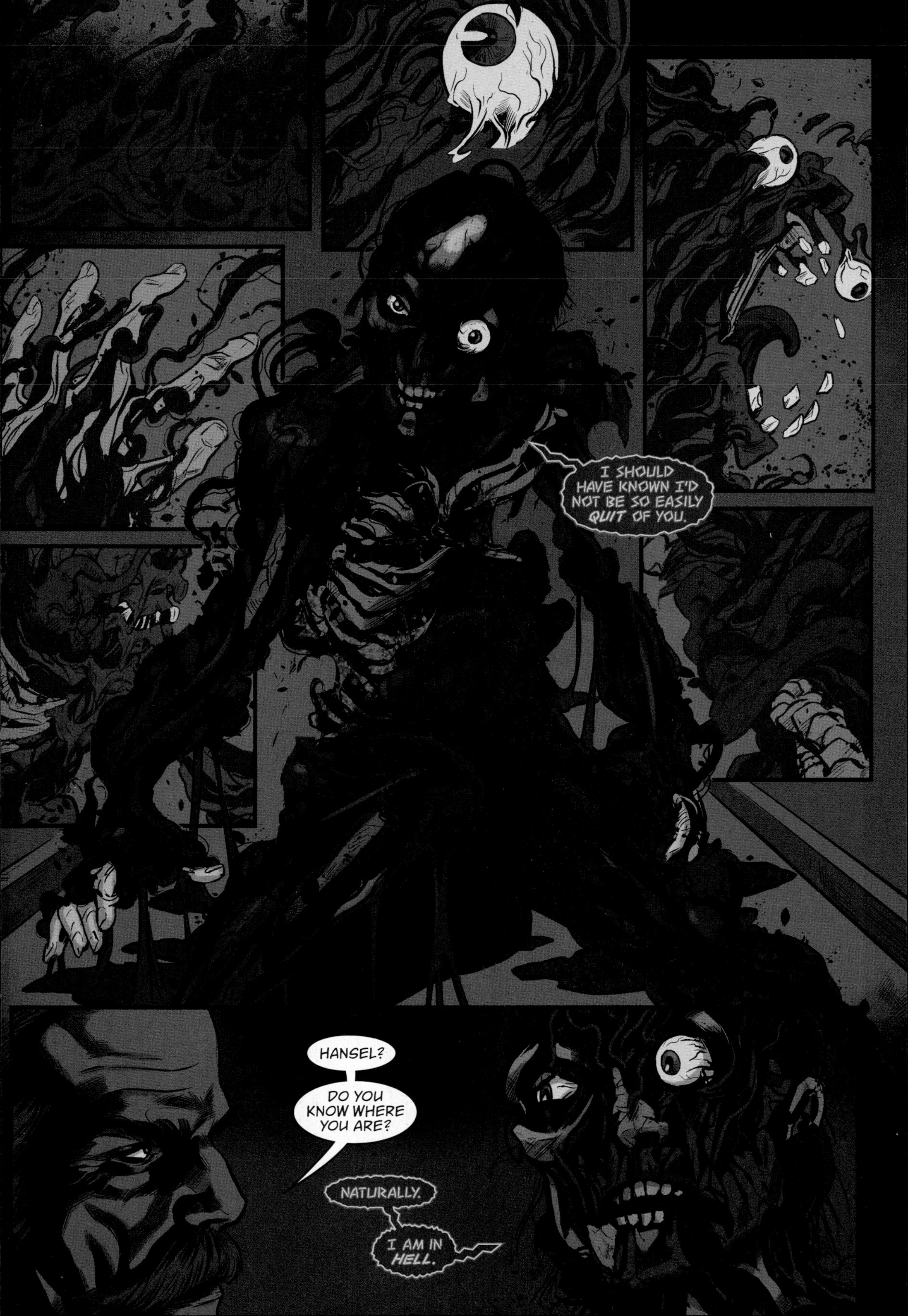
I SHOULD HAVE KNOWN I'D NOT BE SO EASILY QUIT OF YOU.
HANSEL?
DO YOU KNOW WHERE YOU ARE?
NATURALLY.
I AM IN HELL.

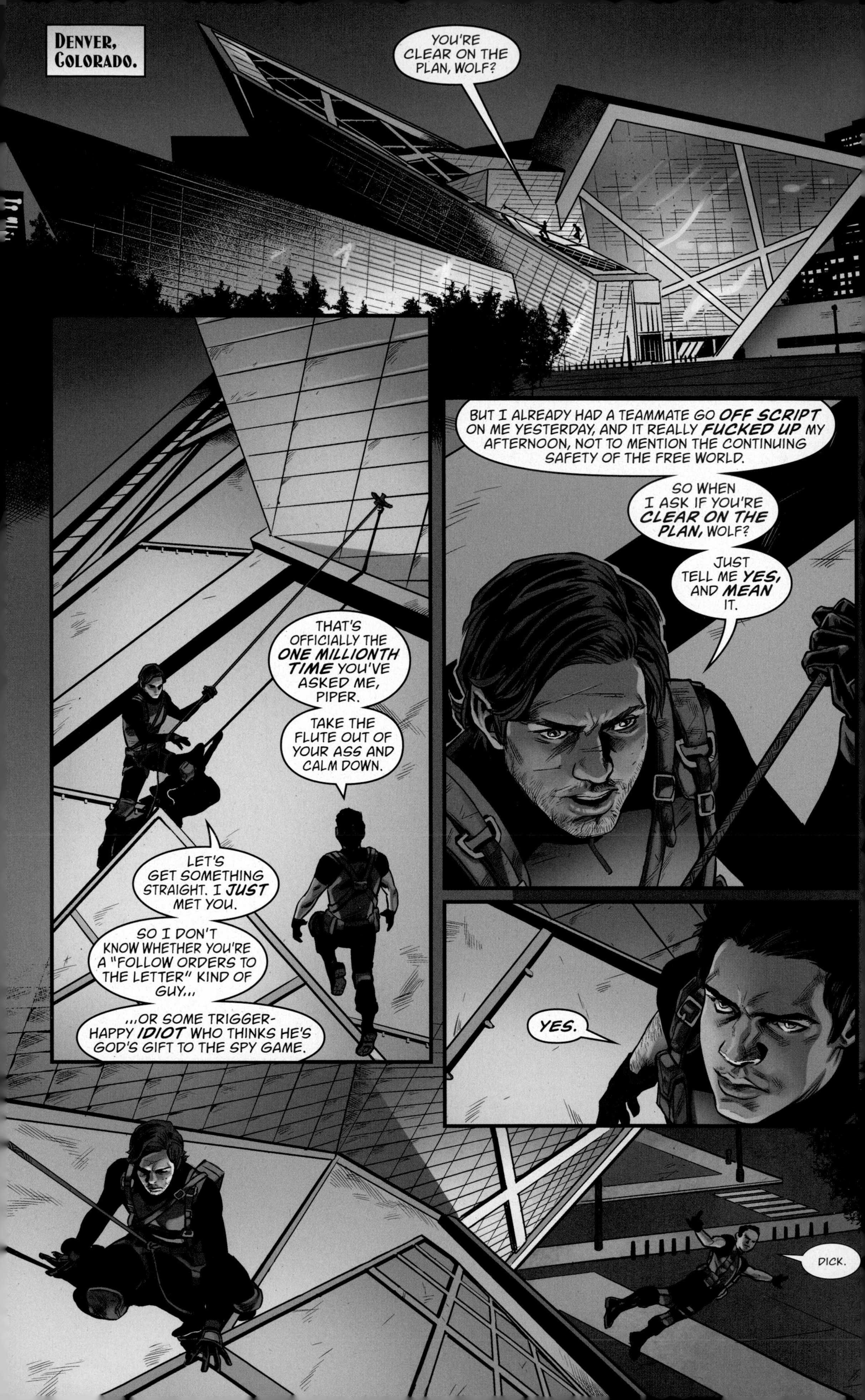
DENVER, COLORADO.
YOU'RE CLEAR ON THE PLAN, WOLF?
THAT'S OFFICIALLY THE ONE MILLIONTH TIME YOU'VE ASKED ME, PIPER.
TAKE THE FLUTE OUT OF YOUR ASS AND CALM DOWN.
LET'S GET SOMETHING STRAIGHT. I JUST MET YOU.
SO I DON'T KNOW WHETHER YOU'RE A "FOLLOW ORDERS TO THE LETTER" KIND OF GUY...
...OR SOME TRIGGER-HAPPY IDIOT WHO THINKS HE'S GOD'S GIFT TO THE SPY GAME.
BUT I ALREADY HAD A TEAMMATE GO OFF SCRIPT ON ME YESTERDAY, AND IT REALLY FUCKED UP MY AFTERNOON, NOT TO MENTION THE CONTINUING SAFETY OF THE FREE WORLD.
SO WHEN I ASK IF YOU'RE CLEAR ON THE PLAN, WOLF?
JUST TELL ME YES, AND MEAN IT.
YES.
DICK.

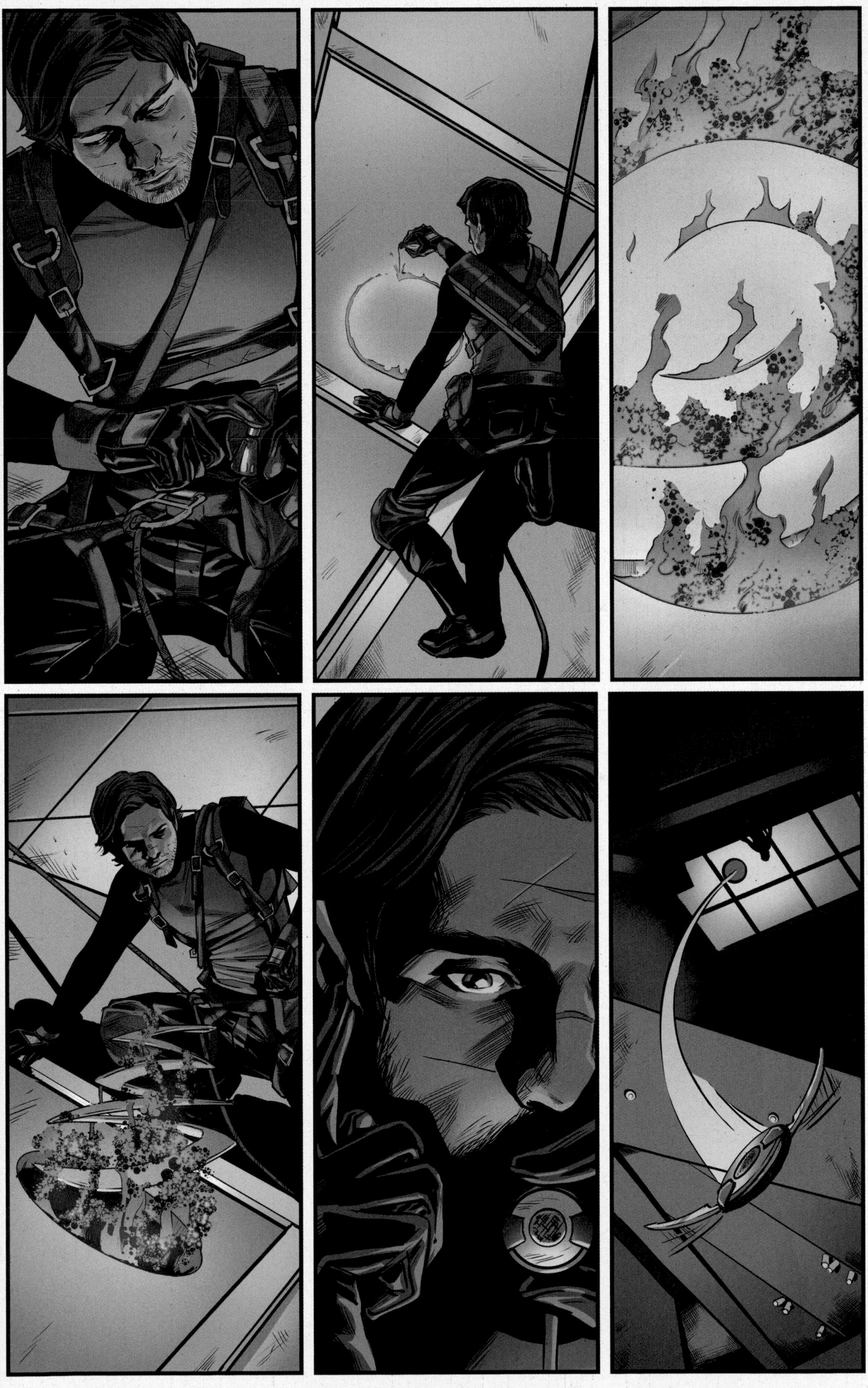

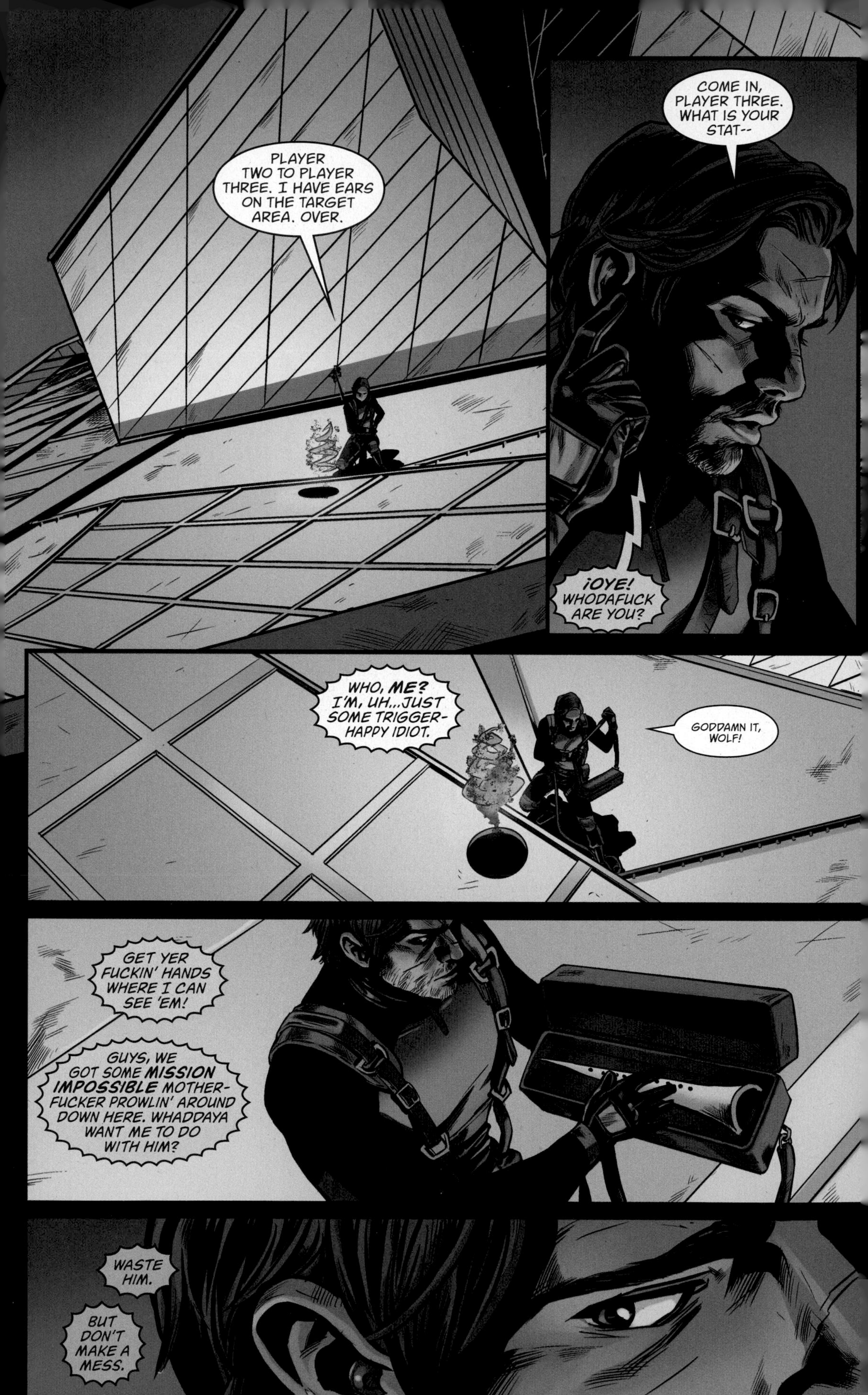
PLAYER TWO TO PLAYER THREE. I HAVE EARS ON THE TARGET AREA. OVER.
COME IN, PLAYER THREE. WHAT IS YOUR STAT--
¡OYE! WHODAFUCK ARE YOU?
WHO, ME? I'M, UH...JUST SOME TRIGGER-HAPPY IDIOT.
GODDAMN IT, WOLF!
GET YER FUCKIN' HANDS WHERE I CAN SEE 'EM!
GUYS, WE GOT SOME MISSION IMPOSSIBLE MOTHER-FUCKER PROWLIN' AROUND DOWN HERE. WHADDAYA WANT ME TO DO WITH HIM?
WASTE HIM.
BUT DON'T MAKE A MESS.

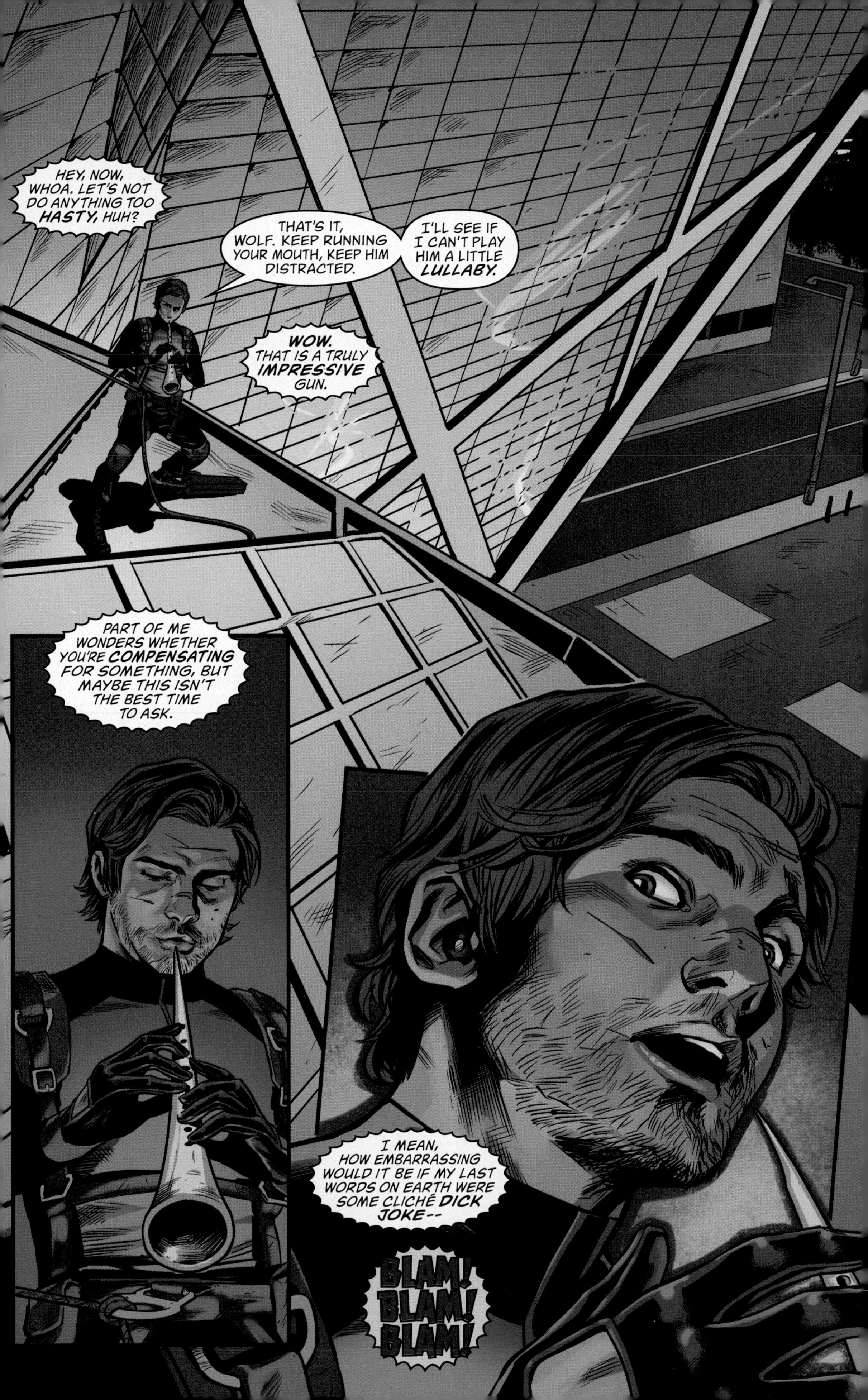
HEY, NOW, WHOA. LET'S NOT DO ANYTHING TOO **HASTY,** HUH?
THAT'S IT, WOLF. KEEP RUNNING YOUR MOUTH, KEEP HIM DISTRACTED.
I'LL SEE IF I CAN'T PLAY HIM A LITTLE **LULLABY.**
WOW. THAT IS A TRULY **IMPRESSIVE** GUN.
PART OF ME WONDERS WHETHER YOU'RE **COMPENSATING** FOR SOMETHING, BUT MAYBE THIS ISN'T THE BEST TIME TO ASK.
I MEAN, HOW EMBARRASSING WOULD IT BE IF MY LAST WORDS ON EARTH WERE SOME CLICHÉ **DICK JOKE--**
BLAM! BLAM! BLAM!

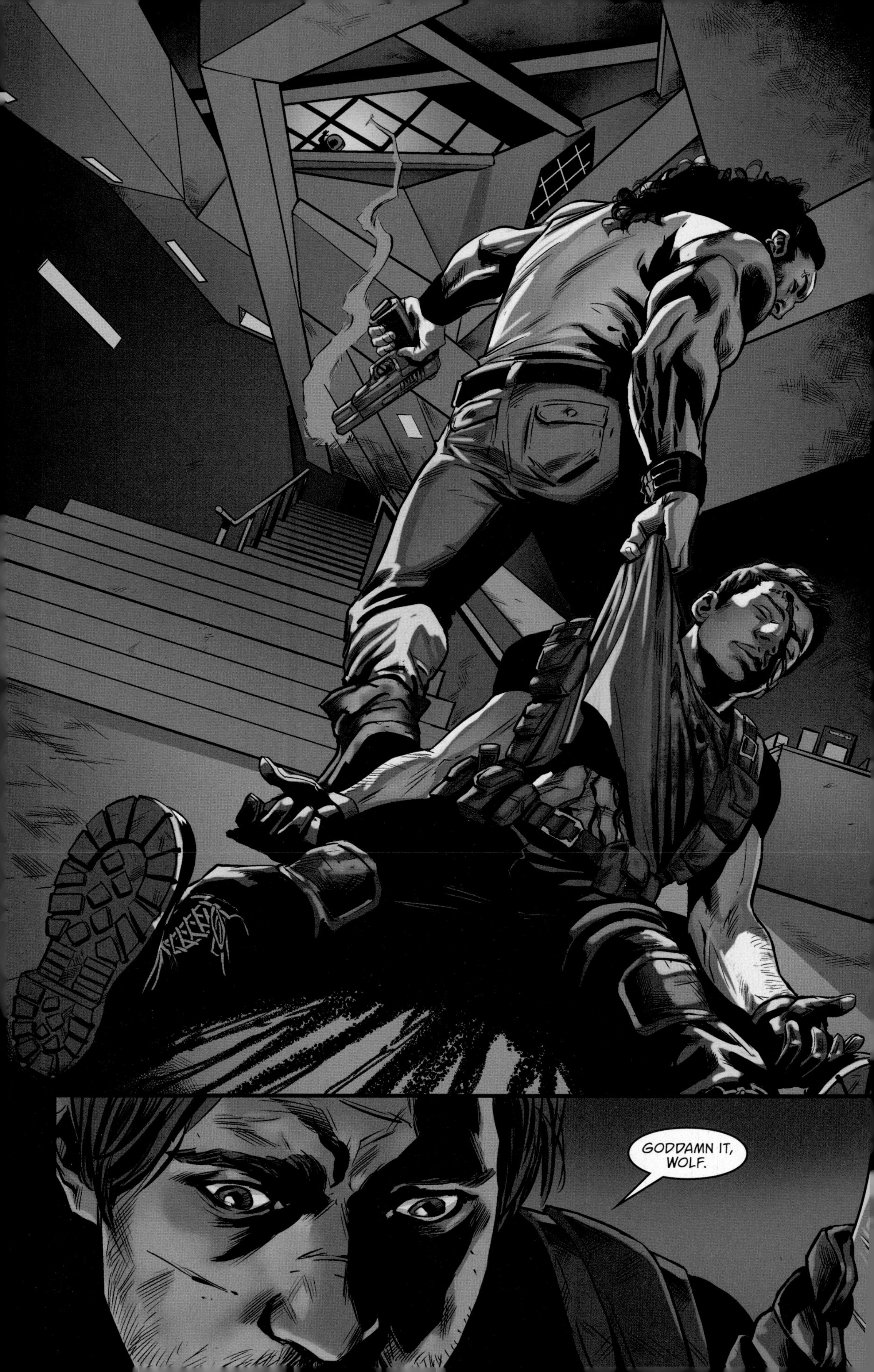
GODDAMN IT, WOLF.

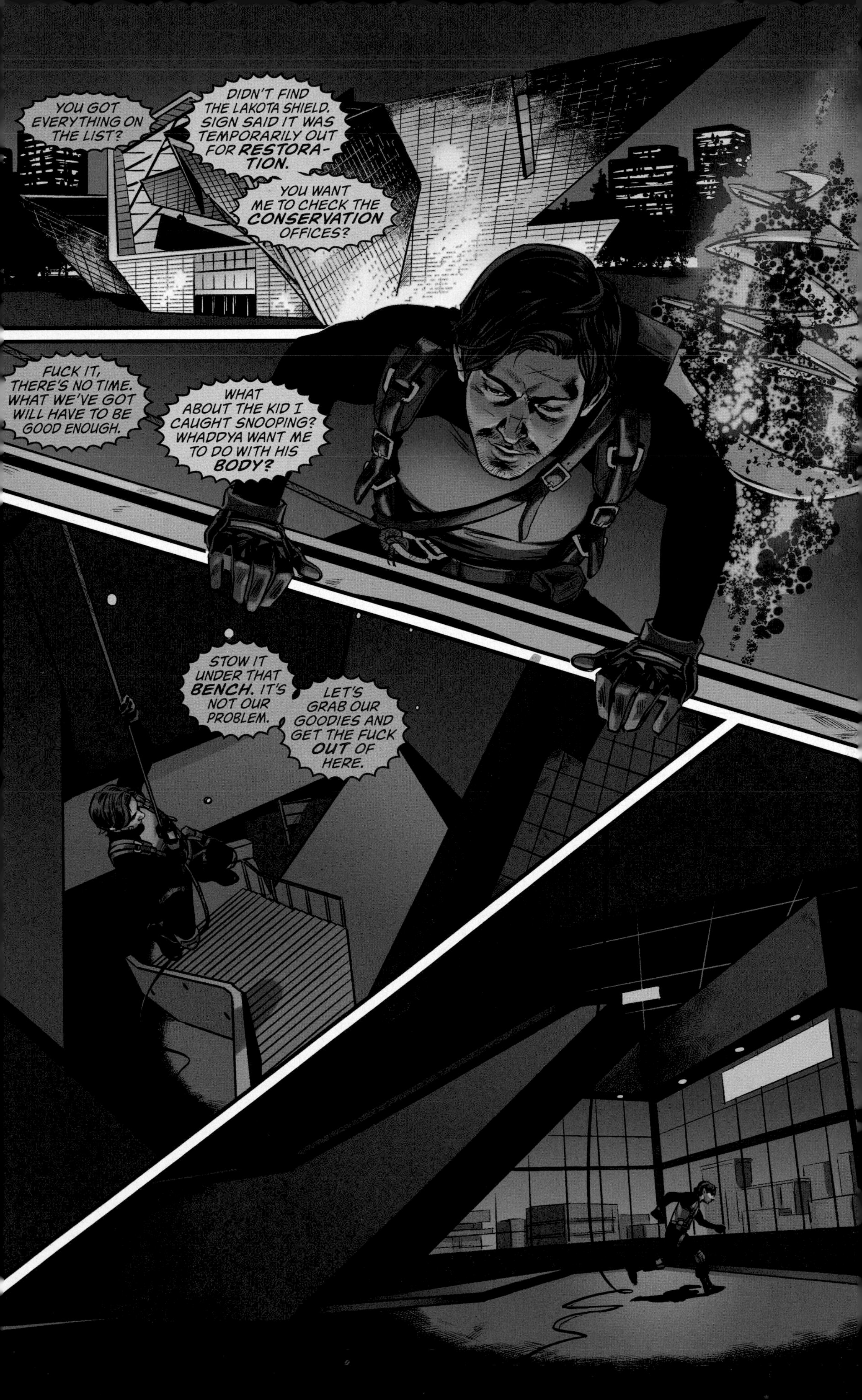
YOU GOT EVERYTHING ON THE LIST?
DIDN'T FIND THE LAKOTA SHIELD. SIGN SAID IT WAS TEMPORARILY OUT FOR RESTORATION.
YOU WANT ME TO CHECK THE CONSERVATION OFFICES?
FUCK IT, THERE'S NO TIME. WHAT WE'VE GOT WILL HAVE TO BE GOOD ENOUGH.
WHAT ABOUT THE KID I CAUGHT SNOOPING? WHADDYA WANT ME TO DO WITH HIS BODY?
STOW IT UNDER THAT BENCH. IT'S NOT OUR PROBLEM.
LET'S GRAB OUR GOODIES AND GET THE FUCK OUT OF HERE.

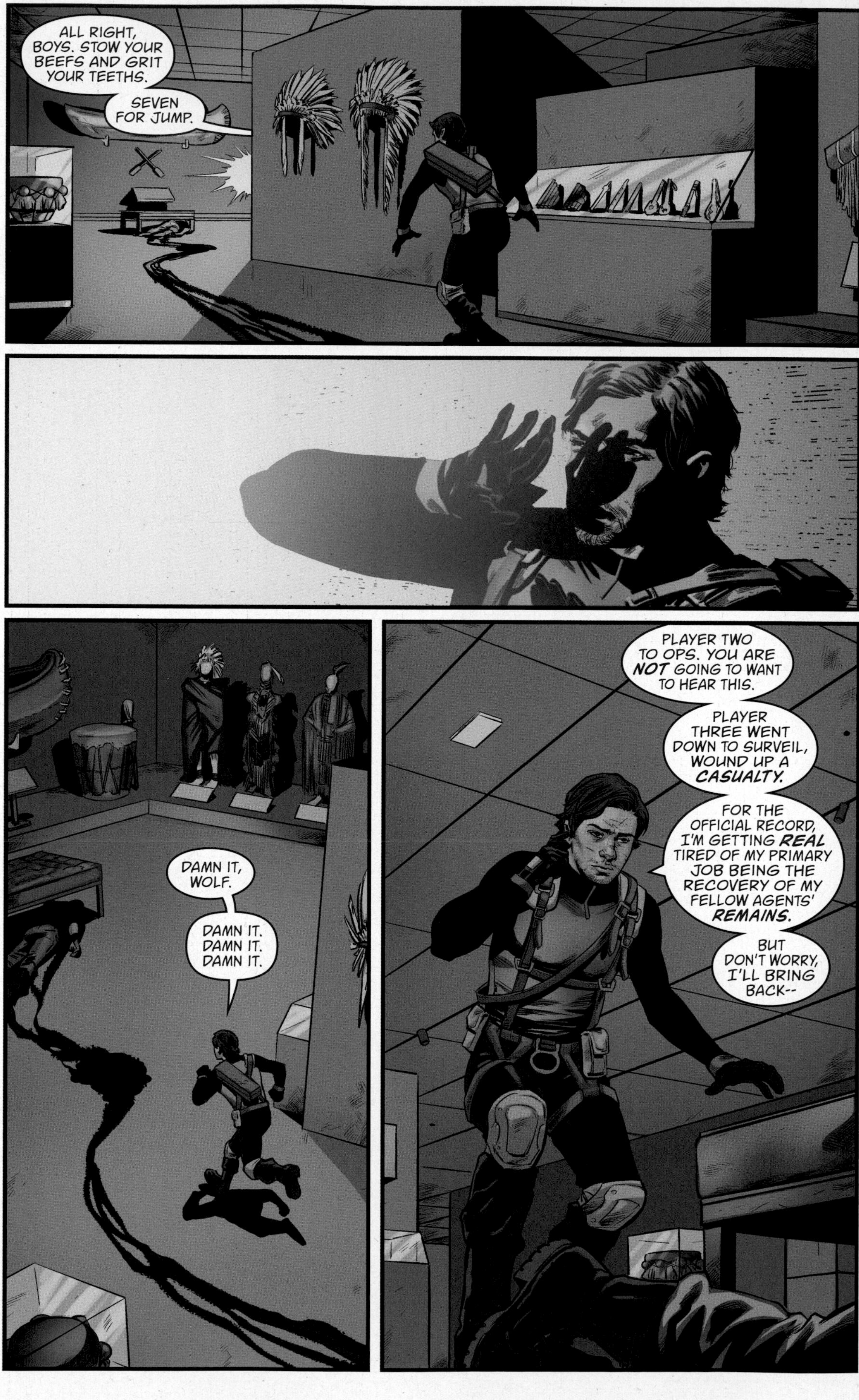
ALL RIGHT, BOYS. STOW YOUR BEEFS AND GRIT YOUR TEETHS.
SEVEN FOR JUMP.
DAMN IT, WOLF.
DAMN IT. DAMN IT. DAMN IT.
PLAYER TWO TO OPS. YOU ARE NOT GOING TO WANT TO HEAR THIS.
PLAYER THREE WENT DOWN TO SURVEIL, WOUND UP A CASUALTY.
FOR THE OFFICIAL RECORD, I'M GETTING REAL TIRED OF MY PRIMARY JOB BEING THE RECOVERY OF MY FELLOW AGENTS' REMAINS.
BUT DON'T WORRY, I'LL BRING BACK--

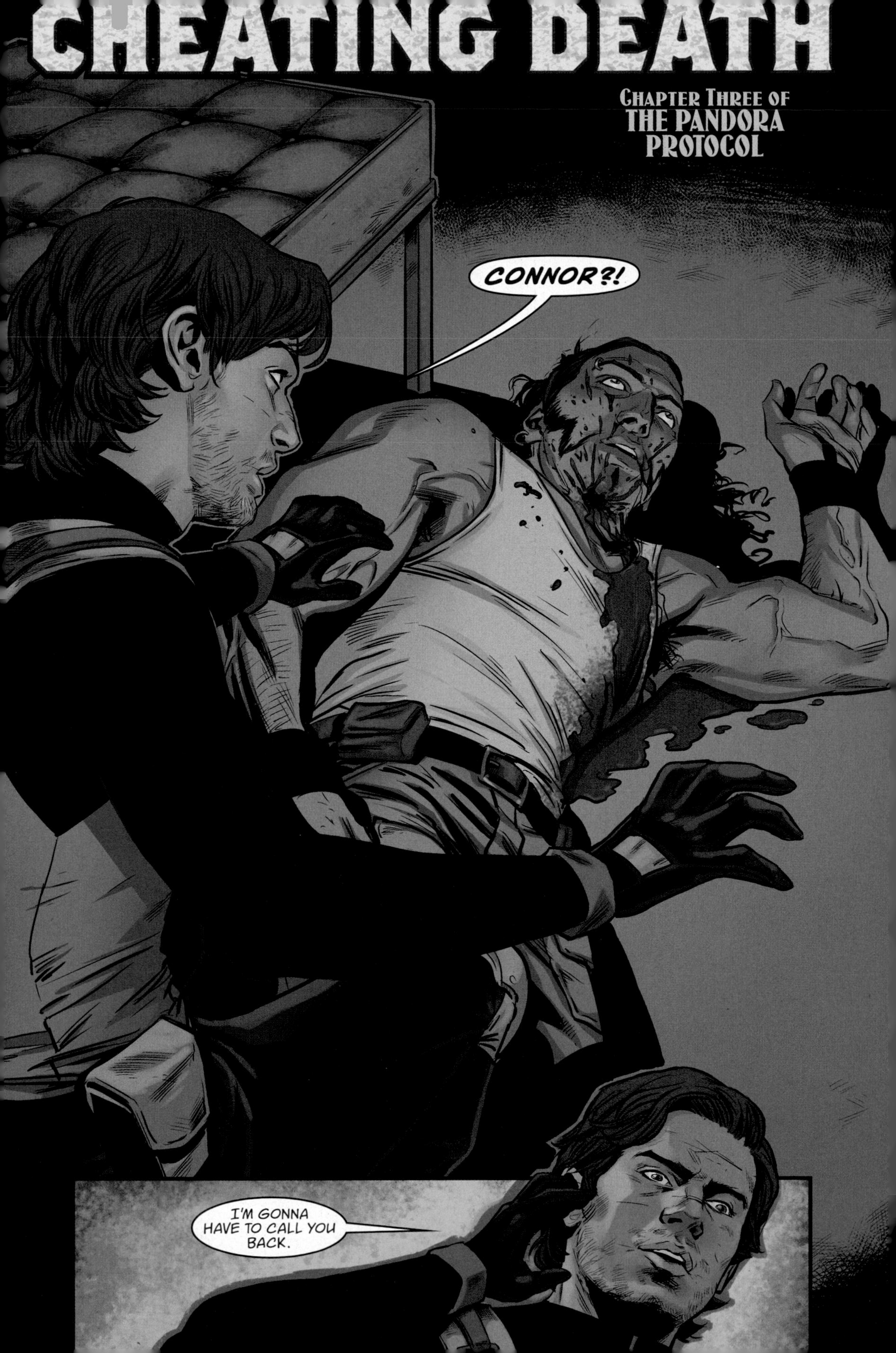
CHEATING DEATH
CHAPTER THREE OF
THE PANDORA PROTOCOL
CONNOR?!
I'M GONNA HAVE TO CALL YOU BACK.

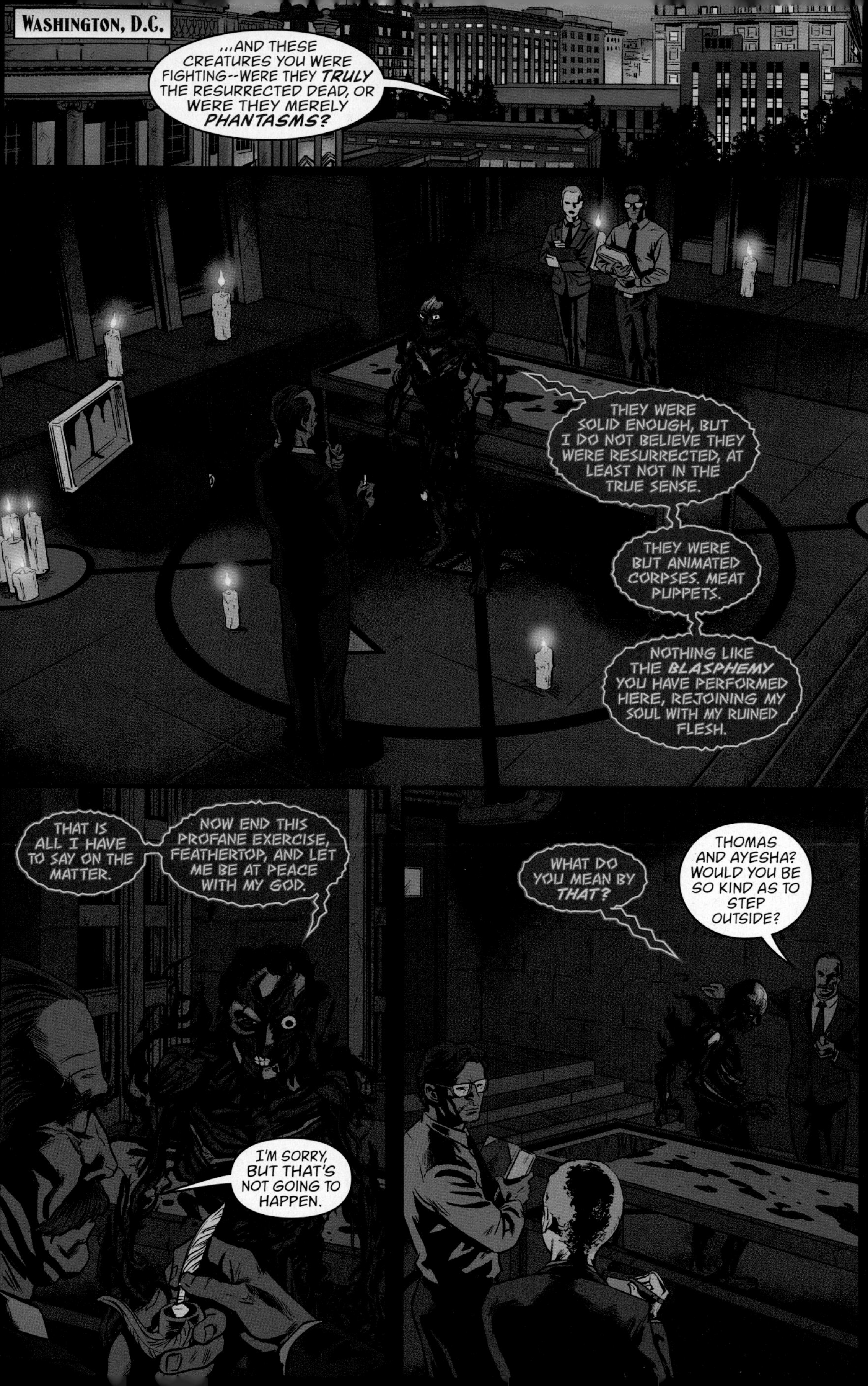
WASHINGTON, D.C.
...AND THESE CREATURES YOU WERE FIGHTING--WERE THEY TRULY THE RESURRECTED DEAD, OR WERE THEY MERELY PHANTASMS?
THEY WERE SOLID ENOUGH, BUT I DO NOT BELIEVE THEY WERE RESURRECTED, AT LEAST NOT IN THE TRUE SENSE.
THEY WERE BUT ANIMATED CORPSES. MEAT PUPPETS.
NOTHING LIKE THE BLASPHEMY YOU HAVE PERFORMED HERE, REJOINING MY SOUL WITH MY RUINED FLESH.
THAT IS ALL I HAVE TO SAY ON THE MATTER.
NOW END THIS PROFANE EXERCISE, FEATHERTOP, AND LET ME BE AT PEACE WITH MY GOD.
I'M SORRY, BUT THAT'S NOT GOING TO HAPPEN.
WHAT DO YOU MEAN BY THAT?
THOMAS AND AYESHA? WOULD YOU BE SO KIND AS TO STEP OUTSIDE?

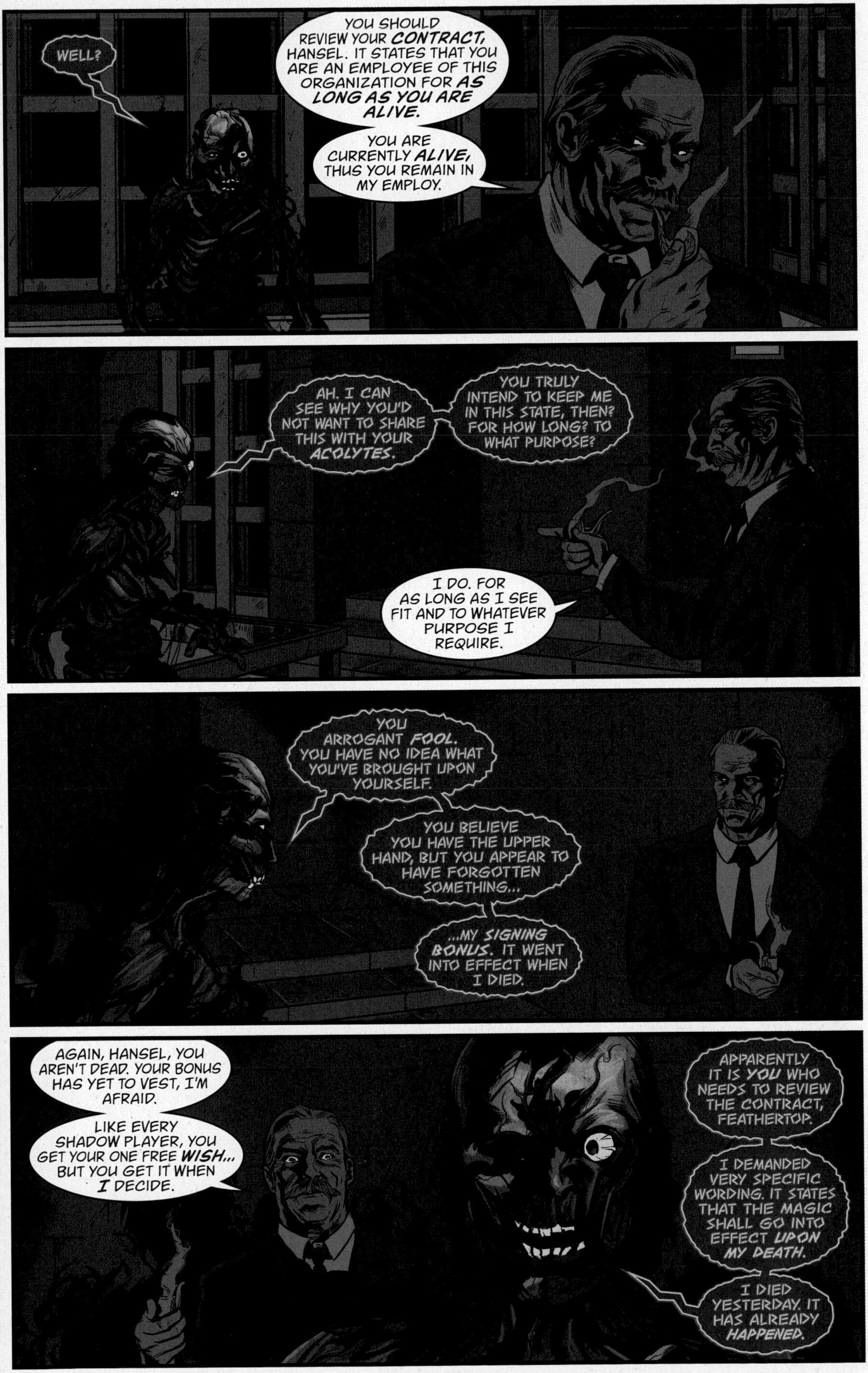
WELL?
YOU SHOULD REVIEW YOUR CONTRACT, HANSEL. IT STATES THAT YOU ARE AN EMPLOYEE OF THIS ORGANIZATION FOR AS LONG AS YOU ARE ALIVE.
YOU ARE CURRENTLY ALIVE, THUS YOU REMAIN IN MY EMPLOY.
AH. I CAN SEE WHY YOU'D NOT WANT TO SHARE THIS WITH YOUR ACOLYTES.
YOU TRULY INTEND TO KEEP ME IN THIS STATE, THEN? FOR HOW LONG? TO WHAT PURPOSE?
I DO. FOR AS LONG AS I SEE FIT AND TO WHATEVER PURPOSE I REQUIRE.
YOU ARROGANT FOOL. YOU HAVE NO IDEA WHAT YOU'VE BROUGHT UPON YOURSELF.
YOU BELIEVE YOU HAVE THE UPPER HAND, BUT YOU APPEAR TO HAVE FORGOTTEN SOMETHING...
...MY SIGNING BONUS. IT WENT INTO EFFECT WHEN I DIED.
AGAIN, HANSEL, YOU AREN'T DEAD. YOUR BONUS HAS YET TO VEST, I'M AFRAID.
LIKE EVERY SHADOW PLAYER, YOU GET YOUR ONE FREE WISH... BUT YOU GET IT WHEN I DECIDE.
APPARENTLY IT IS YOU WHO NEEDS TO REVIEW THE CONTRACT, FEATHERTOP.
I DEMANDED VERY SPECIFIC WORDING. IT STATES THAT THE MAGIC SHALL GO INTO EFFECT UPON MY DEATH.
I DIED YESTERDAY. IT HAS ALREADY HAPPENED.

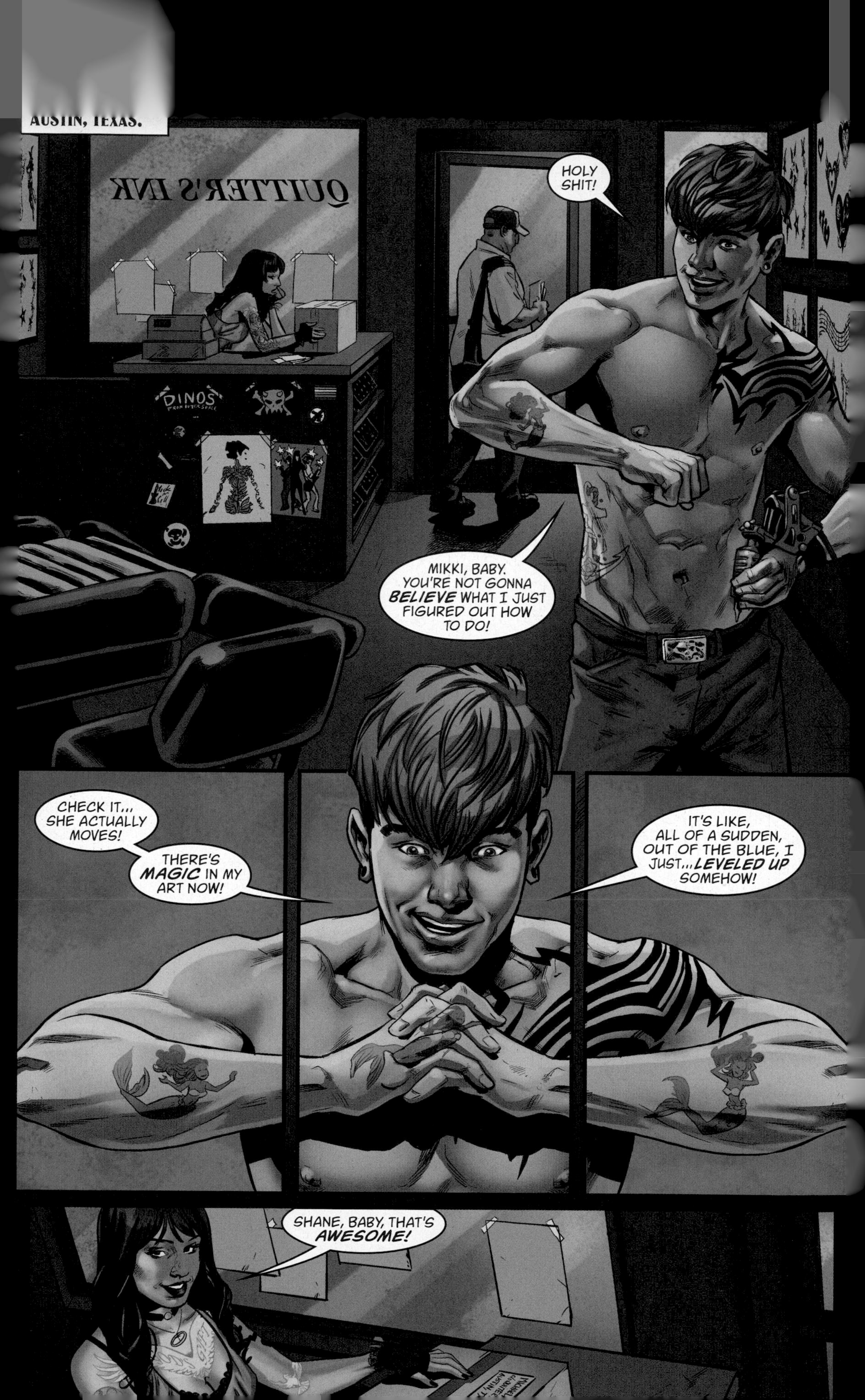
AUSTIN, TEXAS.
QUITTER'S INK
HOLY SHIT!
MIKKI, BABY. YOU'RE NOT GONNA BELIEVE WHAT I JUST FIGURED OUT HOW TO DO!
CHECK IT... SHE ACTUALLY MOVES!
THERE'S MAGIC IN MY ART NOW!
IT'S LIKE, ALL OF A SUDDEN, OUT OF THE BLUE, I JUST...LEVELED UP SOMEHOW!
SHANE, BABY, THAT'S AWESOME!

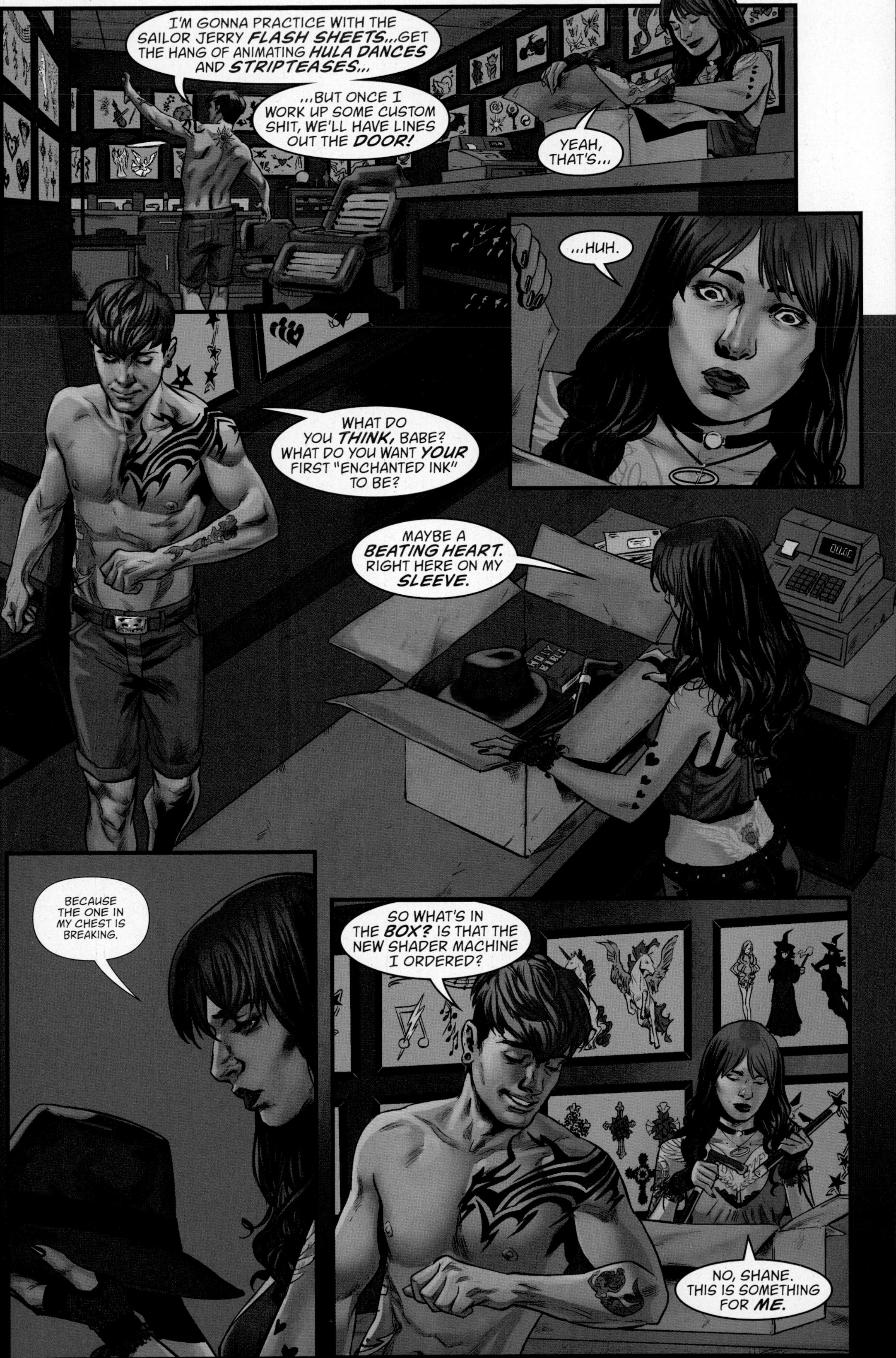
I'M GONNA PRACTICE WITH THE SAILOR JERRY FLASH SHEETS...GET THE HANG OF ANIMATING HULA DANCES AND STRIPTEASES...
...BUT ONCE I WORK UP SOME CUSTOM SHIT, WE'LL HAVE LINES OUT THE DOOR!
YEAH, THAT'S...
...HUH.
WHAT DO YOU THINK, BABE? WHAT DO YOU WANT YOUR FIRST "ENCHANTED INK" TO BE?
MAYBE A BEATING HEART. RIGHT HERE ON MY SLEEVE.
BECAUSE THE ONE IN MY CHEST IS BREAKING.
SO WHAT'S IN THE BOX? IS THAT THE NEW SHADER MACHINE I ORDERED?
NO, SHANE. THIS IS SOMETHING FOR ME.

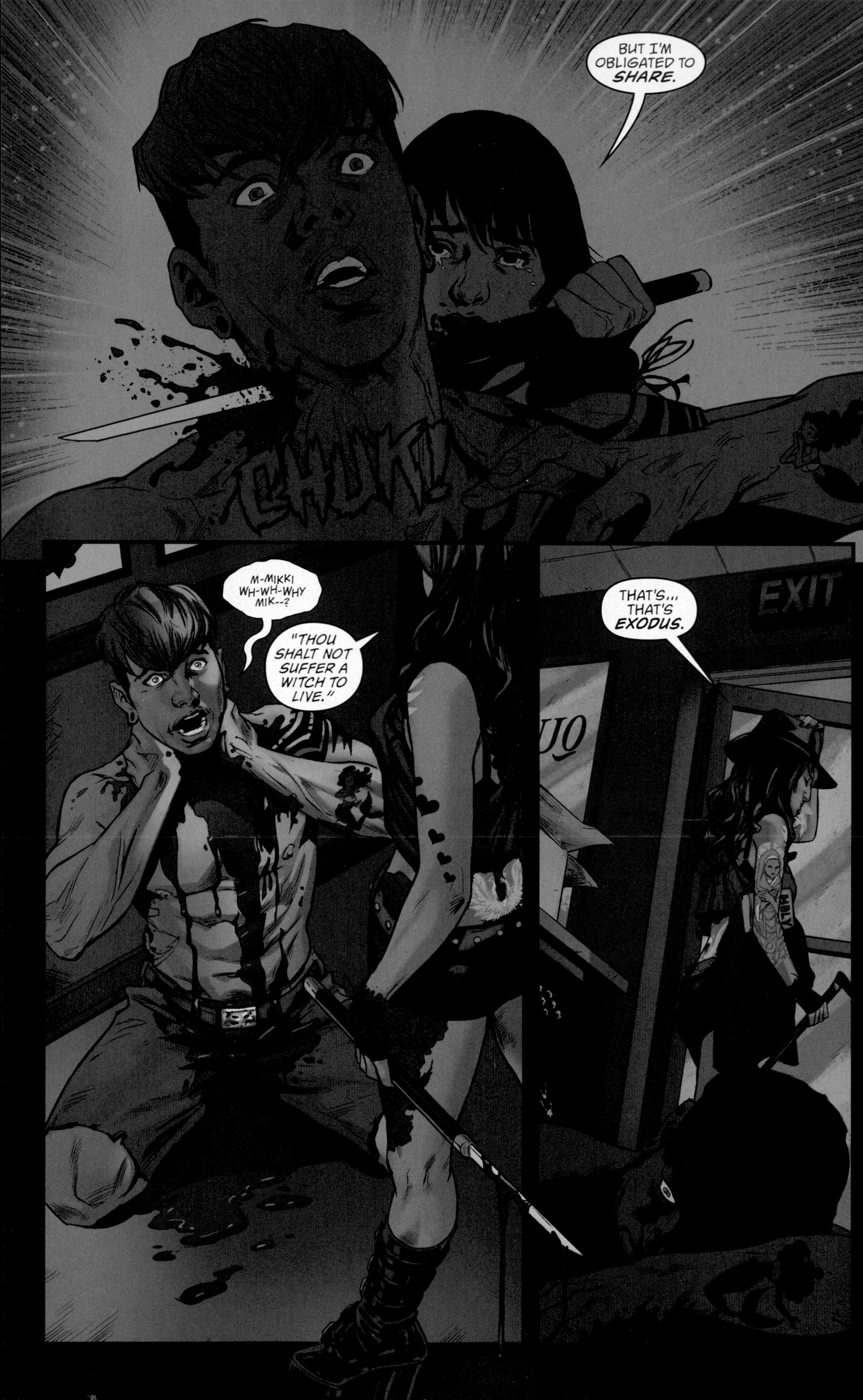
BUT I'M OBLIGATED TO SHARE.
CHUK!
M-MIKKI WH-WH-WHY MIK--?
"THOU SHALT NOT SUFFER A WITCH TO LIVE."
THAT'S... THAT'S EXODUS.
EXIT

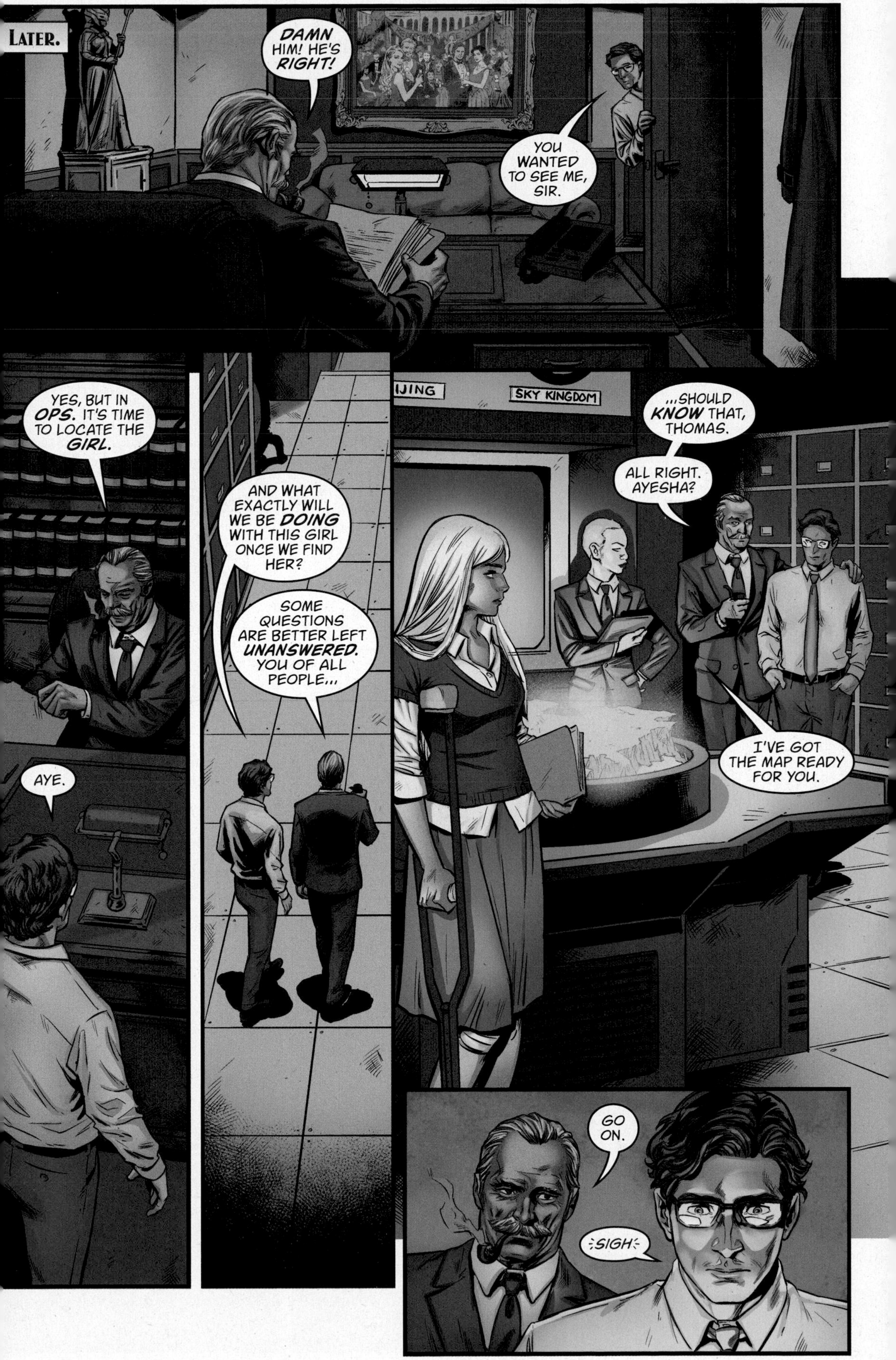
LATER.
DAMN HIM! HE'S RIGHT!
YOU WANTED TO SEE ME, SIR.
YES, BUT IN OPS. IT'S TIME TO LOCATE THE GIRL.
AYE.
AND WHAT EXACTLY WILL WE BE DOING WITH THIS GIRL ONCE WE FIND HER?
SOME QUESTIONS ARE BETTER LEFT UNANSWERED. YOU OF ALL PEOPLE...
IJING
SKY KINGDOM
...SHOULD KNOW THAT, THOMAS.
ALL RIGHT. AYESHA?
I'VE GOT THE MAP READY FOR YOU.
GO ON.
SIGH

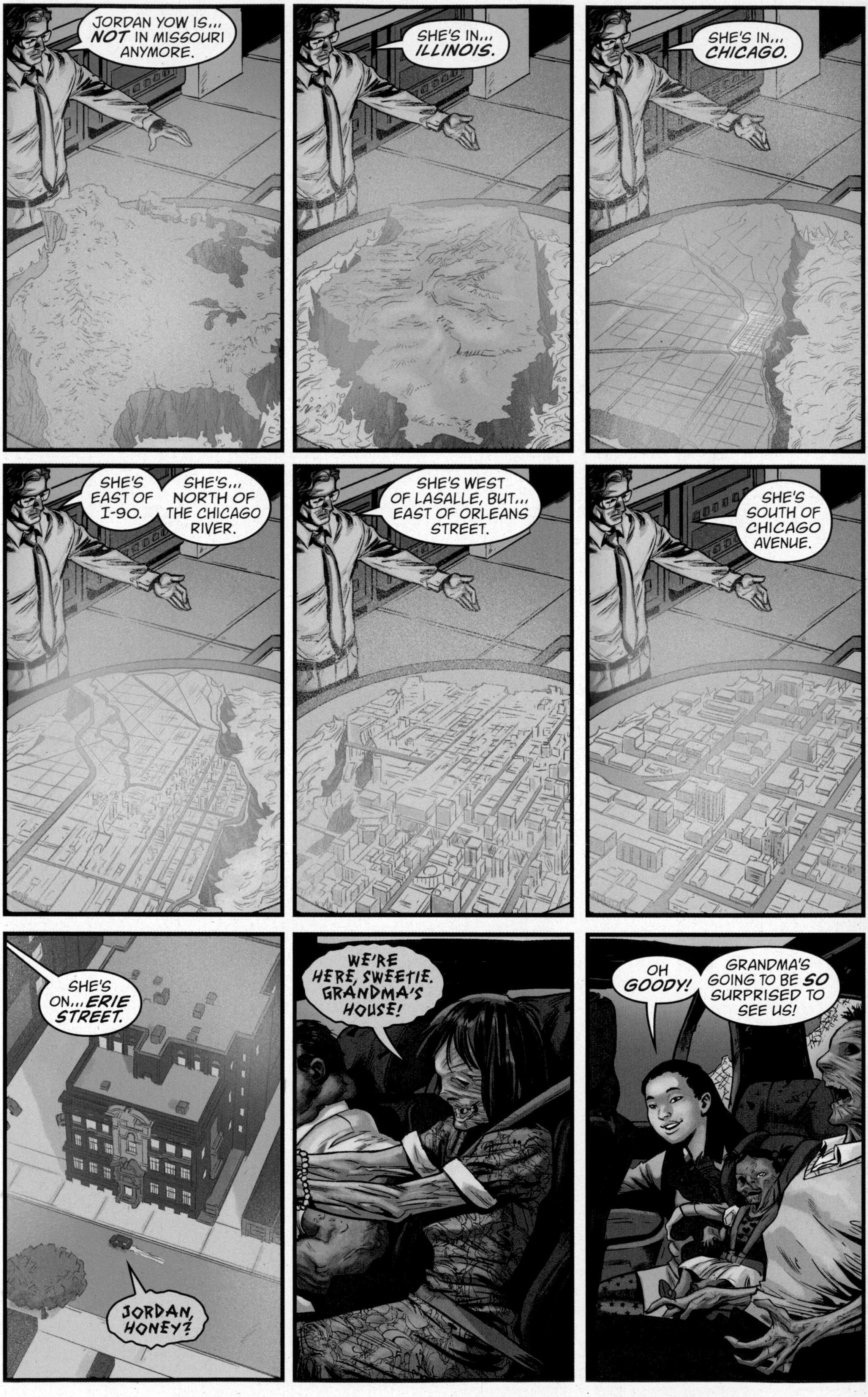
JORDAN YOW IS... NOT IN MISSOURI ANYMORE.
SHE'S IN... ILLINOIS.
SHE'S IN... CHICAGO.
SHE'S EAST OF I-90.
SHE'S... NORTH OF THE CHICAGO RIVER.
SHE'S WEST OF LASALLE, BUT... EAST OF ORLEANS STREET.
SHE'S SOUTH OF CHICAGO AVENUE.
SHE'S ON... ERIE STREET.
JORDAN, HONEY?
WE'RE HERE, SWEETIE. GRANDMA'S HOUSE!
OH GOODY!
GRANDMA'S GOING TO BE SO SURPRISED TO SEE US!

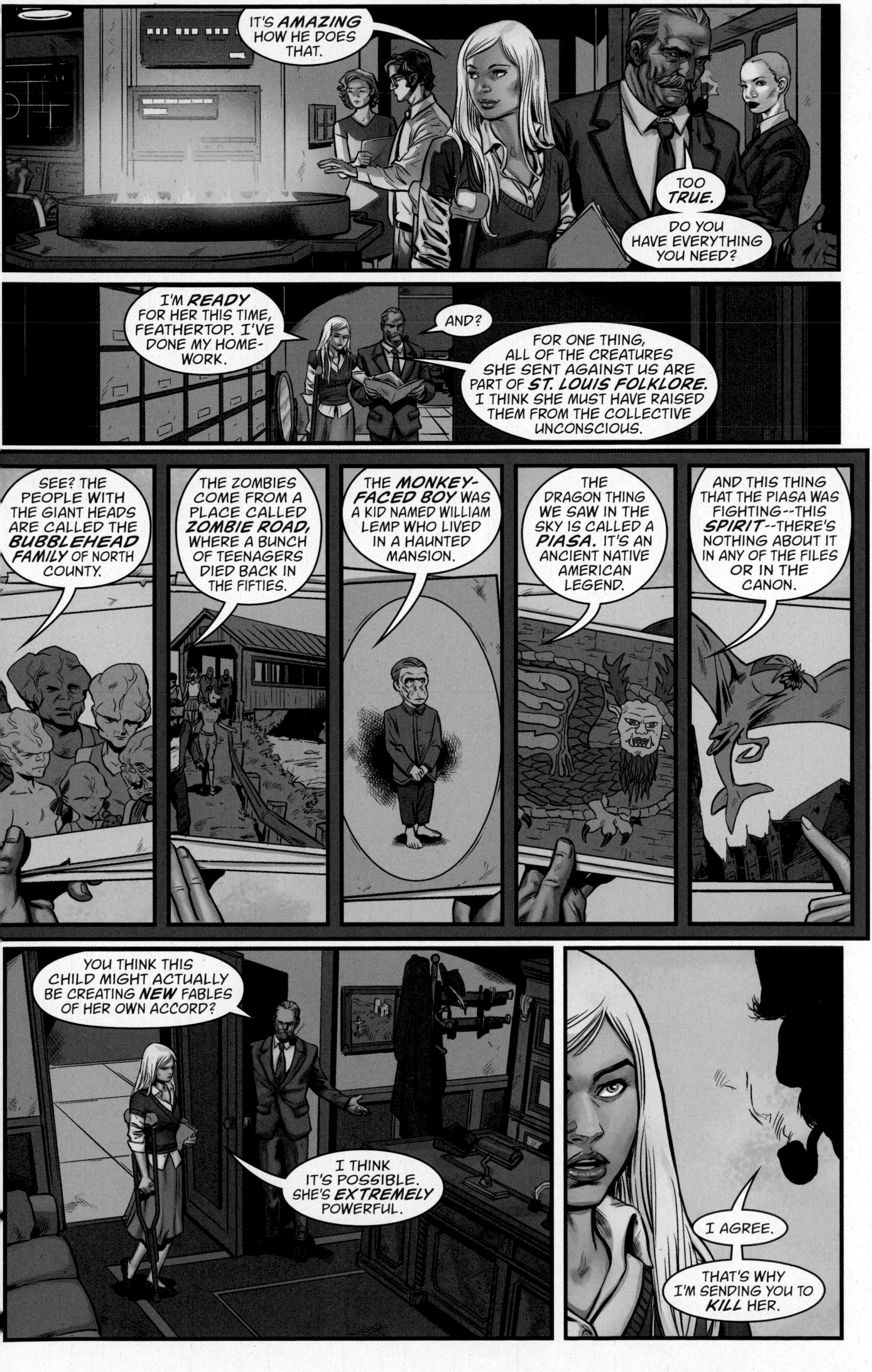
IT'S AMAZING HOW HE DOES THAT.
TOO TRUE.
DO YOU HAVE EVERYTHING YOU NEED?
I'M READY FOR HER THIS TIME, FEATHERTOP. I'VE DONE MY HOME-WORK.
AND?
FOR ONE THING, ALL OF THE CREATURES SHE SENT AGAINST US ARE PART OF ST. LOUIS FOLKLORE. I THINK SHE MUST HAVE RAISED THEM FROM THE COLLECTIVE UNCONSCIOUS.
SEE? THE PEOPLE WITH THE GIANT HEADS ARE CALLED THE BUBBLEHEAD FAMILY OF NORTH COUNTY.
THE ZOMBIES COME FROM A PLACE CALLED ZOMBIE ROAD, WHERE A BUNCH OF TEENAGERS DIED BACK IN THE FIFTIES.
THE MONKEY-FACED BOY WAS A KID NAMED WILLIAM LEMP WHO LIVED IN A HAUNTED MANSION.
THE DRAGON THING WE SAW IN THE SKY IS CALLED A PIASA. IT'S AN ANCIENT NATIVE AMERICAN LEGEND.
AND THIS THING THAT THE PIASA WAS FIGHTING--THIS SPIRIT--THERE'S NOTHING ABOUT IT IN ANY OF THE FILES OR IN THE CANON.
YOU THINK THIS CHILD MIGHT ACTUALLY BE CREATING NEW FABLES OF HER OWN ACCORD?
I THINK IT'S POSSIBLE. SHE'S EXTREMELY POWERFUL.
I AGREE.
THAT'S WHY I'M SENDING YOU TO KILL HER.

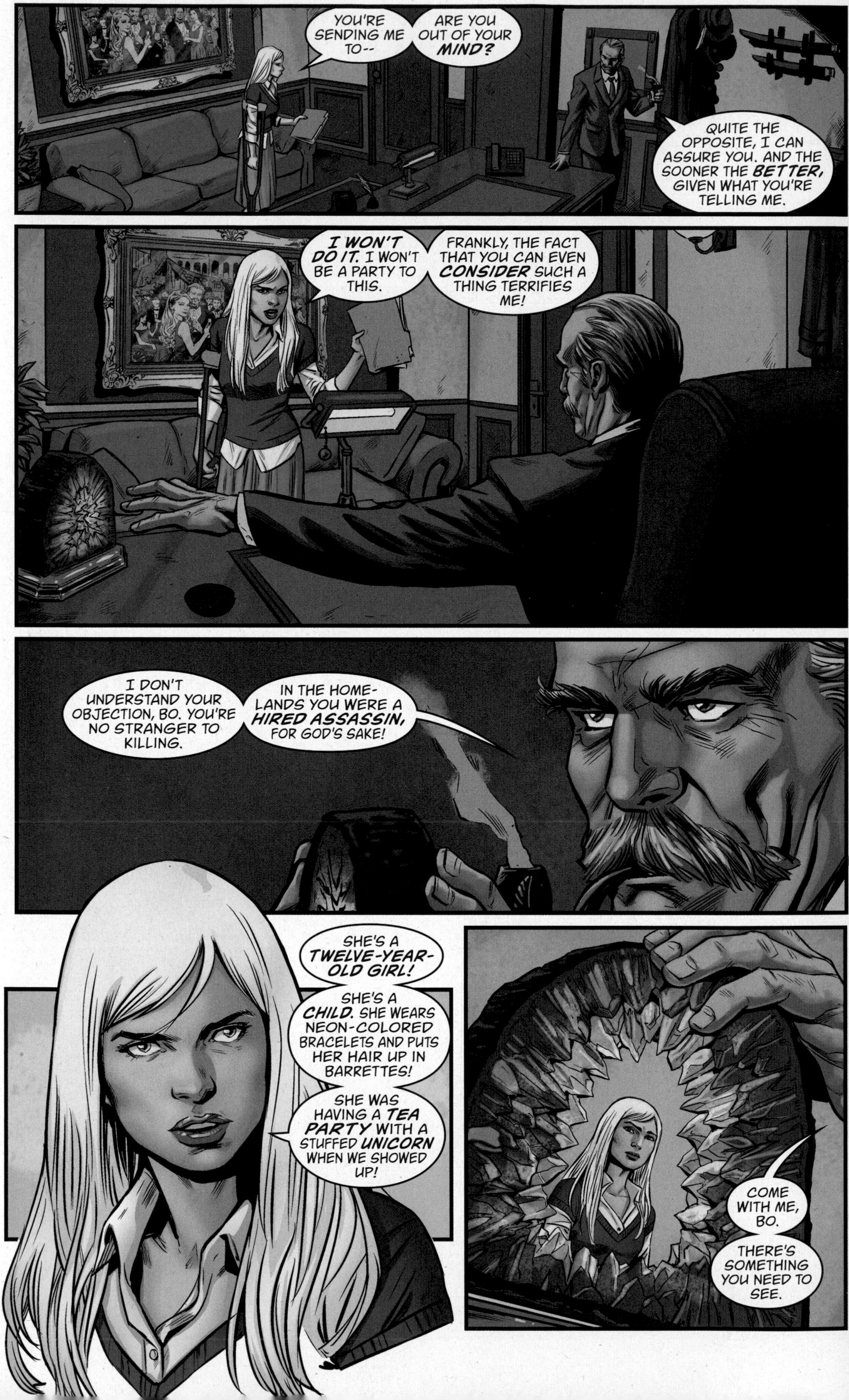
YOU'RE SENDING ME TO--
ARE YOU OUT OF YOUR MIND?
QUITE THE OPPOSITE, I CAN ASSURE YOU. AND THE SOONER THE BETTER, GIVEN WHAT YOU'RE TELLING ME.
I WON'T DO IT. I WON'T BE A PARTY TO THIS.
FRANKLY, THE FACT THAT YOU CAN EVEN CONSIDER SUCH A THING TERRIFIES ME!
I DON'T UNDERSTAND YOUR OBJECTION, BO. YOU'RE NO STRANGER TO KILLING.
IN THE HOME-LANDS YOU WERE A HIRED ASSASSIN, FOR GOD'S SAKE!
SHE'S A TWELVE-YEAR-OLD GIRL!
SHE'S A CHILD. SHE WEARS NEON-COLORED BRACELETS AND PUTS HER HAIR UP IN BARRETTES!
SHE WAS HAVING A TEA PARTY WITH A STUFFED UNICORN WHEN WE SHOWED UP!
COME WITH ME, BO.
THERE'S SOMETHING YOU NEED TO SEE.

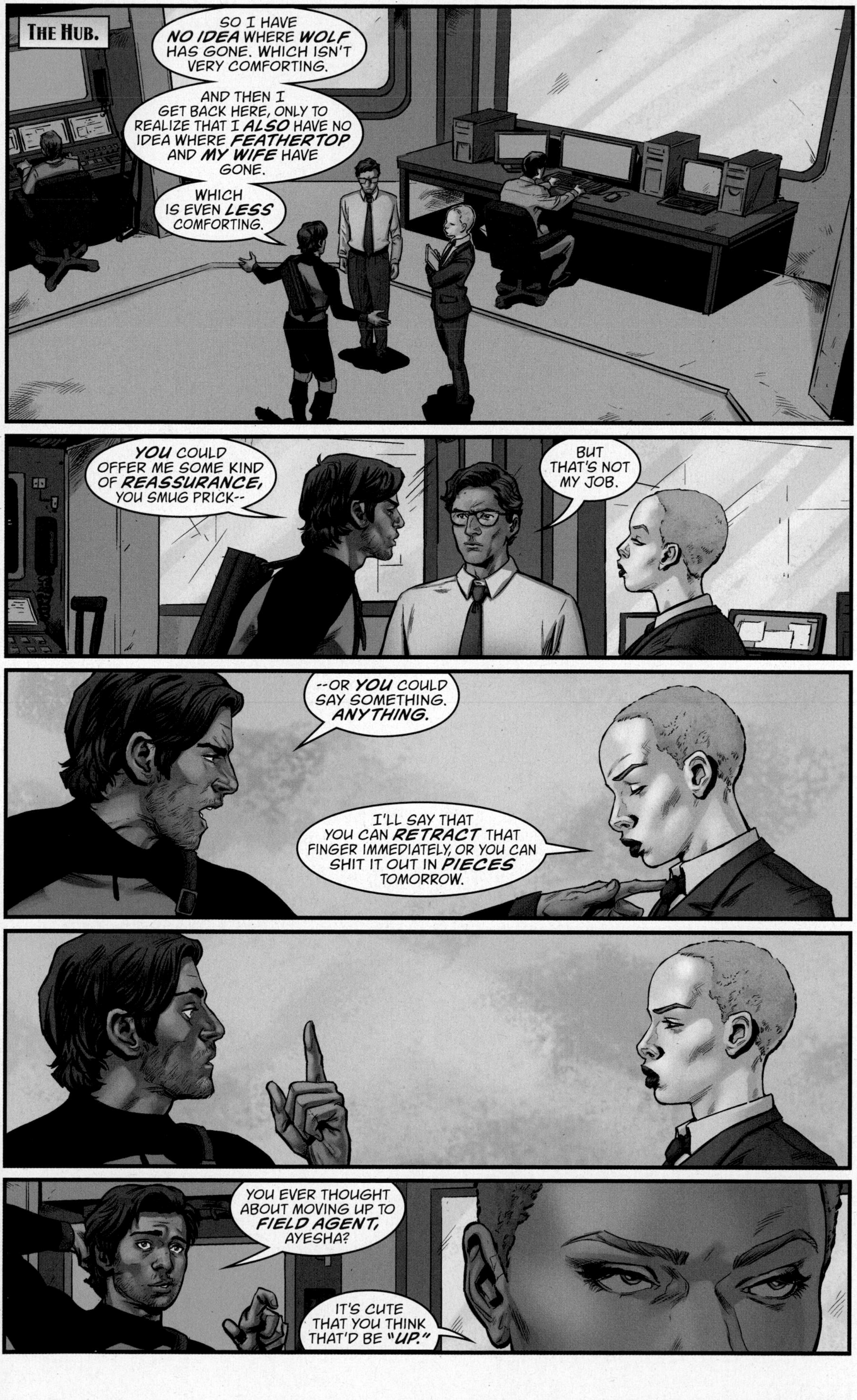
THE HUB.
SO I HAVE NO IDEA WHERE WOLF HAS GONE. WHICH ISN'T VERY COMFORTING.
AND THEN I GET BACK HERE, ONLY TO REALIZE THAT I ALSO HAVE NO IDEA WHERE FEATHERTOP AND MY WIFE HAVE GONE.
WHICH IS EVEN LESS COMFORTING.
YOU COULD OFFER ME SOME KIND OF REASSURANCE, YOU SMUG PRICK--
BUT THAT'S NOT MY JOB.
--OR YOU COULD SAY SOMETHING. ANYTHING.
I'LL SAY THAT YOU CAN RETRACT THAT FINGER IMMEDIATELY, OR YOU CAN SHIT IT OUT IN PIECES TOMORROW.
YOU EVER THOUGHT ABOUT MOVING UP TO FIELD AGENT, AYESHA?
IT'S CUTE THAT YOU THINK THAT'D BE "UP."

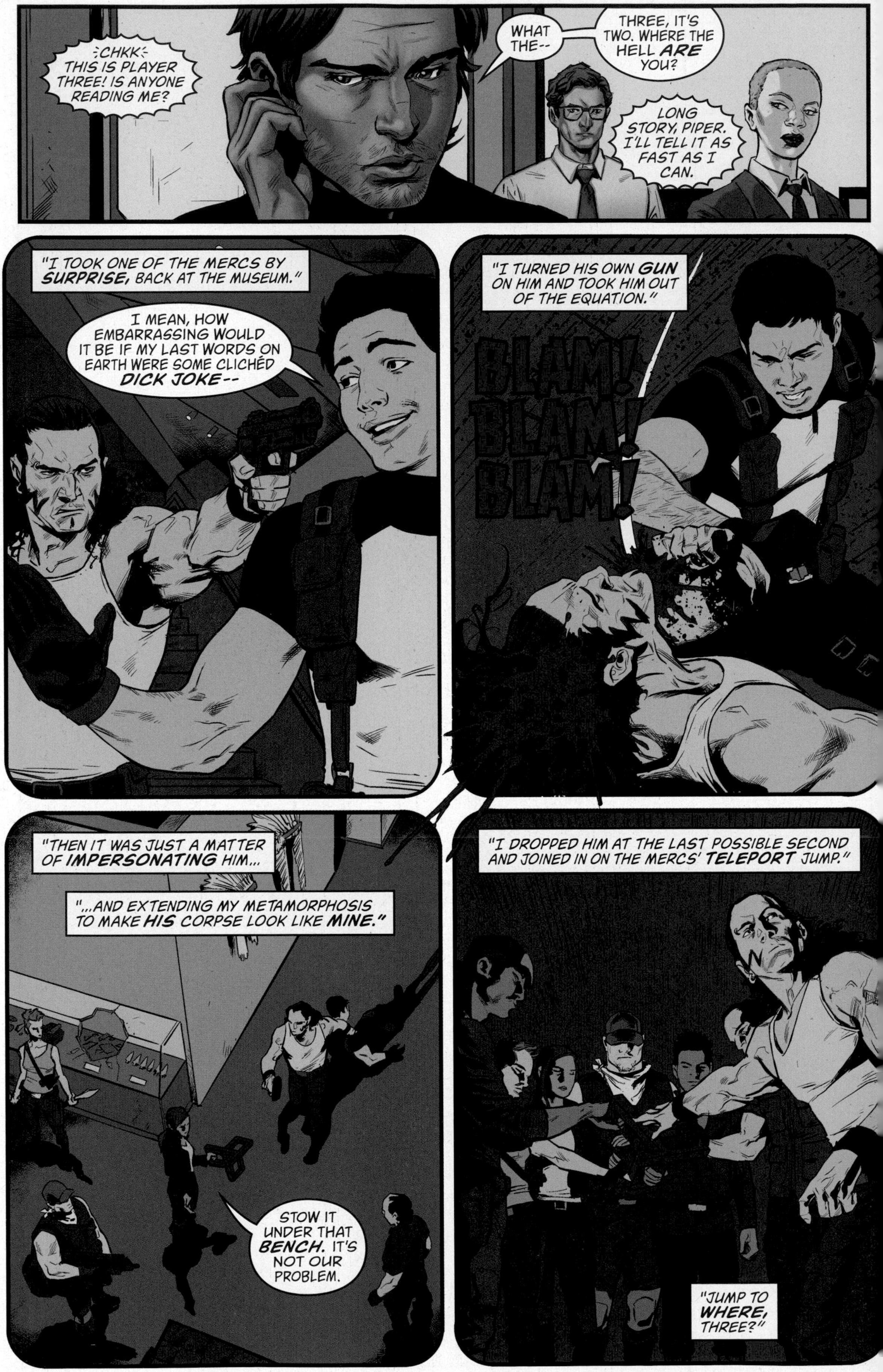
CHKK THIS IS PLAYER THREE! IS ANYONE READING ME?
WHAT THE--
THREE, IT'S TWO. WHERE THE HELL ARE YOU?
LONG STORY, PIPER. I'LL TELL IT AS FAST AS I CAN.
"I TOOK ONE OF THE MERCS BY SURPRISE, BACK AT THE MUSEUM."
I MEAN, HOW EMBARRASSING WOULD IT BE IF MY LAST WORDS ON EARTH WERE SOME CLICHÉD DICK JOKE--
"I TURNED HIS OWN GUN ON HIM AND TOOK HIM OUT OF THE EQUATION."
BLAM! BLAM! BLAM!
"THEN IT WAS JUST A MATTER OF IMPERSONATING HIM...
"...AND EXTENDING MY METAMORPHOSIS TO MAKE HIS CORPSE LOOK LIKE MINE."
STOW IT UNDER THAT BENCH. IT'S NOT OUR PROBLEM.
"I DROPPED HIM AT THE LAST POSSIBLE SECOND AND JOINED IN ON THE MERCS' TELEPORT JUMP."
"JUMP TO WHERE, THREE?"

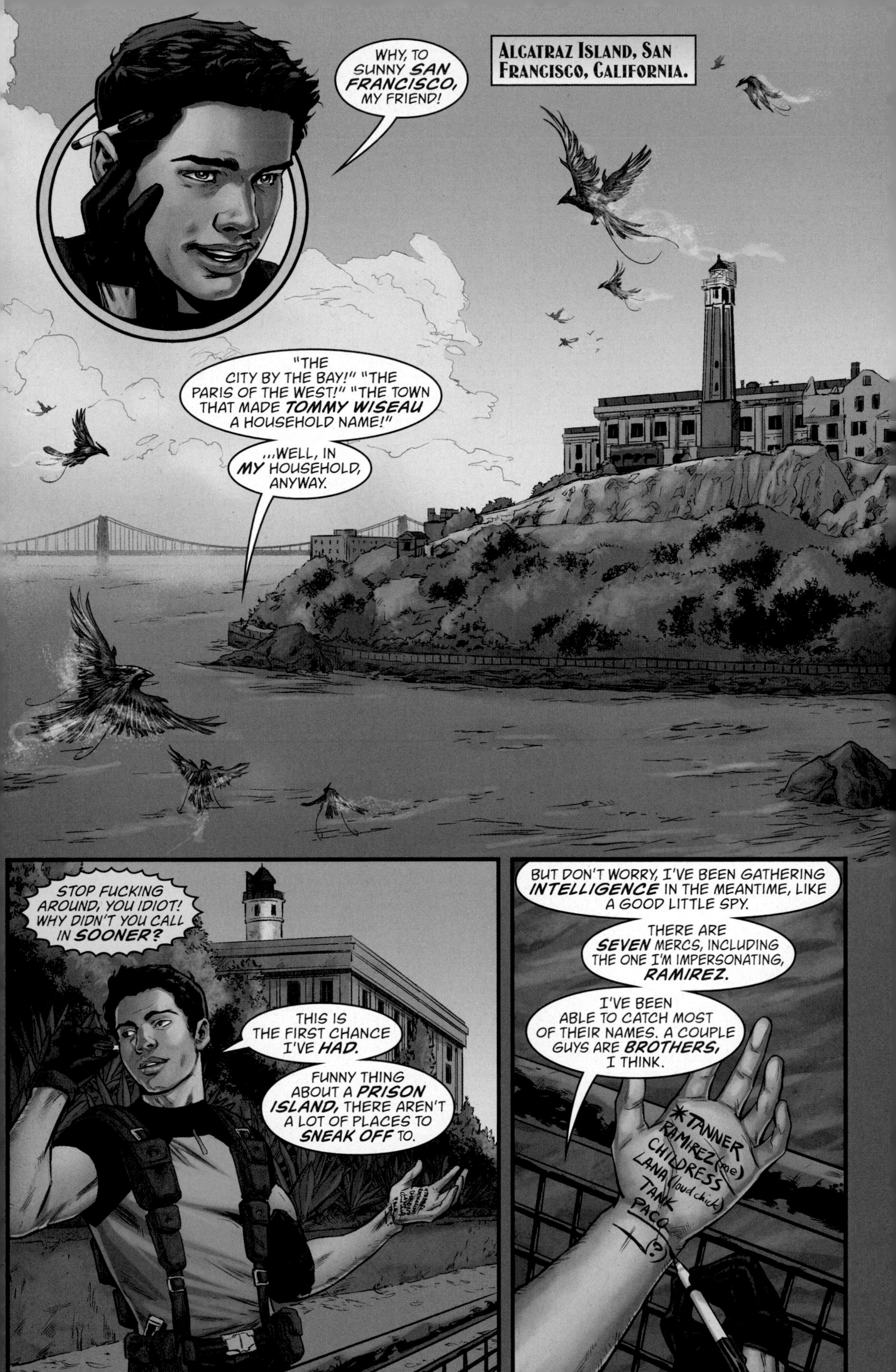
WHY, TO SUNNY SAN FRANCISCO, MY FRIEND!
ALCATRAZ ISLAND, SAN FRANCISCO, CALIFORNIA.
"THE CITY BY THE BAY!" "THE PARIS OF THE WEST!" "THE TOWN THAT MADE TOMMY WISEAU A HOUSEHOLD NAME!"
...WELL, IN MY HOUSEHOLD, ANYWAY.
STOP FUCKING AROUND, YOU IDIOT! WHY DIDN'T YOU CALL IN SOONER?
THIS IS THE FIRST CHANCE I'VE HAD.
FUNNY THING ABOUT A PRISON ISLAND, THERE AREN'T A LOT OF PLACES TO SNEAK OFF TO.
BUT DON'T WORRY, I'VE BEEN GATHERING INTELLIGENCE IN THE MEANTIME, LIKE A GOOD LITTLE SPY.
THERE ARE SEVEN MERCS, INCLUDING THE ONE I'M IMPERSONATING, RAMIREZ.
I'VE BEEN ABLE TO CATCH MOST OF THEIR NAMES. A COUPLE GUYS ARE BROTHERS, I THINK.
*TANNER
RAMIREZ (me)
CHILDRESS
LANA (loud chick)
TANK
PACO
?

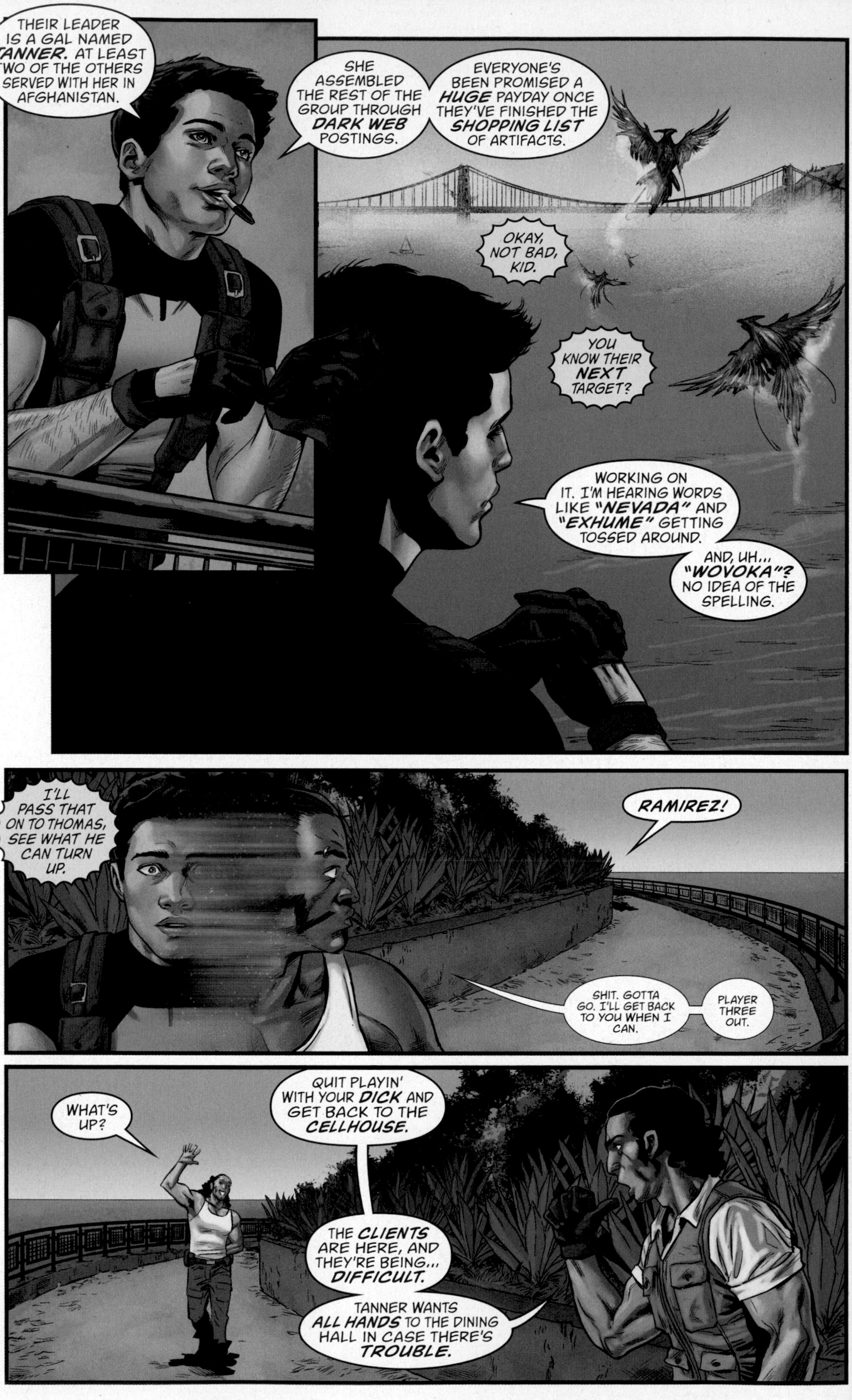
THEIR LEADER IS A GAL NAMED TANNER. AT LEAST TWO OF THE OTHERS SERVED WITH HER IN AFGHANISTAN.
SHE ASSEMBLED THE REST OF THE GROUP THROUGH DARK WEB POSTINGS.
EVERYONE'S BEEN PROMISED A HUGE PAYDAY ONCE THEY'VE FINISHED THE SHOPPING LIST OF ARTIFACTS.
OKAY, NOT BAD, KID.
YOU KNOW THEIR NEXT TARGET?
WORKING ON IT. I'M HEARING WORDS LIKE "NEVADA" AND "EXHUME" GETTING TOSSED AROUND.
AND, UH... "WOVOKA"? NO IDEA OF THE SPELLING.
I'LL PASS THAT ON TO THOMAS, SEE WHAT HE CAN TURN UP.
RAMIREZ!
SHIT. GOTTA GO. I'LL GET BACK TO YOU WHEN I CAN.
PLAYER THREE OUT.
WHAT'S UP?
QUIT PLAYIN' WITH YOUR DICK AND GET BACK TO THE CELLHOUSE.
THE CLIENTS ARE HERE, AND THEY'RE BEING... DIFFICULT.
TANNER WANTS ALL HANDS TO THE DINING HALL IN CASE THERE'S TROUBLE.

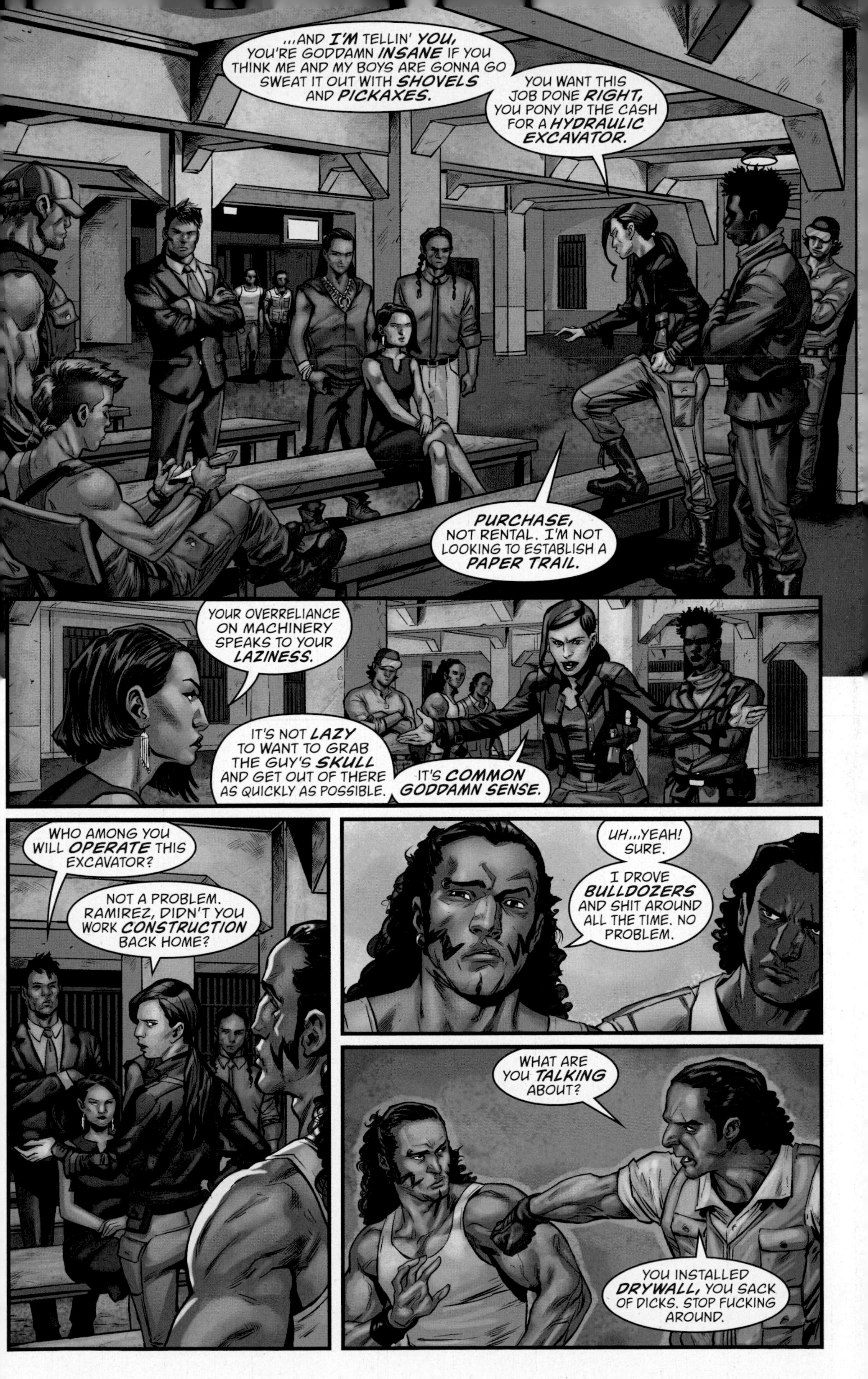
...AND I'M TELLIN' YOU, YOU'RE GODDAMN INSANE IF YOU THINK ME AND MY BOYS ARE GONNA GO SWEAT IT OUT WITH SHOVELS AND PICKAXES.
YOU WANT THIS JOB DONE RIGHT, YOU PONY UP THE CASH FOR A HYDRAULIC EXCAVATOR.
PURCHASE, NOT RENTAL. I'M NOT LOOKING TO ESTABLISH A PAPER TRAIL.
YOUR OVERRELIANCE ON MACHINERY SPEAKS TO YOUR LAZINESS.
IT'S NOT LAZY TO WANT TO GRAB THE GUY'S SKULL AND GET OUT OF THERE AS QUICKLY AS POSSIBLE.
IT'S COMMON GODDAMN SENSE.
WHO AMONG YOU WILL OPERATE THIS EXCAVATOR?
NOT A PROBLEM. RAMIREZ, DIDN'T YOU WORK CONSTRUCTION BACK HOME?
UH...YEAH! SURE.
I DROVE BULLDOZERS AND SHIT AROUND ALL THE TIME. NO PROBLEM.
WHAT ARE YOU TALKING ABOUT?
YOU INSTALLED DRYWALL, YOU SACK OF DICKS. STOP FUCKING AROUND.

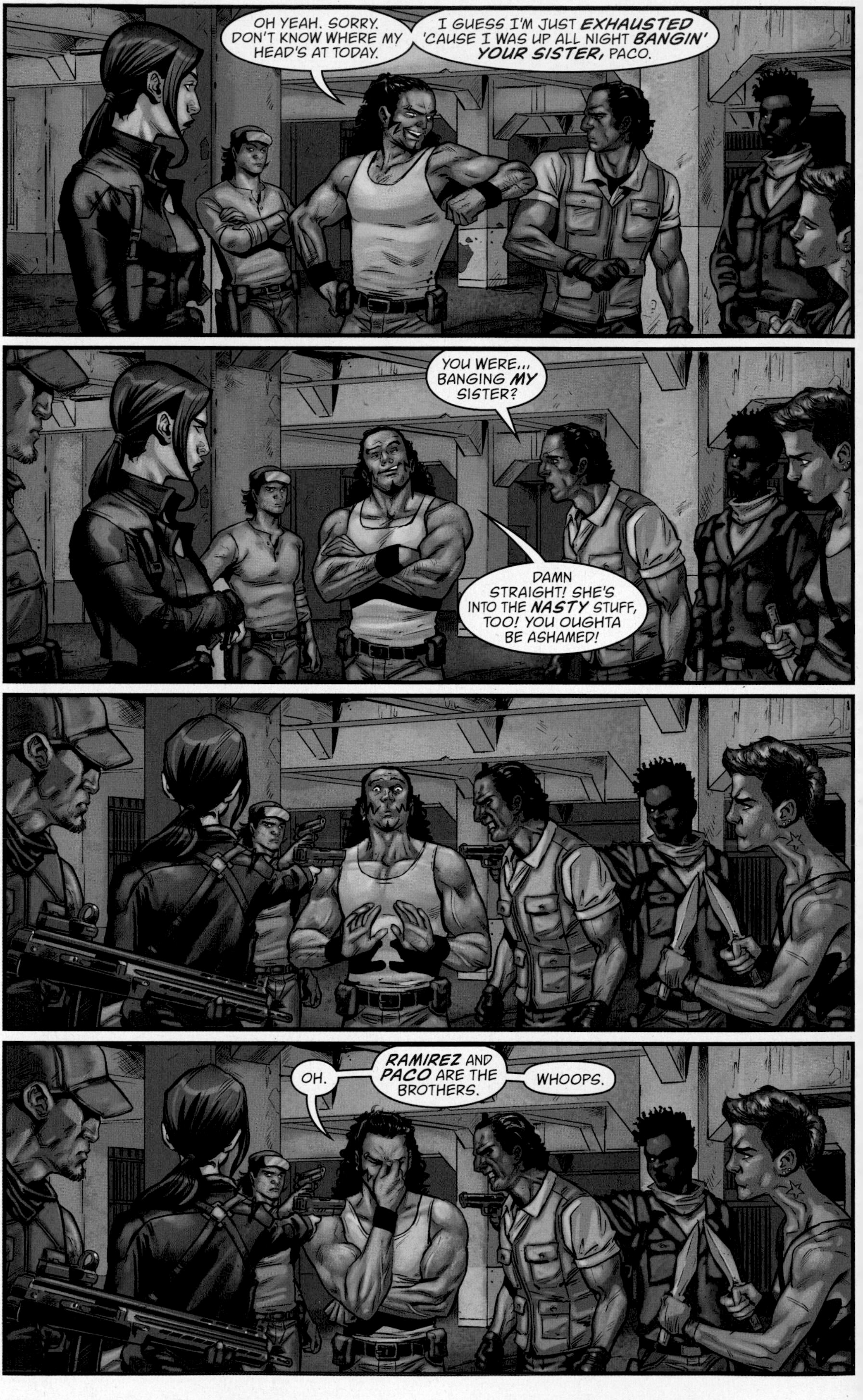
OH YEAH. SORRY. DON'T KNOW WHERE MY HEAD'S AT TODAY.
I GUESS I'M JUST EXHAUSTED 'CAUSE I WAS UP ALL NIGHT BANGIN' YOUR SISTER, PACO.
YOU WERE... BANGING MY SISTER?
DAMN STRAIGHT! SHE'S INTO THE NASTY STUFF, TOO! YOU OUGHTA BE ASHAMED!
OH.
RAMIREZ AND PACO ARE THE BROTHERS.
WHOOPS.

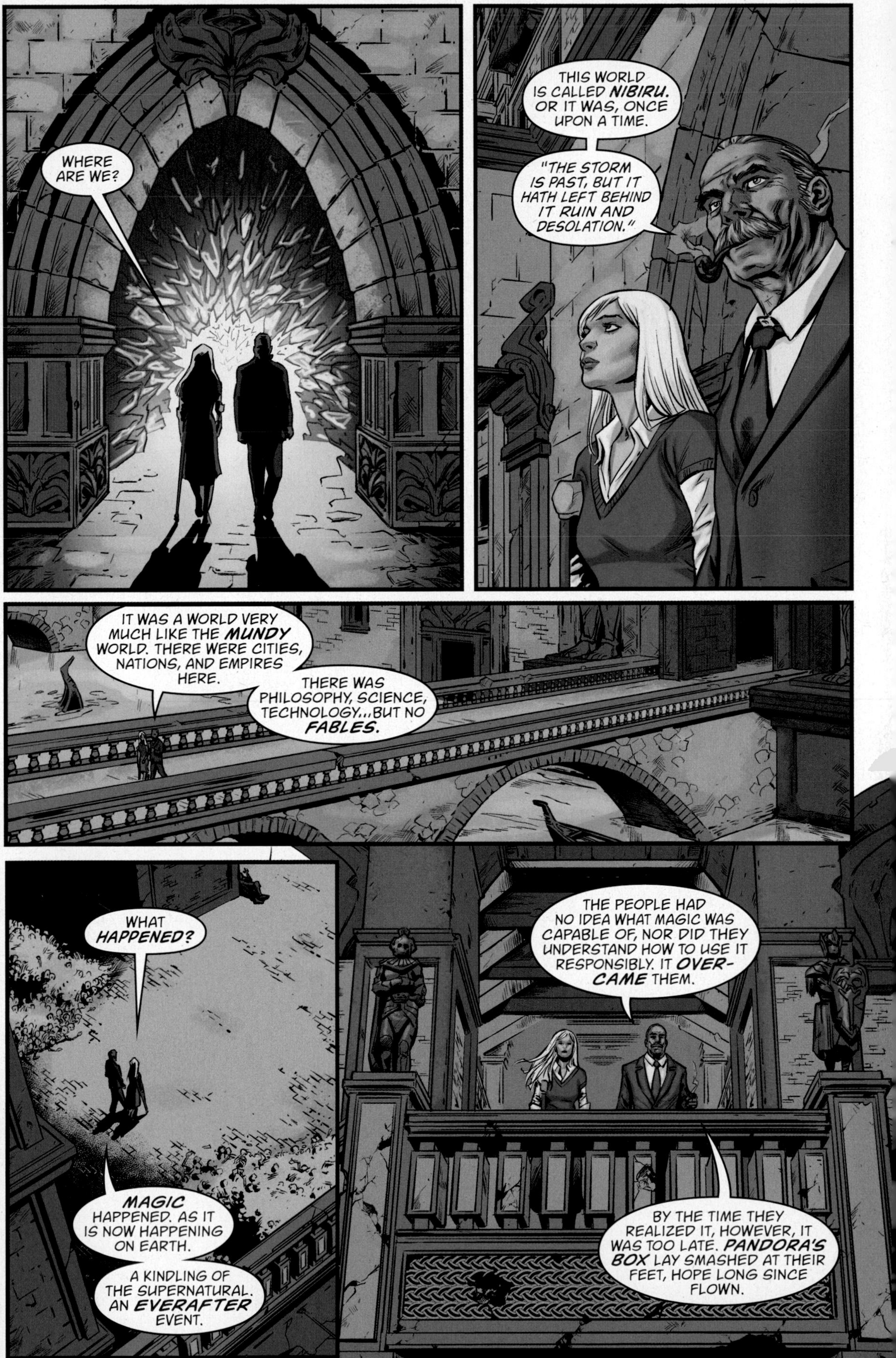
WHERE ARE WE?
THIS WORLD IS CALLED NIBIRU. OR IT WAS, ONCE UPON A TIME.
"THE STORM IS PAST, BUT IT HATH LEFT BEHIND IT RUIN AND DESOLATION."
IT WAS A WORLD VERY MUCH LIKE THE MUNDY WORLD. THERE WERE CITIES, NATIONS, AND EMPIRES HERE.
THERE WAS PHILOSOPHY, SCIENCE, TECHNOLOGY...BUT NO FABLES.
WHAT HAPPENED?
MAGIC HAPPENED. AS IT IS NOW HAPPENING ON EARTH.
A KINDLING OF THE SUPERNATURAL. AN EVERAFTER EVENT.
THE PEOPLE HAD NO IDEA WHAT MAGIC WAS CAPABLE OF, NOR DID THEY UNDERSTAND HOW TO USE IT RESPONSIBLY. IT OVER-CAME THEM.
BY THE TIME THEY REALIZED IT, HOWEVER, IT WAS TOO LATE. PANDORA'S BOX LAY SMASHED AT THEIR FEET, HOPE LONG SINCE FLOWN.

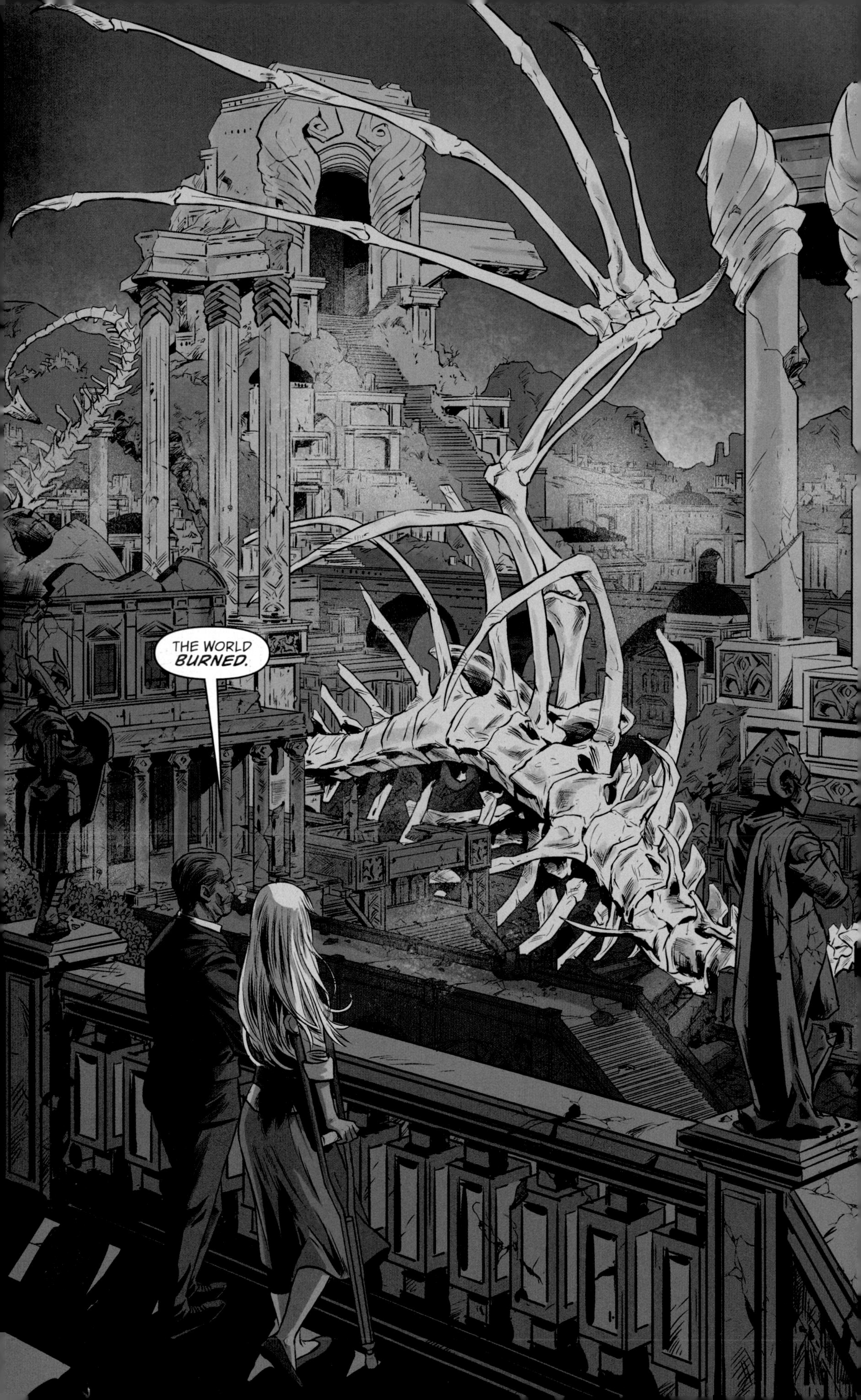
THE WORLD BURNED.

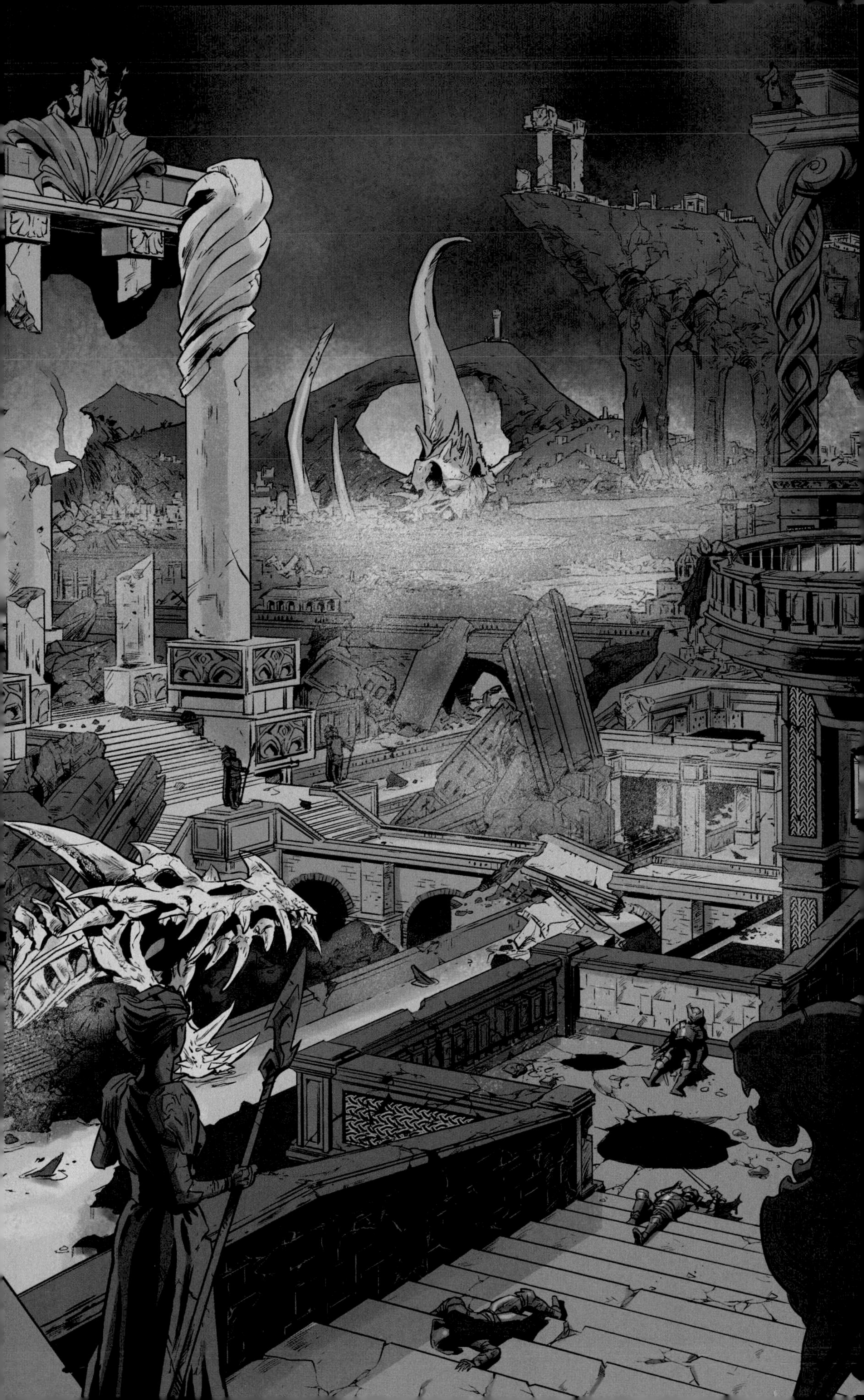

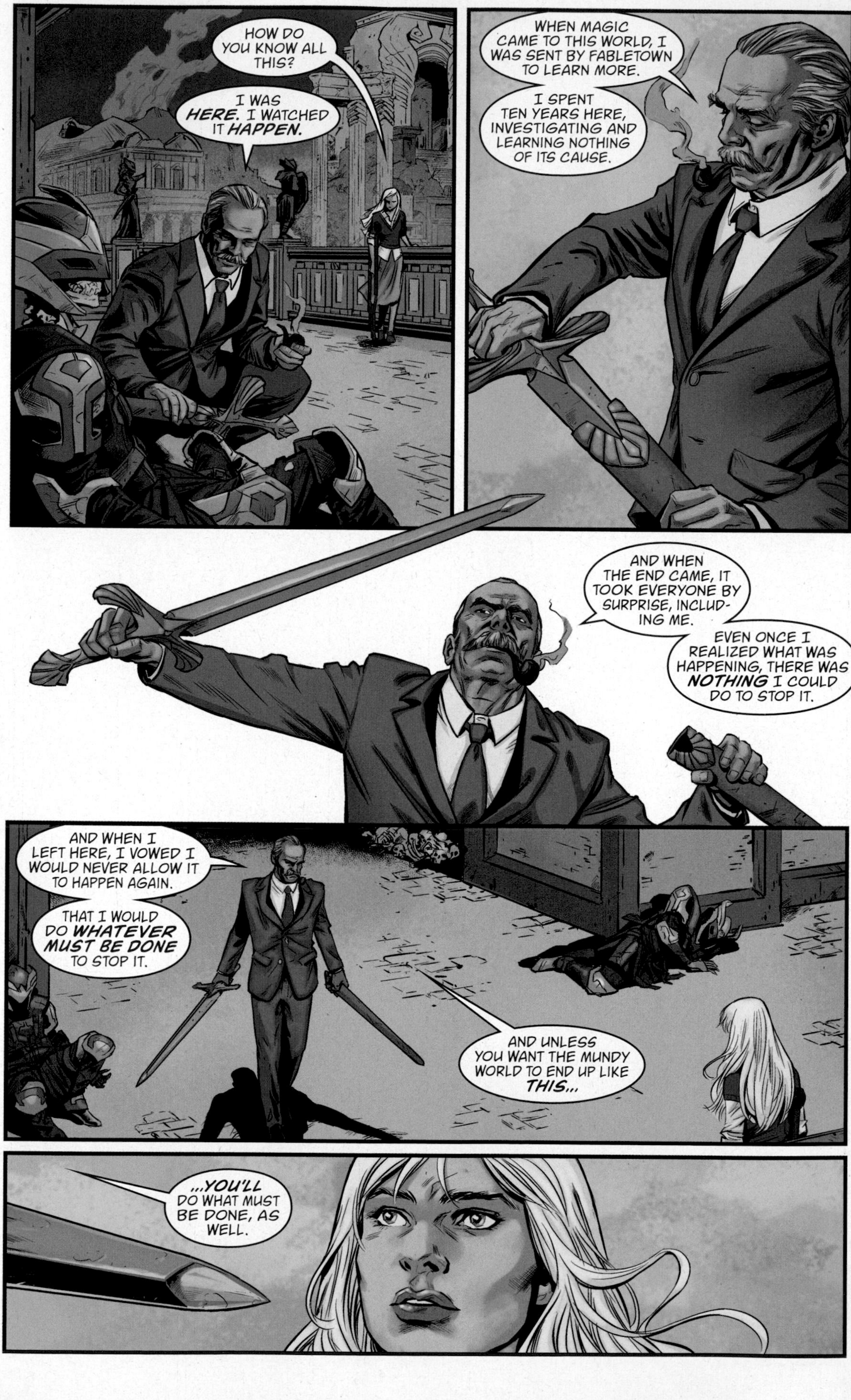
HOW DO YOU KNOW ALL THIS?
I WAS HERE. I WATCHED IT HAPPEN.
WHEN MAGIC CAME TO THIS WORLD, I WAS SENT BY FABLETOWN TO LEARN MORE.
I SPENT TEN YEARS HERE, INVESTIGATING AND LEARNING NOTHING OF ITS CAUSE.
AND WHEN THE END CAME, IT TOOK EVERYONE BY SURPRISE, INCLUDING ME.
EVEN ONCE I REALIZED WHAT WAS HAPPENING, THERE WAS NOTHING I COULD DO TO STOP IT.
AND WHEN I LEFT HERE, I VOWED I WOULD NEVER ALLOW IT TO HAPPEN AGAIN.
THAT I WOULD DO WHATEVER MUST BE DONE TO STOP IT.
AND UNLESS YOU WANT THE MUNDY WORLD TO END UP LIKE THIS...
...YOU'LL DO WHAT MUST BE DONE, AS WELL.

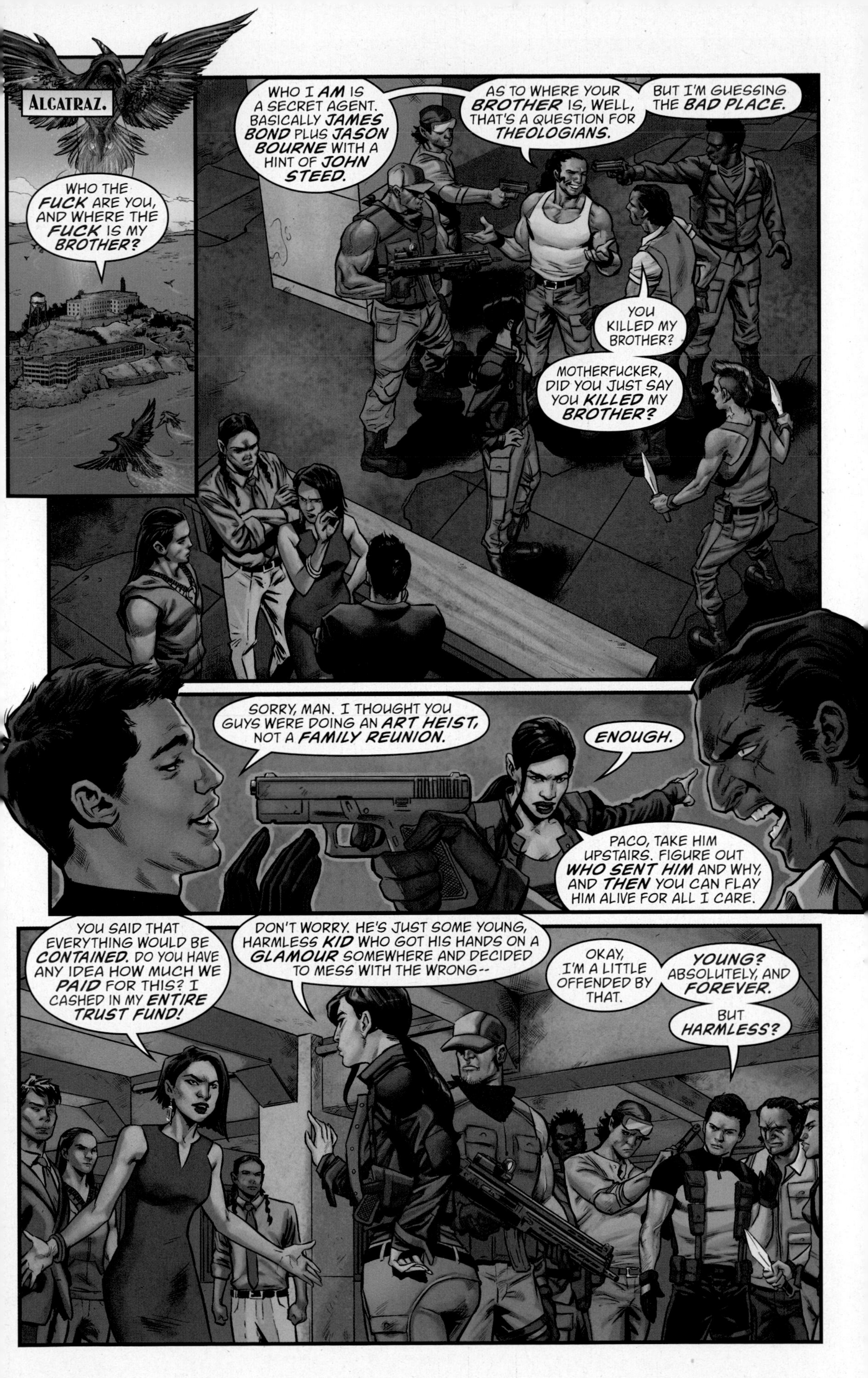
ALCATRAZ.
WHO THE FUCK ARE YOU, AND WHERE THE FUCK IS MY BROTHER?
WHO I AM IS A SECRET AGENT. BASICALLY JAMES BOND PLUS JASON BOURNE WITH A HINT OF JOHN STEED.
AS TO WHERE YOUR BROTHER IS, WELL, THAT'S A QUESTION FOR THEOLOGIANS.
BUT I'M GUESSING THE BAD PLACE.
YOU KILLED MY BROTHER?
MOTHERFUCKER, DID YOU JUST SAY YOU KILLED MY BROTHER?
SORRY, MAN. I THOUGHT YOU GUYS WERE DOING AN ART HEIST, NOT A FAMILY REUNION.
ENOUGH.
PACO, TAKE HIM UPSTAIRS. FIGURE OUT WHO SENT HIM AND WHY, AND THEN YOU CAN FLAY HIM ALIVE FOR ALL I CARE.
YOU SAID THAT EVERYTHING WOULD BE CONTAINED. DO YOU HAVE ANY IDEA HOW MUCH WE PAID FOR THIS? I CASHED IN MY ENTIRE TRUST FUND!
DON'T WORRY. HE'S JUST SOME YOUNG, HARMLESS KID WHO GOT HIS HANDS ON A GLAMOUR SOMEWHERE AND DECIDED TO MESS WITH THE WRONG--
OKAY, I'M A LITTLE OFFENDED BY THAT.
YOUNG? ABSOLUTELY, AND FOREVER.
BUT HARMLESS?

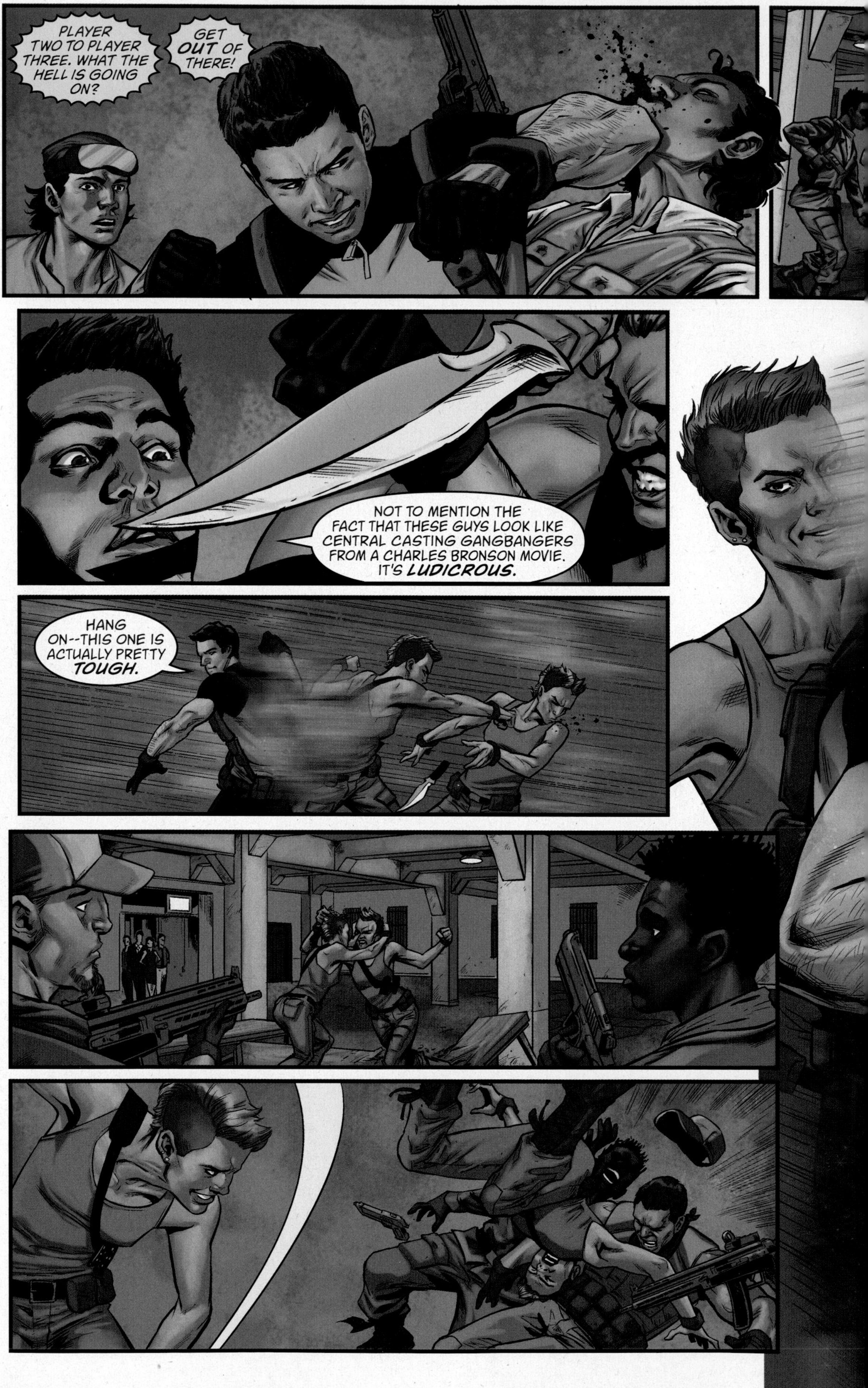
PLAYER TWO TO PLAYER THREE. WHAT THE HELL IS GOING ON?
GET OUT OF THERE!
NOT TO MENTION THE FACT THAT THESE GUYS LOOK LIKE CENTRAL CASTING GANGBANGERS FROM A CHARLES BRONSON MOVIE. IT'S LUDICROUS.
HANG ON--THIS ONE IS ACTUALLY PRETTY TOUGH.

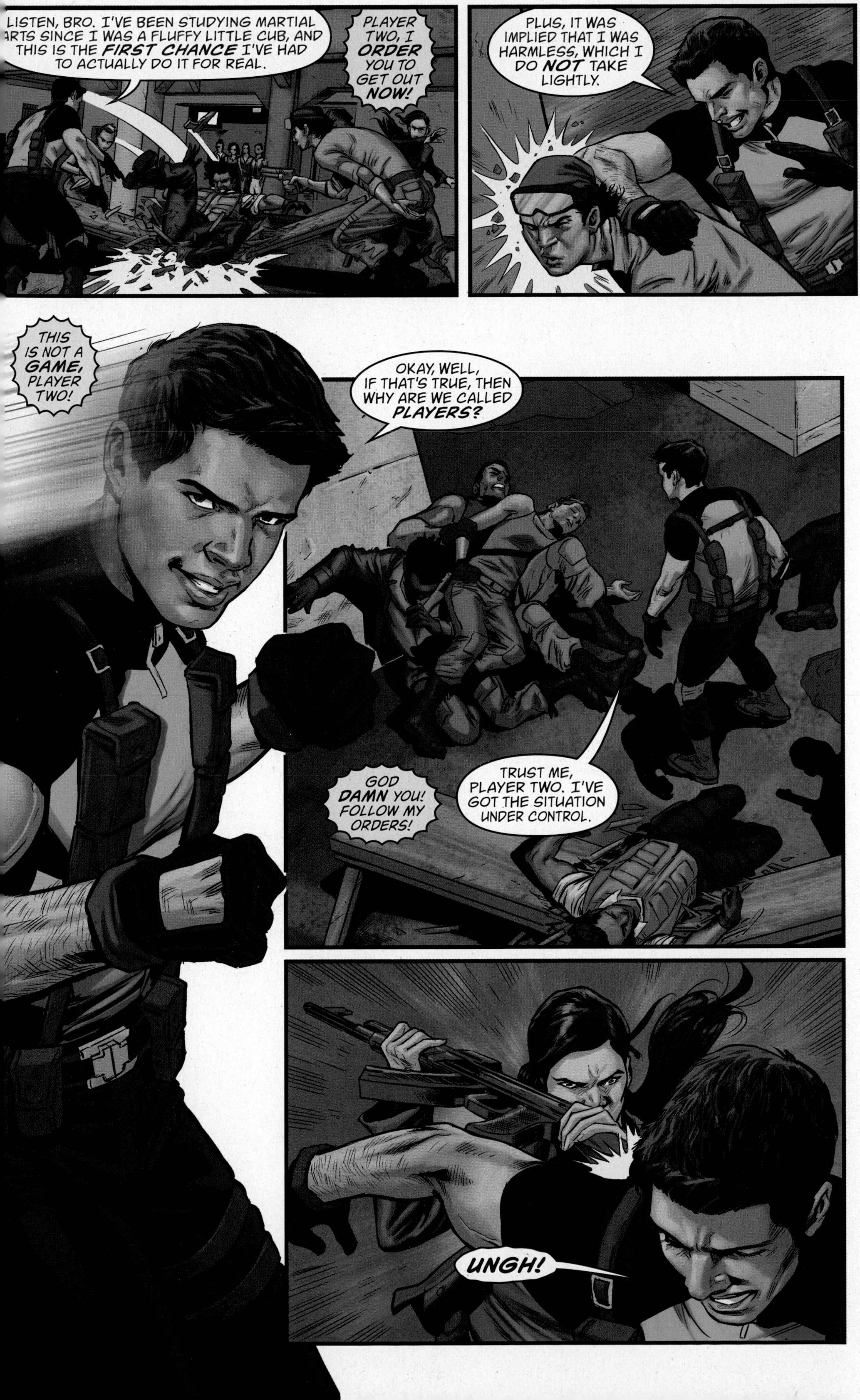
LISTEN, BRO. I'VE BEEN STUDYING MARTIAL ARTS SINCE I WAS A FLUFFY LITTLE CUB, AND THIS IS THE FIRST CHANCE I'VE HAD TO ACTUALLY DO IT FOR REAL.
PLAYER TWO, I ORDER YOU TO GET OUT NOW!
PLUS, IT WAS IMPLIED THAT I WAS HARMLESS, WHICH I DO NOT TAKE LIGHTLY.
THIS IS NOT A GAME, PLAYER TWO!
OKAY, WELL, IF THAT'S TRUE, THEN WHY ARE WE CALLED PLAYERS?
GOD DAMN YOU! FOLLOW MY ORDERS!
TRUST ME, PLAYER TWO. I'VE GOT THE SITUATION UNDER CONTROL.
UNGH!

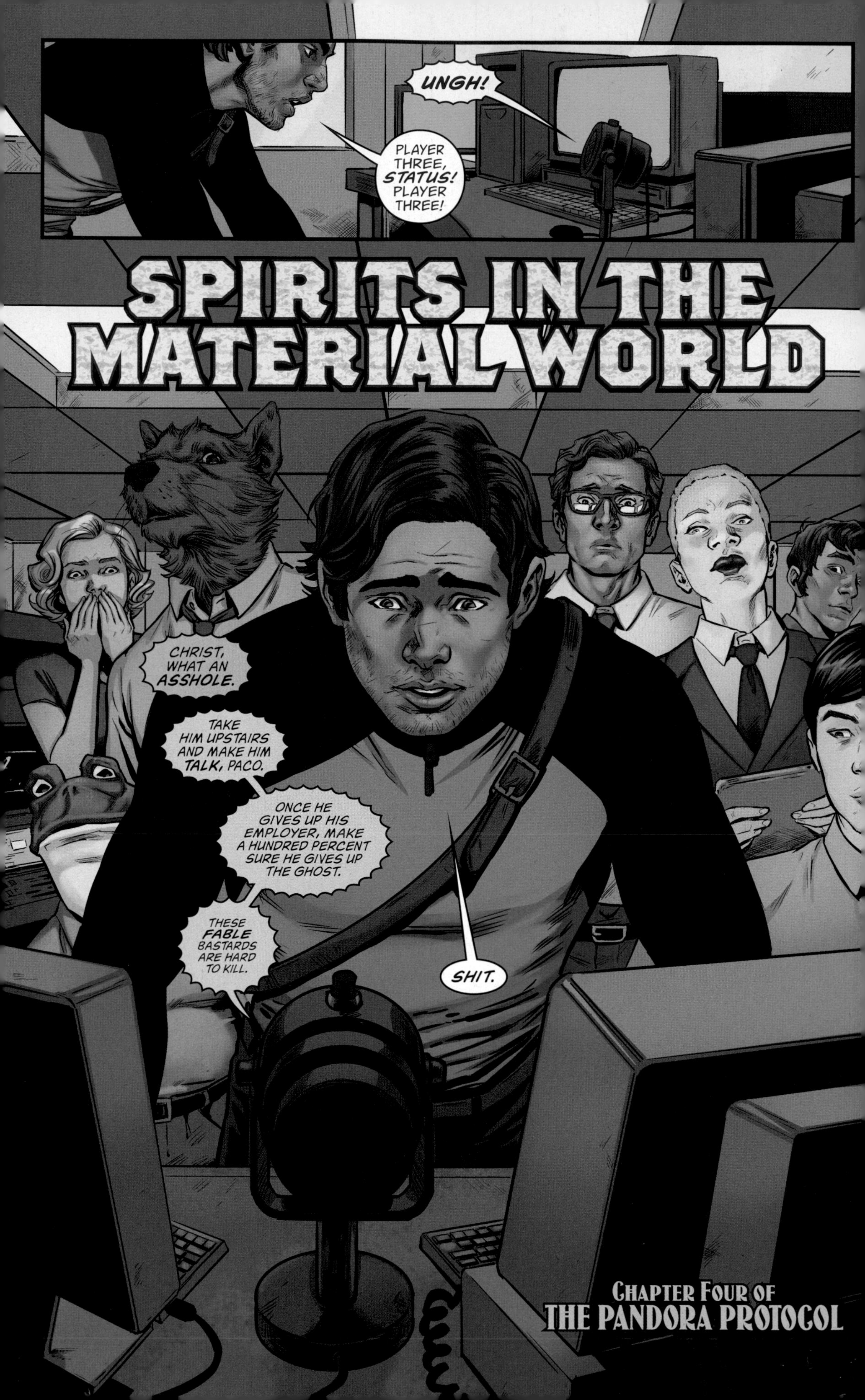
UNGH!
PLAYER THREE, STATUS! PLAYER THREE!
SPIRITS IN THE MATERIAL WORLD
CHRIST, WHAT AN ASSHOLE.
TAKE HIM UPSTAIRS AND MAKE HIM TALK, PACO.
ONCE HE GIVES UP HIS EMPLOYER, MAKE A HUNDRED PERCENT SURE HE GIVES UP THE GHOST.
THESE FABLE BASTARDS ARE HARD TO KILL.
SHIT.
CHAPTER FOUR OF
THE PANDORA PROTOCOL

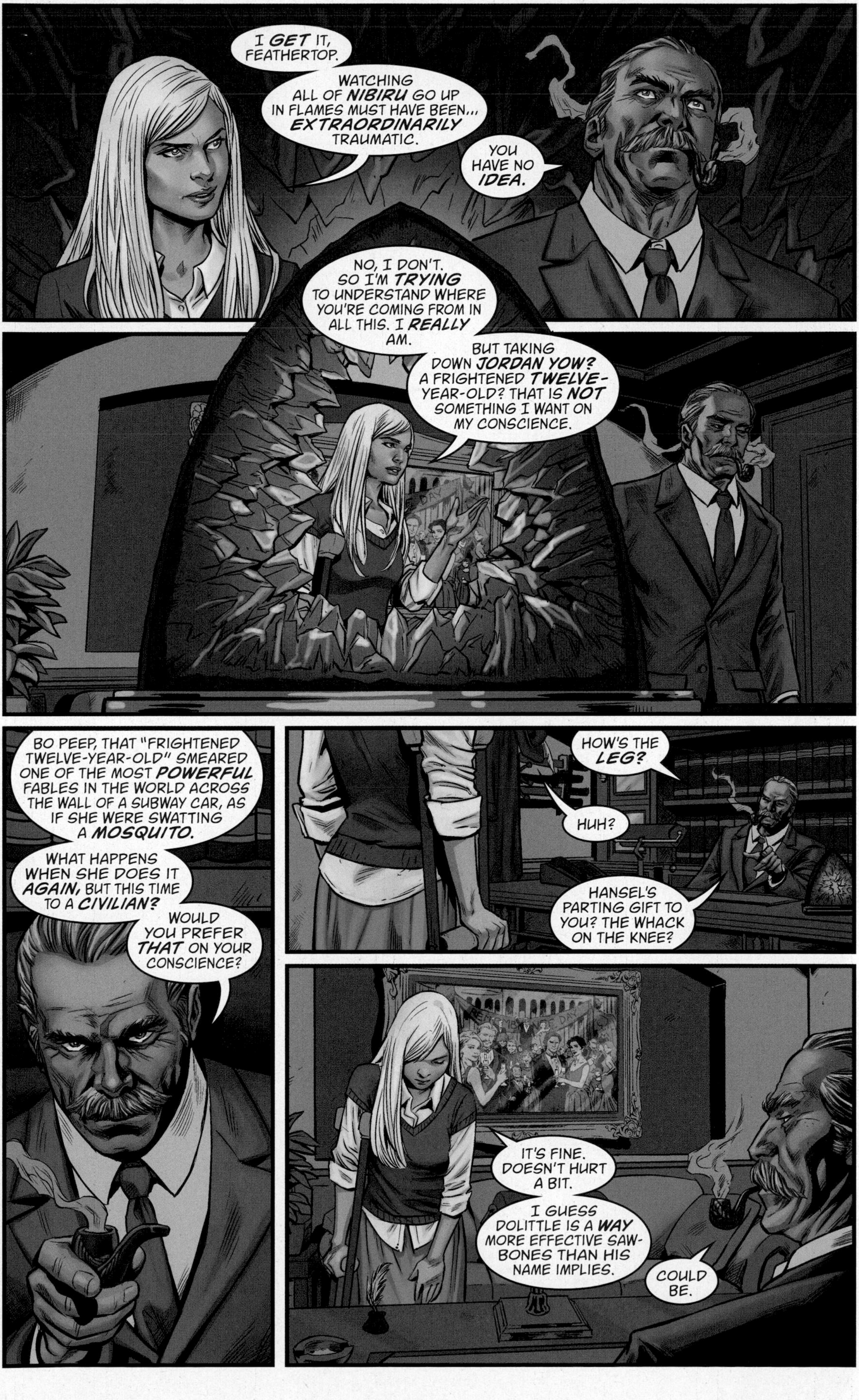
I GET IT, FEATHERTOP.
WATCHING ALL OF NIBIRU GO UP IN FLAMES MUST HAVE BEEN... EXTRAORDINARILY TRAUMATIC.
YOU HAVE NO IDEA.
NO, I DON'T. SO I'M TRYING TO UNDERSTAND WHERE YOU'RE COMING FROM IN ALL THIS. I REALLY AM.
BUT TAKING DOWN JORDAN YOW? A FRIGHTENED TWELVE-YEAR-OLD? THAT IS NOT SOMETHING I WANT ON MY CONSCIENCE.
BO PEEP, THAT "FRIGHTENED TWELVE-YEAR-OLD" SMEARED ONE OF THE MOST POWERFUL FABLES IN THE WORLD ACROSS THE WALL OF A SUBWAY CAR, AS IF SHE WERE SWATTING A MOSQUITO.
WHAT HAPPENS WHEN SHE DOES IT AGAIN, BUT THIS TIME TO A CIVILIAN?
WOULD YOU PREFER THAT ON YOUR CONSCIENCE?
HOW'S THE LEG?
HUH?
HANSEL'S PARTING GIFT TO YOU? THE WHACK ON THE KNEE?
IT'S FINE. DOESN'T HURT A BIT.
I GUESS DOLITTLE IS A WAY MORE EFFECTIVE SAW-BONES THAN HIS NAME IMPLIES.
COULD BE.

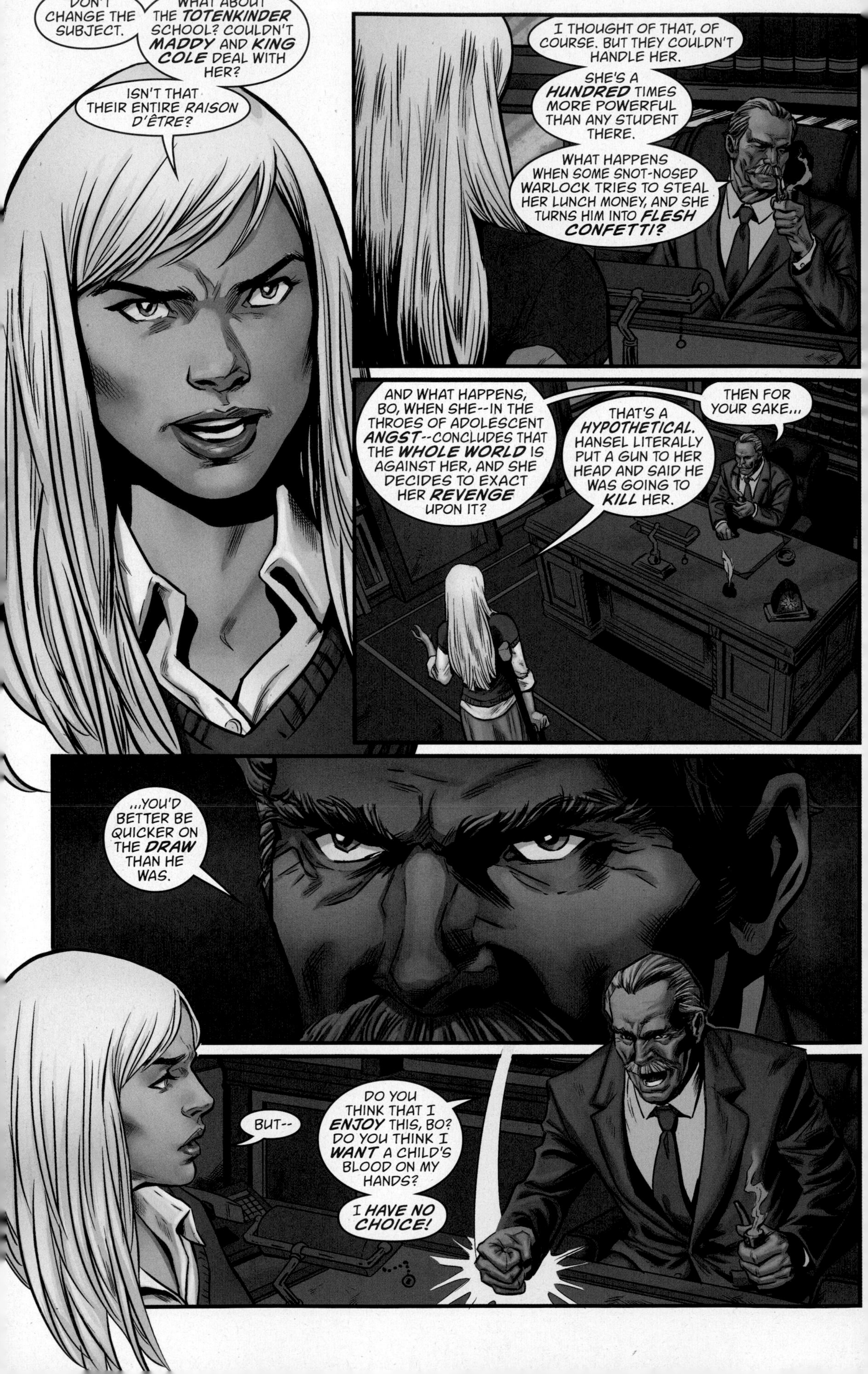
DON'T CHANGE THE SUBJECT.
WHAT ABOUT THE TOTENKINDER SCHOOL? COULDN'T MADDY AND KING COLE DEAL WITH HER?
ISN'T THAT THEIR ENTIRE RAISON D'ÊTRE?
I THOUGHT OF THAT, OF COURSE. BUT THEY COULDN'T HANDLE HER.
SHE'S A HUNDRED TIMES MORE POWERFUL THAN ANY STUDENT THERE.
WHAT HAPPENS WHEN SOME SNOT-NOSED WARLOCK TRIES TO STEAL HER LUNCH MONEY, AND SHE TURNS HIM INTO FLESH CONFETTI?
AND WHAT HAPPENS, BO, WHEN SHE--IN THE THROES OF ADOLESCENT ANGST--CONCLUDES THAT THE WHOLE WORLD IS AGAINST HER, AND SHE DECIDES TO EXACT HER REVENGE UPON IT?
THAT'S A HYPOTHETICAL. HANSEL LITERALLY PUT A GUN TO HER HEAD AND SAID HE WAS GOING TO KILL HER.
THEN FOR YOUR SAKE...
...YOU'D BETTER BE QUICKER ON THE DRAW THAN HE WAS.
BUT--
DO YOU THINK THAT I ENJOY THIS, BO? DO YOU THINK I WANT A CHILD'S BLOOD ON MY HANDS?
I HAVE NO CHOICE!

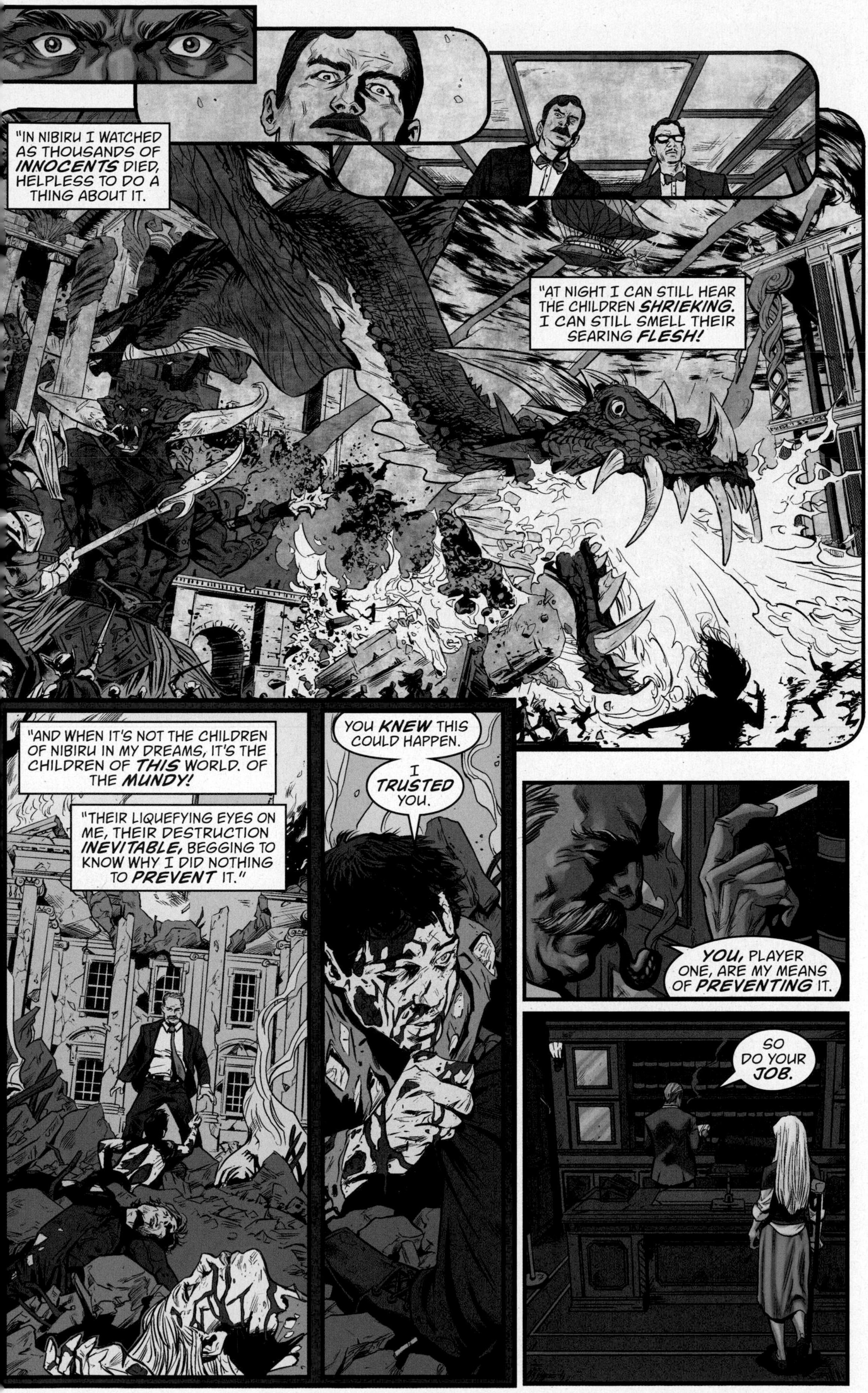
"IN NIBIRU I WATCHED AS THOUSANDS OF INNOCENTS DIED, HELPLESS TO DO A THING ABOUT IT.
"AT NIGHT I CAN STILL HEAR THE CHILDREN SHRIEKING. I CAN STILL SMELL THEIR SEARING FLESH!
"AND WHEN IT'S NOT THE CHILDREN OF NIBIRU IN MY DREAMS, IT'S THE CHILDREN OF THIS WORLD. OF THE MUNDY!
"THEIR LIQUEFYING EYES ON ME, THEIR DESTRUCTION INEVITABLE, BEGGING TO KNOW WHY I DID NOTHING TO PREVENT IT."
YOU KNEW THIS COULD HAPPEN.
I TRUSTED YOU.
YOU, PLAYER ONE, ARE MY MEANS OF PREVENTING IT.
SO DO YOUR JOB.

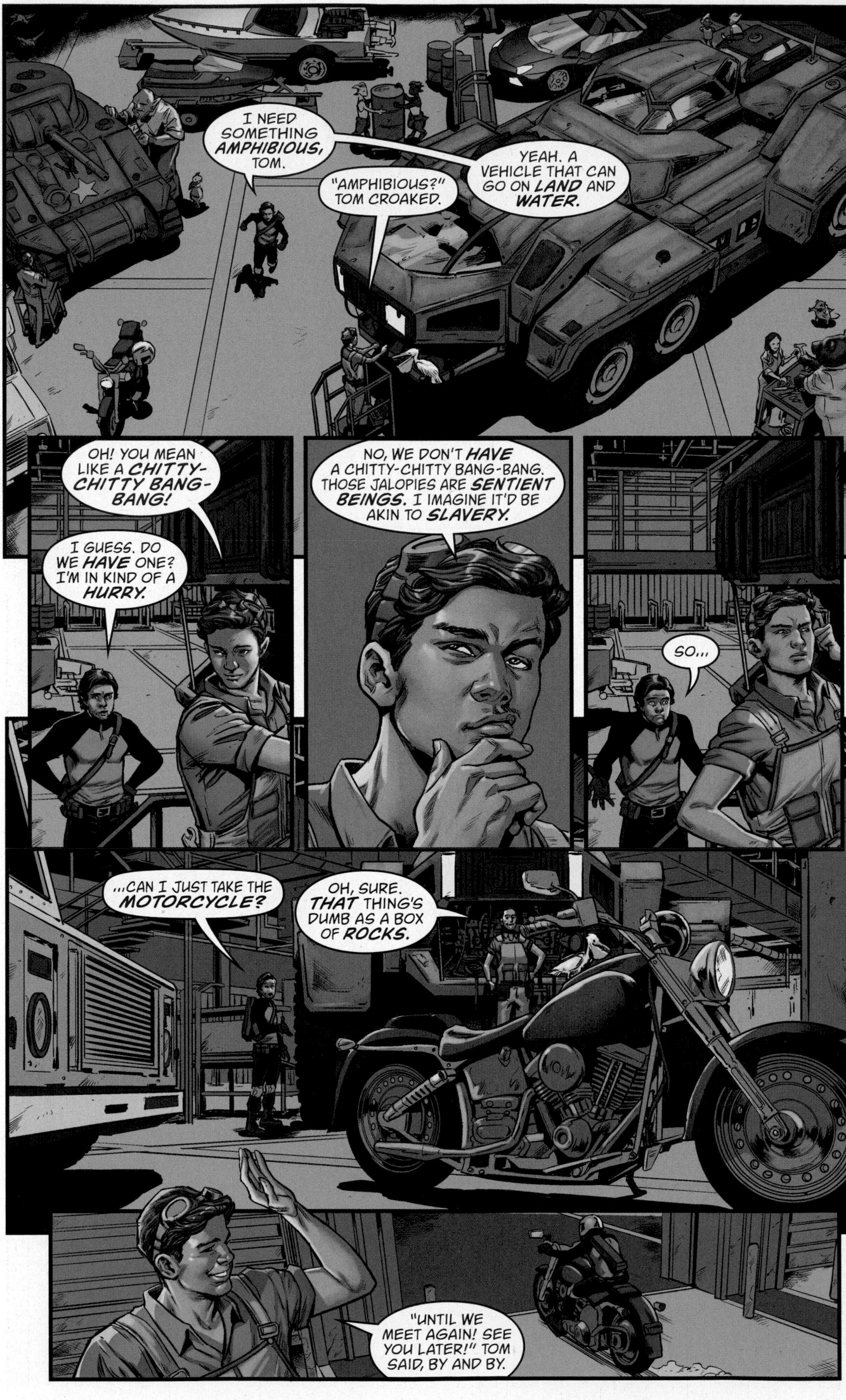

I NEED SOMETHING AMPHIBIOUS, TOM.
"AMPHIBIOUS?" TOM CROAKED.
YEAH. A VEHICLE THAT CAN GO ON LAND AND WATER.
OH! YOU MEAN LIKE A CHITTY-CHITTY BANG-BANG!
I GUESS. DO WE HAVE ONE? I'M IN KIND OF A HURRY.
NO, WE DON'T HAVE A CHITTY-CHITTY BANG-BANG. THOSE JALOPIES ARE SENTIENT BEINGS. I IMAGINE IT'D BE AKIN TO SLAVERY.
SO...
...CAN I JUST TAKE THE MOTORCYCLE?
OH, SURE. THAT THING'S DUMB AS A BOX OF ROCKS.
"UNTIL WE MEET AGAIN! SEE YOU LATER!" TOM SAID, BY AND BY.

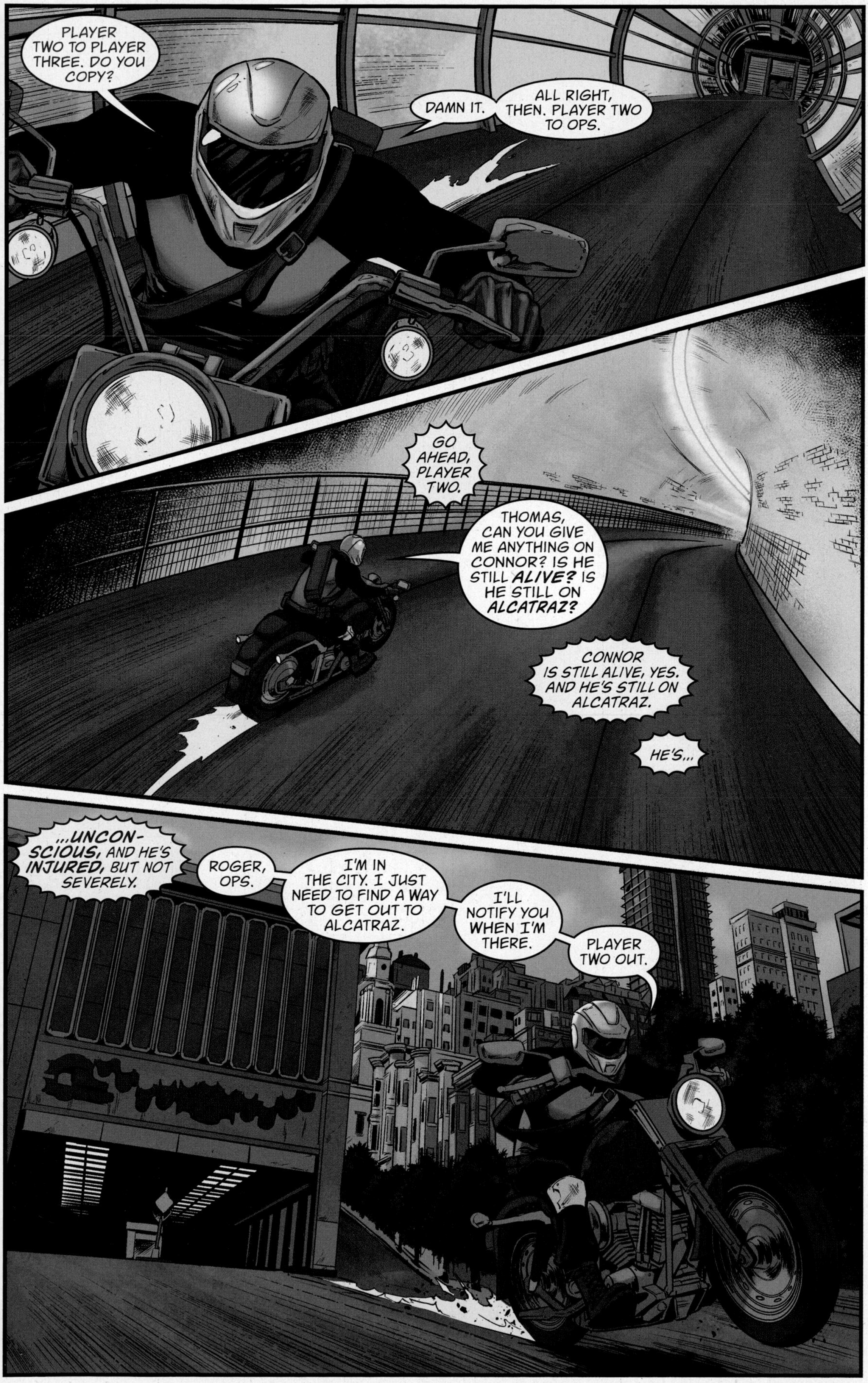
PLAYER TWO TO PLAYER THREE. DO YOU COPY?
DAMN IT.
ALL RIGHT, THEN. PLAYER TWO TO OPS.
GO AHEAD, PLAYER TWO.
THOMAS, CAN YOU GIVE ME ANYTHING ON CONNOR? IS HE STILL ALIVE? IS HE STILL ON ALCATRAZ?
CONNOR IS STILL ALIVE, YES. AND HE'S STILL ON ALCATRAZ.
HE'S...
...UNCONSCIOUS, AND HE'S INJURED, BUT NOT SEVERELY.
ROGER, OPS.
I'M IN THE CITY. I JUST NEED TO FIND A WAY TO GET OUT TO ALCATRAZ.
I'LL NOTIFY YOU WHEN I'M THERE.
PLAYER TWO OUT.

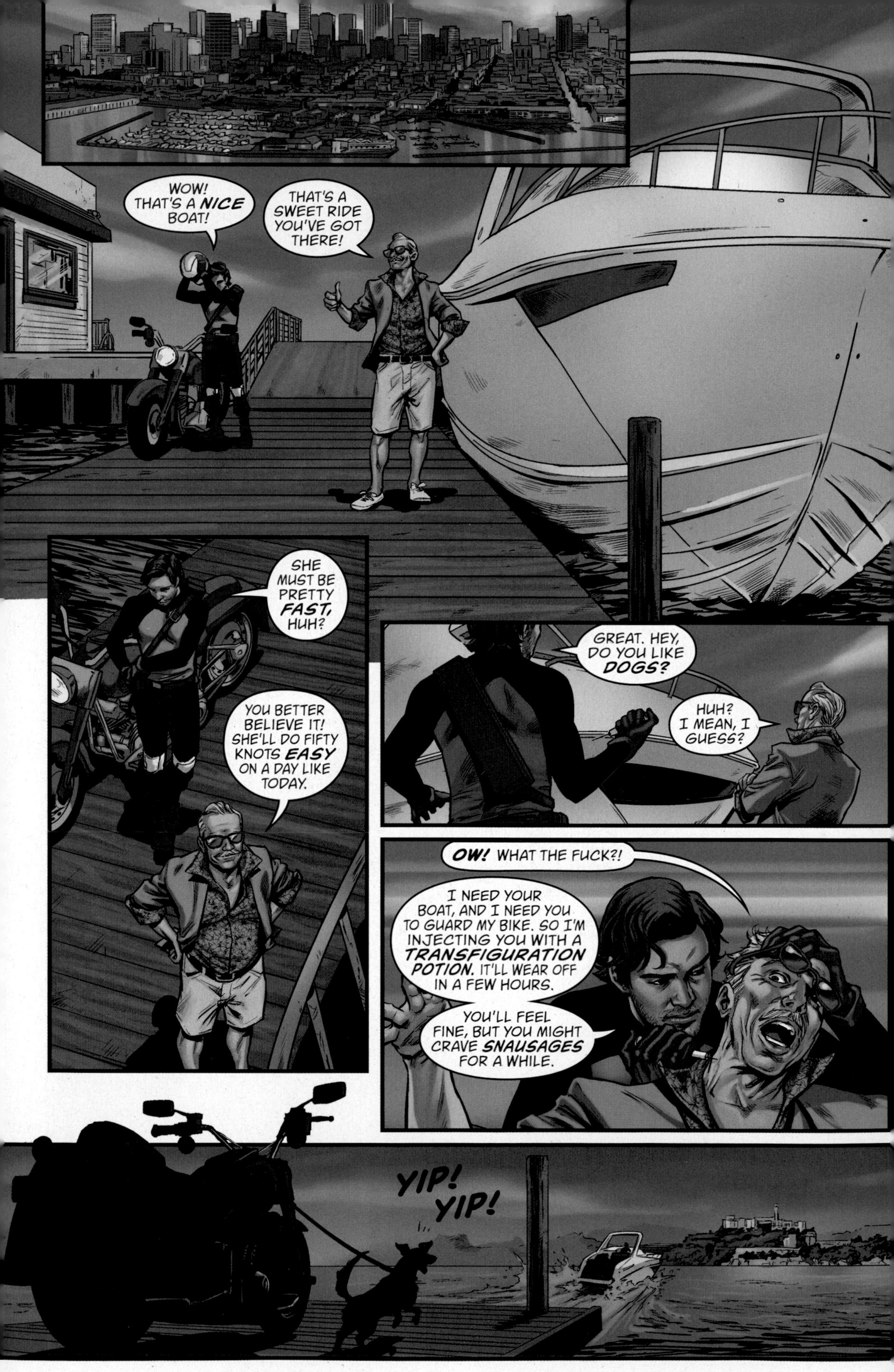

WOW! THAT'S A NICE BOAT!
THAT'S A SWEET RIDE YOU'VE GOT THERE!
SHE MUST BE PRETTY FAST, HUH?
YOU BETTER BELIEVE IT! SHE'LL DO FIFTY KNOTS EASY ON A DAY LIKE TODAY.
GREAT. HEY, DO YOU LIKE DOGS?
HUH? I MEAN, I GUESS?
OW! WHAT THE FUCK?!
I NEED YOUR BOAT, AND I NEED YOU TO GUARD MY BIKE. SO I'M INJECTING YOU WITH A TRANSFIGURATION POTION. IT'LL WEAR OFF IN A FEW HOURS.
YOU'LL FEEL FINE, BUT YOU MIGHT CRAVE SNAUSAGES FOR A WHILE.
YIP! YIP!

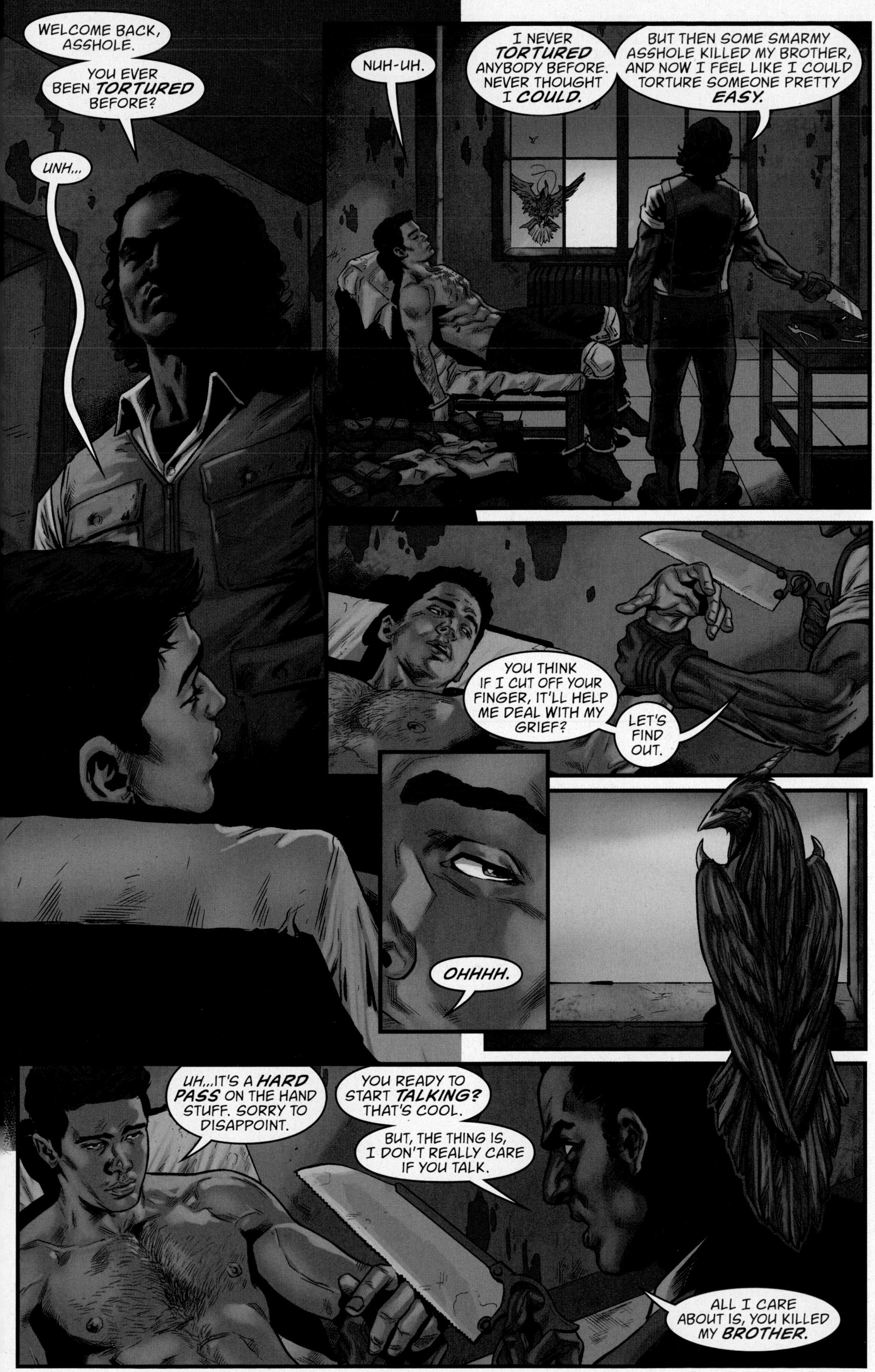
WELCOME BACK, ASSHOLE.
YOU EVER BEEN TORTURED BEFORE?
UNH...
NUH-UH.
I NEVER TORTURED ANYBODY BEFORE. NEVER THOUGHT I COULD.
BUT THEN SOME SMARMY ASSHOLE KILLED MY BROTHER, AND NOW I FEEL LIKE I COULD TORTURE SOMEONE PRETTY EASY.
YOU THINK IF I CUT OFF YOUR FINGER, IT'LL HELP ME DEAL WITH MY GRIEF?
LET'S FIND OUT.
OHHHH.
UH...IT'S A HARD PASS ON THE HAND STUFF. SORRY TO DISAPPOINT.
YOU READY TO START TALKING? THAT'S COOL.
BUT, THE THING IS, I DON'T REALLY CARE IF YOU TALK.
ALL I CARE ABOUT IS, YOU KILLED MY BROTHER.

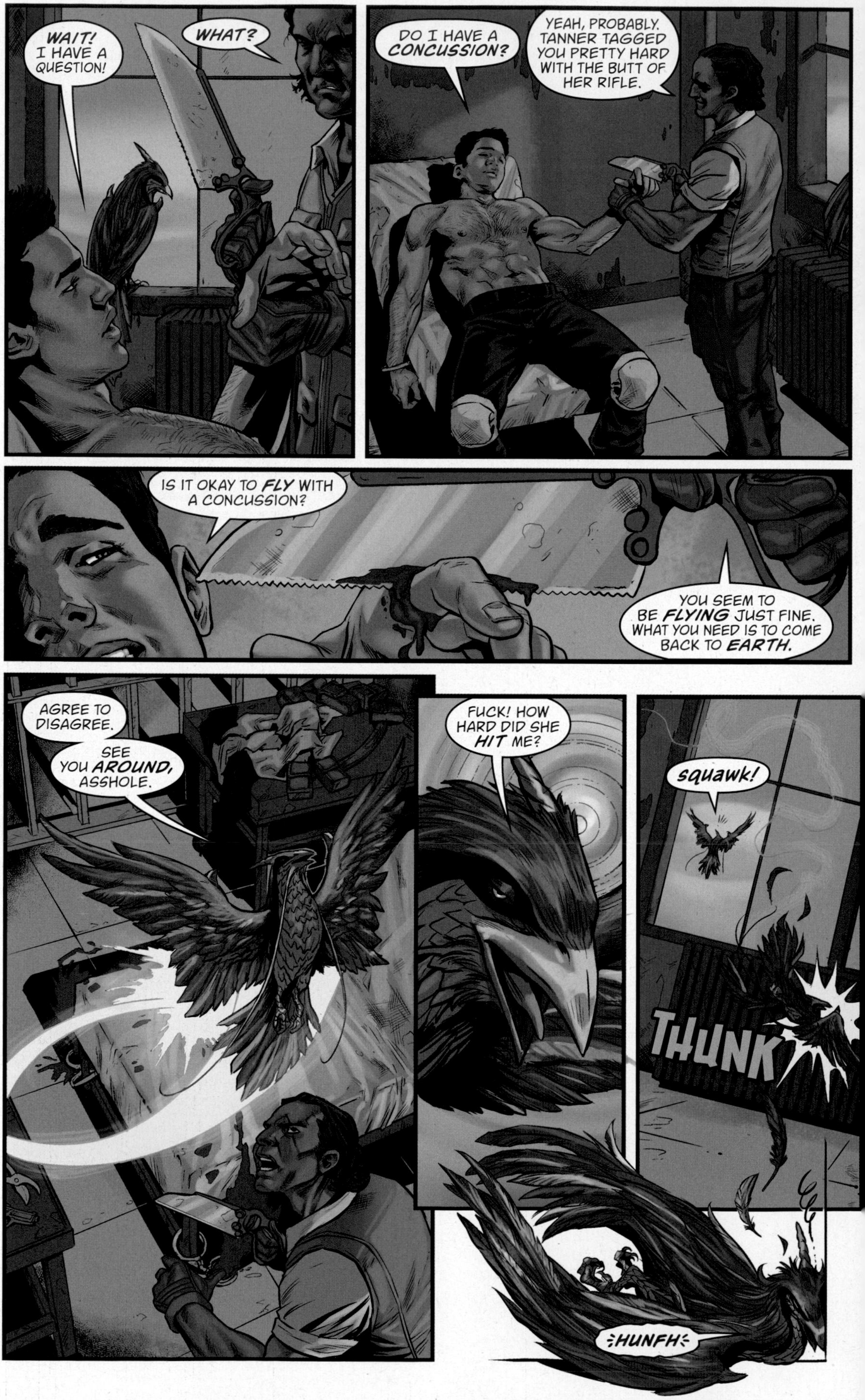
WAIT! I HAVE A QUESTION!
WHAT?
DO I HAVE A CONCUSSION?
YEAH, PROBABLY. TANNER TAGGED YOU PRETTY HARD WITH THE BUTT OF HER RIFLE.
IS IT OKAY TO FLY WITH A CONCUSSION?
YOU SEEM TO BE FLYING JUST FINE. WHAT YOU NEED IS TO COME BACK TO EARTH.
AGREE TO DISAGREE.
SEE YOU AROUND, ASSHOLE.
FUCK! HOW HARD DID SHE HIT ME?
squawk!
THUNK
HUNFH

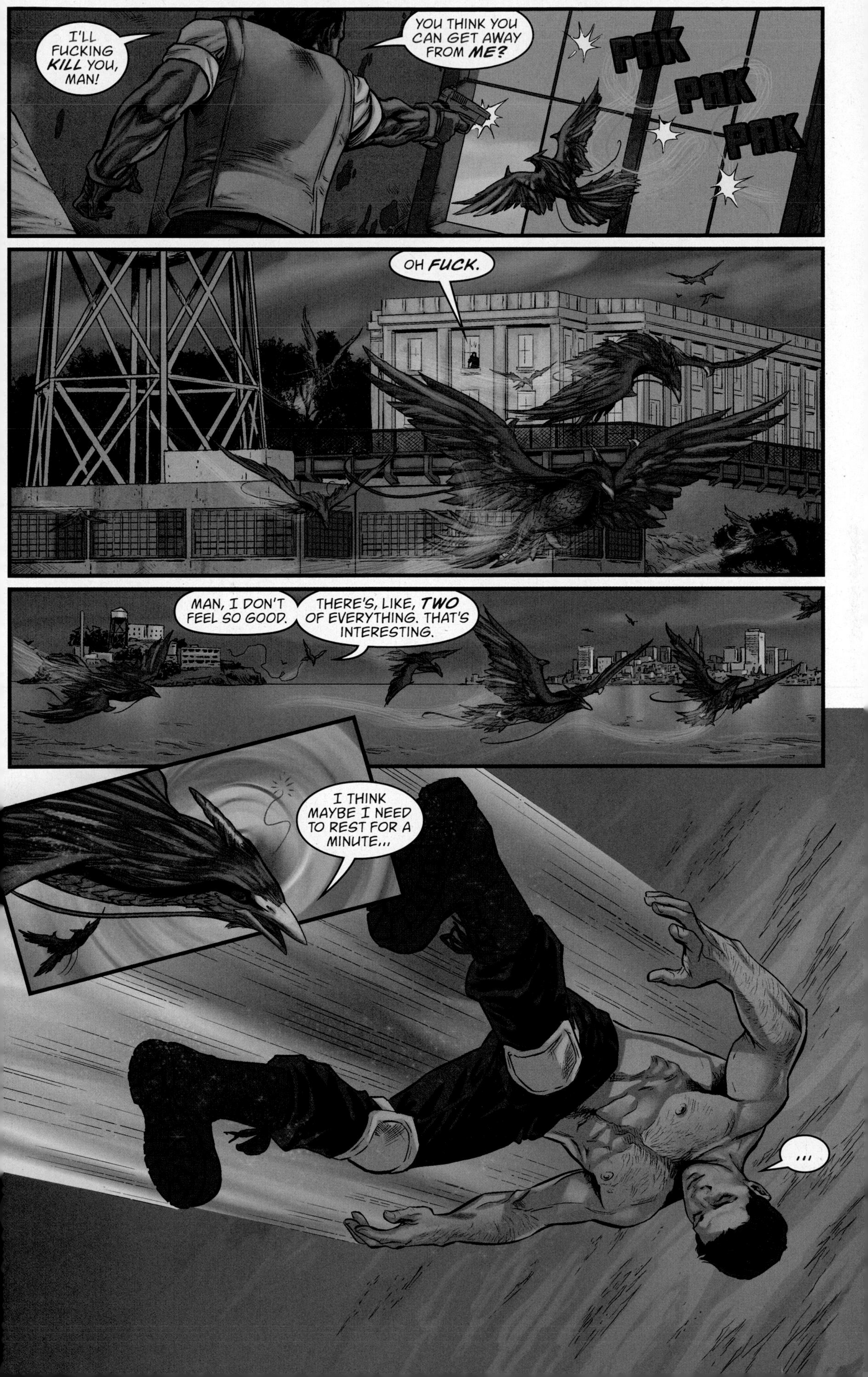
I'LL FUCKING KILL YOU, MAN!
YOU THINK YOU CAN GET AWAY FROM ME?
PAK
PAK
PAK
OH FUCK.
MAN, I DON'T FEEL SO GOOD.
THERE'S, LIKE, TWO OF EVERYTHING. THAT'S INTERESTING.
I THINK MAYBE I NEED TO REST FOR A MINUTE...
...

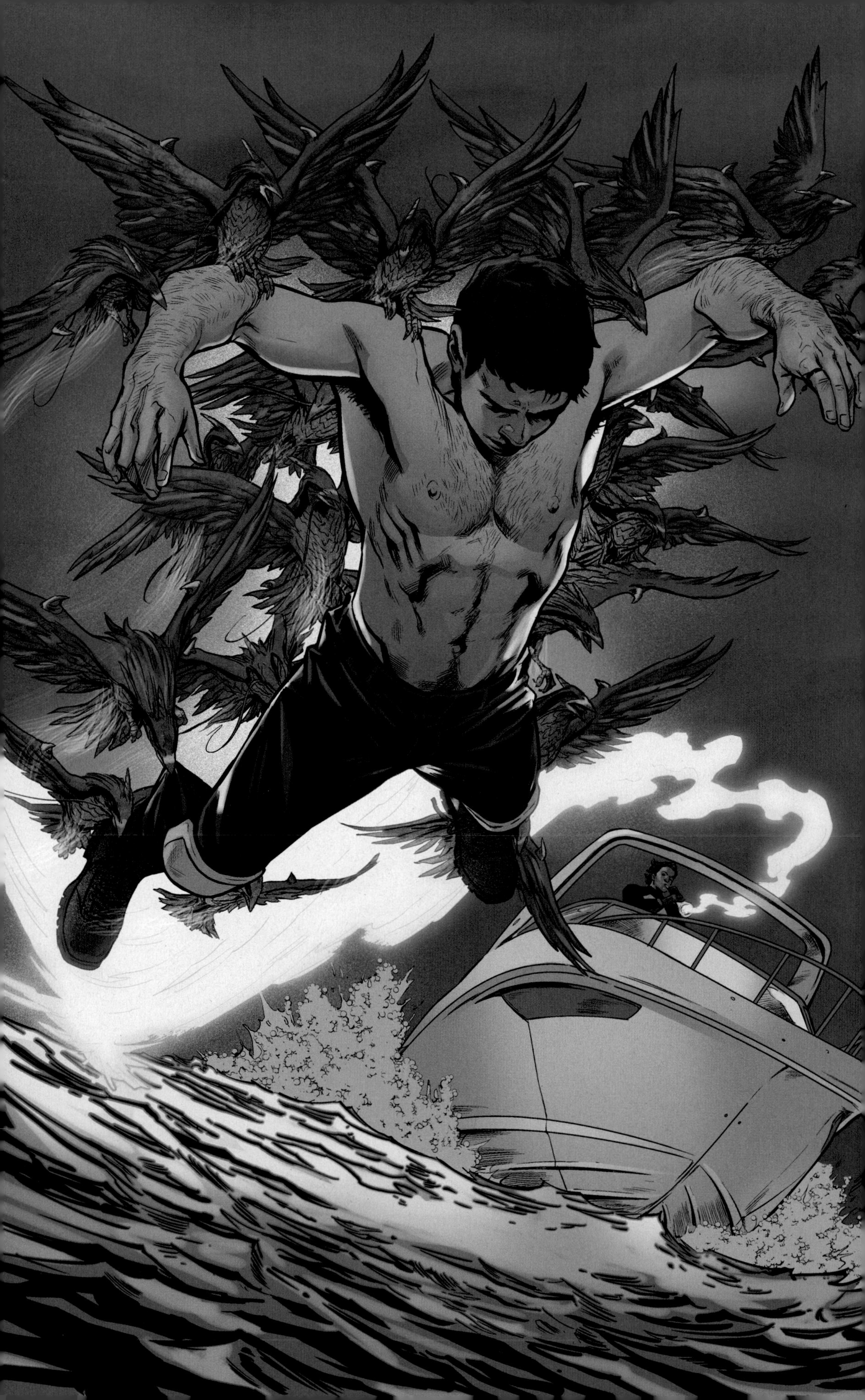

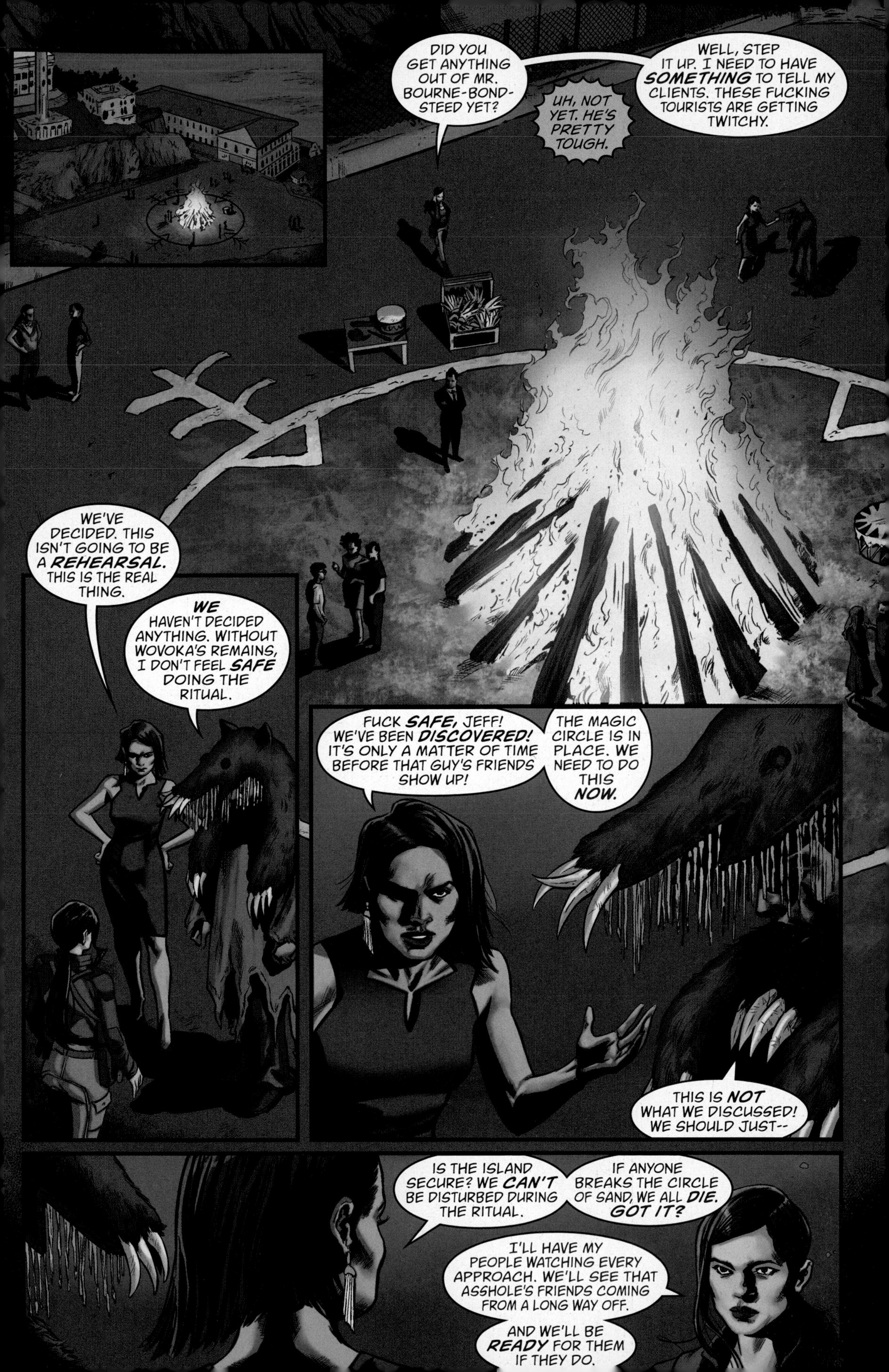
DID YOU GET ANYTHING OUT OF MR. BOURNE-BOND-STEED YET?
UH, NOT YET. HE'S PRETTY TOUGH.
WELL, STEP IT UP. I NEED TO HAVE SOMETHING TO TELL MY CLIENTS. THESE FUCKING TOURISTS ARE GETTING TWITCHY.
WE'VE DECIDED. THIS ISN'T GOING TO BE A REHEARSAL. THIS IS THE REAL THING.
WE HAVEN'T DECIDED ANYTHING. WITHOUT WOVOKA'S REMAINS, I DON'T FEEL SAFE DOING THE RITUAL.
FUCK SAFE, JEFF! WE'VE BEEN DISCOVERED! IT'S ONLY A MATTER OF TIME BEFORE THAT GUY'S FRIENDS SHOW UP!
THE MAGIC CIRCLE IS IN PLACE. WE NEED TO DO THIS NOW.
THIS IS NOT WHAT WE DISCUSSED! WE SHOULD JUST--
IS THE ISLAND SECURE? WE CAN'T BE DISTURBED DURING THE RITUAL.
IF ANYONE BREAKS THE CIRCLE OF SAND, WE ALL DIE. GOT IT?
I'LL HAVE MY PEOPLE WATCHING EVERY APPROACH. WE'LL SEE THAT ASSHOLE'S FRIENDS COMING FROM A LONG WAY OFF.
AND WE'LL BE READY FOR THEM IF THEY DO.

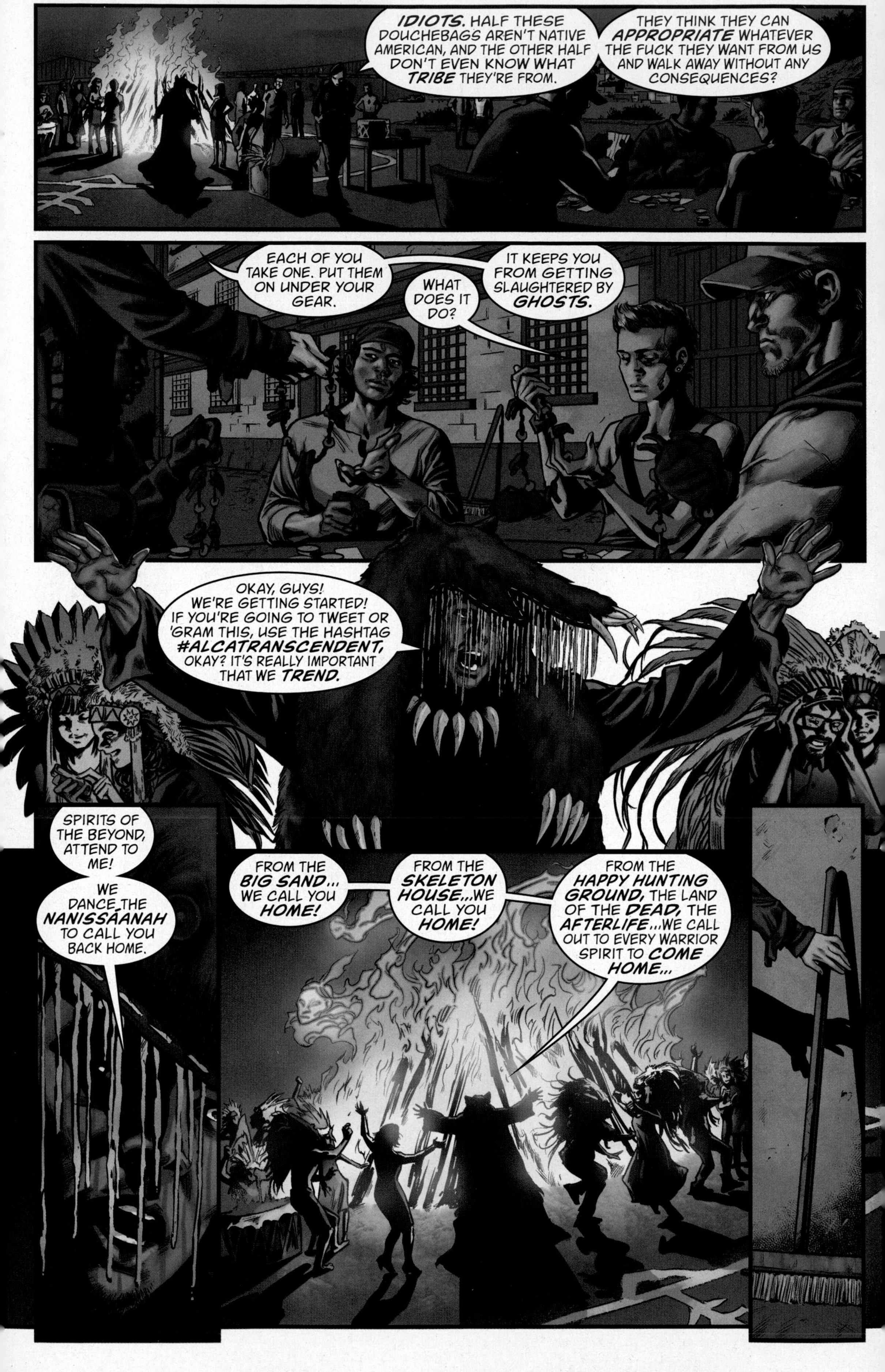
IDIOTS. HALF THESE DOUCHEBAGS AREN'T NATIVE AMERICAN, AND THE OTHER HALF DON'T EVEN KNOW WHAT TRIBE THEY'RE FROM.
THEY THINK THEY CAN APPROPRIATE WHATEVER THE FUCK THEY WANT FROM US AND WALK AWAY WITHOUT ANY CONSEQUENCES?
EACH OF YOU TAKE ONE. PUT THEM ON UNDER YOUR GEAR.
IT KEEPS YOU FROM GETTING SLAUGHTERED BY GHOSTS.
WHAT DOES IT DO?
OKAY, GUYS! WE'RE GETTING STARTED! IF YOU'RE GOING TO TWEET OR 'GRAM THIS, USE THE HASHTAG #ALCATRANSCENDENT, OKAY? IT'S REALLY IMPORTANT THAT WE TREND.
SPIRITS OF THE BEYOND, ATTEND TO ME!
WE DANCE THE NANISSÁANAH TO CALL YOU BACK HOME.
FROM THE BIG SAND... WE CALL YOU HOME!
FROM THE SKELETON HOUSE...WE CALL YOU HOME!
FROM THE HAPPY HUNTING GROUND, THE LAND OF THE DEAD, THE AFTERLIFE...WE CALL OUT TO EVERY WARRIOR SPIRIT TO COME HOME...

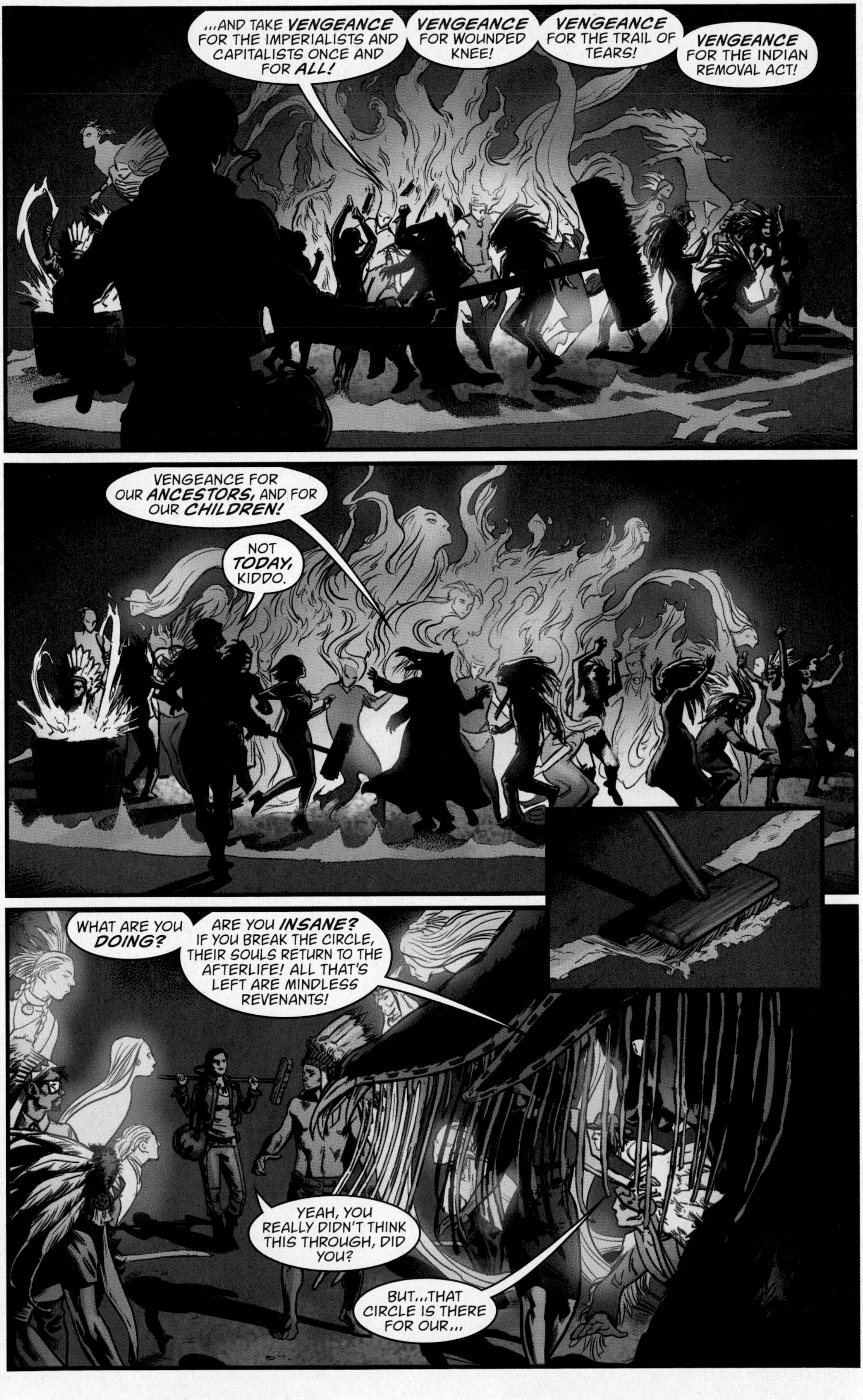
...AND TAKE VENGEANCE FOR THE IMPERIALISTS AND CAPITALISTS ONCE AND FOR ALL!
VENGEANCE FOR WOUNDED KNEE!
VENGEANCE FOR THE TRAIL OF TEARS!
VENGEANCE FOR THE INDIAN REMOVAL ACT!
VENGEANCE FOR OUR ANCESTORS, AND FOR OUR CHILDREN!
NOT TODAY, KIDDO.
WHAT ARE YOU DOING?
ARE YOU INSANE? IF YOU BREAK THE CIRCLE, THEIR SOULS RETURN TO THE AFTERLIFE! ALL THAT'S LEFT ARE MINDLESS REVENANTS!
YEAH, YOU REALLY DIDN'T THINK THIS THROUGH, DID YOU?
BUT...THAT CIRCLE IS THERE FOR OUR...

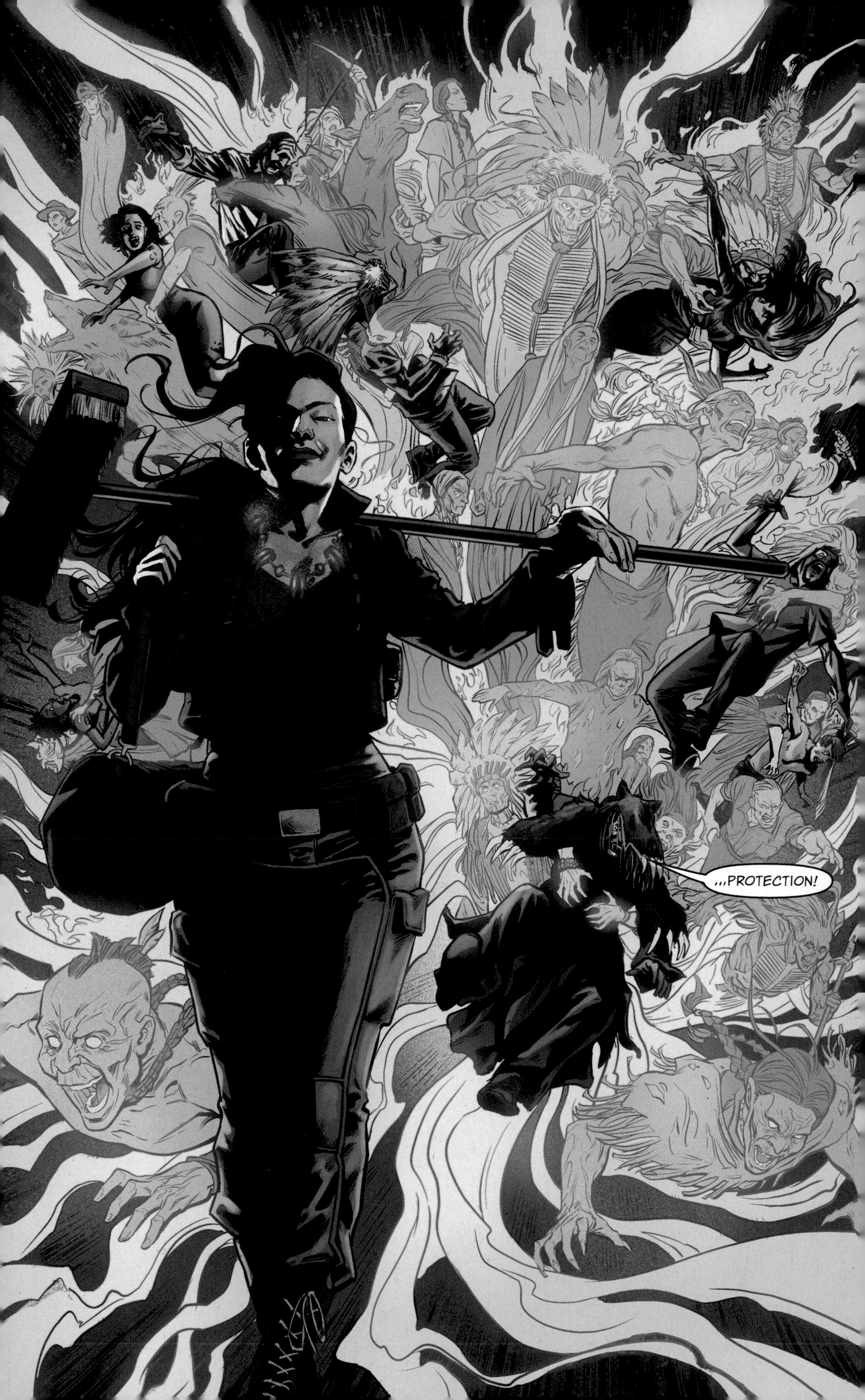
...PROTECTION!

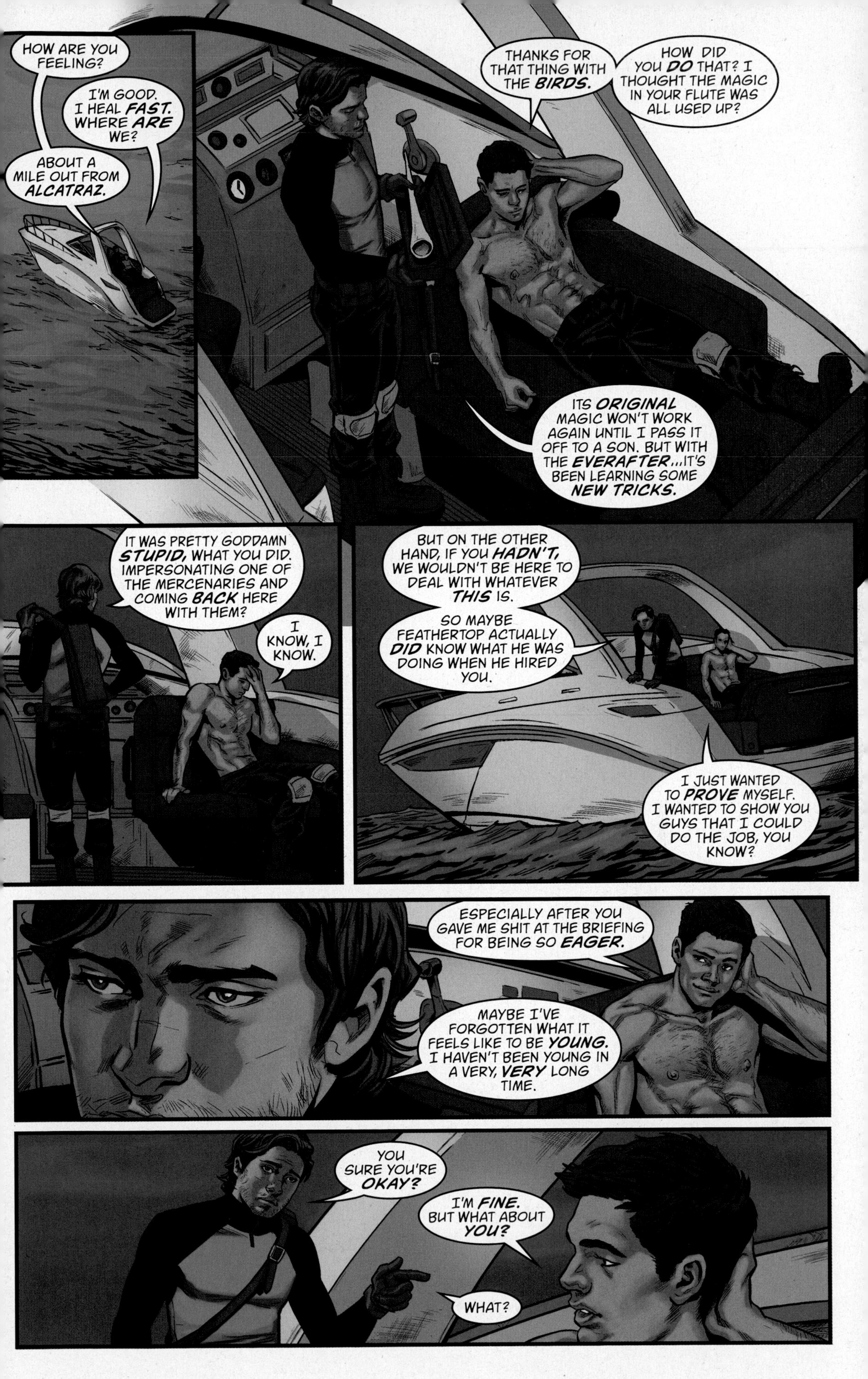
HOW ARE YOU FEELING?
I'M GOOD. I HEAL FAST. WHERE ARE WE?
ABOUT A MILE OUT FROM ALCATRAZ.
THANKS FOR THAT THING WITH THE BIRDS.
HOW DID YOU DO THAT? I THOUGHT THE MAGIC IN YOUR FLUTE WAS ALL USED UP?
ITS ORIGINAL MAGIC WON'T WORK AGAIN UNTIL I PASS IT OFF TO A SON. BUT WITH THE EVERAFTER...IT'S BEEN LEARNING SOME NEW TRICKS.
IT WAS PRETTY GODDAMN STUPID, WHAT YOU DID. IMPERSONATING ONE OF THE MERCENARIES AND COMING BACK HERE WITH THEM?
I KNOW, I KNOW.
BUT ON THE OTHER HAND, IF YOU HADN'T, WE WOULDN'T BE HERE TO DEAL WITH WHATEVER THIS IS.
SO MAYBE FEATHERTOP ACTUALLY DID KNOW WHAT HE WAS DOING WHEN HE HIRED YOU.
I JUST WANTED TO PROVE MYSELF. I WANTED TO SHOW YOU GUYS THAT I COULD DO THE JOB, YOU KNOW?
ESPECIALLY AFTER YOU GAVE ME SHIT AT THE BRIEFING FOR BEING SO EAGER.
MAYBE I'VE FORGOTTEN WHAT IT FEELS LIKE TO BE YOUNG. I HAVEN'T BEEN YOUNG IN A VERY, VERY LONG TIME.
YOU SURE YOU'RE OKAY?
I'M FINE. BUT WHAT ABOUT YOU?
WHAT?

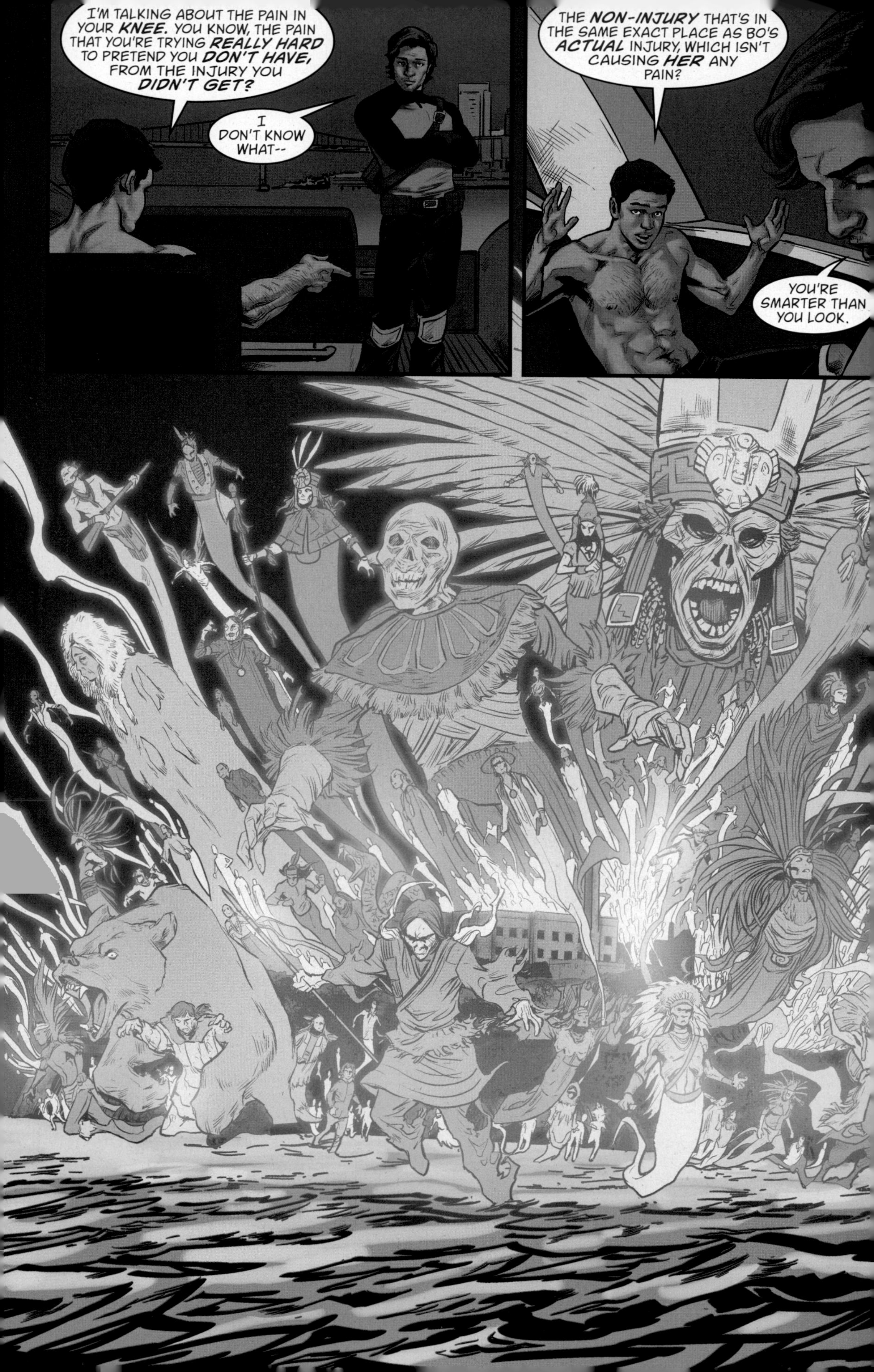
I'M TALKING ABOUT THE PAIN IN YOUR KNEE. YOU KNOW, THE PAIN THAT YOU'RE TRYING REALLY HARD TO PRETEND YOU DON'T HAVE, FROM THE INJURY YOU DIDN'T GET?
I DON'T KNOW WHAT--
THE NON-INJURY THAT'S IN THE SAME EXACT PLACE AS BO'S ACTUAL INJURY, WHICH ISN'T CAUSING HER ANY PAIN?
YOU'RE SMARTER THAN YOU LOOK.

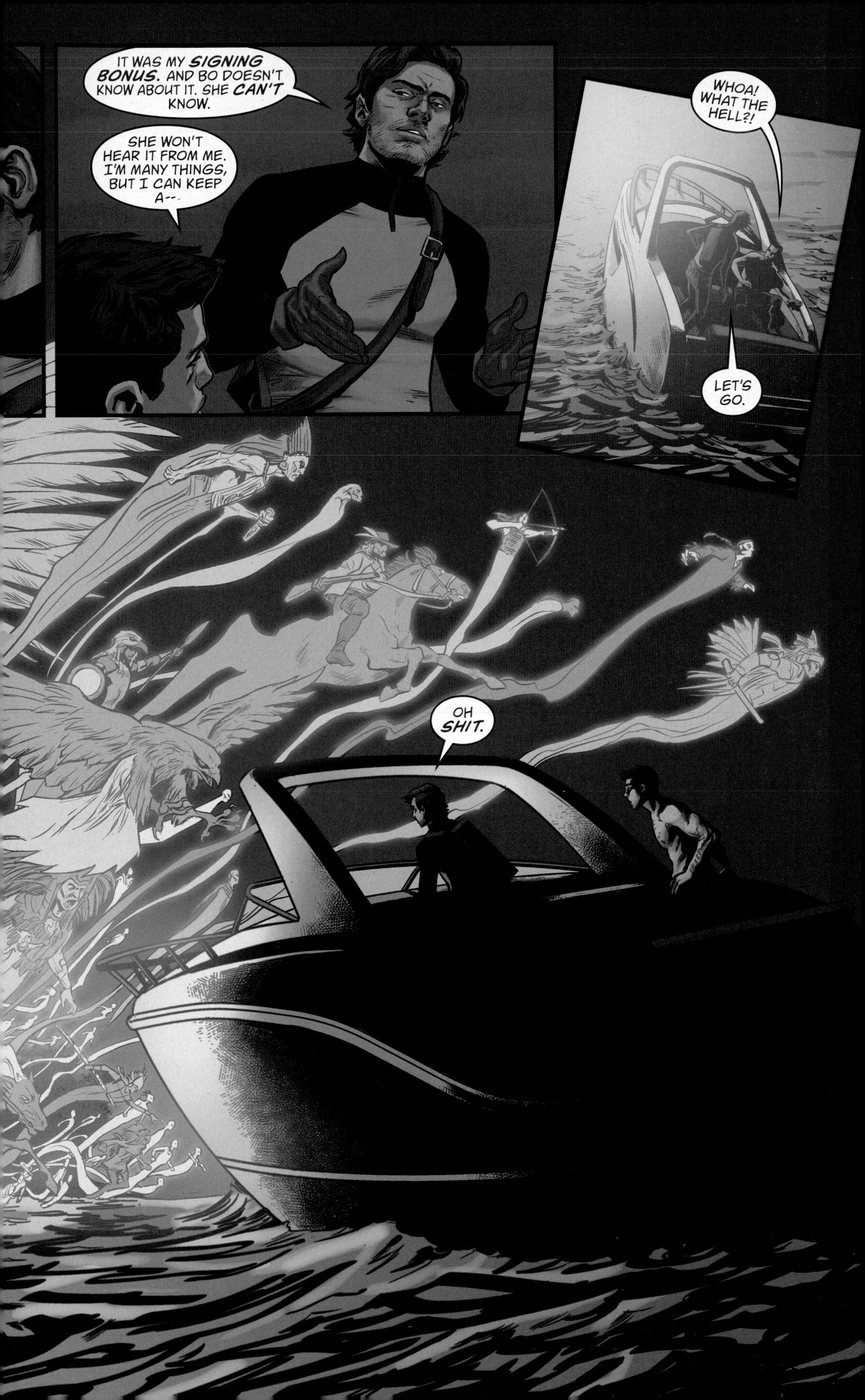
IT WAS MY **SIGNING BONUS.** AND BO DOESN'T KNOW ABOUT IT. SHE ***CAN'T*** KNOW.
SHE WON'T HEAR IT FROM ME. I'M MANY THINGS, BUT I CAN KEEP A--
WHOA! WHAT THE HELL?!
LET'S GO.
OH ***SHIT.***

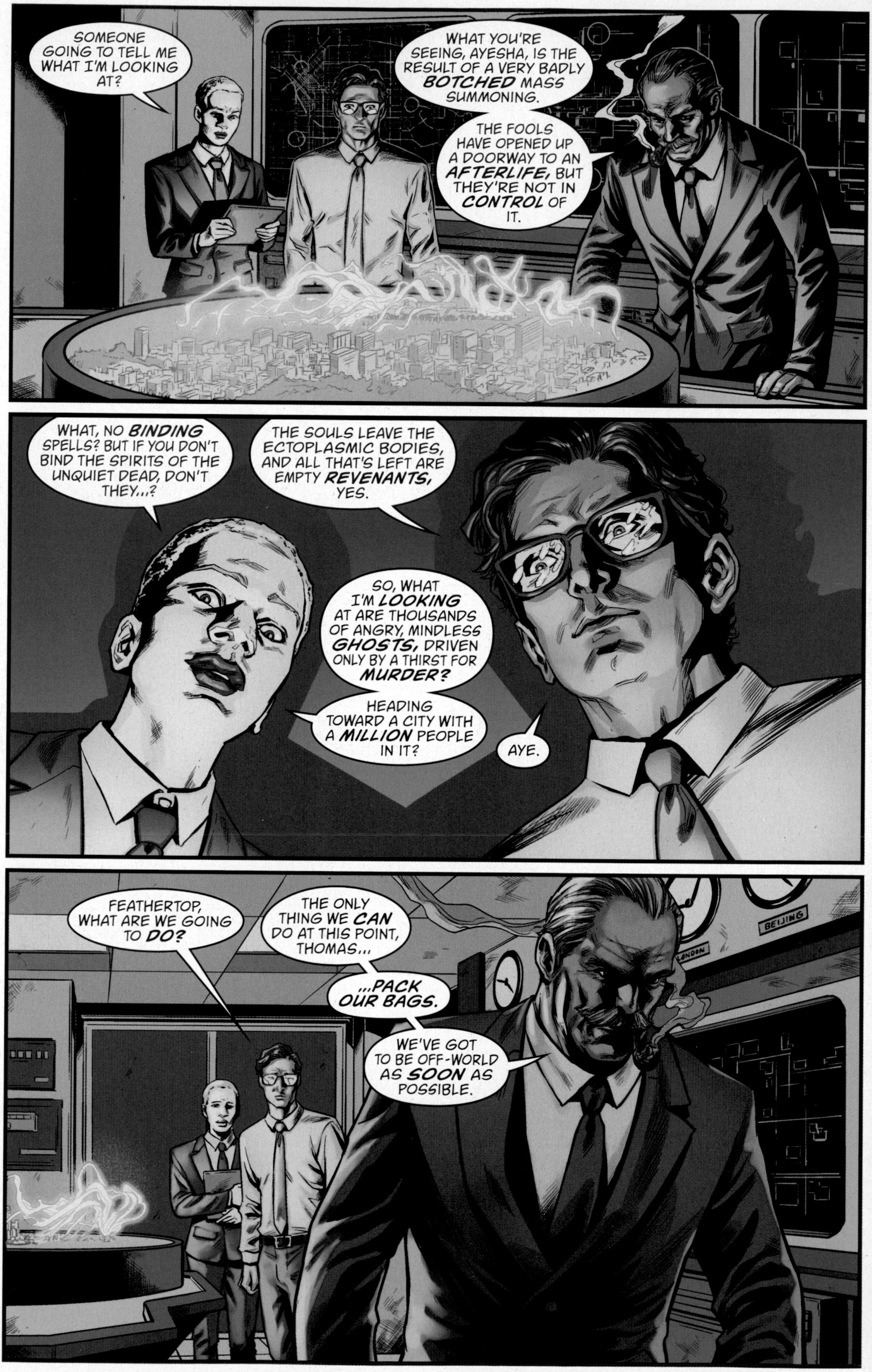
SOMEONE GOING TO TELL ME WHAT I'M LOOKING AT?
WHAT YOU'RE SEEING, AYESHA, IS THE RESULT OF A VERY BADLY BOTCHED MASS SUMMONING.
THE FOOLS HAVE OPENED UP A DOORWAY TO AN AFTERLIFE, BUT THEY'RE NOT IN CONTROL OF IT.
WHAT, NO BINDING SPELLS? BUT IF YOU DON'T BIND THE SPIRITS OF THE UNQUIET DEAD, DON'T THEY...?
THE SOULS LEAVE THE ECTOPLASMIC BODIES, AND ALL THAT'S LEFT ARE EMPTY REVENANTS, YES.
SO, WHAT I'M LOOKING AT ARE THOUSANDS OF ANGRY, MINDLESS GHOSTS, DRIVEN ONLY BY A THIRST FOR MURDER?
HEADING TOWARD A CITY WITH A MILLION PEOPLE IN IT?
AYE.
FEATHERTOP, WHAT ARE WE GOING TO DO?
THE ONLY THING WE CAN DO AT THIS POINT, THOMAS...
...PACK OUR BAGS.
WE'VE GOT TO BE OFF-WORLD AS SOON AS POSSIBLE.
BEIJING
LONDON

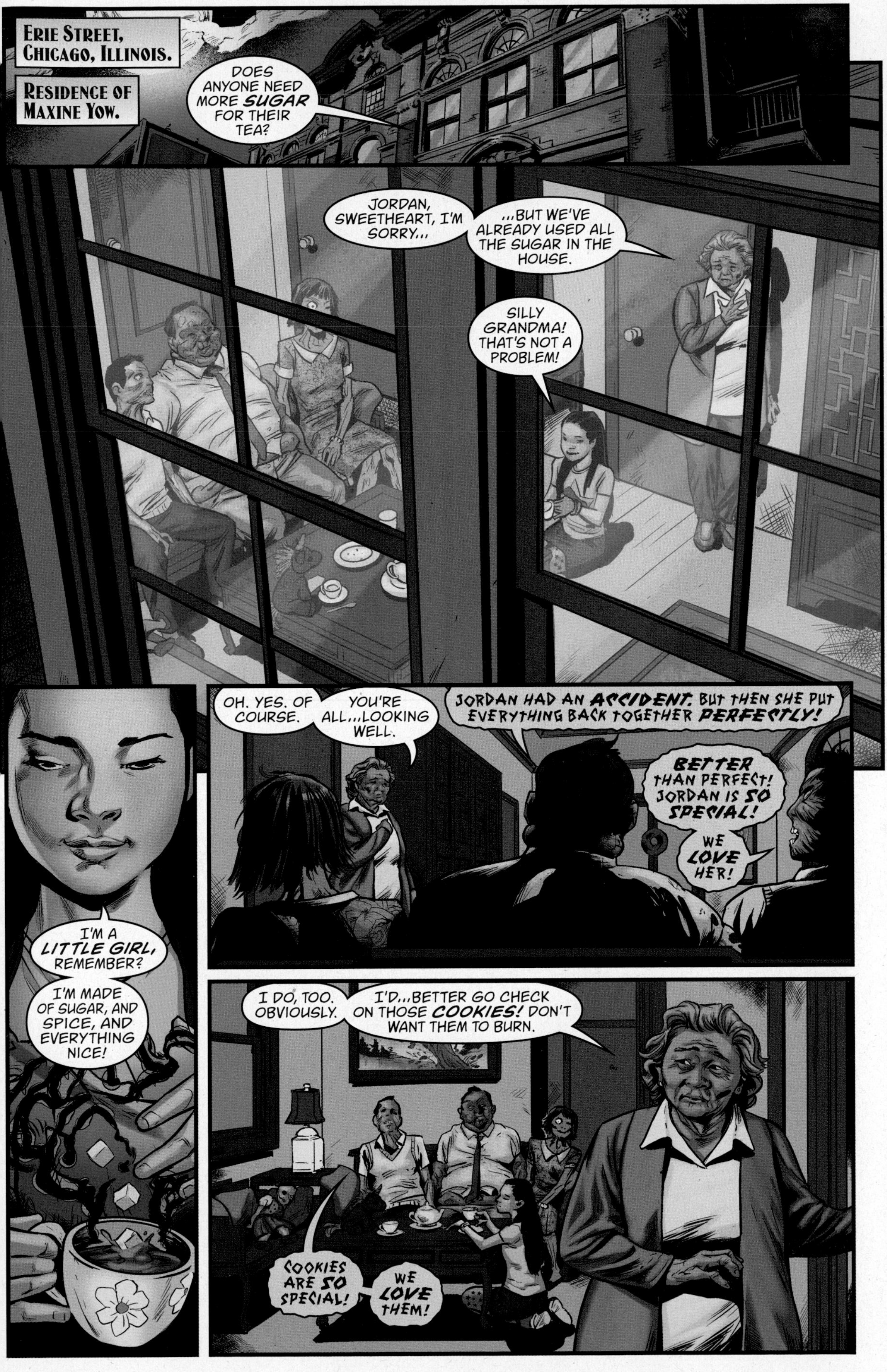
ERIE STREET, CHICAGO, ILLINOIS.
RESIDENCE OF MAXINE YOW.
DOES ANYONE NEED MORE SUGAR FOR THEIR TEA?
JORDAN, SWEETHEART, I'M SORRY...
...BUT WE'VE ALREADY USED ALL THE SUGAR IN THE HOUSE.
SILLY GRANDMA! THAT'S NOT A PROBLEM!
I'M A LITTLE GIRL, REMEMBER?
I'M MADE OF SUGAR, AND SPICE, AND EVERYTHING NICE!
OH. YES. OF COURSE.
YOU'RE ALL...LOOKING WELL.
JORDAN HAD AN ACCIDENT. BUT THEN SHE PUT EVERYTHING BACK TOGETHER PERFECTLY!
BETTER THAN PERFECT! JORDAN IS SO SPECIAL!
WE LOVE HER!
I DO, TOO. OBVIOUSLY.
I'D...BETTER GO CHECK ON THOSE COOKIES! DON'T WANT THEM TO BURN.
COOKIES ARE SO SPECIAL!
WE LOVE THEM!

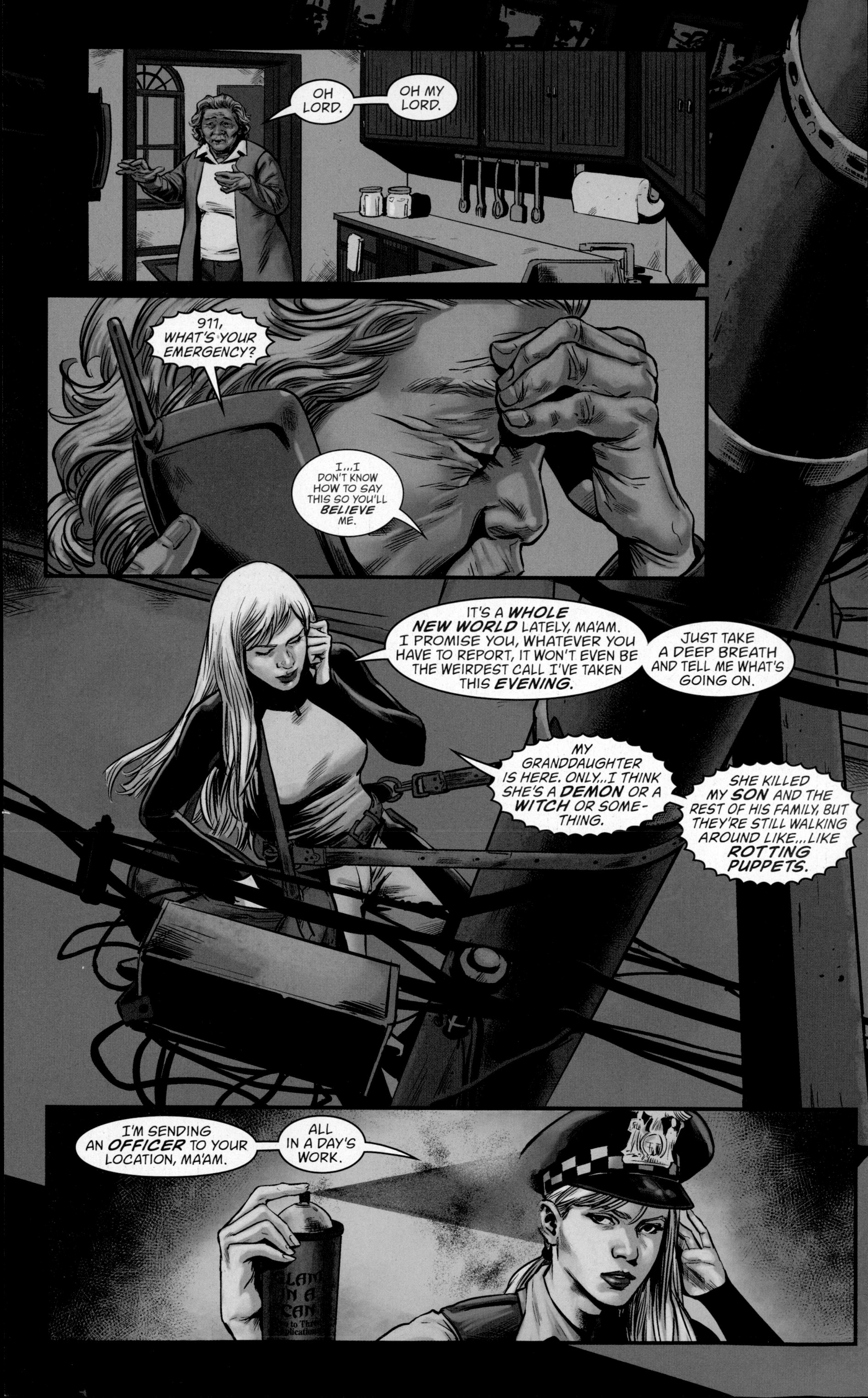
OH LORD.
OH MY LORD.
911, WHAT'S YOUR EMERGENCY?
I...I DON'T KNOW HOW TO SAY THIS SO YOU'LL BELIEVE ME.
IT'S A WHOLE NEW WORLD LATELY, MA'AM. I PROMISE YOU, WHATEVER YOU HAVE TO REPORT, IT WON'T EVEN BE THE WEIRDEST CALL I'VE TAKEN THIS EVENING.
JUST TAKE A DEEP BREATH AND TELL ME WHAT'S GOING ON.
MY GRANDDAUGHTER IS HERE. ONLY...I THINK SHE'S A DEMON OR A WITCH OR SOME-THING.
SHE KILLED MY SON AND THE REST OF HIS FAMILY, BUT THEY'RE STILL WALKING AROUND LIKE...LIKE ROTTING PUPPETS.
I'M SENDING AN OFFICER TO YOUR LOCATION, MA'AM.
ALL IN A DAY'S WORK.

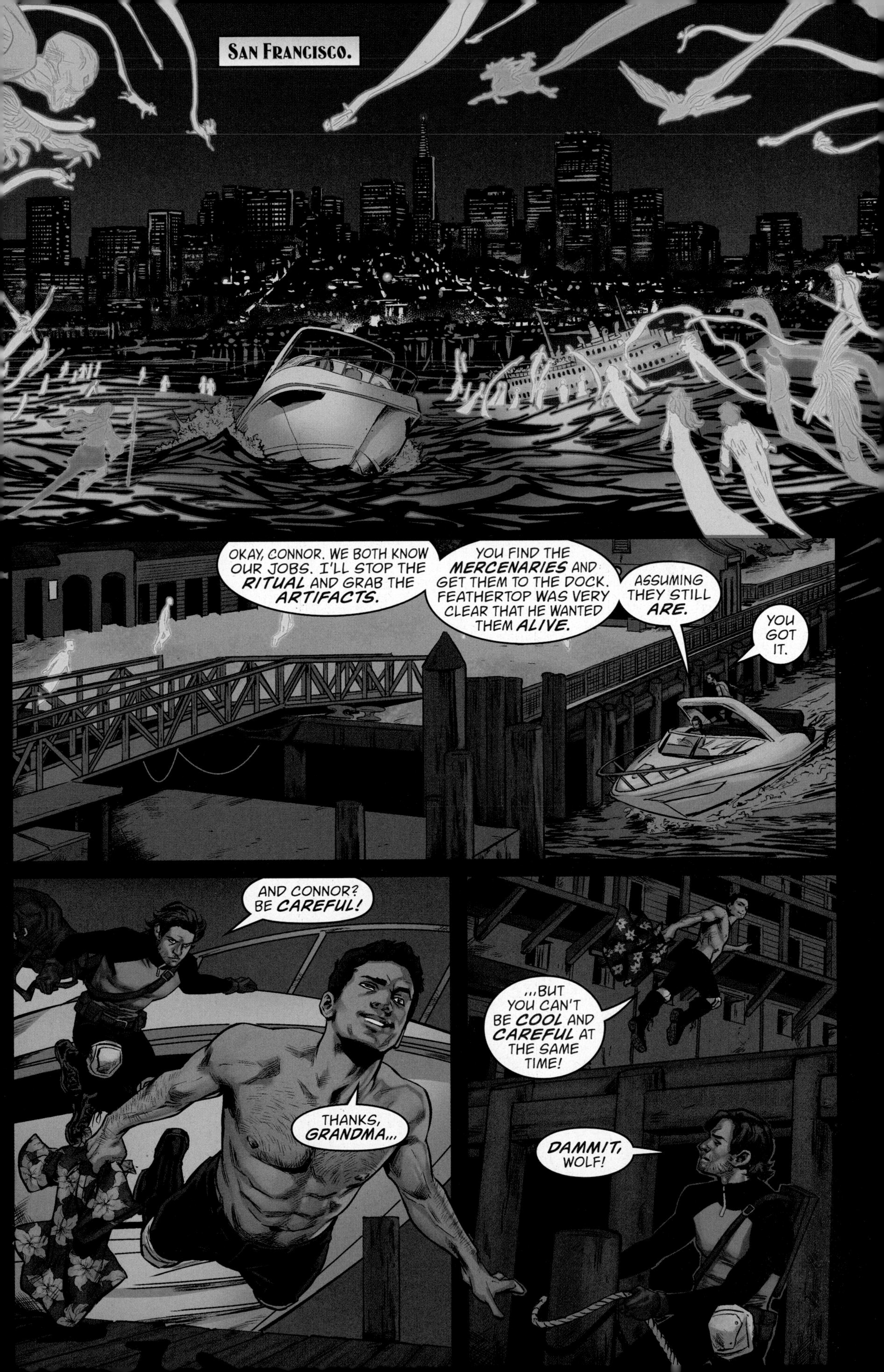
SAN FRANCISCO.
OKAY, CONNOR. WE BOTH KNOW OUR JOBS. I'LL STOP THE RITUAL AND GRAB THE ARTIFACTS.
YOU FIND THE MERCENARIES AND GET THEM TO THE DOCK. FEATHERTOP WAS VERY CLEAR THAT HE WANTED THEM ALIVE.
ASSUMING THEY STILL ARE.
YOU GOT IT.
AND CONNOR? BE CAREFUL!
THANKS, GRANDMA...
...BUT YOU CAN'T BE COOL AND CAREFUL AT THE SAME TIME!
DAMMIT, WOLF!

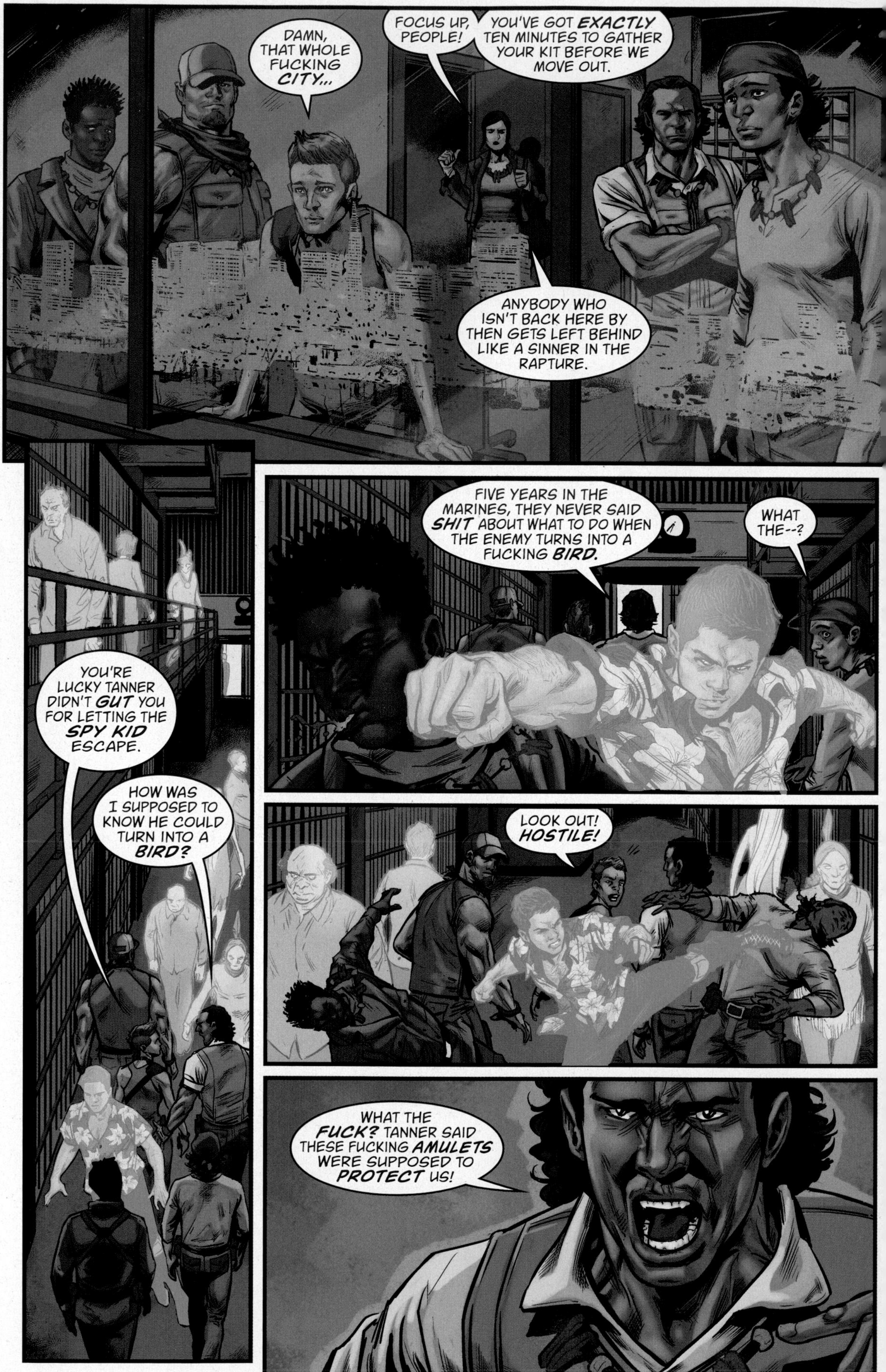
DAMN, THAT WHOLE FUCKING CITY...
FOCUS UP, PEOPLE!
YOU'VE GOT EXACTLY TEN MINUTES TO GATHER YOUR KIT BEFORE WE MOVE OUT.
ANYBODY WHO ISN'T BACK HERE BY THEN GETS LEFT BEHIND LIKE A SINNER IN THE RAPTURE.
YOU'RE LUCKY TANNER DIDN'T GUT YOU FOR LETTING THE SPY KID ESCAPE.
HOW WAS I SUPPOSED TO KNOW HE COULD TURN INTO A BIRD?
FIVE YEARS IN THE MARINES, THEY NEVER SAID SHIT ABOUT WHAT TO DO WHEN THE ENEMY TURNS INTO A FUCKING BIRD.
WHAT THE--?
LOOK OUT! HOSTILE!
WHAT THE FUCK? TANNER SAID THESE FUCKING AMULETS WERE SUPPOSED TO PROTECT US!

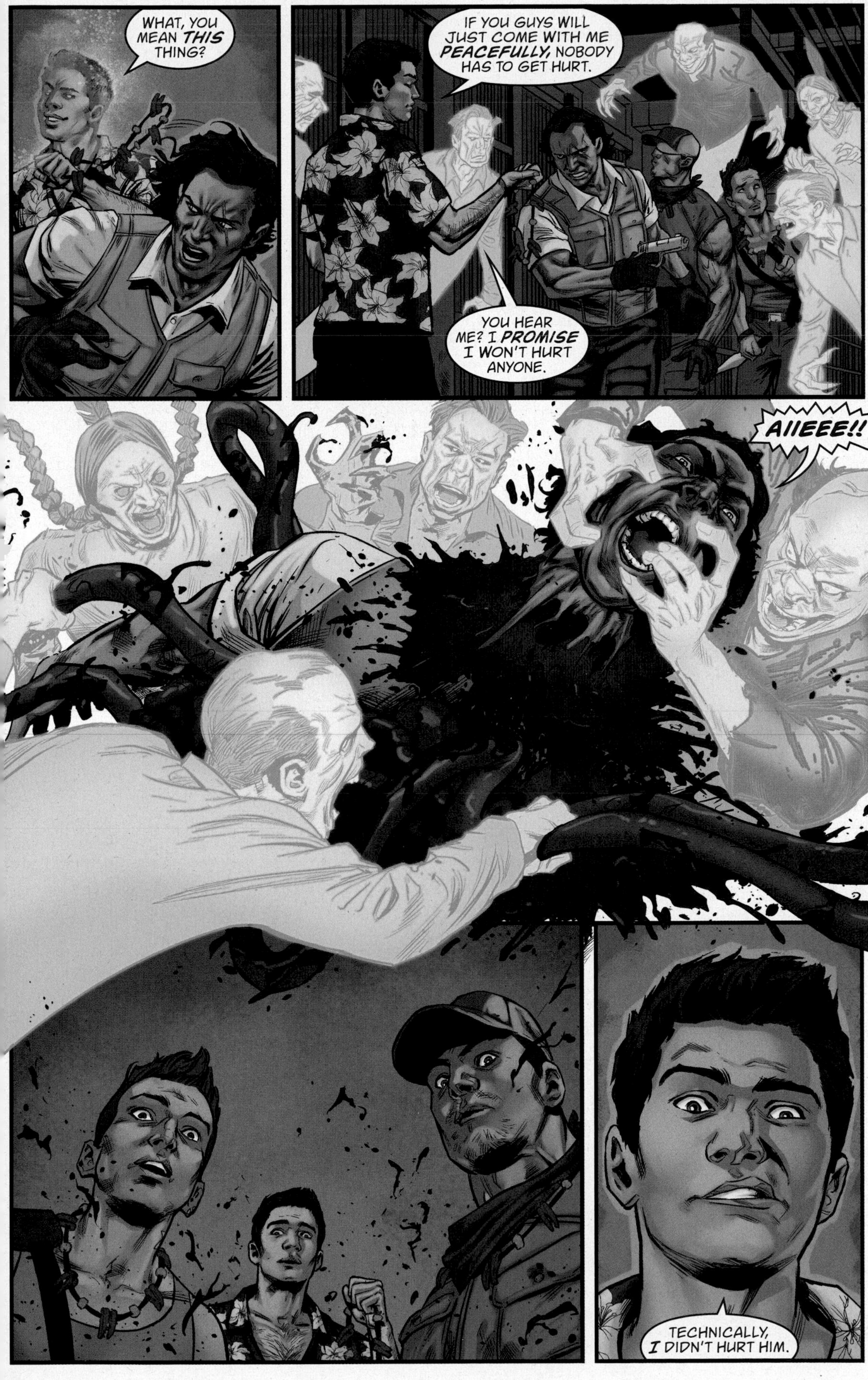
WHAT, YOU MEAN **THIS** THING?
IF YOU GUYS WILL JUST COME WITH ME **PEACEFULLY,** NOBODY HAS TO GET HURT.
YOU HEAR ME? I **PROMISE** I WON'T HURT ANYONE.
AIIEEE!!
TECHNICALLY, **I** DIDN'T HURT HIM.

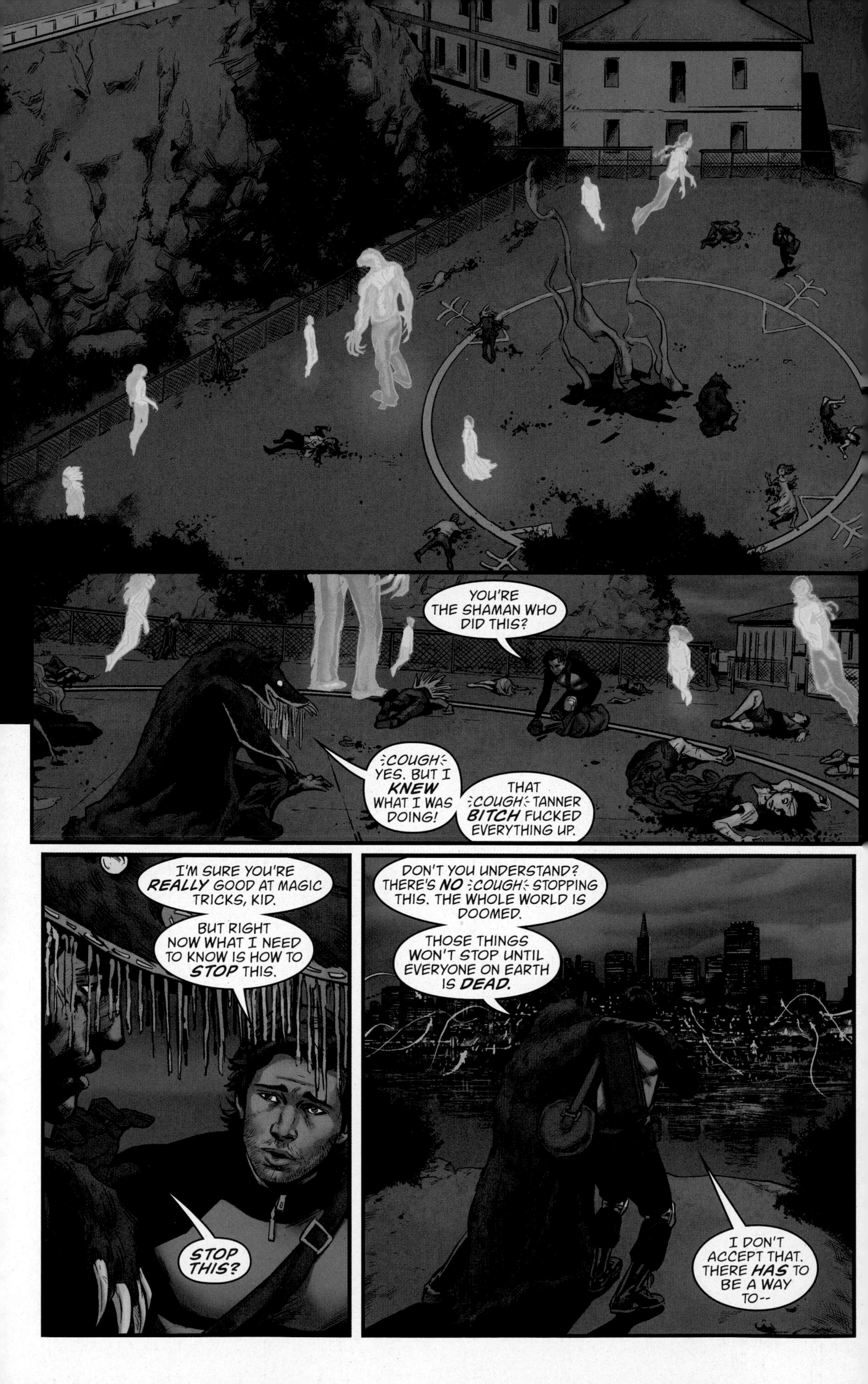
YOU'RE THE SHAMAN WHO DID THIS?
COUGH YES. BUT I KNEW WHAT I WAS DOING!
THAT COUGH TANNER BITCH FUCKED EVERYTHING UP.
I'M SURE YOU'RE REALLY GOOD AT MAGIC TRICKS, KID.
BUT RIGHT NOW WHAT I NEED TO KNOW IS HOW TO STOP THIS.
STOP THIS?
DON'T YOU UNDERSTAND? THERE'S NO COUGH STOPPING THIS. THE WHOLE WORLD IS DOOMED.
THOSE THINGS WON'T STOP UNTIL EVERYONE ON EARTH IS DEAD.
I DON'T ACCEPT THAT. THERE HAS TO BE A WAY TO--

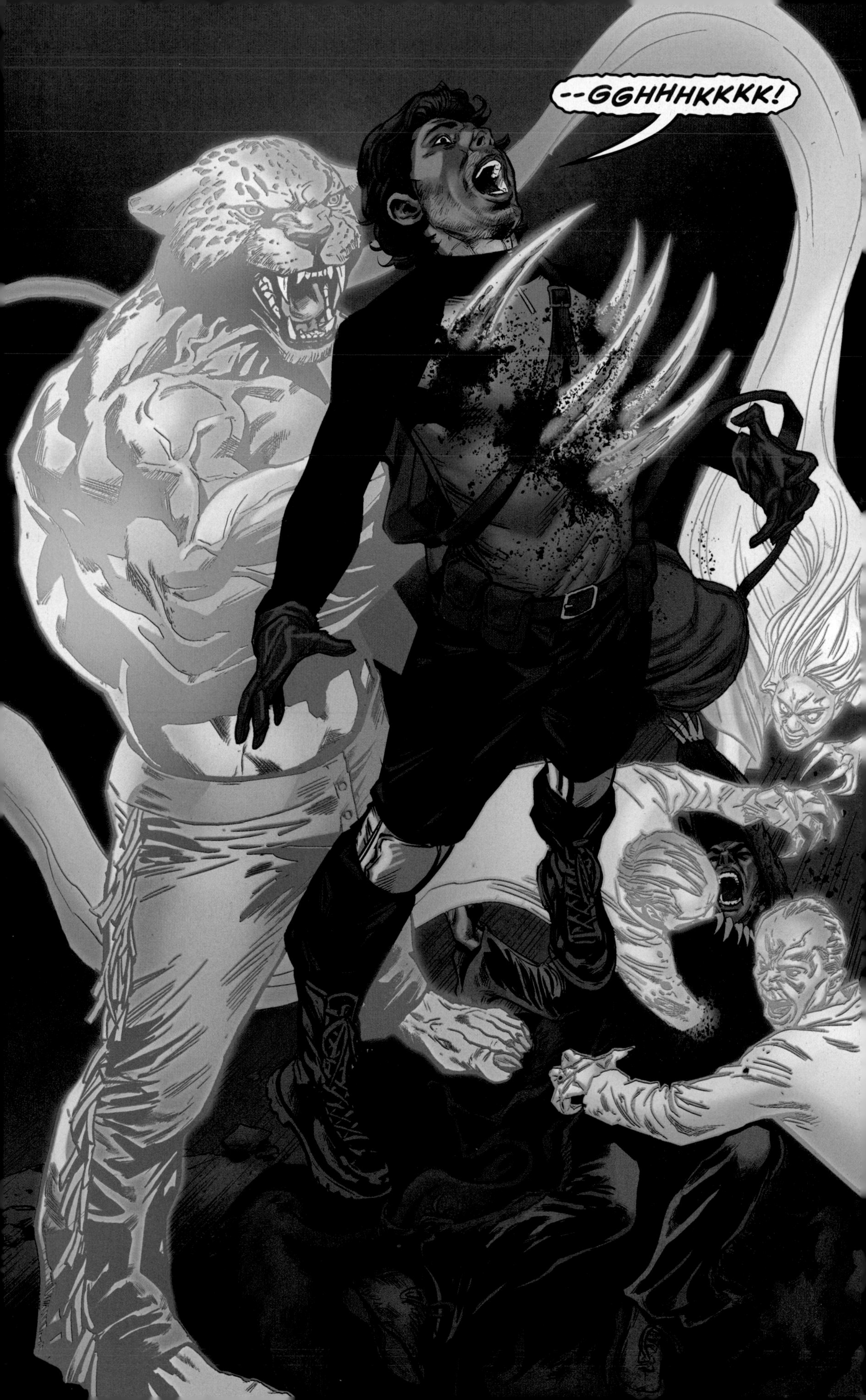
--GGHHHKKKK!

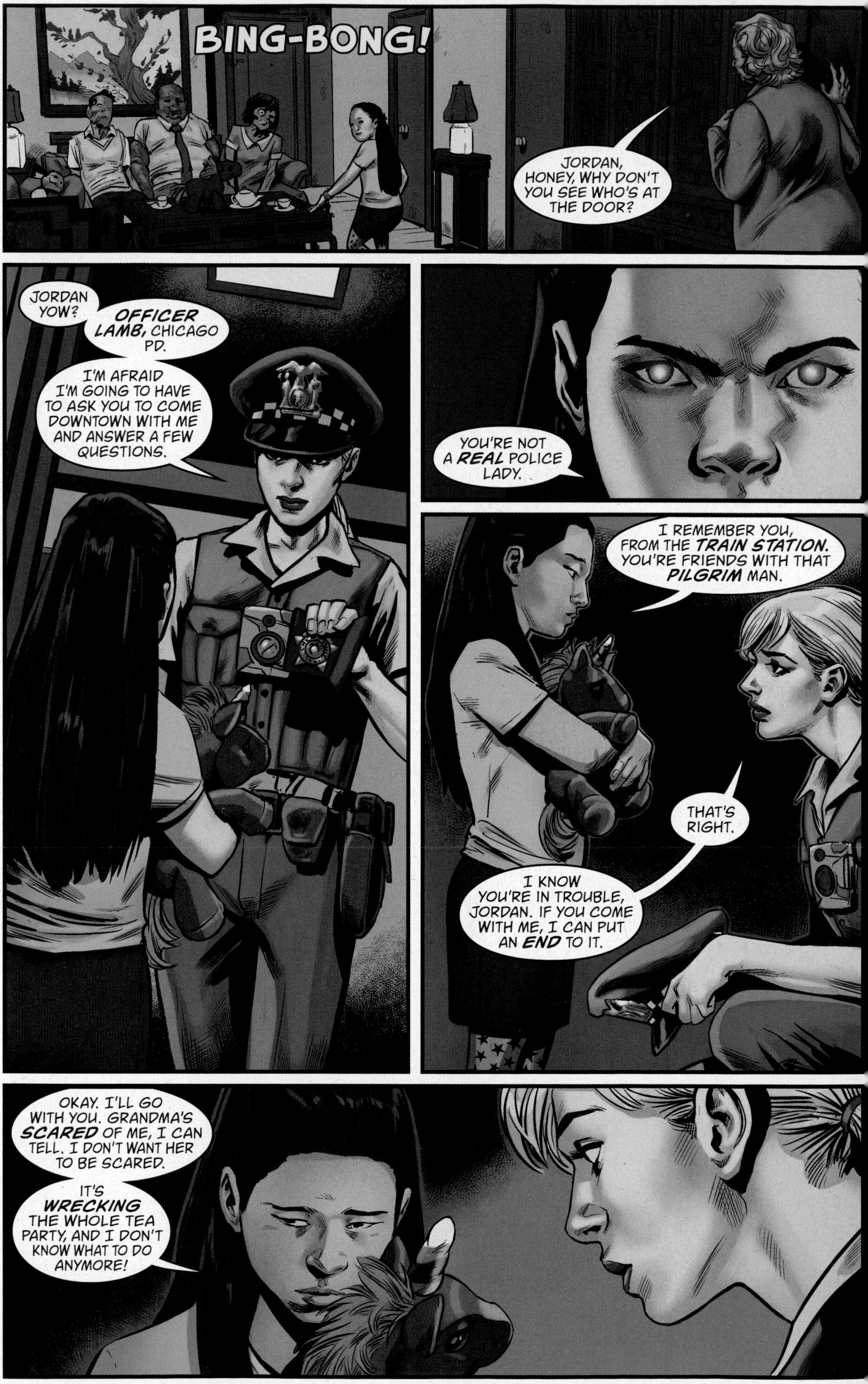
BING-BONG!
JORDAN, HONEY, WHY DON'T YOU SEE WHO'S AT THE DOOR?
JORDAN YOW?
OFFICER LAMB, CHICAGO PD.
I'M AFRAID I'M GOING TO HAVE TO ASK YOU TO COME DOWNTOWN WITH ME AND ANSWER A FEW QUESTIONS.
YOU'RE NOT A REAL POLICE LADY.
I REMEMBER YOU, FROM THE TRAIN STATION. YOU'RE FRIENDS WITH THAT PILGRIM MAN.
THAT'S RIGHT.
I KNOW YOU'RE IN TROUBLE, JORDAN. IF YOU COME WITH ME, I CAN PUT AN END TO IT.
OKAY. I'LL GO WITH YOU. GRANDMA'S SCARED OF ME, I CAN TELL. I DON'T WANT HER TO BE SCARED.
IT'S WRECKING THE WHOLE TEA PARTY, AND I DON'T KNOW WHAT TO DO ANYMORE!

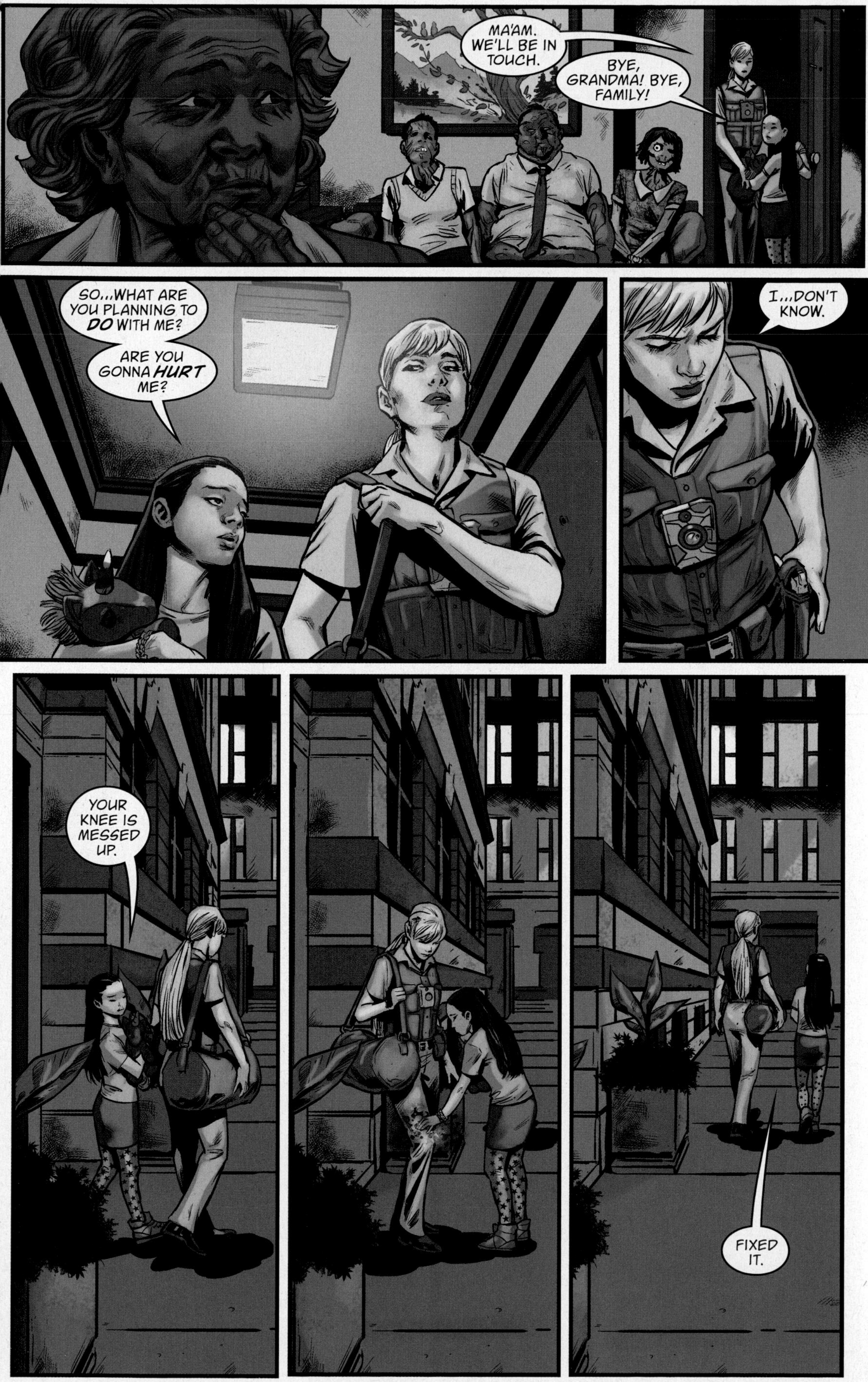
MA'AM. WE'LL BE IN TOUCH.
BYE, GRANDMA! BYE, FAMILY!
SO...WHAT ARE YOU PLANNING TO DO WITH ME?
ARE YOU GONNA HURT ME?
I...DON'T KNOW.
YOUR KNEE IS MESSED UP.
FIXED IT.

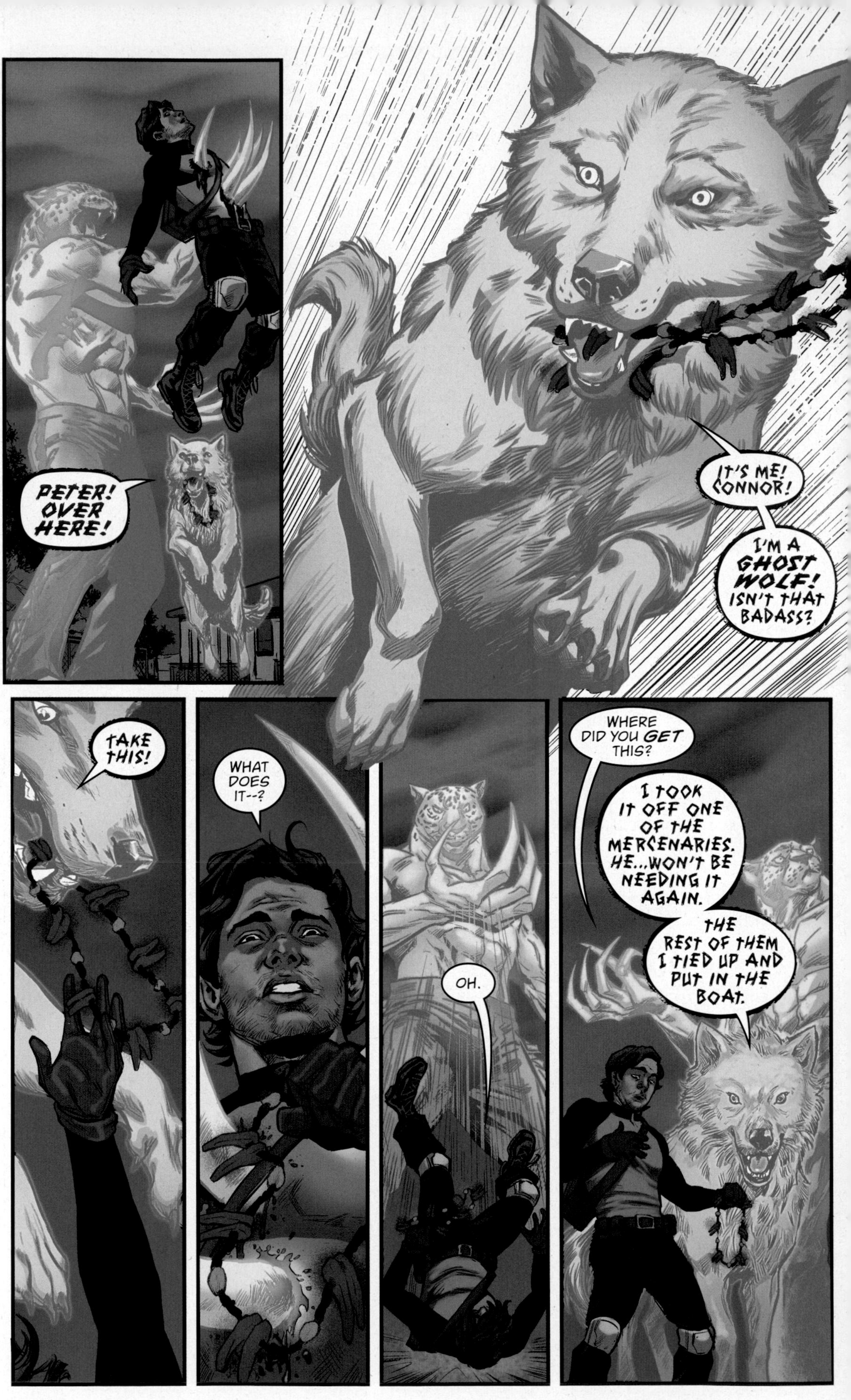
PETER! OVER HERE!
IT'S ME! CONNOR!
I'M A GHOST WOLF! ISN'T THAT BADASS?
TAKE THIS!
WHAT DOES IT--?
OH.
WHERE DID YOU GET THIS?
I TOOK IT OFF ONE OF THE MERCENARIES. HE...WON'T BE NEEDING IT AGAIN.
THE REST OF THEM I TIED UP AND PUT IN THE BOAT.

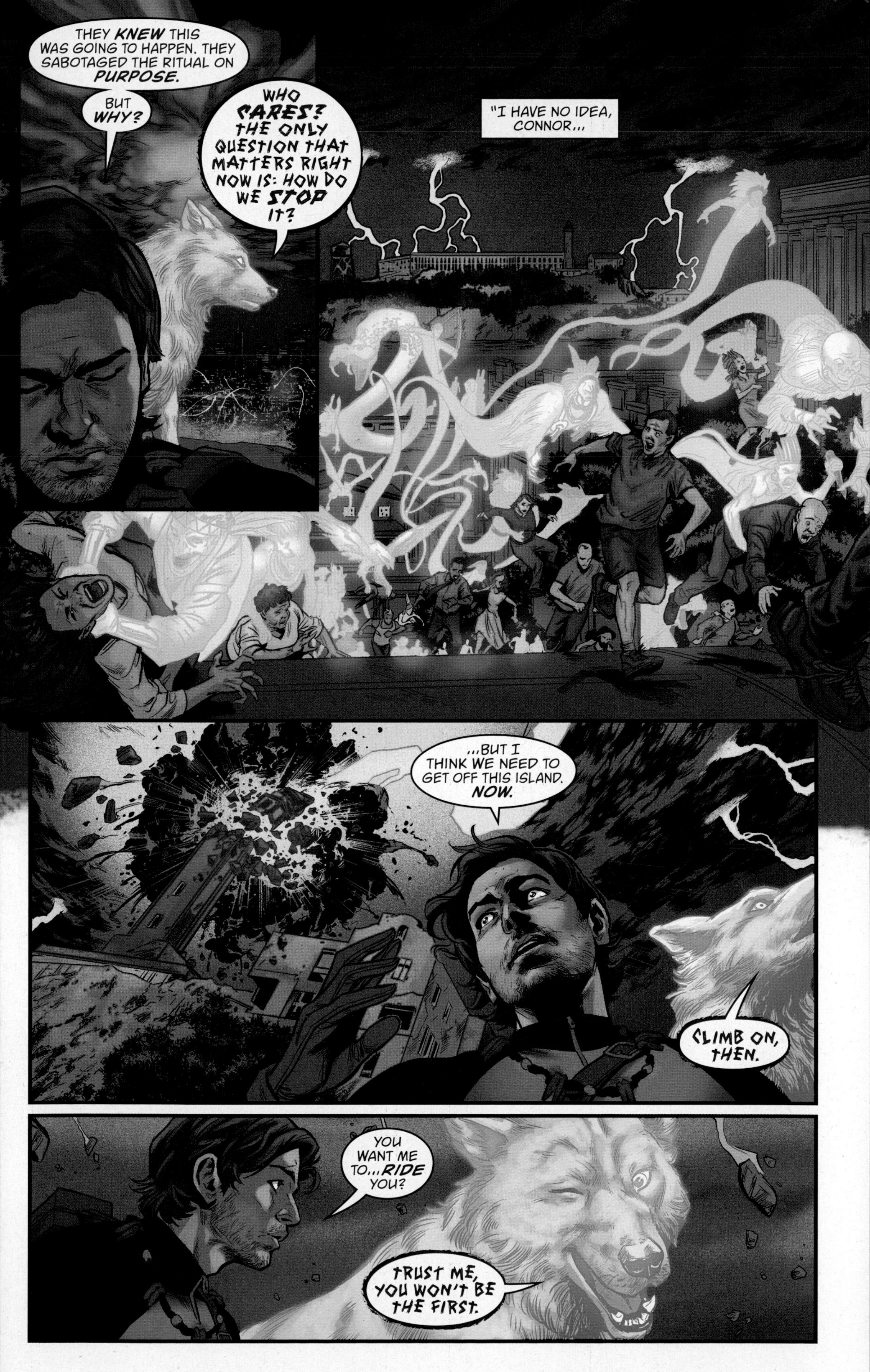
THEY KNEW THIS WAS GOING TO HAPPEN. THEY SABOTAGED THE RITUAL ON PURPOSE.
BUT WHY?
WHO CARES? THE ONLY QUESTION THAT MATTERS RIGHT NOW IS: HOW DO WE STOP IT?
"I HAVE NO IDEA, CONNOR...
...BUT I THINK WE NEED TO GET OFF THIS ISLAND. NOW.
CLIMB ON, THEN.
YOU WANT ME TO...RIDE YOU?
TRUST ME, YOU WON'T BE THE FIRST.

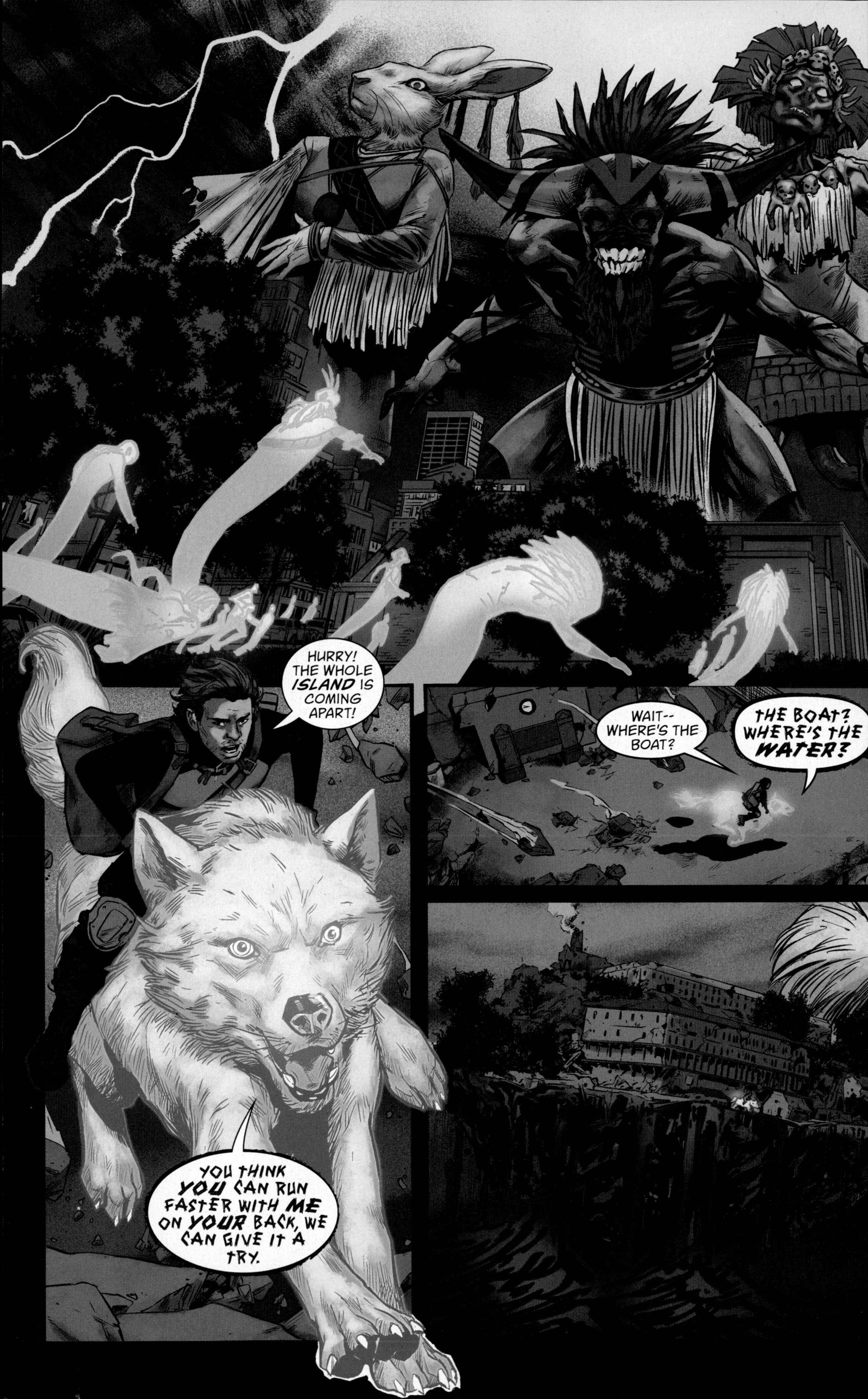
HURRY! THE WHOLE ISLAND IS COMING APART!
WAIT-- WHERE'S THE BOAT?
THE BOAT? WHERE'S THE WATER?
YOU THINK YOU CAN RUN FASTER WITH ME ON YOUR BACK, WE CAN GIVE IT A TRY.

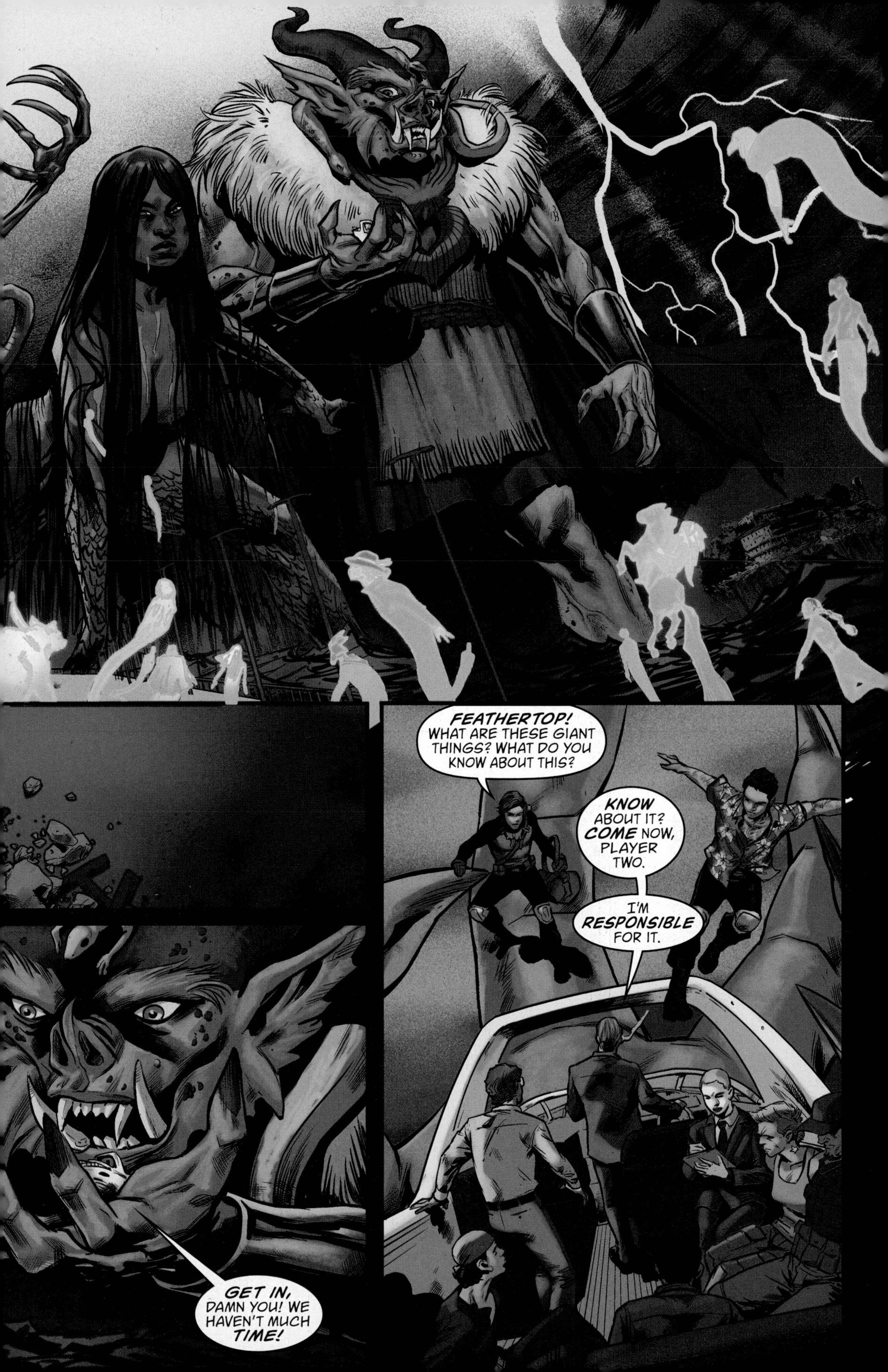
FEATHERTOP! WHAT ARE THESE GIANT THINGS? WHAT DO YOU KNOW ABOUT THIS?
KNOW ABOUT IT? COME NOW, PLAYER TWO.
I'M RESPONSIBLE FOR IT.
GET IN, DAMN YOU! WE HAVEN'T MUCH TIME!

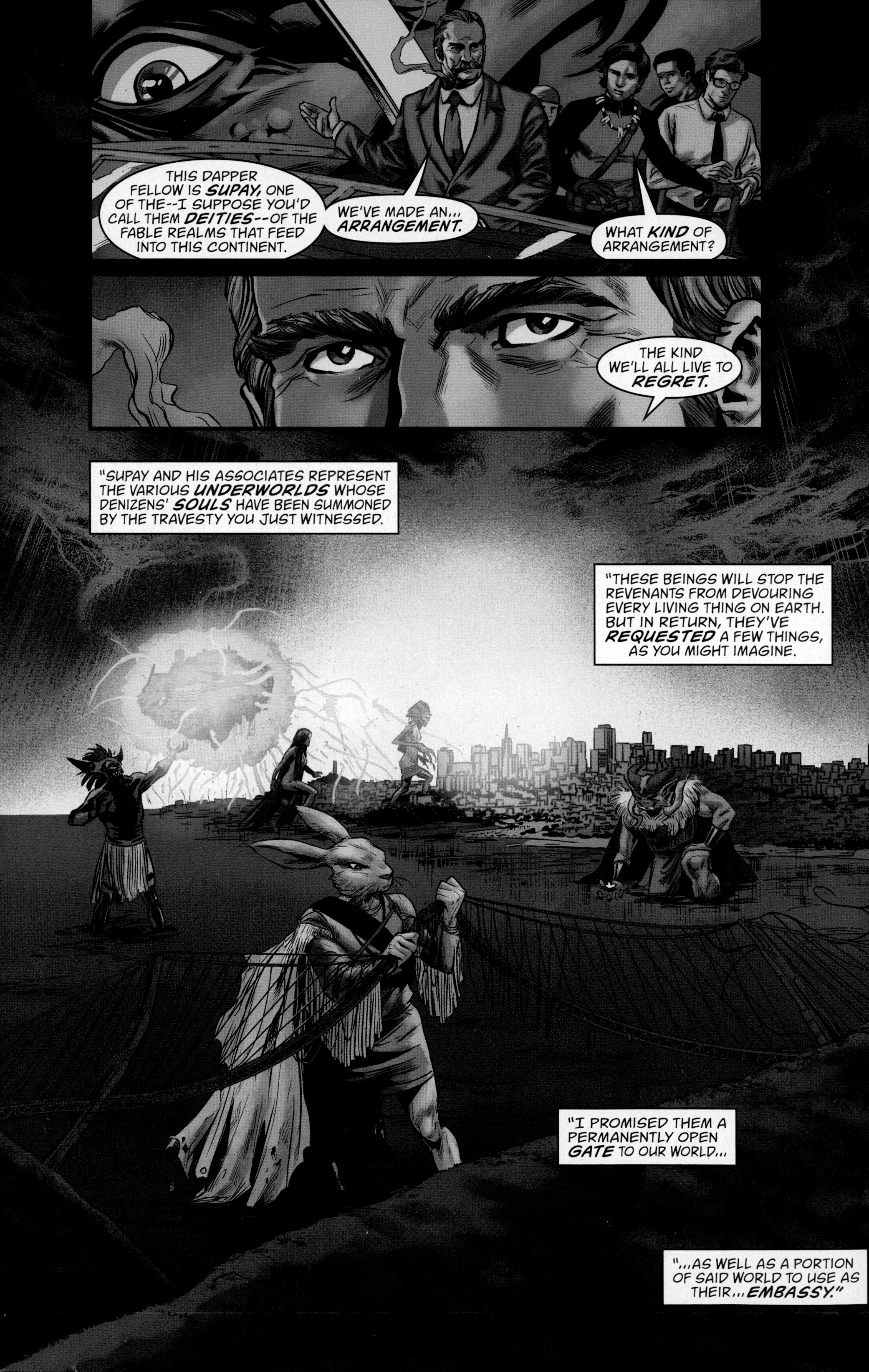
THIS DAPPER FELLOW IS SUPAY, ONE OF THE--I SUPPOSE YOU'D CALL THEM DEITIES--OF THE FABLE REALMS THAT FEED INTO THIS CONTINENT.
WE'VE MADE AN... ARRANGEMENT.
WHAT KIND OF ARRANGEMENT?
THE KIND WE'LL ALL LIVE TO REGRET.
"SUPAY AND HIS ASSOCIATES REPRESENT THE VARIOUS UNDERWORLDS WHOSE DENIZENS' SOULS HAVE BEEN SUMMONED BY THE TRAVESTY YOU JUST WITNESSED.
"THESE BEINGS WILL STOP THE REVENANTS FROM DEVOURING EVERY LIVING THING ON EARTH. BUT IN RETURN, THEY'VE REQUESTED A FEW THINGS, AS YOU MIGHT IMAGINE.
"I PROMISED THEM A PERMANENTLY OPEN GATE TO OUR WORLD...
"...AS WELL AS A PORTION OF SAID WORLD TO USE AS THEIR... EMBASSY."

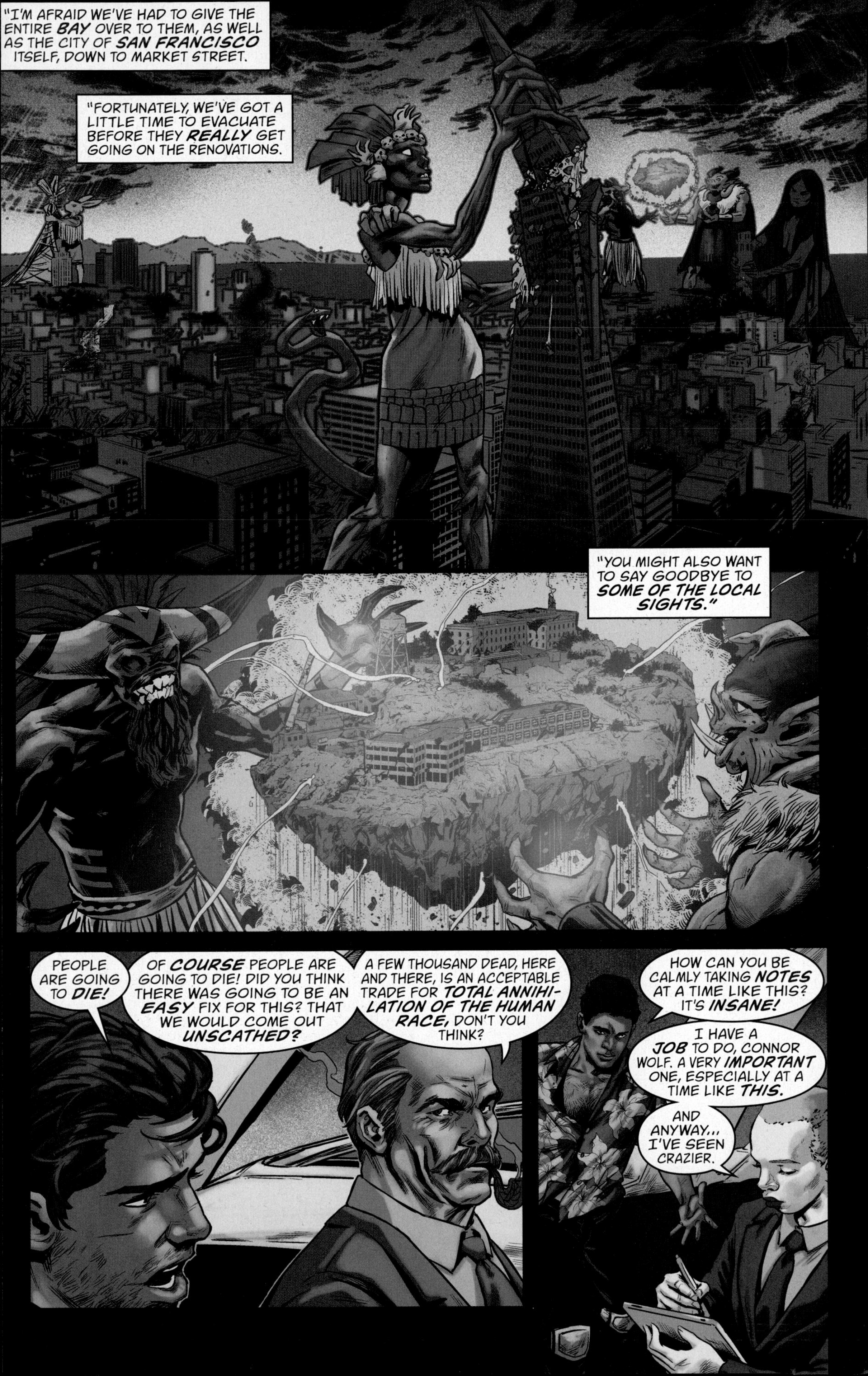
"I'M AFRAID WE'VE HAD TO GIVE THE ENTIRE BAY OVER TO THEM, AS WELL AS THE CITY OF SAN FRANCISCO ITSELF, DOWN TO MARKET STREET.
"FORTUNATELY, WE'VE GOT A LITTLE TIME TO EVACUATE BEFORE THEY REALLY GET GOING ON THE RENOVATIONS.
"YOU MIGHT ALSO WANT TO SAY GOODBYE TO SOME OF THE LOCAL SIGHTS."
PEOPLE ARE GOING TO DIE!
OF COURSE PEOPLE ARE GOING TO DIE! DID YOU THINK THERE WAS GOING TO BE AN EASY FIX FOR THIS? THAT WE WOULD COME OUT UNSCATHED?
A FEW THOUSAND DEAD, HERE AND THERE, IS AN ACCEPTABLE TRADE FOR TOTAL ANNIHILATION OF THE HUMAN RACE, DON'T YOU THINK?
HOW CAN YOU BE CALMLY TAKING NOTES AT A TIME LIKE THIS? IT'S INSANE!
I HAVE A JOB TO DO, CONNOR WOLF. A VERY IMPORTANT ONE, ESPECIALLY AT A TIME LIKE THIS.
AND ANYWAY... I'VE SEEN CRAZIER.

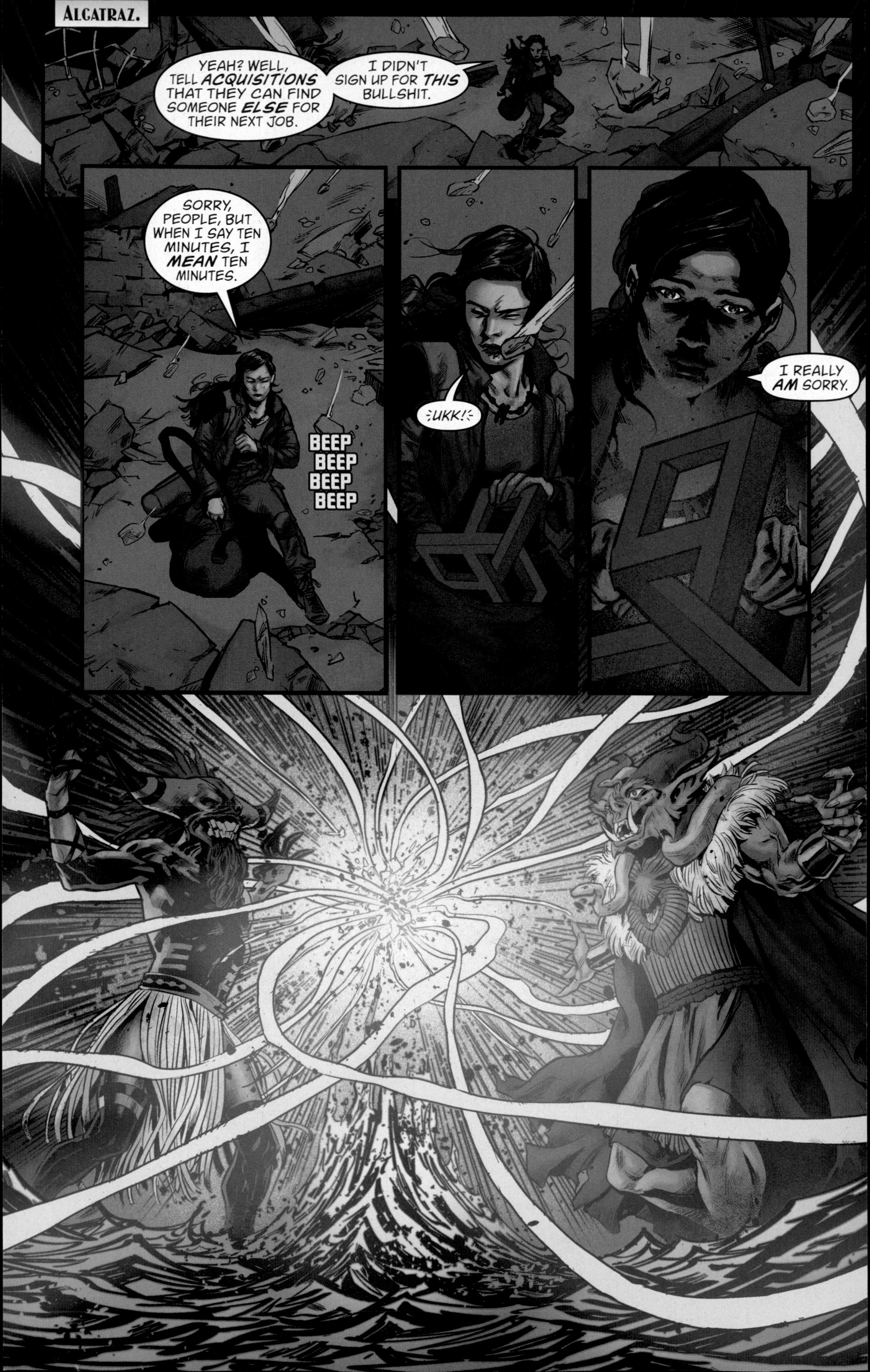
ALCATRAZ.
YEAH? WELL, TELL ACQUISITIONS THAT THEY CAN FIND SOMEONE ELSE FOR THEIR NEXT JOB.
I DIDN'T SIGN UP FOR THIS BULLSHIT.
SORRY, PEOPLE, BUT WHEN I SAY TEN MINUTES, I MEAN TEN MINUTES.
BEEP BEEP BEEP BEEP
UKK!
I REALLY AM SORRY.

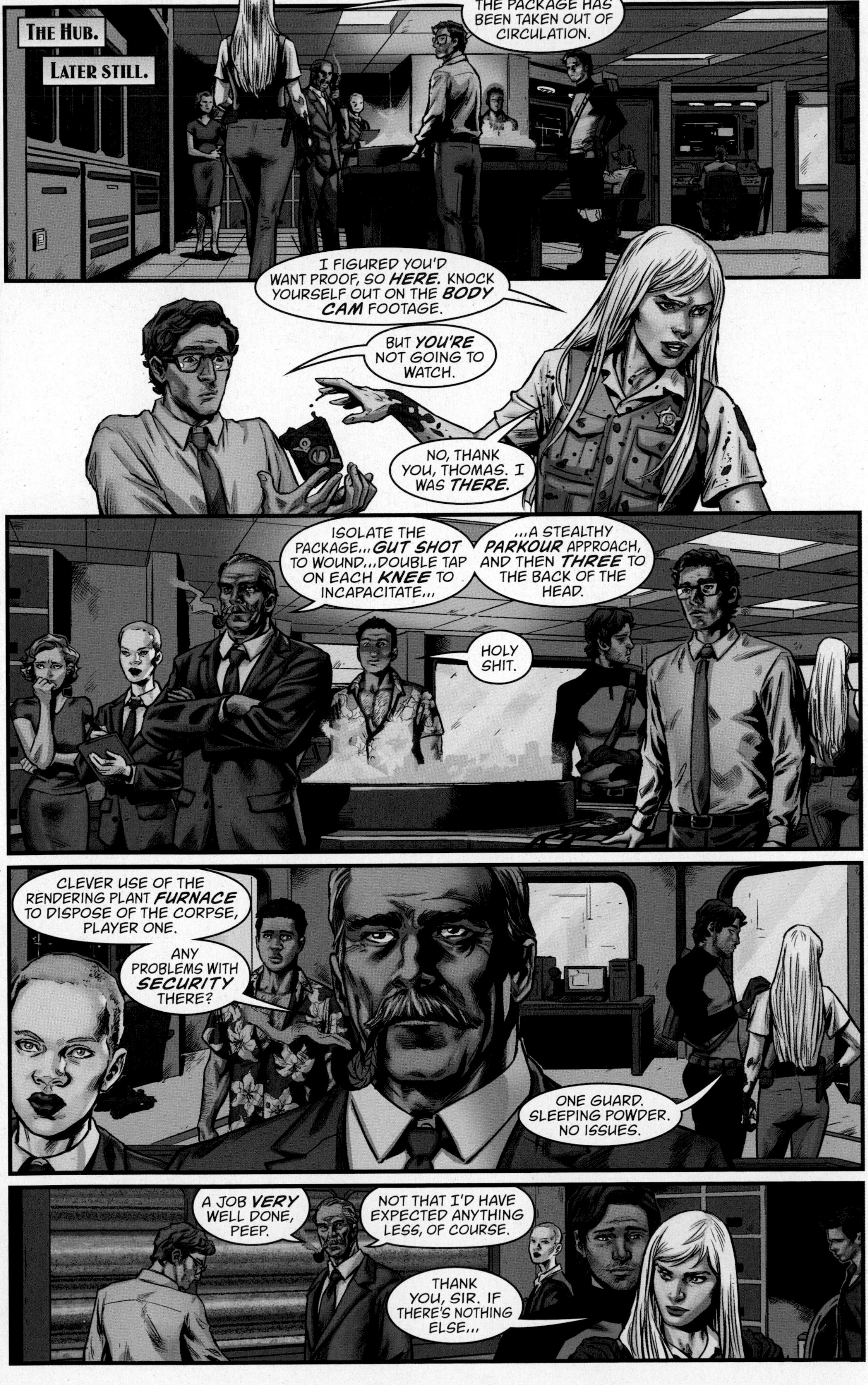
THE HUB.
LATER STILL.
IT'S DONE. THE PACKAGE HAS BEEN TAKEN OUT OF CIRCULATION.
I FIGURED YOU'D WANT PROOF, SO HERE. KNOCK YOURSELF OUT ON THE BODY CAM FOOTAGE.
BUT YOU'RE NOT GOING TO WATCH.
NO, THANK YOU, THOMAS. I WAS THERE.
ISOLATE THE PACKAGE... GUT SHOT TO WOUND... DOUBLE TAP ON EACH KNEE TO INCAPACITATE...
...A STEALTHY PARKOUR APPROACH, AND THEN THREE TO THE BACK OF THE HEAD.
HOLY SHIT.
CLEVER USE OF THE RENDERING PLANT FURNACE TO DISPOSE OF THE CORPSE, PLAYER ONE.
ANY PROBLEMS WITH SECURITY THERE?
ONE GUARD. SLEEPING POWDER. NO ISSUES.
A JOB VERY WELL DONE, PEEP.
NOT THAT I'D HAVE EXPECTED ANYTHING LESS, OF COURSE.
THANK YOU, SIR. IF THERE'S NOTHING ELSE...

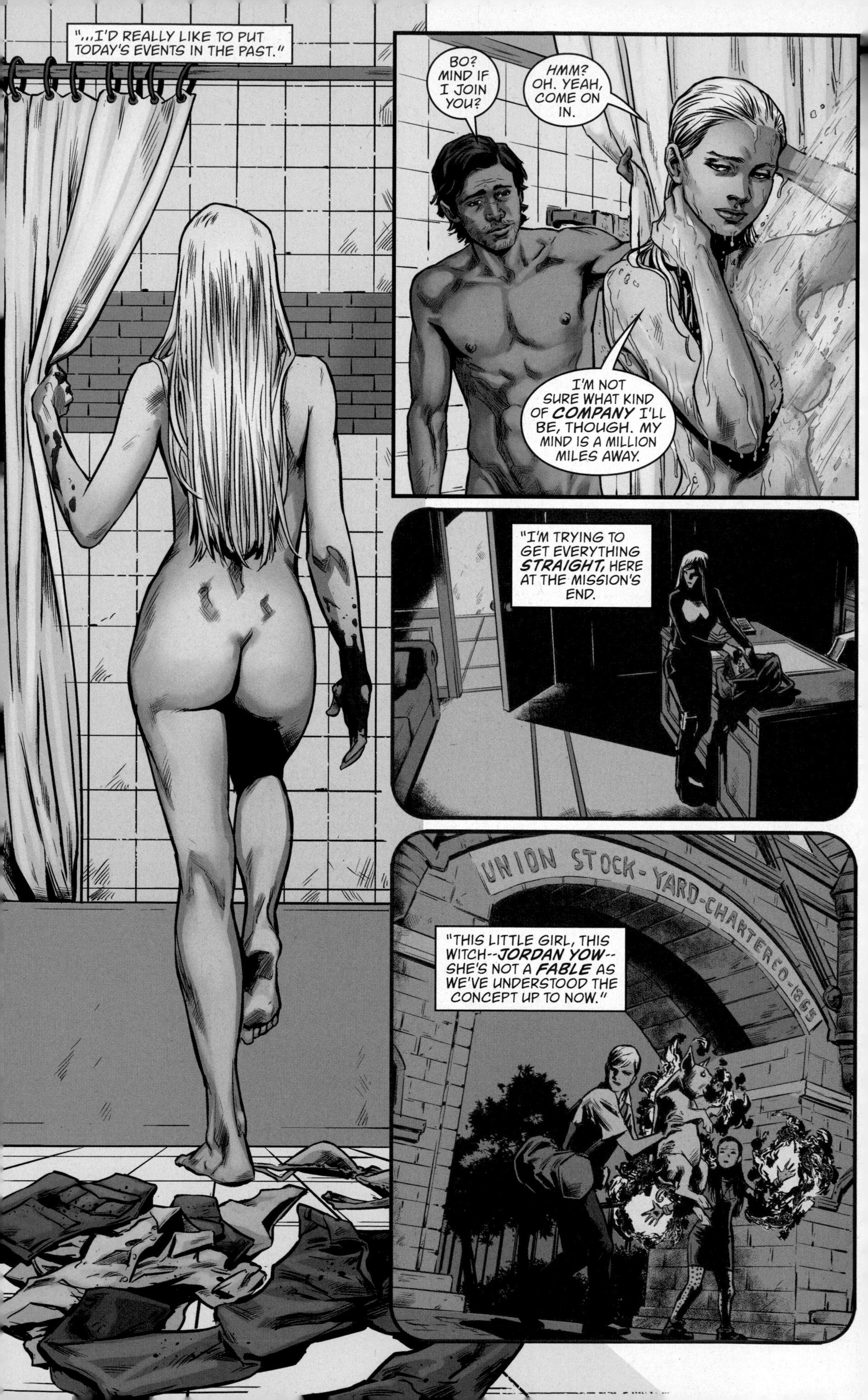
"...I'D REALLY LIKE TO PUT TODAY'S EVENTS IN THE PAST."
BO? MIND IF I JOIN YOU?
HMM? OH. YEAH, COME ON IN.
I'M NOT SURE WHAT KIND OF COMPANY I'LL BE, THOUGH. MY MIND IS A MILLION MILES AWAY.
"I'M TRYING TO GET EVERYTHING STRAIGHT, HERE AT THE MISSION'S END.
UNION STOCK-YARD-CHARTERED-1865
"THIS LITTLE GIRL, THIS WITCH--JORDAN YOW--SHE'S NOT A FABLE AS WE'VE UNDERSTOOD THE CONCEPT UP TO NOW."

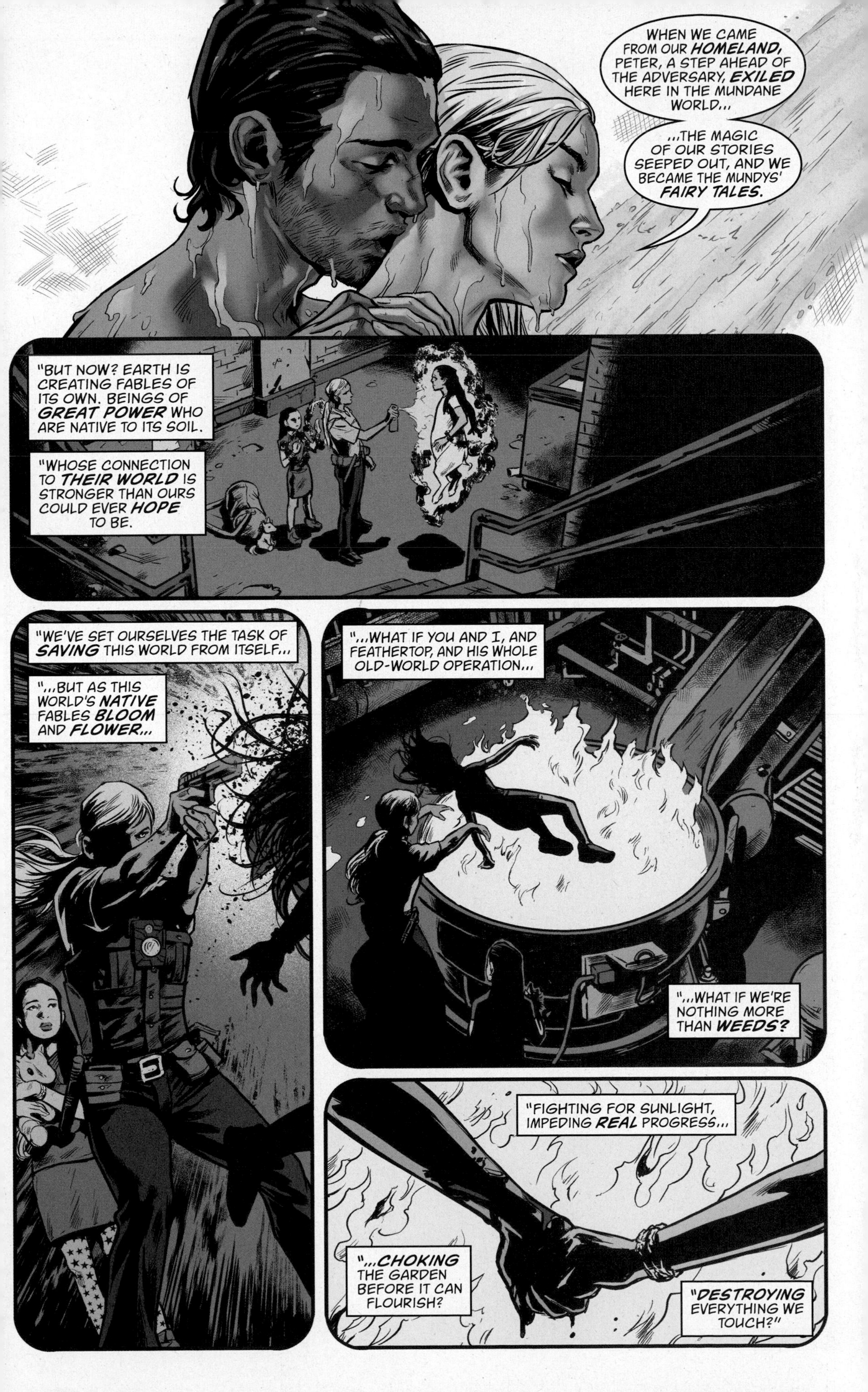

WHEN WE CAME FROM OUR HOMELAND, PETER, A STEP AHEAD OF THE ADVERSARY, EXILED HERE IN THE MUNDANE WORLD...
...THE MAGIC OF OUR STORIES SEEPED OUT, AND WE BECAME THE MUNDYS' FAIRY TALES.
"BUT NOW? EARTH IS CREATING FABLES OF ITS OWN. BEINGS OF GREAT POWER WHO ARE NATIVE TO ITS SOIL.
"WHOSE CONNECTION TO THEIR WORLD IS STRONGER THAN OURS COULD EVER HOPE TO BE.
"WE'VE SET OURSELVES THE TASK OF SAVING THIS WORLD FROM ITSELF...
"...BUT AS THIS WORLD'S NATIVE FABLES BLOOM AND FLOWER...
"...WHAT IF YOU AND I, AND FEATHERTOP, AND HIS WHOLE OLD-WORLD OPERATION...
"...WHAT IF WE'RE NOTHING MORE THAN WEEDS?
"FIGHTING FOR SUNLIGHT, IMPEDING REAL PROGRESS...
"...CHOKING THE GARDEN BEFORE IT CAN FLOURISH?
"DESTROYING EVERYTHING WE TOUCH?"

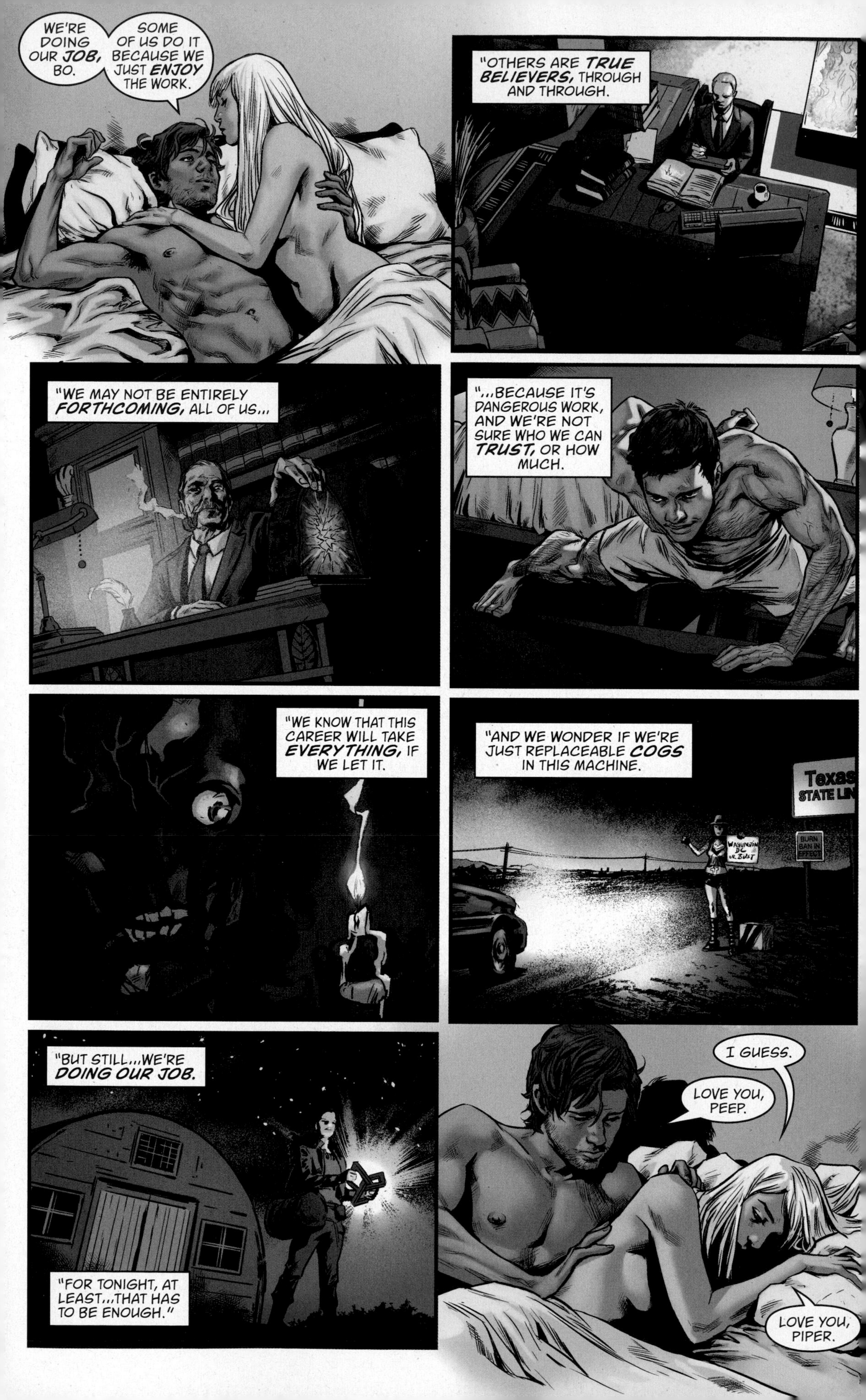

WE'RE DOING OUR JOB, BO.
SOME OF US DO IT BECAUSE WE JUST ENJOY THE WORK.
"OTHERS ARE TRUE BELIEVERS, THROUGH AND THROUGH.
"WE MAY NOT BE ENTIRELY FORTHCOMING, ALL OF US...
"...BECAUSE IT'S DANGEROUS WORK, AND WE'RE NOT SURE WHO WE CAN TRUST, OR HOW MUCH.
"WE KNOW THAT THIS CAREER WILL TAKE EVERYTHING, IF WE LET IT.
"AND WE WONDER IF WE'RE JUST REPLACEABLE COGS IN THIS MACHINE.
Texas
BURN BAN IN EFFECT
"BUT STILL...WE'RE DOING OUR JOB.
"FOR TONIGHT, AT LEAST...THAT HAS TO BE ENOUGH."
I GUESS.
LOVE YOU, PEEP.
LOVE YOU, PIPER.

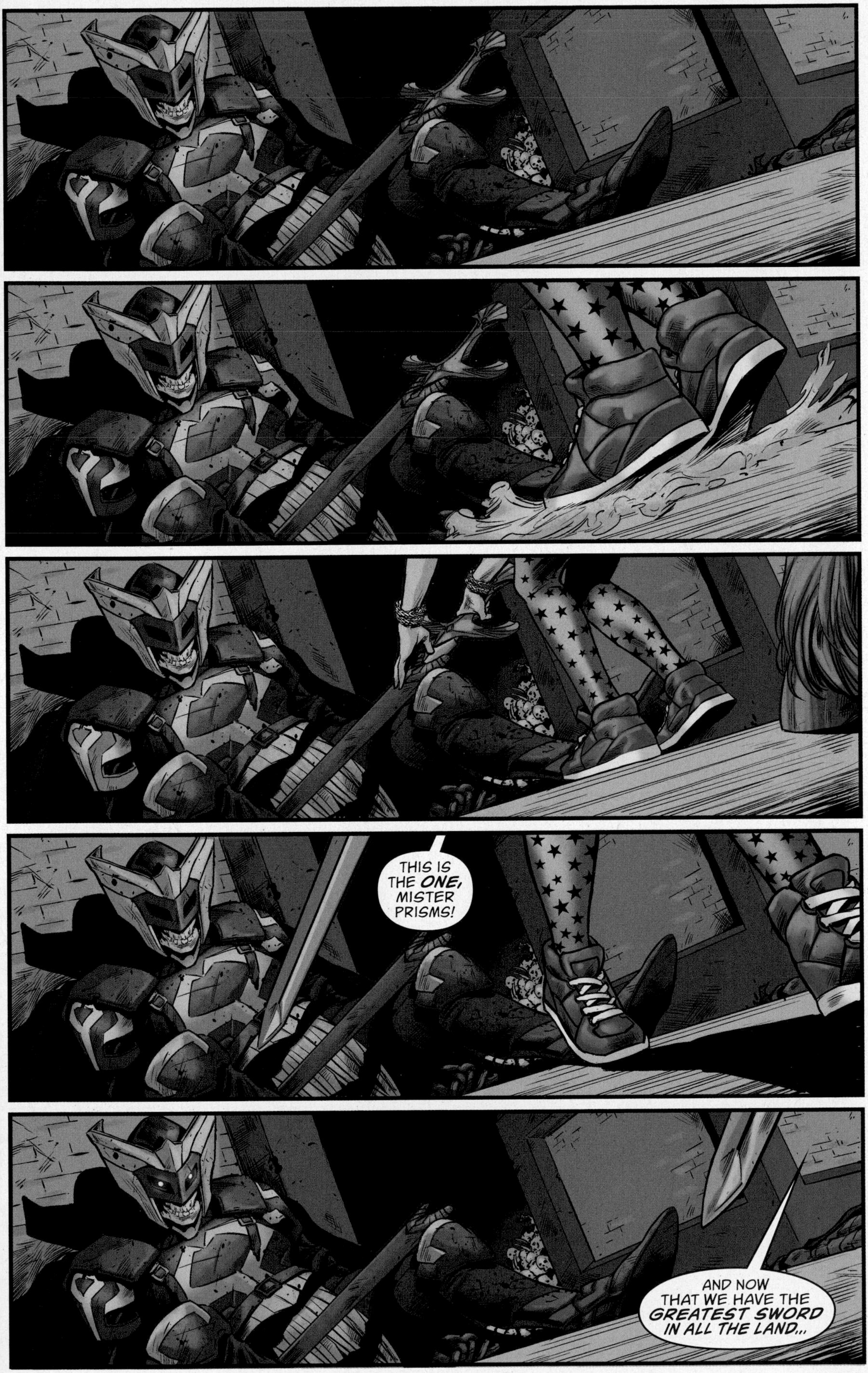
THIS IS THE *ONE,* MISTER PRISMS!
AND NOW THAT WE HAVE THE ***GREATEST SWORD IN ALL THE LAND...***

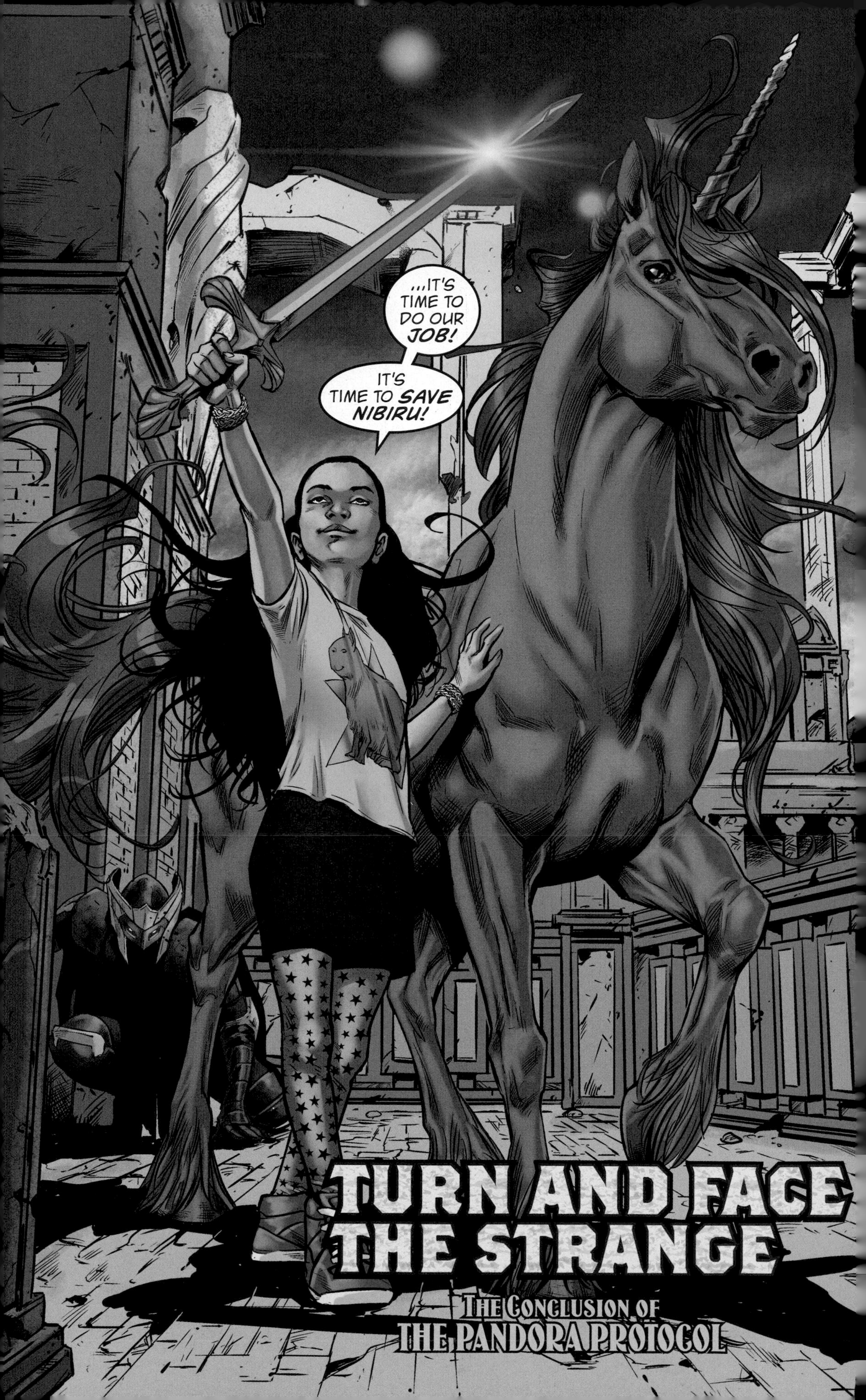
...IT'S TIME TO DO OUR JOB!
IT'S TIME TO SAVE NIBIRU!
TURN AND FACE THE STRANGE
THE CONCLUSION OF THE PANDORA PROTOCOL

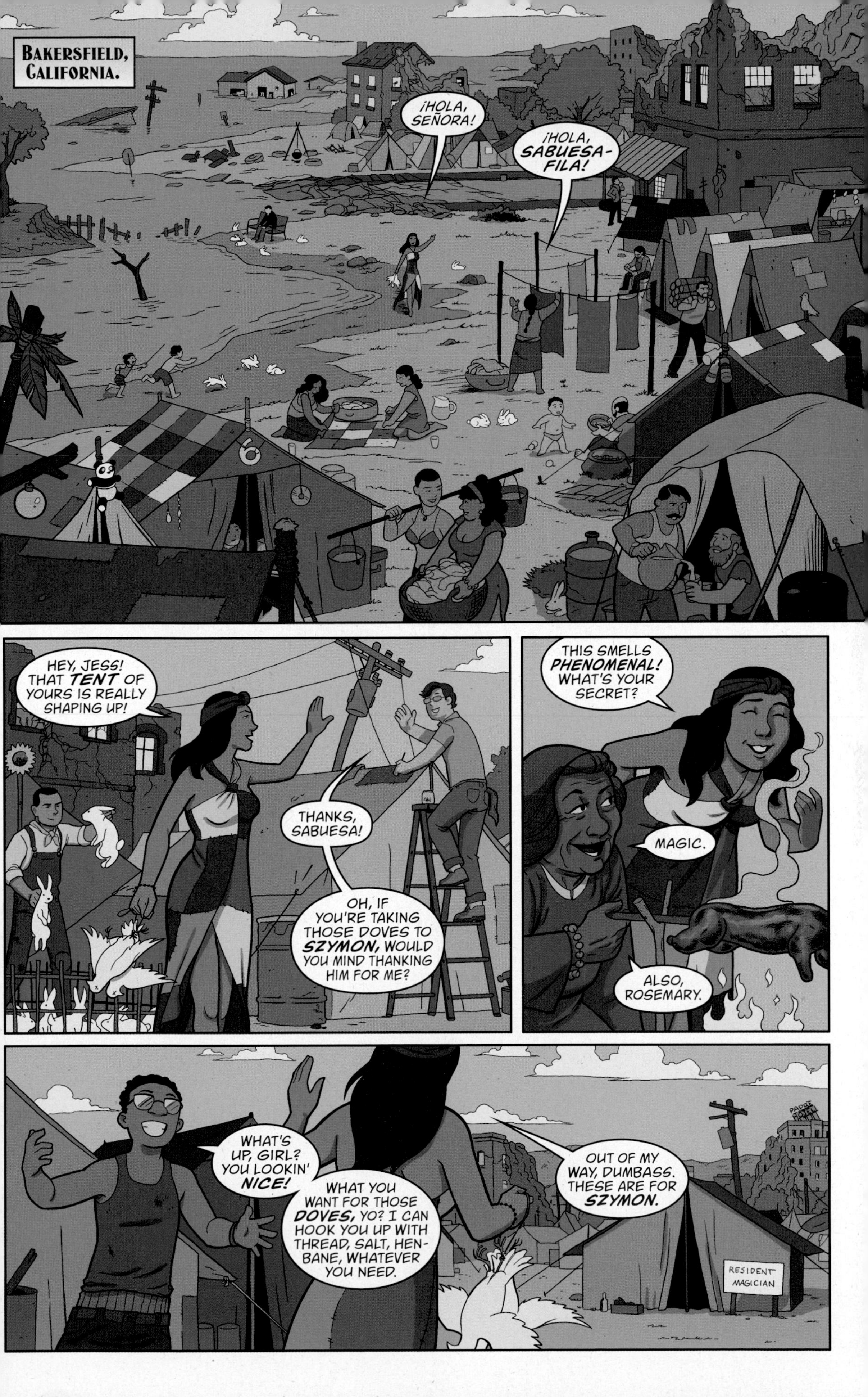
BAKERSFIELD, CALIFORNIA.
¡HOLA, SEÑORA!
¡HOLA, SABUESA-FILA!
HEY, JESS! THAT TENT OF YOURS IS REALLY SHAPING UP!
THANKS, SABUESA!
OH, IF YOU'RE TAKING THOSE DOVES TO SZYMON, WOULD YOU MIND THANKING HIM FOR ME?
THIS SMELLS PHENOMENAL! WHAT'S YOUR SECRET?
MAGIC.
ALSO, ROSEMARY.
WHAT'S UP, GIRL? YOU LOOKIN' NICE!
WHAT YOU WANT FOR THOSE DOVES, YO? I CAN HOOK YOU UP WITH THREAD, SALT, HENBANE, WHATEVER YOU NEED.
OUT OF MY WAY, DUMBASS. THESE ARE FOR SZYMON.
RESIDENT MAGICIAN

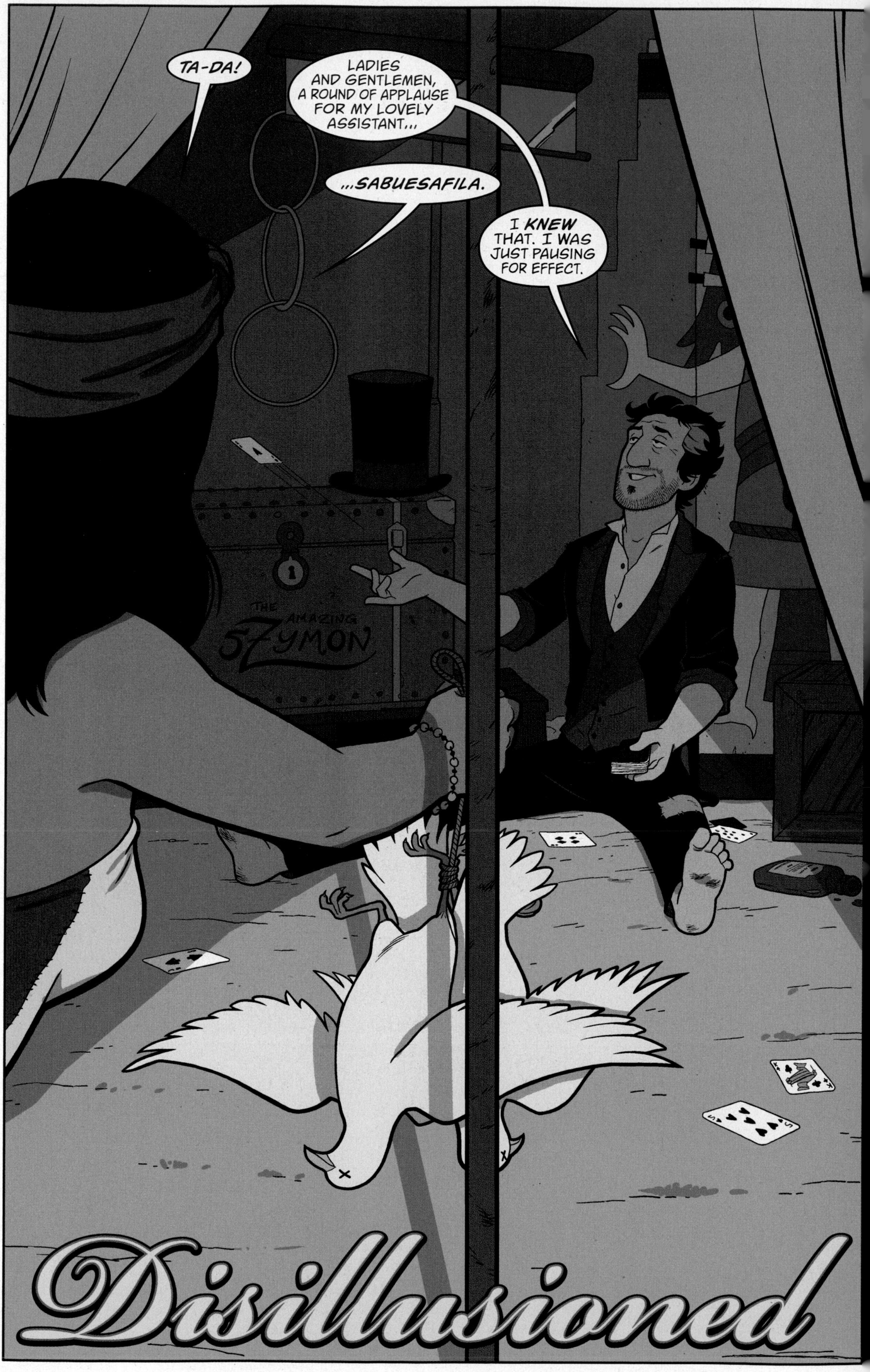
TA-DA!
LADIES AND GENTLEMEN, A ROUND OF APPLAUSE FOR MY LOVELY ASSISTANT...
...SABUESAFILA.
I KNEW THAT. I WAS JUST PAUSING FOR EFFECT.
THE AMAZING SZYMON
Disillusioned

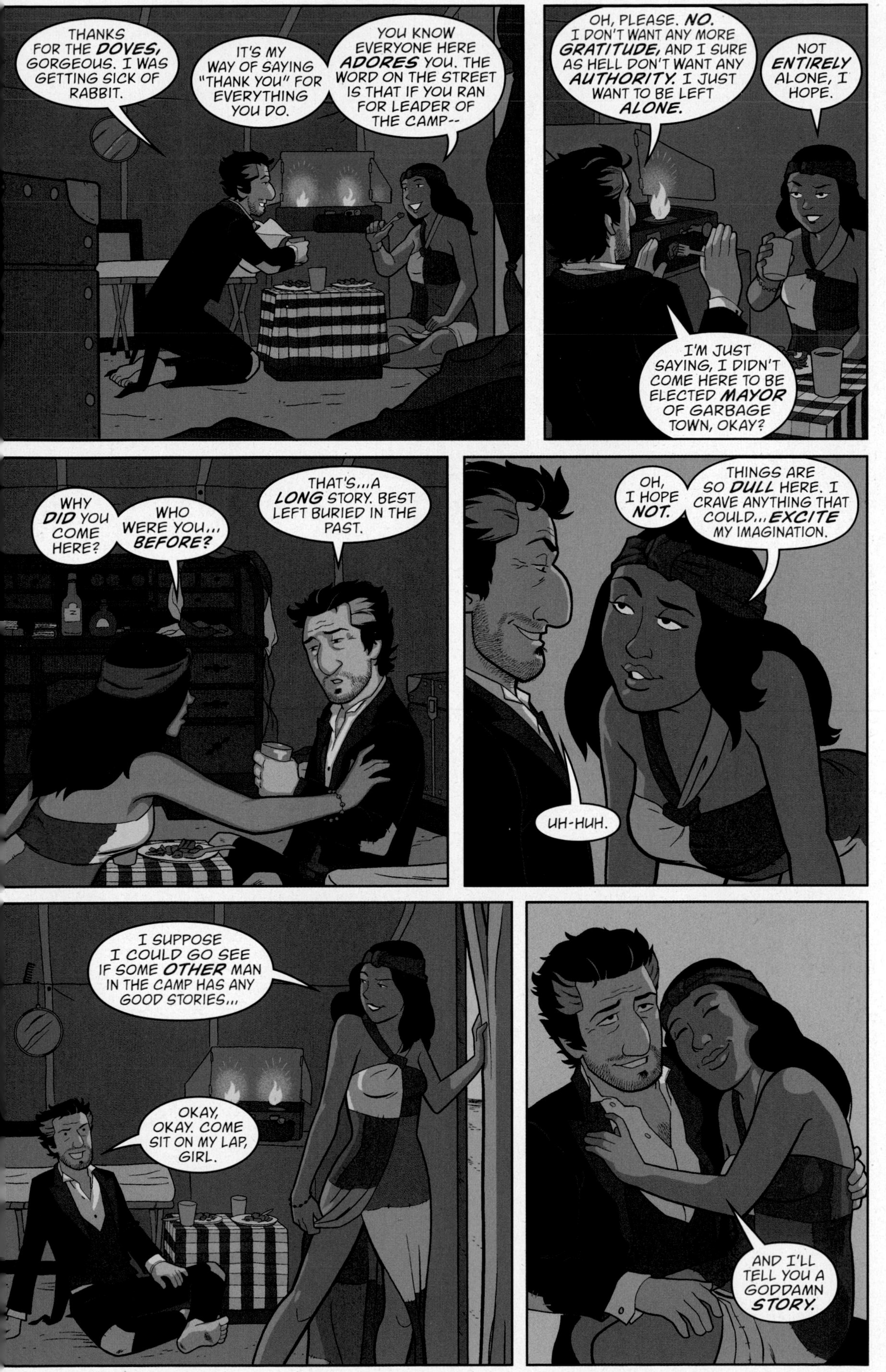
THANKS FOR THE DOVES, GORGEOUS. I WAS GETTING SICK OF RABBIT.
IT'S MY WAY OF SAYING "THANK YOU" FOR EVERYTHING YOU DO.
YOU KNOW EVERYONE HERE ADORES YOU. THE WORD ON THE STREET IS THAT IF YOU RAN FOR LEADER OF THE CAMP--
OH, PLEASE. NO. I DON'T WANT ANY MORE GRATITUDE, AND I SURE AS HELL DON'T WANT ANY AUTHORITY. I JUST WANT TO BE LEFT ALONE.
NOT ENTIRELY ALONE, I HOPE.
I'M JUST SAYING, I DIDN'T COME HERE TO BE ELECTED MAYOR OF GARBAGE TOWN, OKAY?
WHY DID YOU COME HERE?
WHO WERE YOU... BEFORE?
THAT'S...A LONG STORY. BEST LEFT BURIED IN THE PAST.
OH, I HOPE NOT.
THINGS ARE SO DULL HERE. I CRAVE ANYTHING THAT COULD...EXCITE MY IMAGINATION.
UH-HUH.
I SUPPOSE I COULD GO SEE IF SOME OTHER MAN IN THE CAMP HAS ANY GOOD STORIES...
OKAY, OKAY. COME SIT ON MY LAP, GIRL.
AND I'LL TELL YOU A GODDAMN STORY.

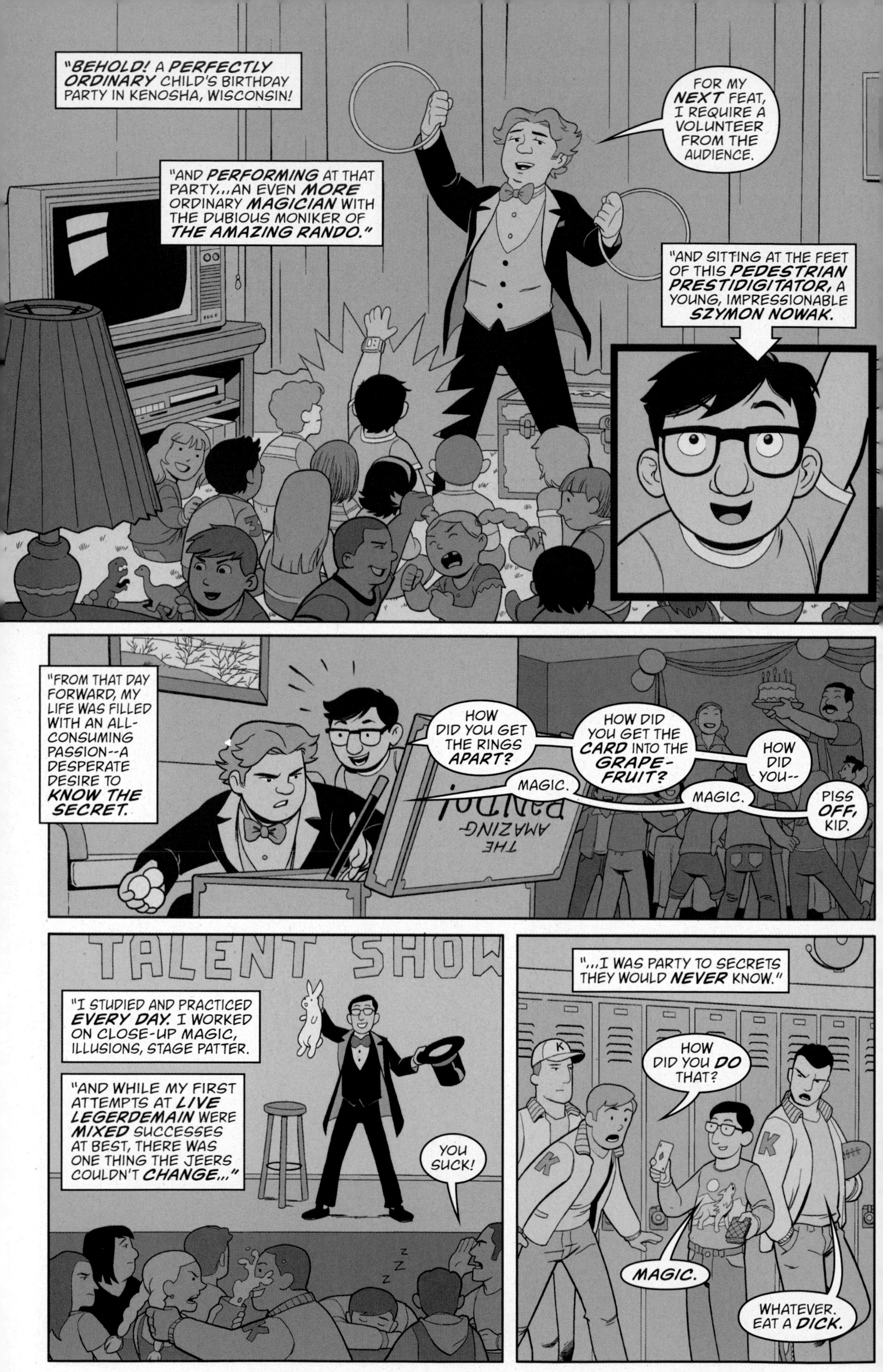
"BEHOLD! A PERFECTLY ORDINARY CHILD'S BIRTHDAY PARTY IN KENOSHA, WISCONSIN!
"AND PERFORMING AT THAT PARTY...AN EVEN MORE ORDINARY MAGICIAN WITH THE DUBIOUS MONIKER OF THE AMAZING RANDO."
FOR MY NEXT FEAT, I REQUIRE A VOLUNTEER FROM THE AUDIENCE.
"AND SITTING AT THE FEET OF THIS PEDESTRIAN PRESTIDIGITATOR, A YOUNG, IMPRESSIONABLE SZYMON NOWAK.
"FROM THAT DAY FORWARD, MY LIFE WAS FILLED WITH AN ALL-CONSUMING PASSION--A DESPERATE DESIRE TO KNOW THE SECRET.
HOW DID YOU GET THE RINGS APART?
MAGIC.
HOW DID YOU GET THE CARD INTO THE GRAPE-FRUIT?
MAGIC.
HOW DID YOU--
PISS OFF, KID.
TALENT SHOW
"I STUDIED AND PRACTICED EVERY DAY. I WORKED ON CLOSE-UP MAGIC, ILLUSIONS, STAGE PATTER.
"AND WHILE MY FIRST ATTEMPTS AT LIVE LEGERDEMAIN WERE MIXED SUCCESSES AT BEST, THERE WAS ONE THING THE JEERS COULDN'T CHANGE..."
YOU SUCK!
"...I WAS PARTY TO SECRETS THEY WOULD NEVER KNOW."
HOW DID YOU DO THAT?
MAGIC.
WHATEVER. EAT A DICK.

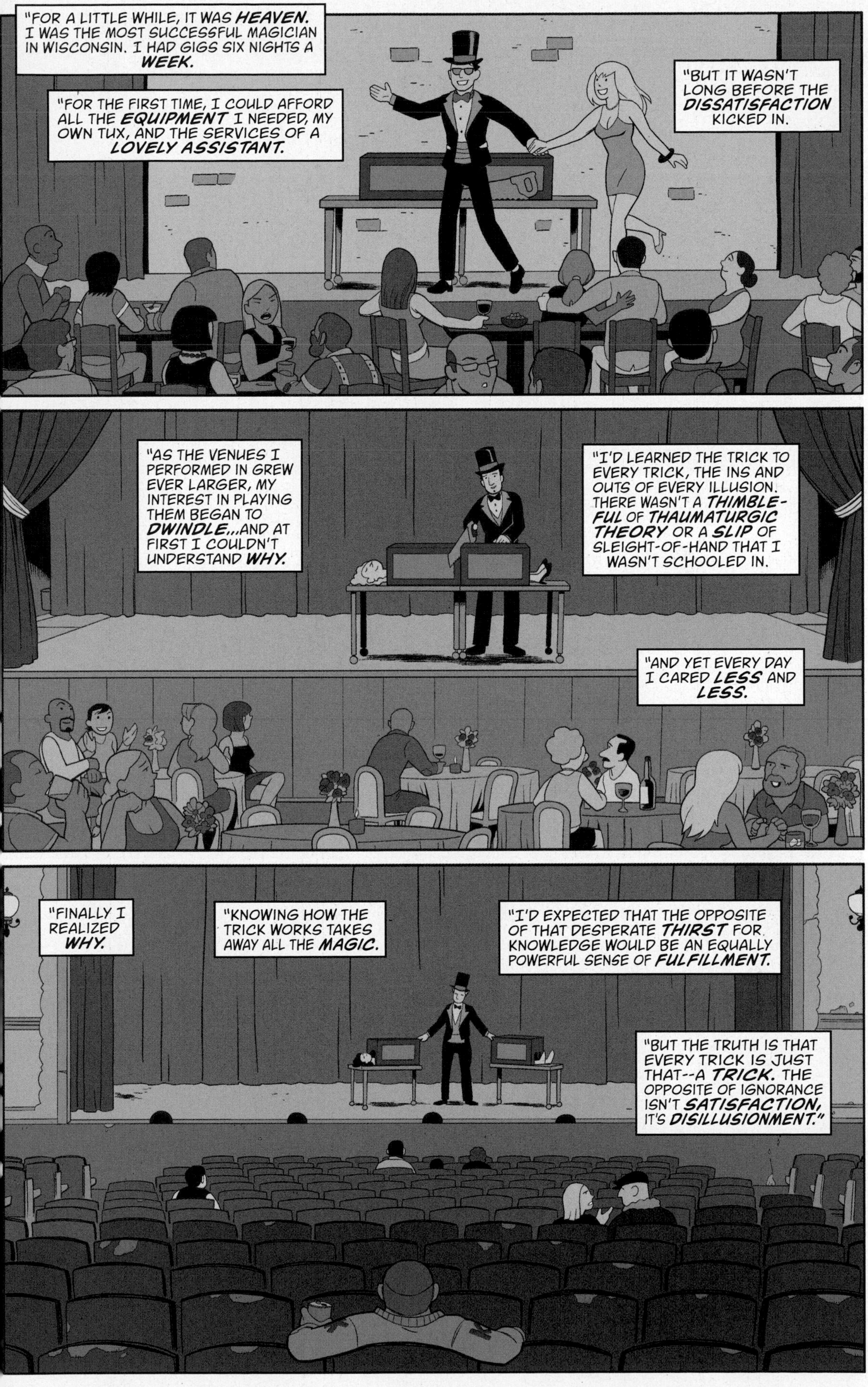
"FOR A LITTLE WHILE, IT WAS HEAVEN. I WAS THE MOST SUCCESSFUL MAGICIAN IN WISCONSIN. I HAD GIGS SIX NIGHTS A WEEK.
"FOR THE FIRST TIME, I COULD AFFORD ALL THE EQUIPMENT I NEEDED, MY OWN TUX, AND THE SERVICES OF A LOVELY ASSISTANT.
"BUT IT WASN'T LONG BEFORE THE DISSATISFACTION KICKED IN.
"AS THE VENUES I PERFORMED IN GREW EVER LARGER, MY INTEREST IN PLAYING THEM BEGAN TO DWINDLE...AND AT FIRST I COULDN'T UNDERSTAND WHY.
"I'D LEARNED THE TRICK TO EVERY TRICK, THE INS AND OUTS OF EVERY ILLUSION. THERE WASN'T A THIMBLE-FUL OF THAUMATURGIC THEORY OR A SLIP OF SLEIGHT-OF-HAND THAT I WASN'T SCHOOLED IN.
"AND YET EVERY DAY I CARED LESS AND LESS.
"FINALLY I REALIZED WHY.
"KNOWING HOW THE TRICK WORKS TAKES AWAY ALL THE MAGIC.
"I'D EXPECTED THAT THE OPPOSITE OF THAT DESPERATE THIRST FOR KNOWLEDGE WOULD BE AN EQUALLY POWERFUL SENSE OF FULFILLMENT.
"BUT THE TRUTH IS THAT EVERY TRICK IS JUST THAT--A TRICK. THE OPPOSITE OF IGNORANCE ISN'T SATISFACTION, IT'S DISILLUSIONMENT."

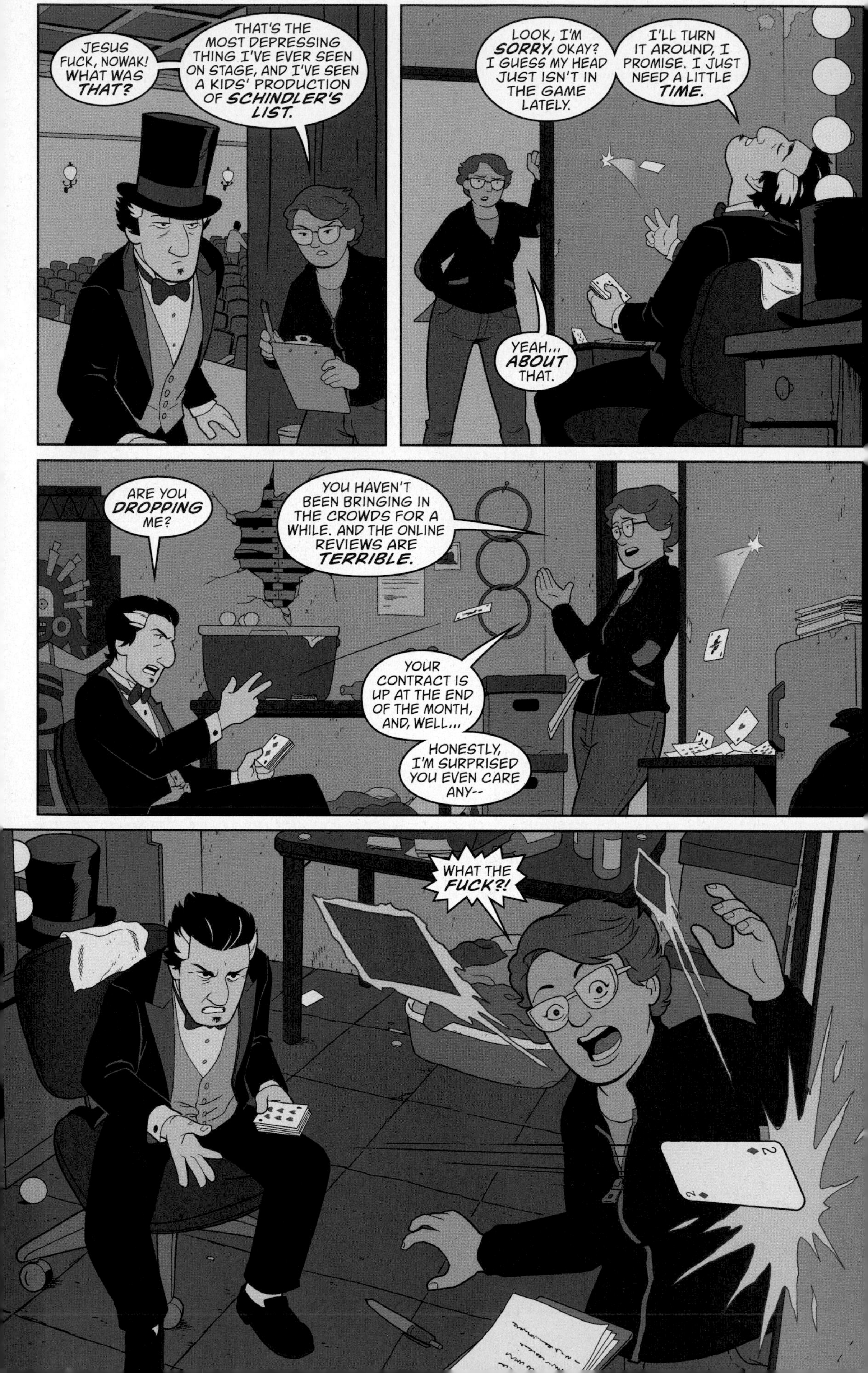
JESUS FUCK, NOWAK! WHAT WAS THAT?
THAT'S THE MOST DEPRESSING THING I'VE EVER SEEN ON STAGE, AND I'VE SEEN A KIDS' PRODUCTION OF SCHINDLER'S LIST.
LOOK, I'M SORRY, OKAY? I GUESS MY HEAD JUST ISN'T IN THE GAME LATELY.
I'LL TURN IT AROUND, I PROMISE. I JUST NEED A LITTLE TIME.
YEAH... ABOUT THAT.
ARE YOU DROPPING ME?
YOU HAVEN'T BEEN BRINGING IN THE CROWDS FOR A WHILE. AND THE ONLINE REVIEWS ARE TERRIBLE.
YOUR CONTRACT IS UP AT THE END OF THE MONTH, AND, WELL...
HONESTLY, I'M SURPRISED YOU EVEN CARE ANY--
WHAT THE FUCK?!

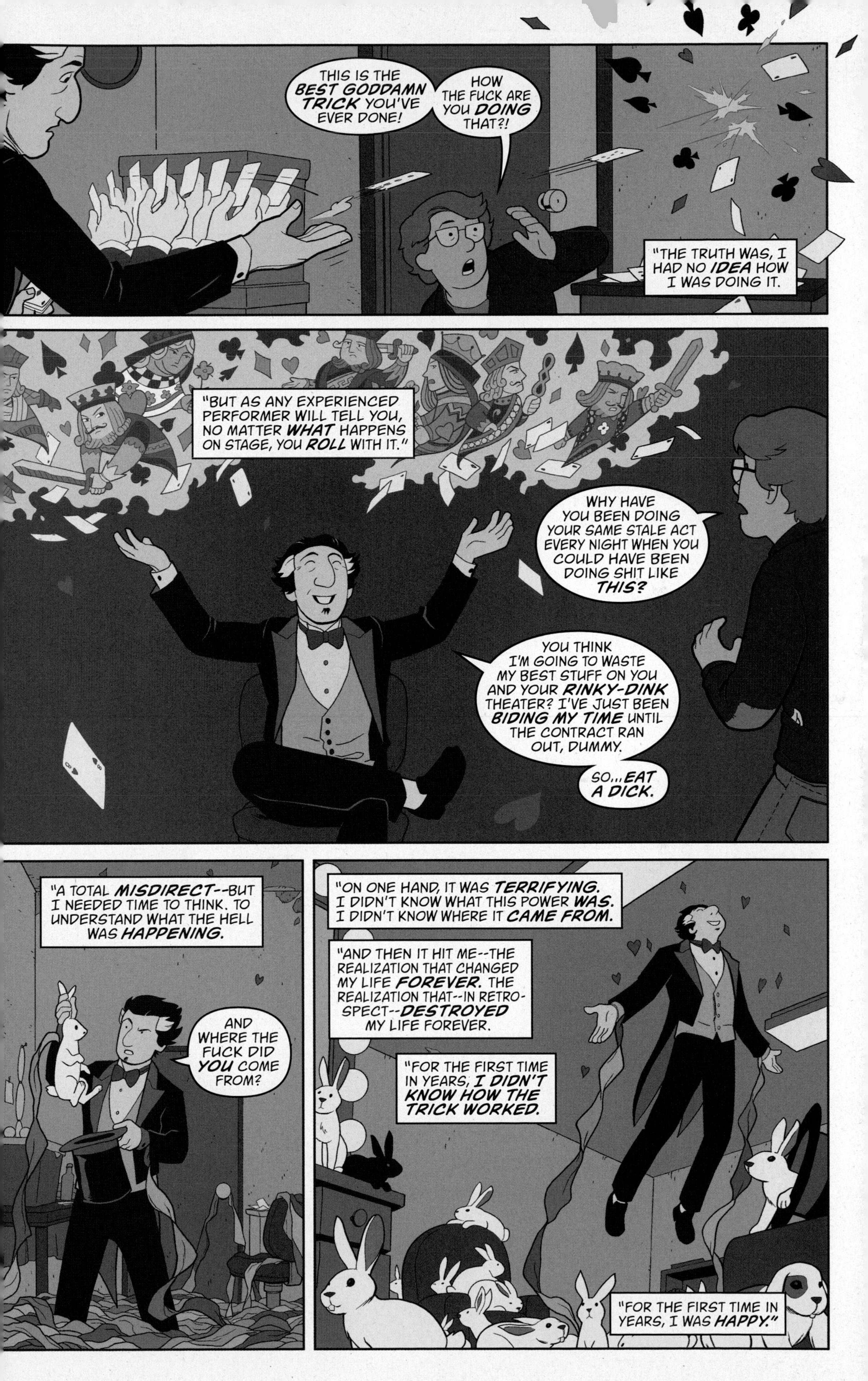
THIS IS THE BEST GODDAMN TRICK YOU'VE EVER DONE!
HOW THE FUCK ARE YOU DOING THAT?!
"THE TRUTH WAS, I HAD NO IDEA HOW I WAS DOING IT.
"BUT AS ANY EXPERIENCED PERFORMER WILL TELL YOU, NO MATTER WHAT HAPPENS ON STAGE, YOU ROLL WITH IT."
WHY HAVE YOU BEEN DOING YOUR SAME STALE ACT EVERY NIGHT WHEN YOU COULD HAVE BEEN DOING SHIT LIKE THIS?
YOU THINK I'M GOING TO WASTE MY BEST STUFF ON YOU AND YOUR RINKY-DINK THEATER? I'VE JUST BEEN BIDING MY TIME UNTIL THE CONTRACT RAN OUT, DUMMY.
SO...EAT A DICK.
"A TOTAL MISDIRECT--BUT I NEEDED TIME TO THINK. TO UNDERSTAND WHAT THE HELL WAS HAPPENING.
AND WHERE THE FUCK DID YOU COME FROM?
"ON ONE HAND, IT WAS TERRIFYING. I DIDN'T KNOW WHAT THIS POWER WAS. I DIDN'T KNOW WHERE IT CAME FROM.
"AND THEN IT HIT ME--THE REALIZATION THAT CHANGED MY LIFE FOREVER. THE REALIZATION THAT--IN RETRO-SPECT--DESTROYED MY LIFE FOREVER.
"FOR THE FIRST TIME IN YEARS, I DIDN'T KNOW HOW THE TRICK WORKED.
"FOR THE FIRST TIME IN YEARS, I WAS HAPPY."

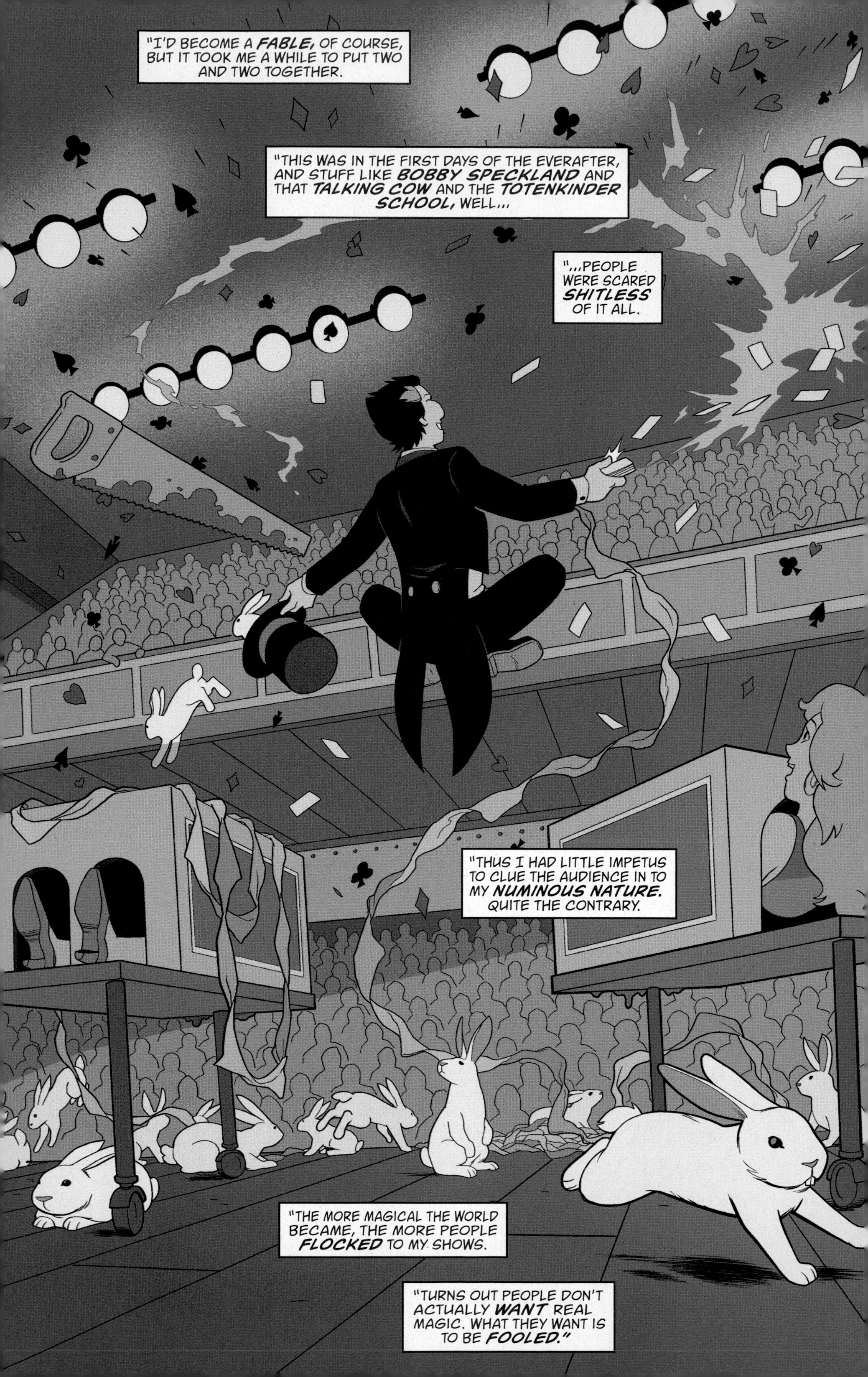
"I'D BECOME A FABLE, OF COURSE, BUT IT TOOK ME A WHILE TO PUT TWO AND TWO TOGETHER.
"THIS WAS IN THE FIRST DAYS OF THE EVERAFTER, AND STUFF LIKE BOBBY SPECKLAND AND THAT TALKING COW AND THE TOTENKINDER SCHOOL, WELL...
"...PEOPLE WERE SCARED SHITLESS OF IT ALL.
"THUS I HAD LITTLE IMPETUS TO CLUE THE AUDIENCE IN TO MY NUMINOUS NATURE. QUITE THE CONTRARY.
"THE MORE MAGICAL THE WORLD BECAME, THE MORE PEOPLE FLOCKED TO MY SHOWS.
"TURNS OUT PEOPLE DON'T ACTUALLY WANT REAL MAGIC. WHAT THEY WANT IS TO BE FOOLED."

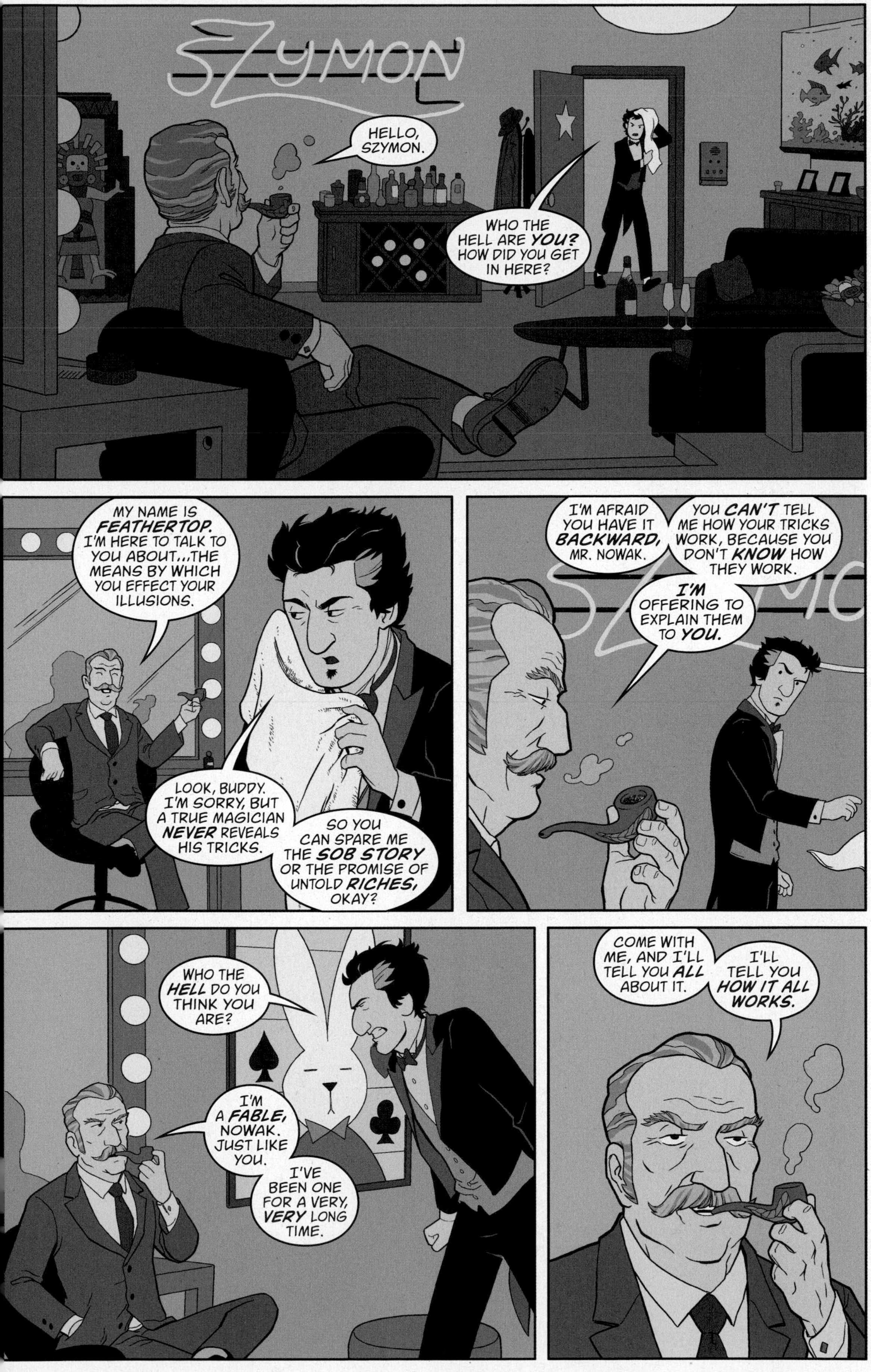
SZYMON
HELLO, SZYMON.
WHO THE HELL ARE YOU? HOW DID YOU GET IN HERE?
MY NAME IS FEATHERTOP. I'M HERE TO TALK TO YOU ABOUT...THE MEANS BY WHICH YOU EFFECT YOUR ILLUSIONS.
LOOK, BUDDY. I'M SORRY, BUT A TRUE MAGICIAN NEVER REVEALS HIS TRICKS.
SO YOU CAN SPARE ME THE SOB STORY OR THE PROMISE OF UNTOLD RICHES, OKAY?
I'M AFRAID YOU HAVE IT BACKWARD, MR. NOWAK.
YOU CAN'T TELL ME HOW YOUR TRICKS WORK, BECAUSE YOU DON'T KNOW HOW THEY WORK.
I'M OFFERING TO EXPLAIN THEM TO YOU.
WHO THE HELL DO YOU THINK YOU ARE?
I'M A FABLE, NOWAK. JUST LIKE YOU.
I'VE BEEN ONE FOR A VERY, VERY LONG TIME.
COME WITH ME, AND I'LL TELL YOU ALL ABOUT IT.
I'LL TELL YOU HOW IT ALL WORKS.

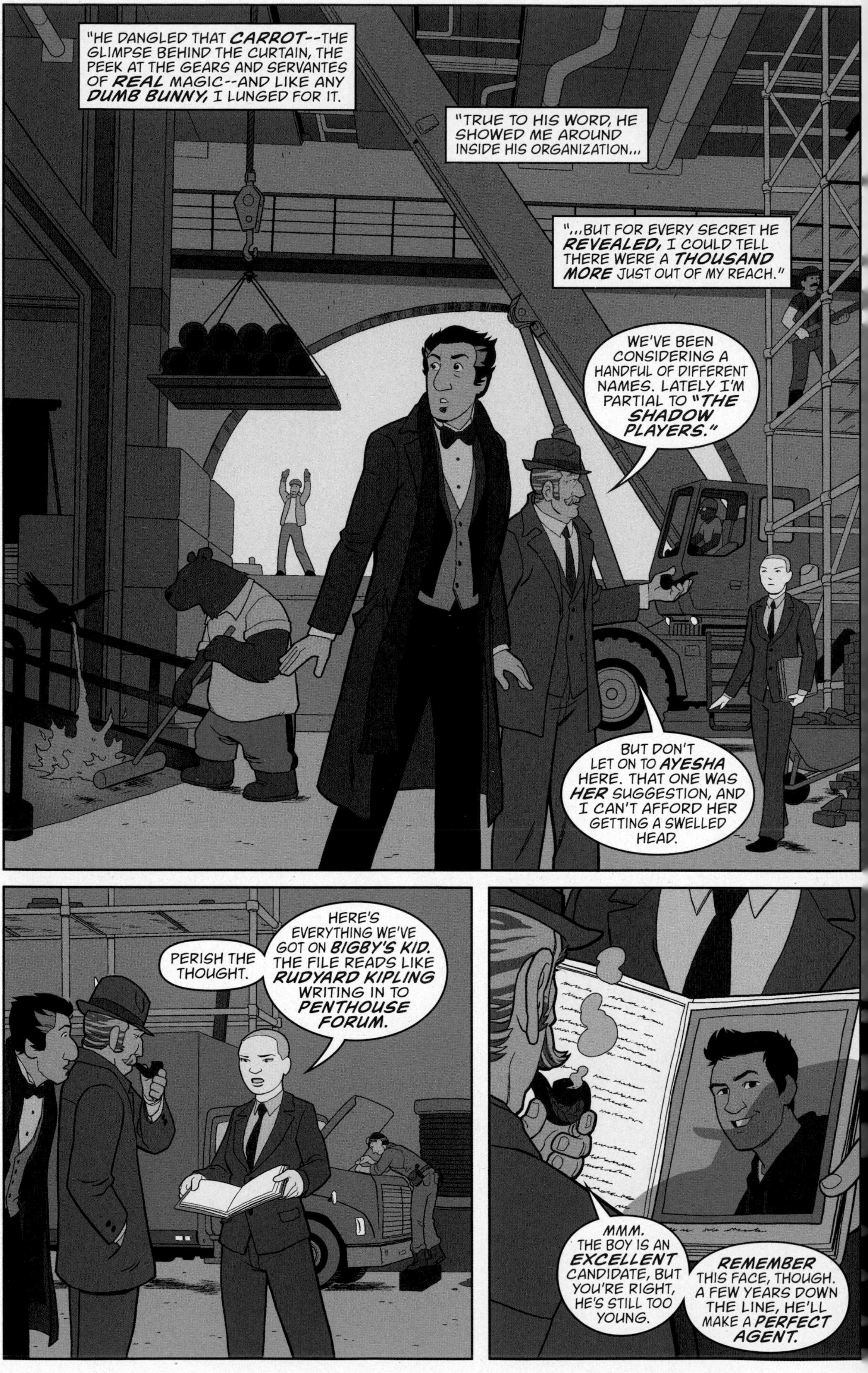

"HE DANGLED THAT CARROT--THE GLIMPSE BEHIND THE CURTAIN, THE PEEK AT THE GEARS AND SERVANTES OF REAL MAGIC--AND LIKE ANY DUMB BUNNY, I LUNGED FOR IT.
"TRUE TO HIS WORD, HE SHOWED ME AROUND INSIDE HIS ORGANIZATION...
"...BUT FOR EVERY SECRET HE REVEALED, I COULD TELL THERE WERE A THOUSAND MORE JUST OUT OF MY REACH."
WE'VE BEEN CONSIDERING A HANDFUL OF DIFFERENT NAMES. LATELY I'M PARTIAL TO "THE SHADOW PLAYERS."
BUT DON'T LET ON TO AYESHA HERE. THAT ONE WAS HER SUGGESTION, AND I CAN'T AFFORD HER GETTING A SWELLED HEAD.
PERISH THE THOUGHT.
HERE'S EVERYTHING WE'VE GOT ON BIGBY'S KID. THE FILE READS LIKE RUDYARD KIPLING WRITING IN TO PENTHOUSE FORUM.
MMM. THE BOY IS AN EXCELLENT CANDIDATE, BUT YOU'RE RIGHT, HE'S STILL TOO YOUNG.
REMEMBER THIS FACE, THOUGH. A FEW YEARS DOWN THE LINE, HE'LL MAKE A PERFECT AGENT.

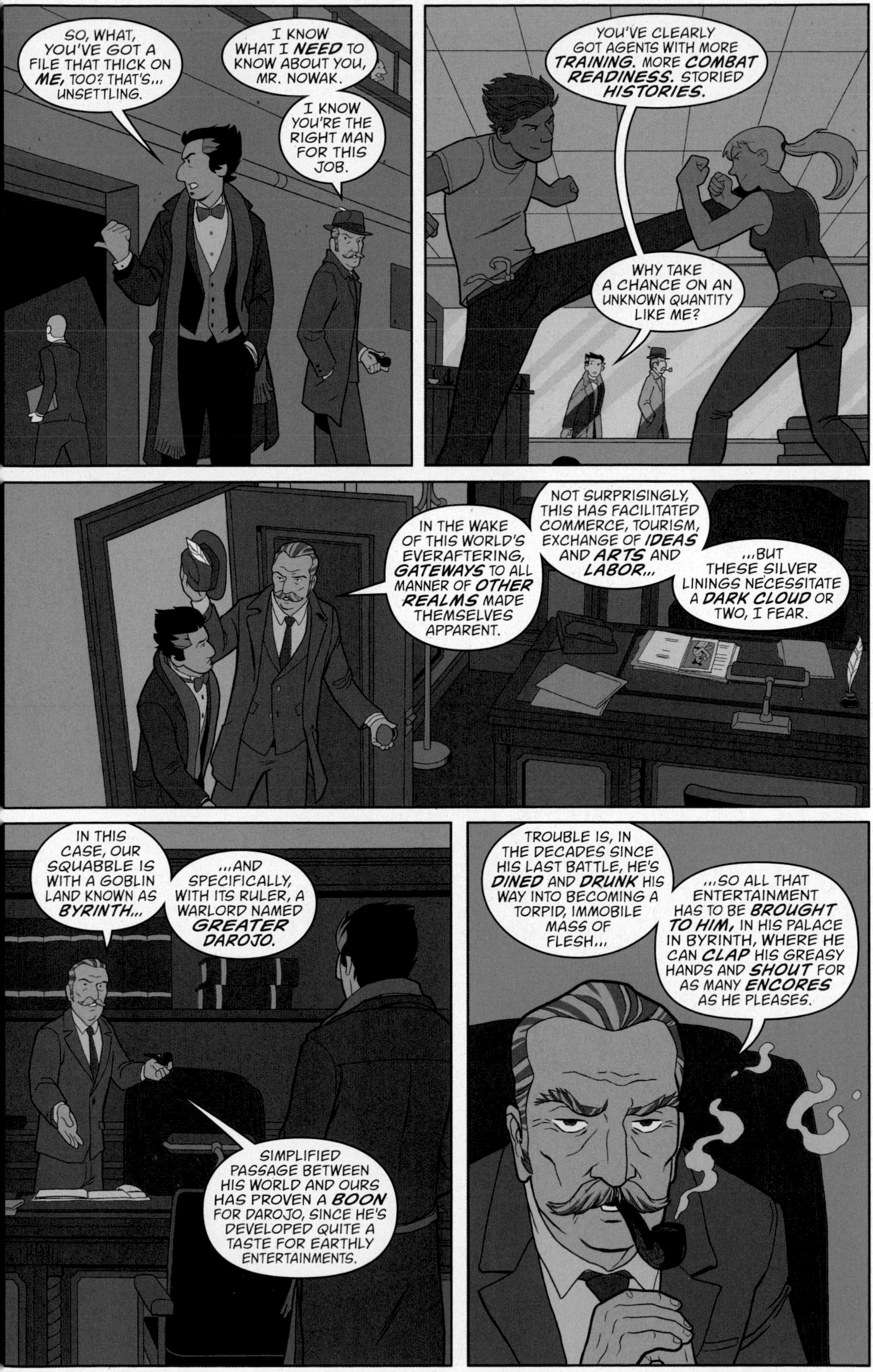
SO, WHAT, YOU'VE GOT A FILE THAT THICK ON ME, TOO? THAT'S... UNSETTLING.
I KNOW WHAT I NEED TO KNOW ABOUT YOU, MR. NOWAK.
I KNOW YOU'RE THE RIGHT MAN FOR THIS JOB.
YOU'VE CLEARLY GOT AGENTS WITH MORE TRAINING. MORE COMBAT READINESS. STORIED HISTORIES.
WHY TAKE A CHANCE ON AN UNKNOWN QUANTITY LIKE ME?
IN THE WAKE OF THIS WORLD'S EVERAFTERING, GATEWAYS TO ALL MANNER OF OTHER REALMS MADE THEMSELVES APPARENT.
NOT SURPRISINGLY, THIS HAS FACILITATED COMMERCE, TOURISM, EXCHANGE OF IDEAS AND ARTS AND LABOR...
...BUT THESE SILVER LININGS NECESSITATE A DARK CLOUD OR TWO, I FEAR.
IN THIS CASE, OUR SQUABBLE IS WITH A GOBLIN LAND KNOWN AS BYRINTH...
...AND SPECIFICALLY, WITH ITS RULER, A WARLORD NAMED GREATER DAROJO.
SIMPLIFIED PASSAGE BETWEEN HIS WORLD AND OURS HAS PROVEN A BOON FOR DAROJO, SINCE HE'S DEVELOPED QUITE A TASTE FOR EARTHLY ENTERTAINMENTS.
TROUBLE IS, IN THE DECADES SINCE HIS LAST BATTLE, HE'S DINED AND DRUNK HIS WAY INTO BECOMING A TORPID, IMMOBILE MASS OF FLESH...
...SO ALL THAT ENTERTAINMENT HAS TO BE BROUGHT TO HIM, IN HIS PALACE IN BYRINTH, WHERE HE CAN CLAP HIS GREASY HANDS AND SHOUT FOR AS MANY ENCORES AS HE PLEASES.

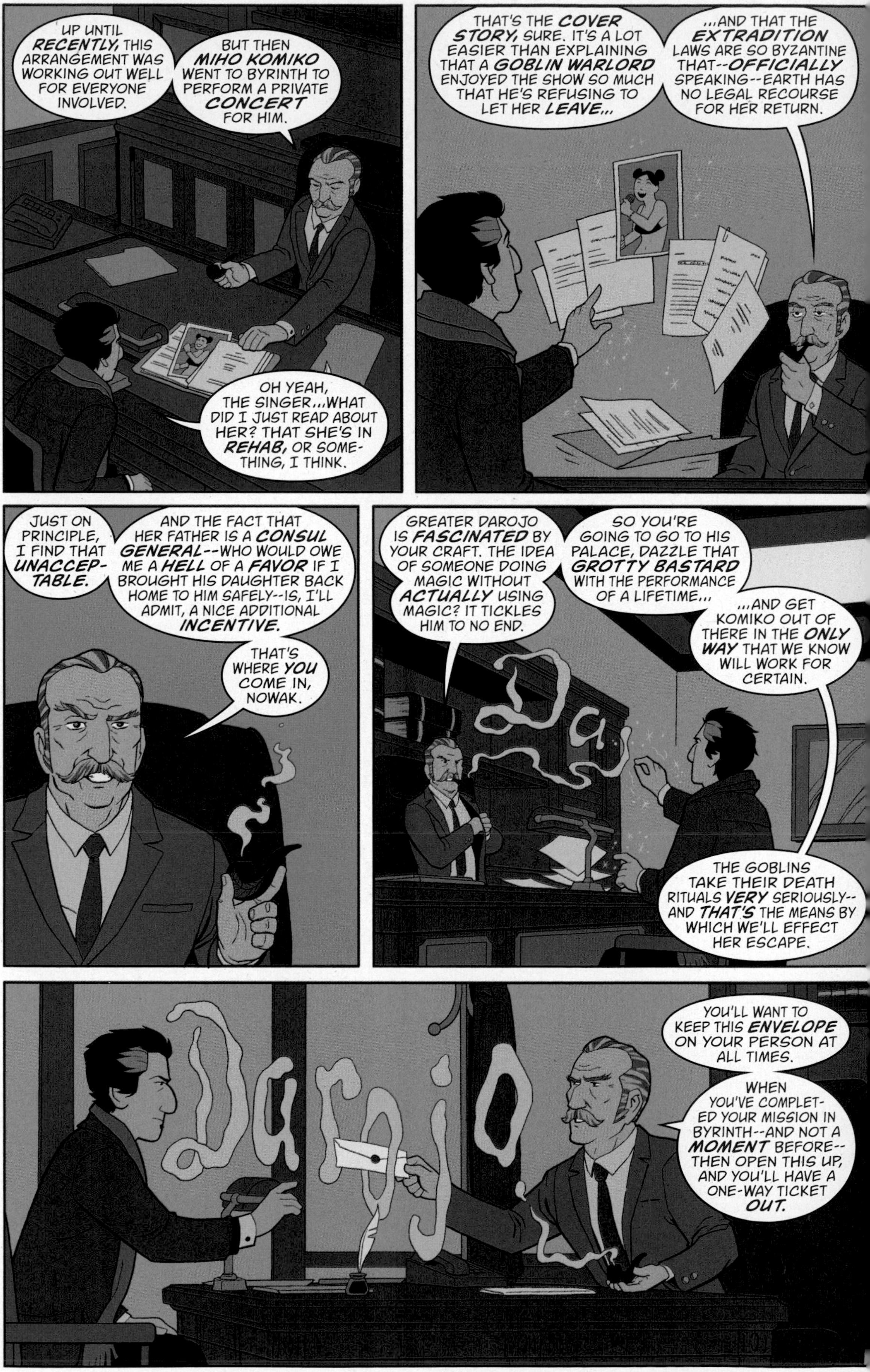
UP UNTIL RECENTLY, THIS ARRANGEMENT WAS WORKING OUT WELL FOR EVERYONE INVOLVED.
BUT THEN MIHO KOMIKO WENT TO BYRINTH TO PERFORM A PRIVATE CONCERT FOR HIM.
OH YEAH, THE SINGER...WHAT DID I JUST READ ABOUT HER? THAT SHE'S IN REHAB, OR SOME-THING, I THINK.
THAT'S THE COVER STORY, SURE. IT'S A LOT EASIER THAN EXPLAINING THAT A GOBLIN WARLORD ENJOYED THE SHOW SO MUCH THAT HE'S REFUSING TO LET HER LEAVE...
...AND THAT THE EXTRADITION LAWS ARE SO BYZANTINE THAT--OFFICIALLY SPEAKING--EARTH HAS NO LEGAL RECOURSE FOR HER RETURN.
JUST ON PRINCIPLE, I FIND THAT UNACCEP-TABLE.
AND THE FACT THAT HER FATHER IS A CONSUL GENERAL--WHO WOULD OWE ME A HELL OF A FAVOR IF I BROUGHT HIS DAUGHTER BACK HOME TO HIM SAFELY--IS, I'LL ADMIT, A NICE ADDITIONAL INCENTIVE.
THAT'S WHERE YOU COME IN, NOWAK.
GREATER DAROJO IS FASCINATED BY YOUR CRAFT. THE IDEA OF SOMEONE DOING MAGIC WITHOUT ACTUALLY USING MAGIC? IT TICKLES HIM TO NO END.
SO YOU'RE GOING TO GO TO HIS PALACE, DAZZLE THAT GROTTY BASTARD WITH THE PERFORMANCE OF A LIFETIME...
...AND GET KOMIKO OUT OF THERE IN THE ONLY WAY THAT WE KNOW WILL WORK FOR CERTAIN.
Dar
THE GOBLINS TAKE THEIR DEATH RITUALS VERY SERIOUSLY--AND THAT'S THE MEANS BY WHICH WE'LL EFFECT HER ESCAPE.
Darojo
YOU'LL WANT TO KEEP THIS ENVELOPE ON YOUR PERSON AT ALL TIMES.
WHEN YOU'VE COMPLET-ED YOUR MISSION IN BYRINTH--AND NOT A MOMENT BEFORE--THEN OPEN THIS UP, AND YOU'LL HAVE A ONE-WAY TICKET OUT.

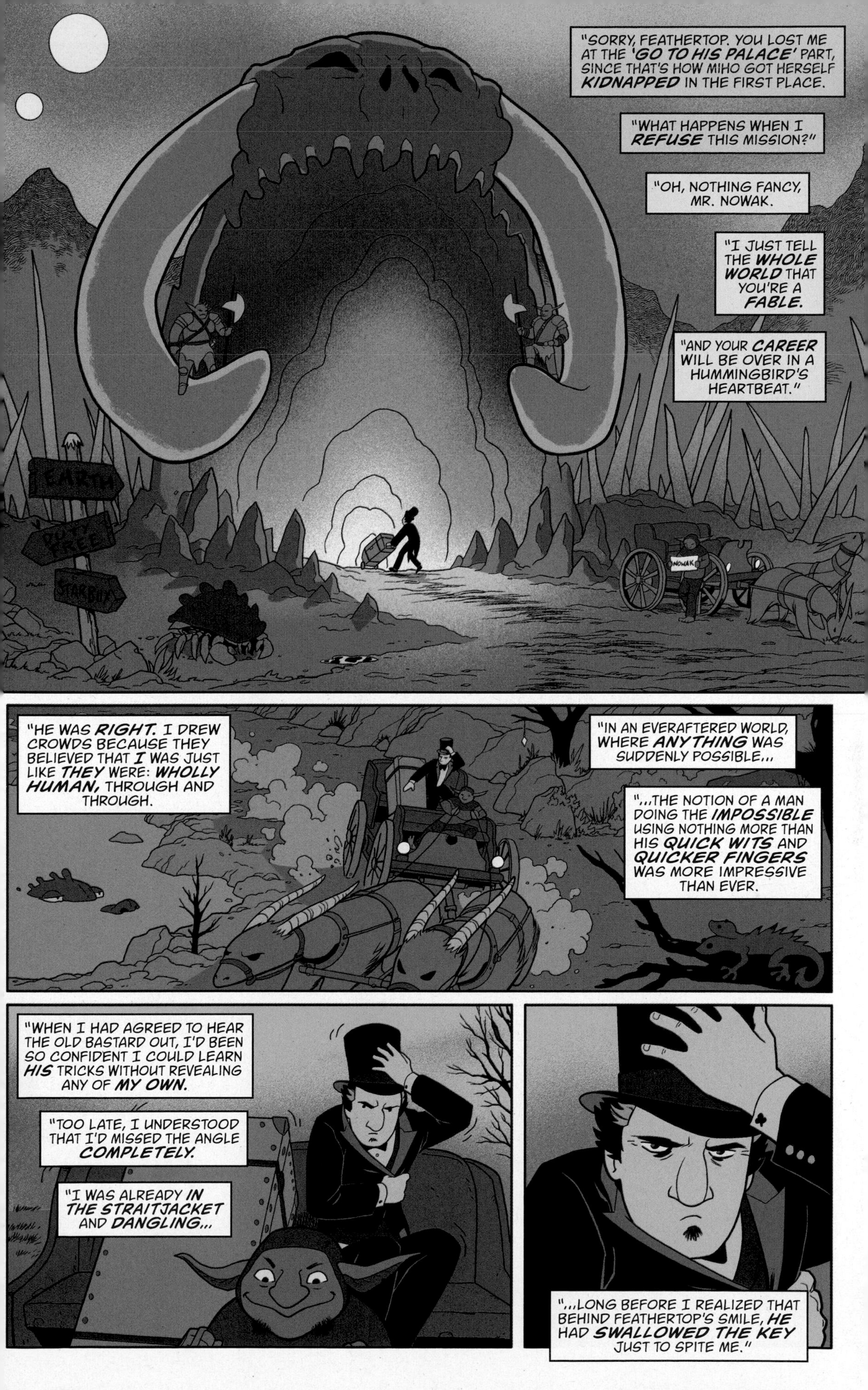
"SORRY, FEATHERTOP. YOU LOST ME AT THE 'GO TO HIS PALACE' PART, SINCE THAT'S HOW MIHO GOT HERSELF KIDNAPPED IN THE FIRST PLACE.
"WHAT HAPPENS WHEN I REFUSE THIS MISSION?"
"OH, NOTHING FANCY, MR. NOWAK.
"I JUST TELL THE WHOLE WORLD THAT YOU'RE A FABLE.
"AND YOUR CAREER WILL BE OVER IN A HUMMINGBIRD'S HEARTBEAT."
EARTH
DUTY FREE
STARBUX
NOWAK
"HE WAS RIGHT. I DREW CROWDS BECAUSE THEY BELIEVED THAT I WAS JUST LIKE THEY WERE: WHOLLY HUMAN, THROUGH AND THROUGH.
"IN AN EVERAFTERED WORLD, WHERE ANYTHING WAS SUDDENLY POSSIBLE...
"...THE NOTION OF A MAN DOING THE IMPOSSIBLE USING NOTHING MORE THAN HIS QUICK WITS AND QUICKER FINGERS WAS MORE IMPRESSIVE THAN EVER.
"WHEN I HAD AGREED TO HEAR THE OLD BASTARD OUT, I'D BEEN SO CONFIDENT I COULD LEARN HIS TRICKS WITHOUT REVEALING ANY OF MY OWN.
"TOO LATE, I UNDERSTOOD THAT I'D MISSED THE ANGLE COMPLETELY.
"I WAS ALREADY IN THE STRAITJACKET AND DANGLING...
"...LONG BEFORE I REALIZED THAT BEHIND FEATHERTOP'S SMILE, HE HAD SWALLOWED THE KEY JUST TO SPITE ME."

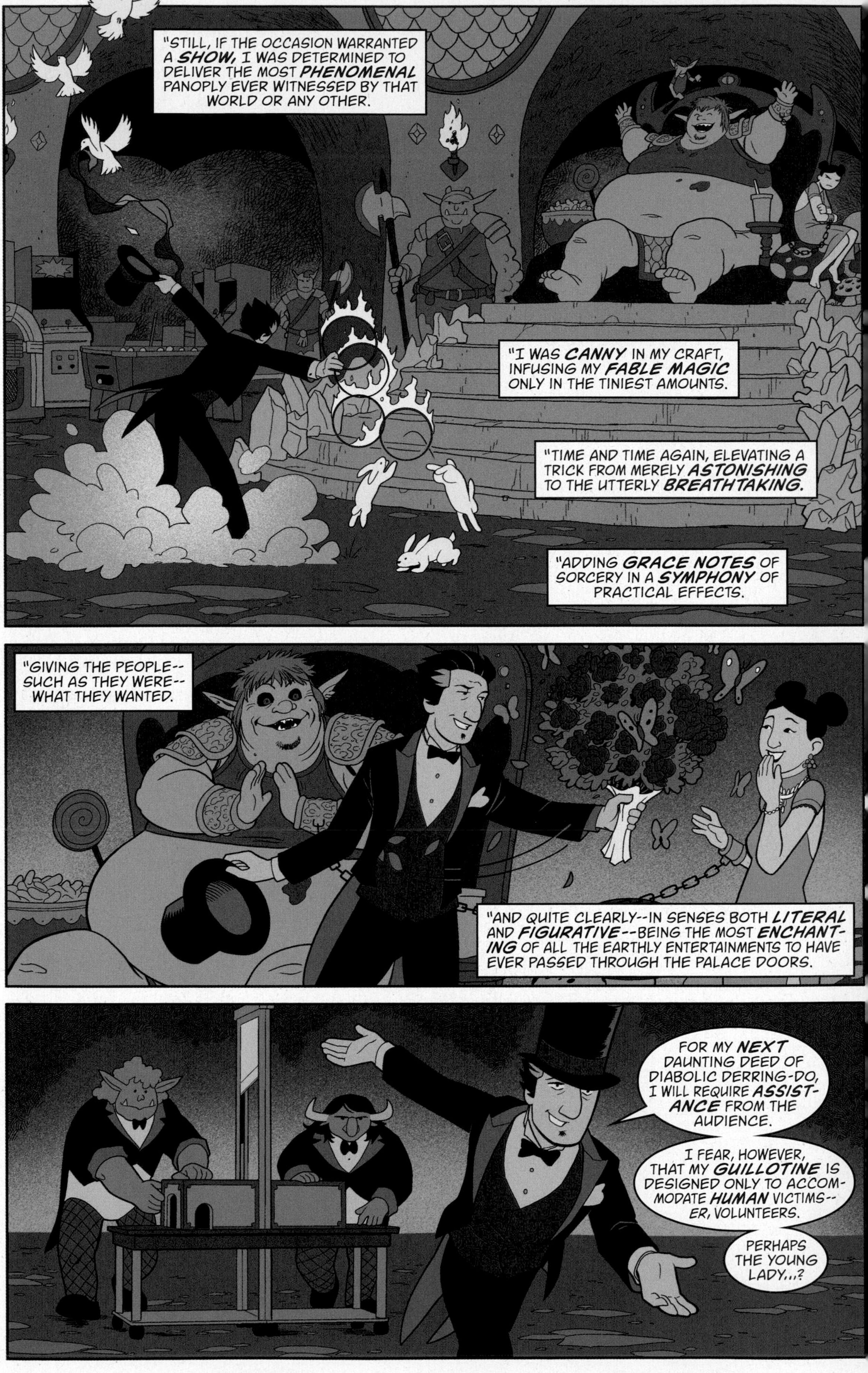
"STILL, IF THE OCCASION WARRANTED A SHOW, I WAS DETERMINED TO DELIVER THE MOST PHENOMENAL PANOPLY EVER WITNESSED BY THAT WORLD OR ANY OTHER.
"I WAS CANNY IN MY CRAFT, INFUSING MY FABLE MAGIC ONLY IN THE TINIEST AMOUNTS.
"TIME AND TIME AGAIN, ELEVATING A TRICK FROM MERELY ASTONISHING TO THE UTTERLY BREATHTAKING.
"ADDING GRACE NOTES OF SORCERY IN A SYMPHONY OF PRACTICAL EFFECTS.
"GIVING THE PEOPLE--SUCH AS THEY WERE--WHAT THEY WANTED.
"AND QUITE CLEARLY--IN SENSES BOTH LITERAL AND FIGURATIVE--BEING THE MOST ENCHANTING OF ALL THE EARTHLY ENTERTAINMENTS TO HAVE EVER PASSED THROUGH THE PALACE DOORS.
FOR MY NEXT DAUNTING DEED OF DIABOLIC DERRING-DO, I WILL REQUIRE ASSISTANCE FROM THE AUDIENCE.
I FEAR, HOWEVER, THAT MY GUILLOTINE IS DESIGNED ONLY TO ACCOMMODATE HUMAN VICTIMS--ER, VOLUNTEERS.
PERHAPS THE YOUNG LADY...?

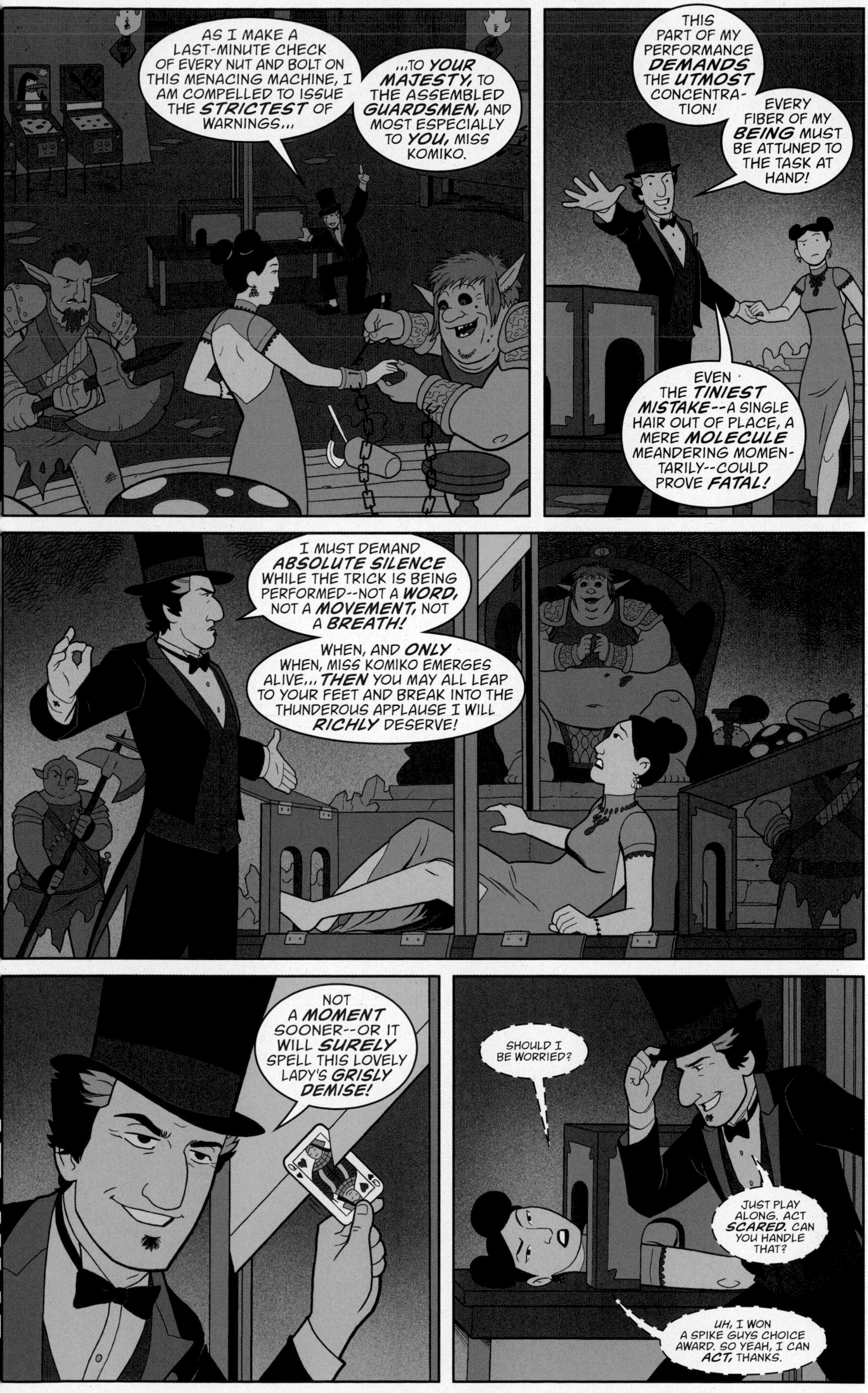
AS I MAKE A LAST-MINUTE CHECK OF EVERY NUT AND BOLT ON THIS MENACING MACHINE, I AM COMPELLED TO ISSUE THE STRICTEST OF WARNINGS...
...TO YOUR MAJESTY, TO THE ASSEMBLED GUARDSMEN, AND MOST ESPECIALLY TO YOU, MISS KOMIKO.
THIS PART OF MY PERFORMANCE DEMANDS THE UTMOST CONCENTRATION!
EVERY FIBER OF MY BEING MUST BE ATTUNED TO THE TASK AT HAND!
EVEN THE TINIEST MISTAKE--A SINGLE HAIR OUT OF PLACE, A MERE MOLECULE MEANDERING MOMENTARILY--COULD PROVE FATAL!
I MUST DEMAND ABSOLUTE SILENCE WHILE THE TRICK IS BEING PERFORMED--NOT A WORD, NOT A MOVEMENT, NOT A BREATH!
WHEN, AND ONLY WHEN, MISS KOMIKO EMERGES ALIVE... THEN YOU MAY ALL LEAP TO YOUR FEET AND BREAK INTO THE THUNDEROUS APPLAUSE I WILL RICHLY DESERVE!
NOT A MOMENT SOONER--OR IT WILL SURELY SPELL THIS LOVELY LADY'S GRISLY DEMISE!
SHOULD I BE WORRIED?
JUST PLAY ALONG. ACT SCARED. CAN YOU HANDLE THAT?
UH, I WON A SPIKE GUYS CHOICE AWARD. SO YEAH, I CAN ACT, THANKS.

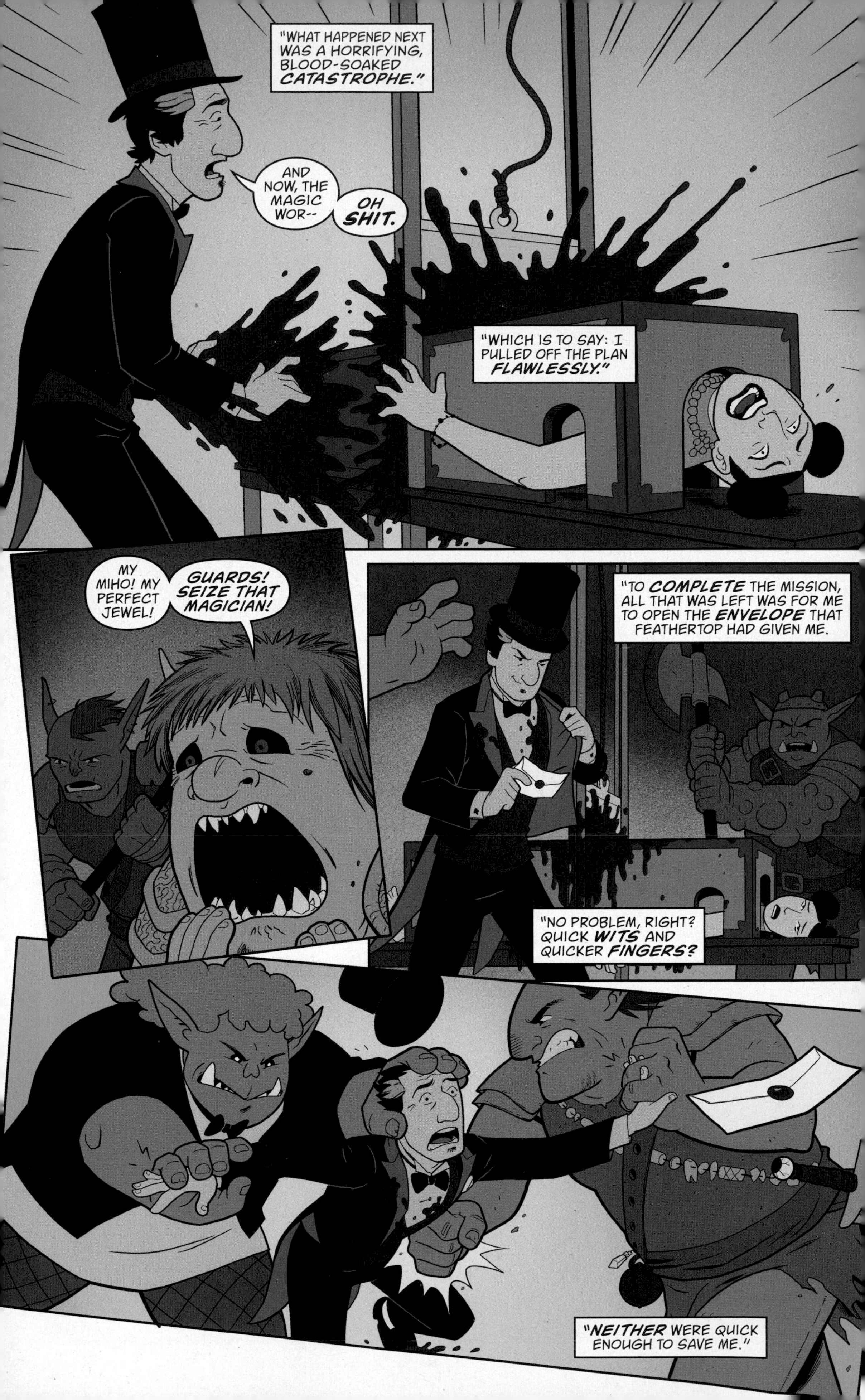
"WHAT HAPPENED NEXT WAS A HORRIFYING, BLOOD-SOAKED *CATASTROPHE.*"
AND NOW, THE MAGIC WOR--
OH *SHIT.*
"WHICH IS TO SAY: I PULLED OFF THE PLAN *FLAWLESSLY.*"
MY MIHO! MY PERFECT JEWEL!
GUARDS! SEIZE THAT MAGICIAN!
"TO *COMPLETE* THE MISSION, ALL THAT WAS LEFT WAS FOR ME TO OPEN THE *ENVELOPE* THAT FEATHERTOP HAD GIVEN ME.
"NO PROBLEM, RIGHT? QUICK *WITS* AND QUICKER *FINGERS?*
"*NEITHER* WERE QUICK ENOUGH TO SAVE ME."

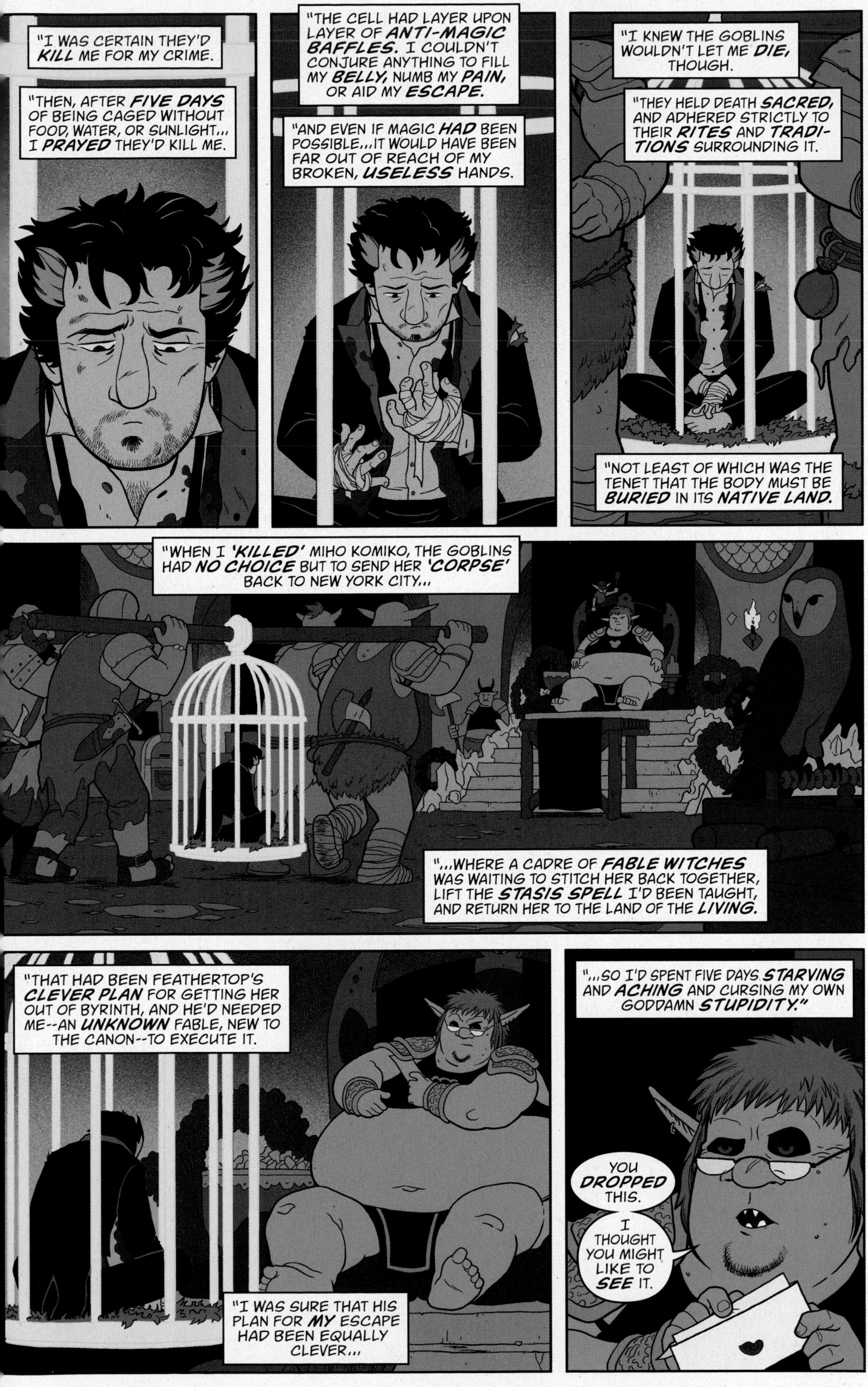
"I WAS CERTAIN THEY'D KILL ME FOR MY CRIME.
"THEN, AFTER FIVE DAYS OF BEING CAGED WITHOUT FOOD, WATER, OR SUNLIGHT... I PRAYED THEY'D KILL ME.
"THE CELL HAD LAYER UPON LAYER OF ANTI-MAGIC BAFFLES. I COULDN'T CONJURE ANYTHING TO FILL MY BELLY, NUMB MY PAIN, OR AID MY ESCAPE.
"AND EVEN IF MAGIC HAD BEEN POSSIBLE...IT WOULD HAVE BEEN FAR OUT OF REACH OF MY BROKEN, USELESS HANDS.
"I KNEW THE GOBLINS WOULDN'T LET ME DIE, THOUGH.
"THEY HELD DEATH SACRED, AND ADHERED STRICTLY TO THEIR RITES AND TRADITIONS SURROUNDING IT.
"NOT LEAST OF WHICH WAS THE TENET THAT THE BODY MUST BE BURIED IN ITS NATIVE LAND.
"WHEN I 'KILLED' MIHO KOMIKO, THE GOBLINS HAD NO CHOICE BUT TO SEND HER 'CORPSE' BACK TO NEW YORK CITY...
"...WHERE A CADRE OF FABLE WITCHES WAS WAITING TO STITCH HER BACK TOGETHER, LIFT THE STASIS SPELL I'D BEEN TAUGHT, AND RETURN HER TO THE LAND OF THE LIVING.
"THAT HAD BEEN FEATHERTOP'S CLEVER PLAN FOR GETTING HER OUT OF BYRINTH, AND HE'D NEEDED ME--AN UNKNOWN FABLE, NEW TO THE CANON--TO EXECUTE IT.
"I WAS SURE THAT HIS PLAN FOR MY ESCAPE HAD BEEN EQUALLY CLEVER...
"...SO I'D SPENT FIVE DAYS STARVING AND ACHING AND CURSING MY OWN GODDAMN STUPIDITY."
YOU DROPPED THIS.
I THOUGHT YOU MIGHT LIKE TO SEE IT.

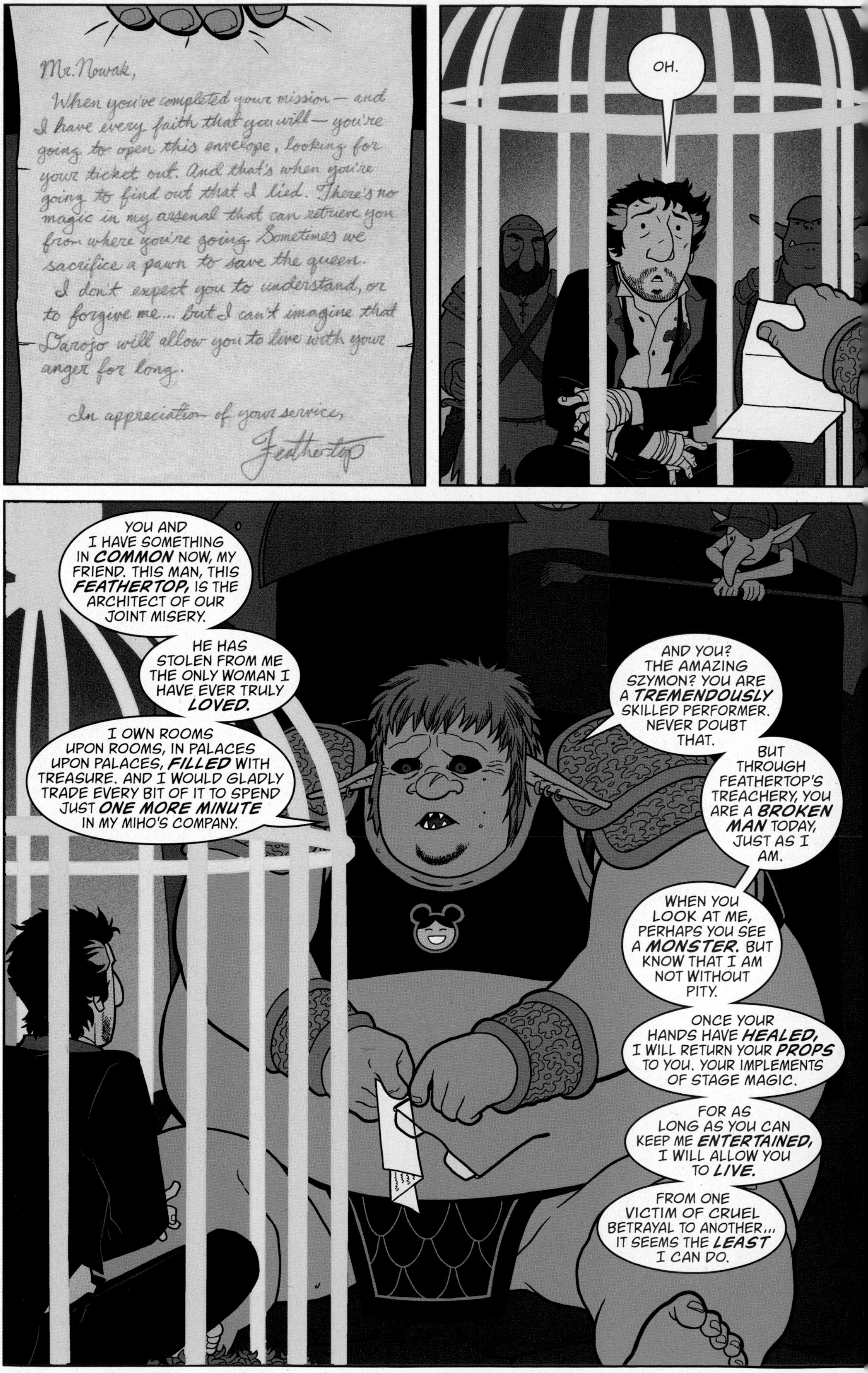
Mr. Nowak,
When you've completed your mission — and I have every faith that you will — you're going to open this envelope, looking for your ticket out. And that's when you're going to find out that I lied. There's no magic in my arsenal that can retrieve you from where you're going. Sometimes we sacrifice a pawn to save the queen.
I don't expect you to understand, or to forgive me... but I can't imagine that Darojo will allow you to live with your anger for long.
In appreciation of your service,
Feathertop
OH.
YOU AND I HAVE SOMETHING IN COMMON NOW, MY FRIEND. THIS MAN, THIS FEATHERTOP, IS THE ARCHITECT OF OUR JOINT MISERY.
HE HAS STOLEN FROM ME THE ONLY WOMAN I HAVE EVER TRULY LOVED.
I OWN ROOMS UPON ROOMS, IN PALACES UPON PALACES, FILLED WITH TREASURE. AND I WOULD GLADLY TRADE EVERY BIT OF IT TO SPEND JUST ONE MORE MINUTE IN MY MIHO'S COMPANY.
AND YOU? THE AMAZING SZYMON? YOU ARE A TREMENDOUSLY SKILLED PERFORMER. NEVER DOUBT THAT.
BUT THROUGH FEATHERTOP'S TREACHERY, YOU ARE A BROKEN MAN TODAY, JUST AS I AM.
WHEN YOU LOOK AT ME, PERHAPS YOU SEE A MONSTER. BUT KNOW THAT I AM NOT WITHOUT PITY.
ONCE YOUR HANDS HAVE HEALED, I WILL RETURN YOUR PROPS TO YOU. YOUR IMPLEMENTS OF STAGE MAGIC.
FOR AS LONG AS YOU CAN KEEP ME ENTERTAINED, I WILL ALLOW YOU TO LIVE.
FROM ONE VICTIM OF CRUEL BETRAYAL TO ANOTHER... IT SEEMS THE LEAST I CAN DO.

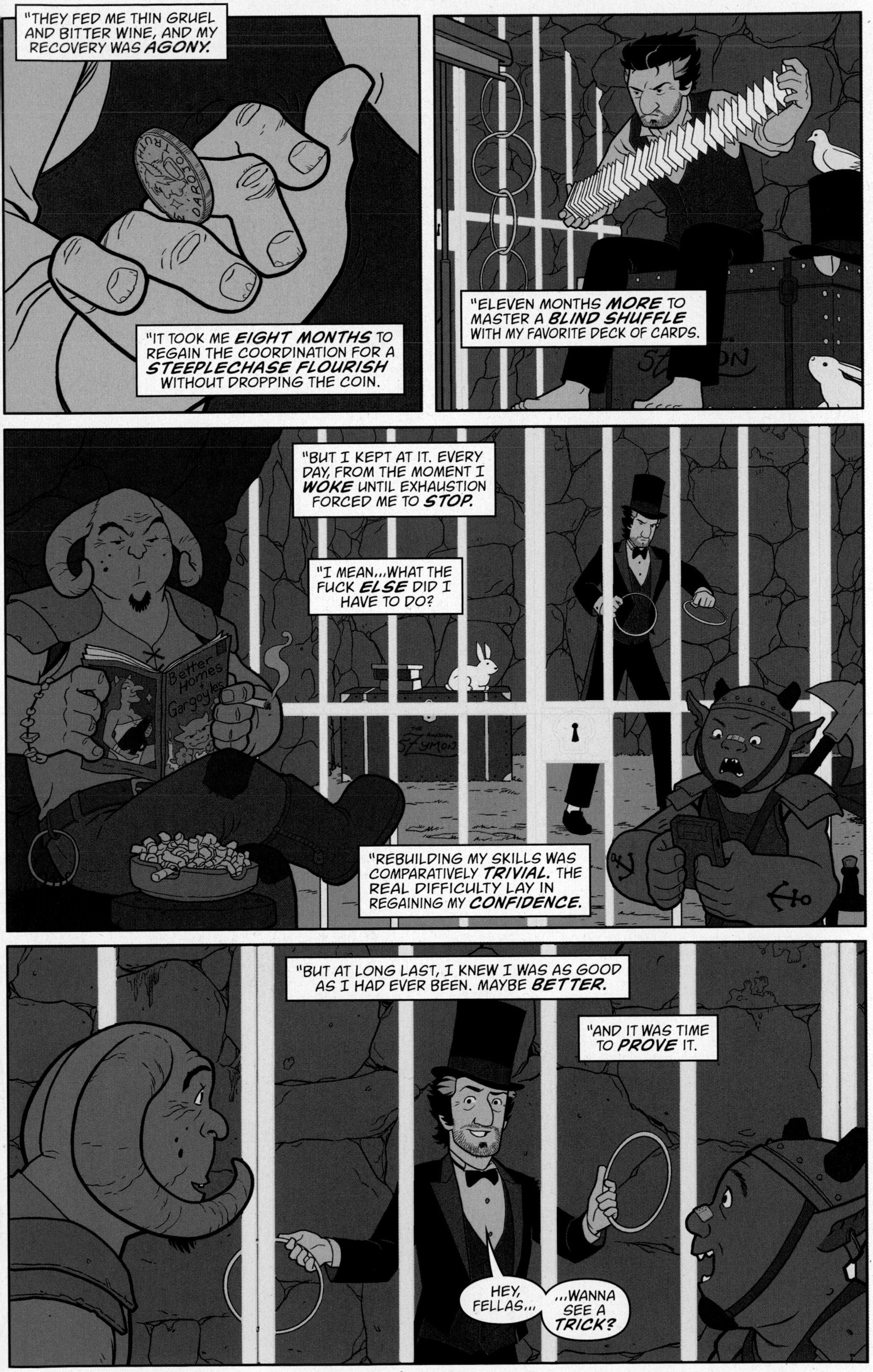
"THEY FED ME THIN GRUEL AND BITTER WINE, AND MY RECOVERY WAS AGONY.
"IT TOOK ME EIGHT MONTHS TO REGAIN THE COORDINATION FOR A STEEPLECHASE FLOURISH WITHOUT DROPPING THE COIN.
"ELEVEN MONTHS MORE TO MASTER A BLIND SHUFFLE WITH MY FAVORITE DECK OF CARDS.
"BUT I KEPT AT IT. EVERY DAY, FROM THE MOMENT I WOKE UNTIL EXHAUSTION FORCED ME TO STOP.
"I MEAN...WHAT THE FUCK ELSE DID I HAVE TO DO?
Better Homes + Gargoyles
"REBUILDING MY SKILLS WAS COMPARATIVELY TRIVIAL. THE REAL DIFFICULTY LAY IN REGAINING MY CONFIDENCE.
"BUT AT LONG LAST, I KNEW I WAS AS GOOD AS I HAD EVER BEEN. MAYBE BETTER.
"AND IT WAS TIME TO PROVE IT.
HEY, FELLAS...
...WANNA SEE A TRICK?

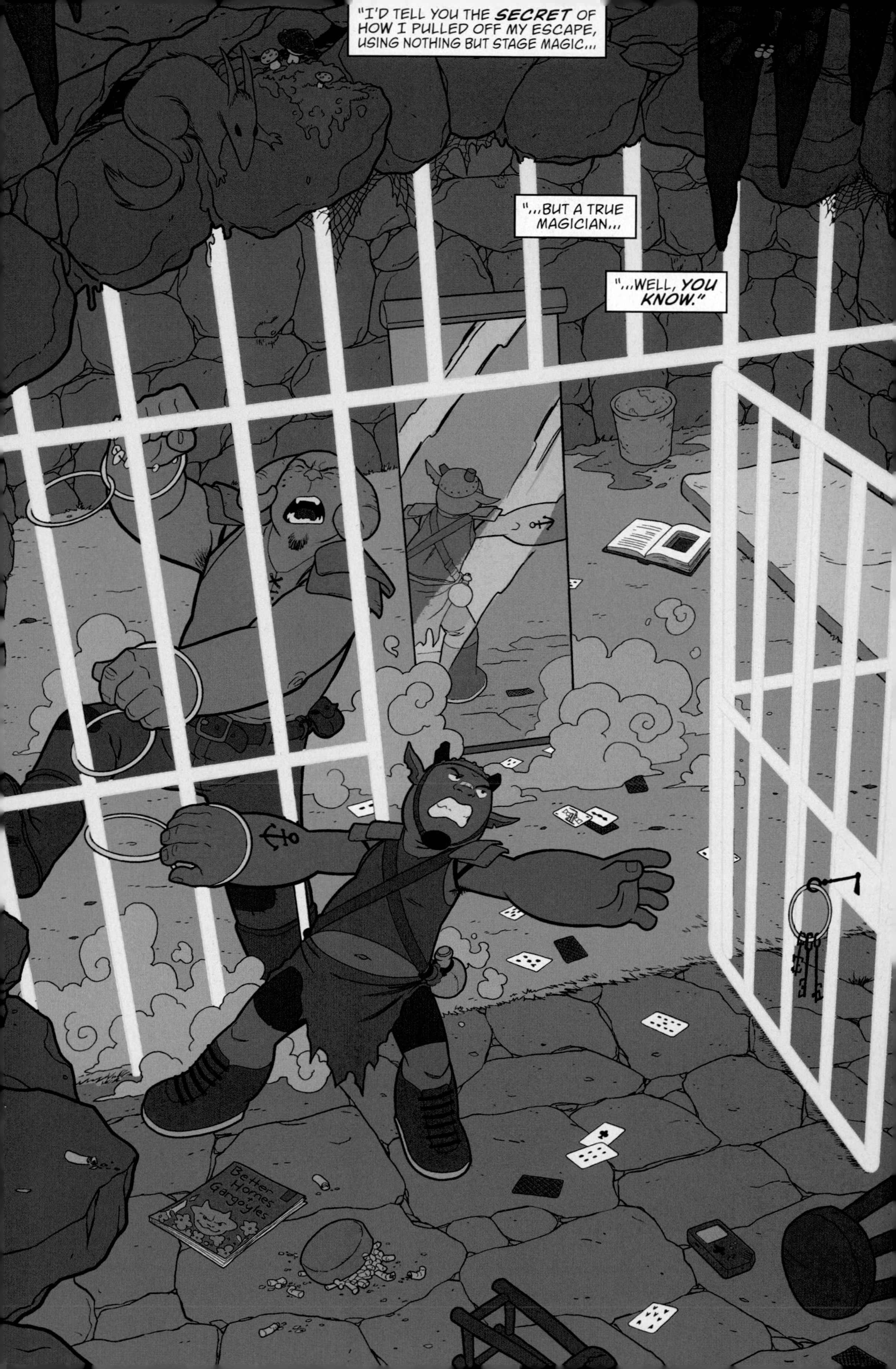
"I'D TELL YOU THE SECRET OF HOW I PULLED OFF MY ESCAPE, USING NOTHING BUT STAGE MAGIC...
"...BUT A TRUE MAGICIAN...
"...WELL, YOU KNOW."
Better Homes Gargoyles

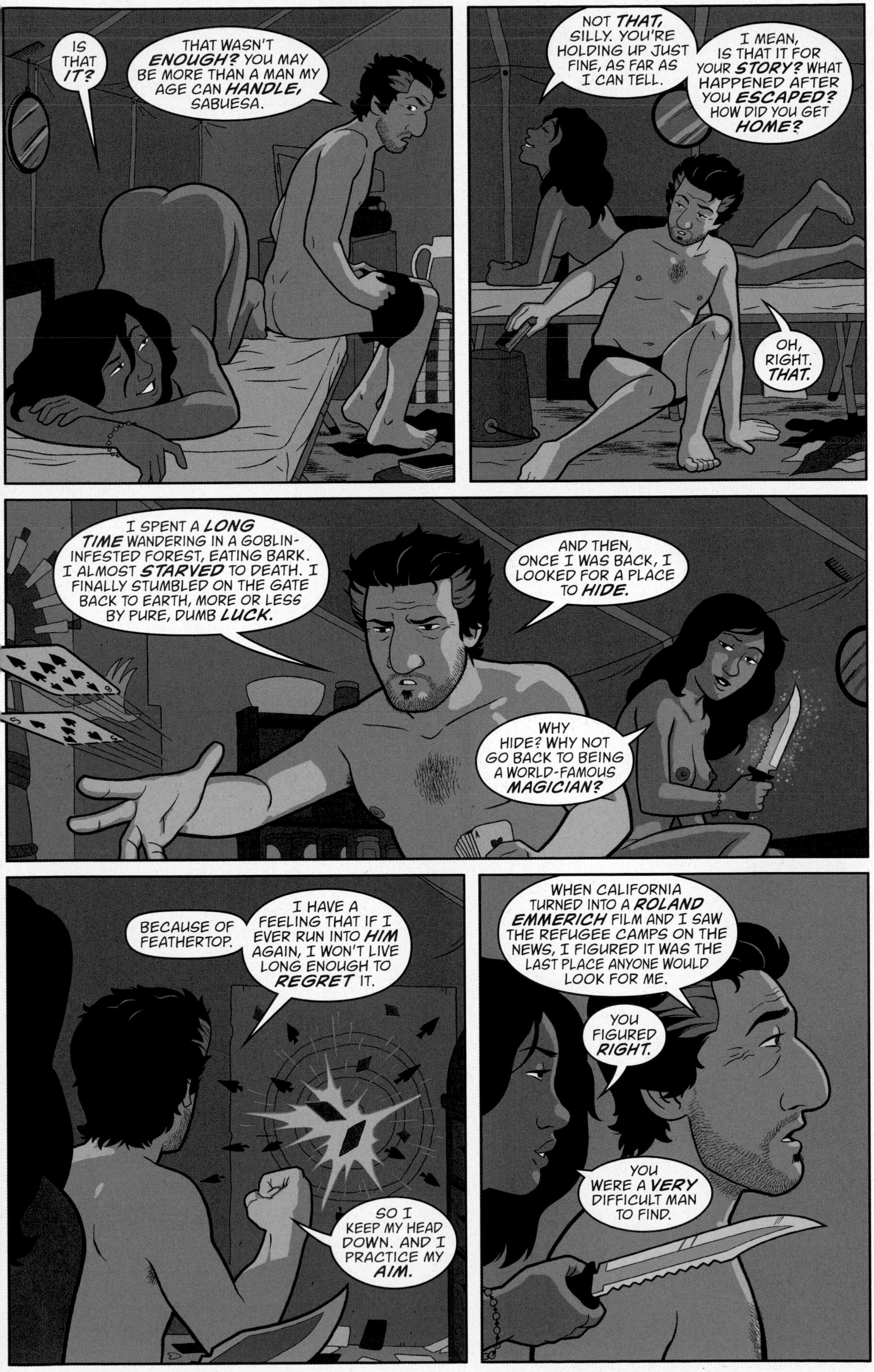
IS THAT IT?
THAT WASN'T ENOUGH? YOU MAY BE MORE THAN A MAN MY AGE CAN HANDLE, SABUESA.
NOT THAT, SILLY. YOU'RE HOLDING UP JUST FINE, AS FAR AS I CAN TELL.
I MEAN, IS THAT IT FOR YOUR STORY? WHAT HAPPENED AFTER YOU ESCAPED? HOW DID YOU GET HOME?
OH, RIGHT. THAT.
I SPENT A LONG TIME WANDERING IN A GOBLIN-INFESTED FOREST, EATING BARK. I ALMOST STARVED TO DEATH. I FINALLY STUMBLED ON THE GATE BACK TO EARTH, MORE OR LESS BY PURE, DUMB LUCK.
AND THEN, ONCE I WAS BACK, I LOOKED FOR A PLACE TO HIDE.
WHY HIDE? WHY NOT GO BACK TO BEING A WORLD-FAMOUS MAGICIAN?
BECAUSE OF FEATHERTOP.
I HAVE A FEELING THAT IF I EVER RUN INTO HIM AGAIN, I WON'T LIVE LONG ENOUGH TO REGRET IT.
SO I KEEP MY HEAD DOWN. AND I PRACTICE MY AIM.
WHEN CALIFORNIA TURNED INTO A ROLAND EMMERICH FILM AND I SAW THE REFUGEE CAMPS ON THE NEWS, I FIGURED IT WAS THE LAST PLACE ANYONE WOULD LOOK FOR ME.
YOU FIGURED RIGHT.
YOU WERE A VERY DIFFICULT MAN TO FIND.

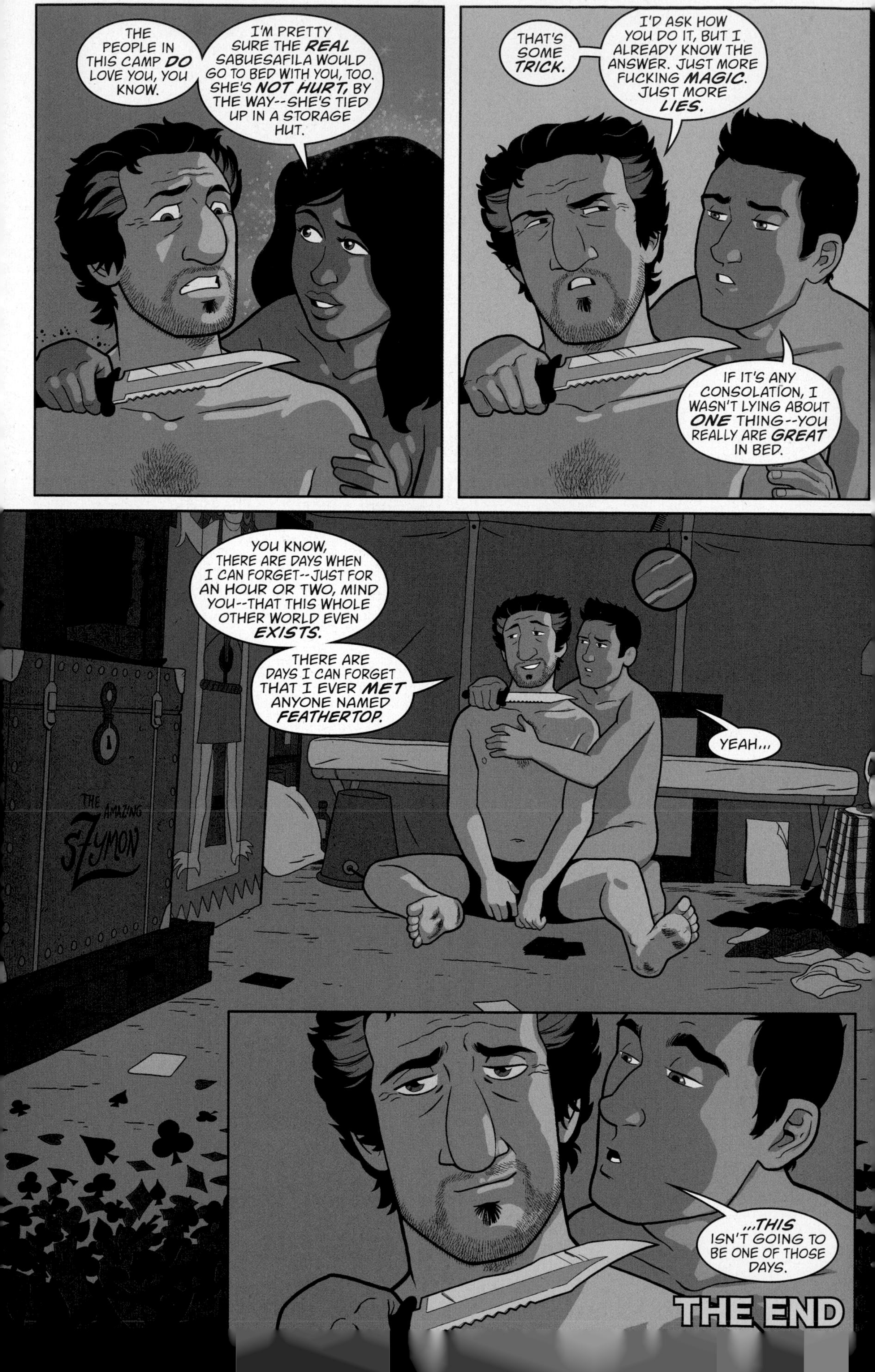
THE PEOPLE IN THIS CAMP DO LOVE YOU, YOU KNOW.
I'M PRETTY SURE THE REAL SABUESAFILA WOULD GO TO BED WITH YOU, TOO. SHE'S NOT HURT, BY THE WAY--SHE'S TIED UP IN A STORAGE HUT.
THAT'S SOME TRICK.
I'D ASK HOW YOU DO IT, BUT I ALREADY KNOW THE ANSWER. JUST MORE FUCKING MAGIC. JUST MORE LIES.
IF IT'S ANY CONSOLATION, I WASN'T LYING ABOUT ONE THING--YOU REALLY ARE GREAT IN BED.
YOU KNOW, THERE ARE DAYS WHEN I CAN FORGET--JUST FOR AN HOUR OR TWO, MIND YOU--THAT THIS WHOLE OTHER WORLD EVEN EXISTS.
THERE ARE DAYS I CAN FORGET THAT I EVER MET ANYONE NAMED FEATHERTOP.
YEAH...
THE AMAZING SZYMON
...THIS ISN'T GOING TO BE ONE OF THOSE DAYS.
THE END

COVER GALLERY

art by
TULA LOTAY

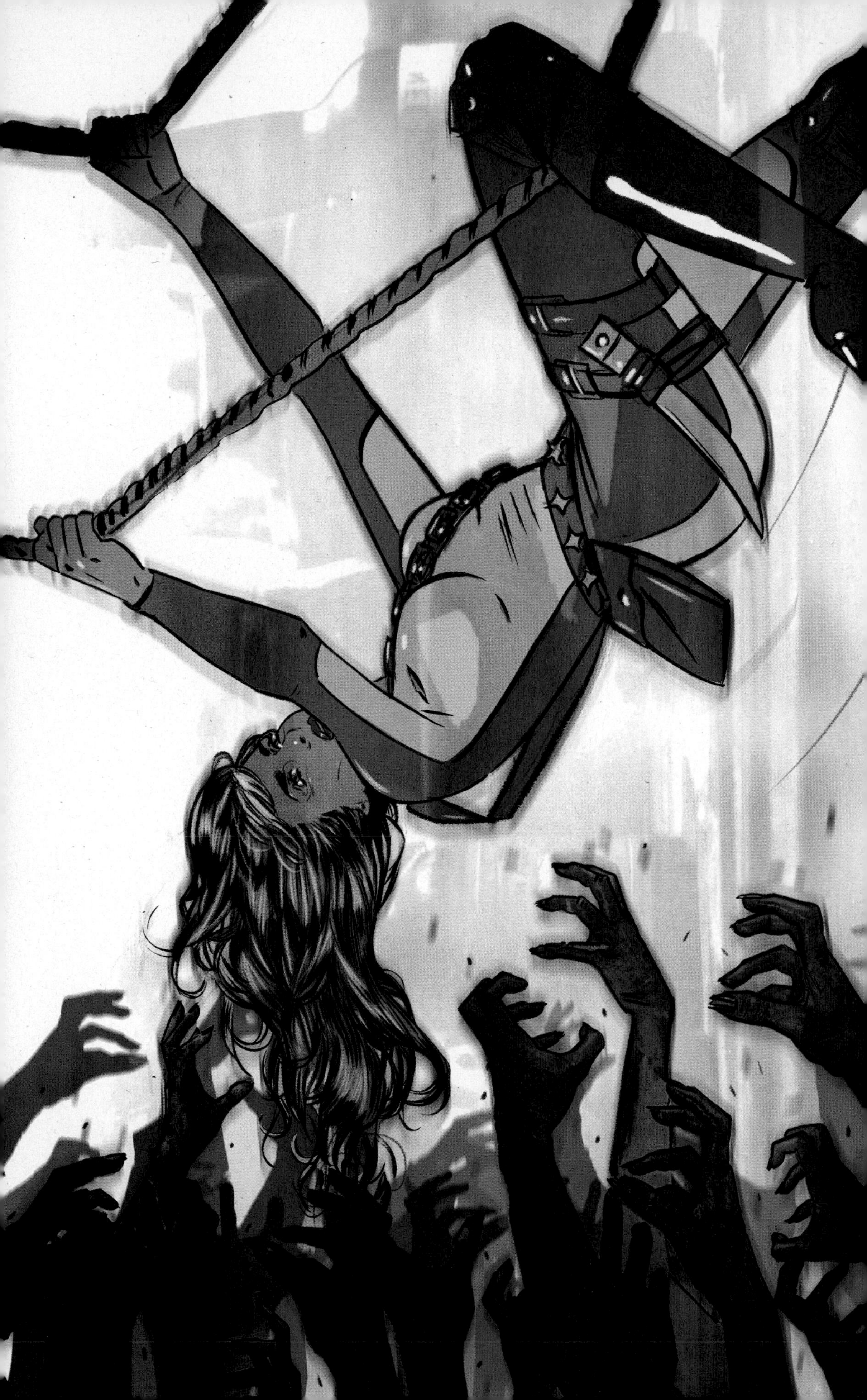

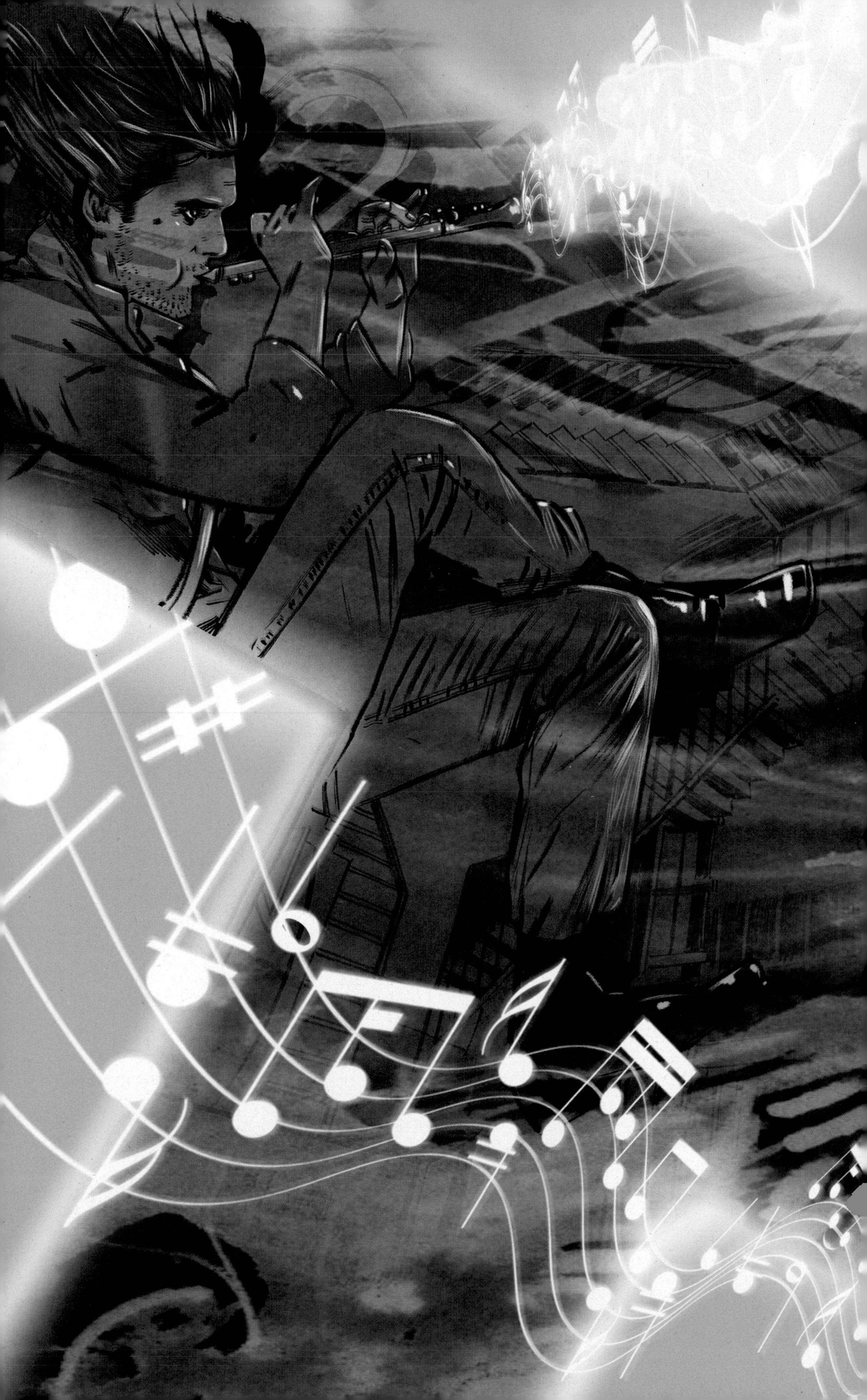

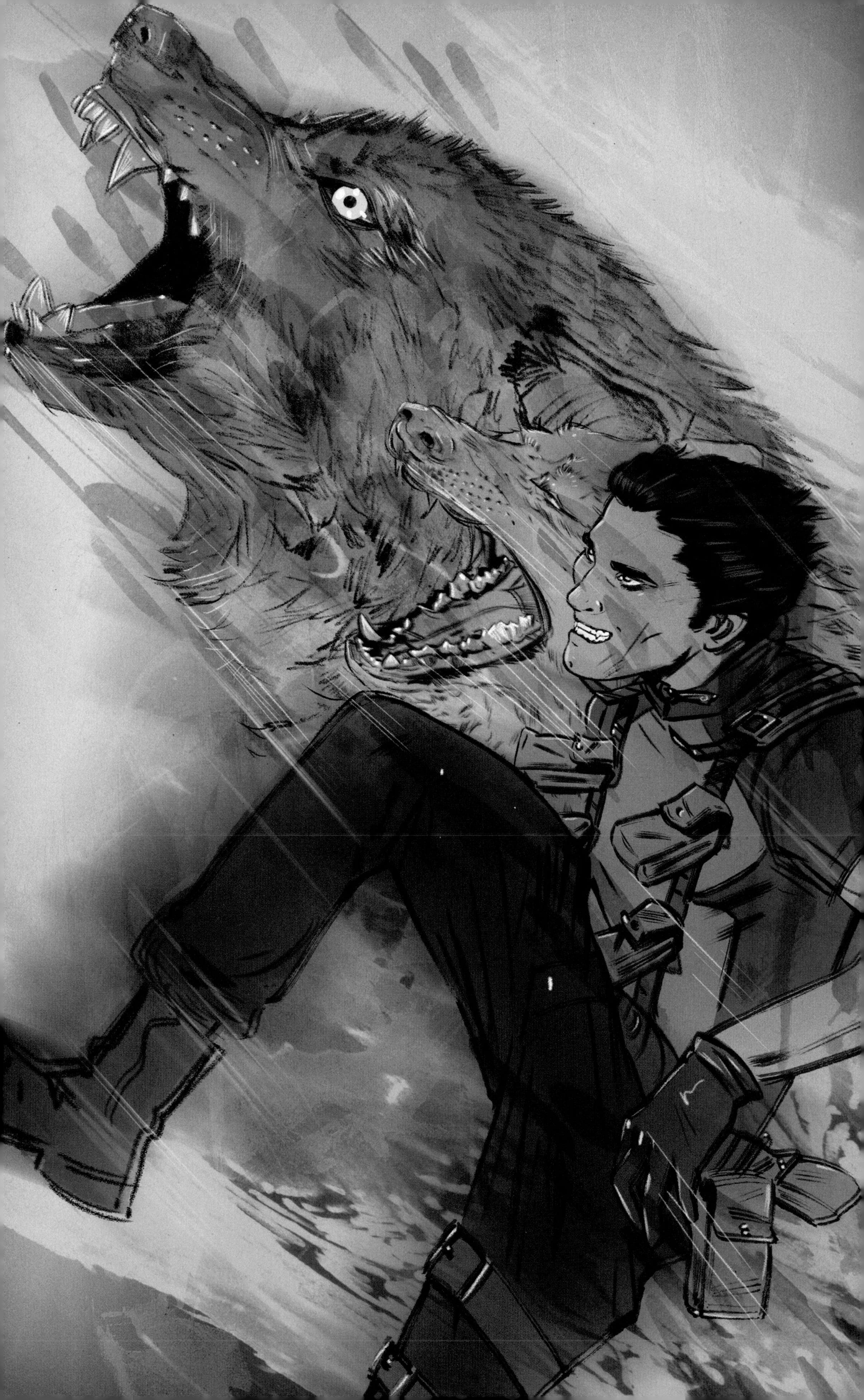

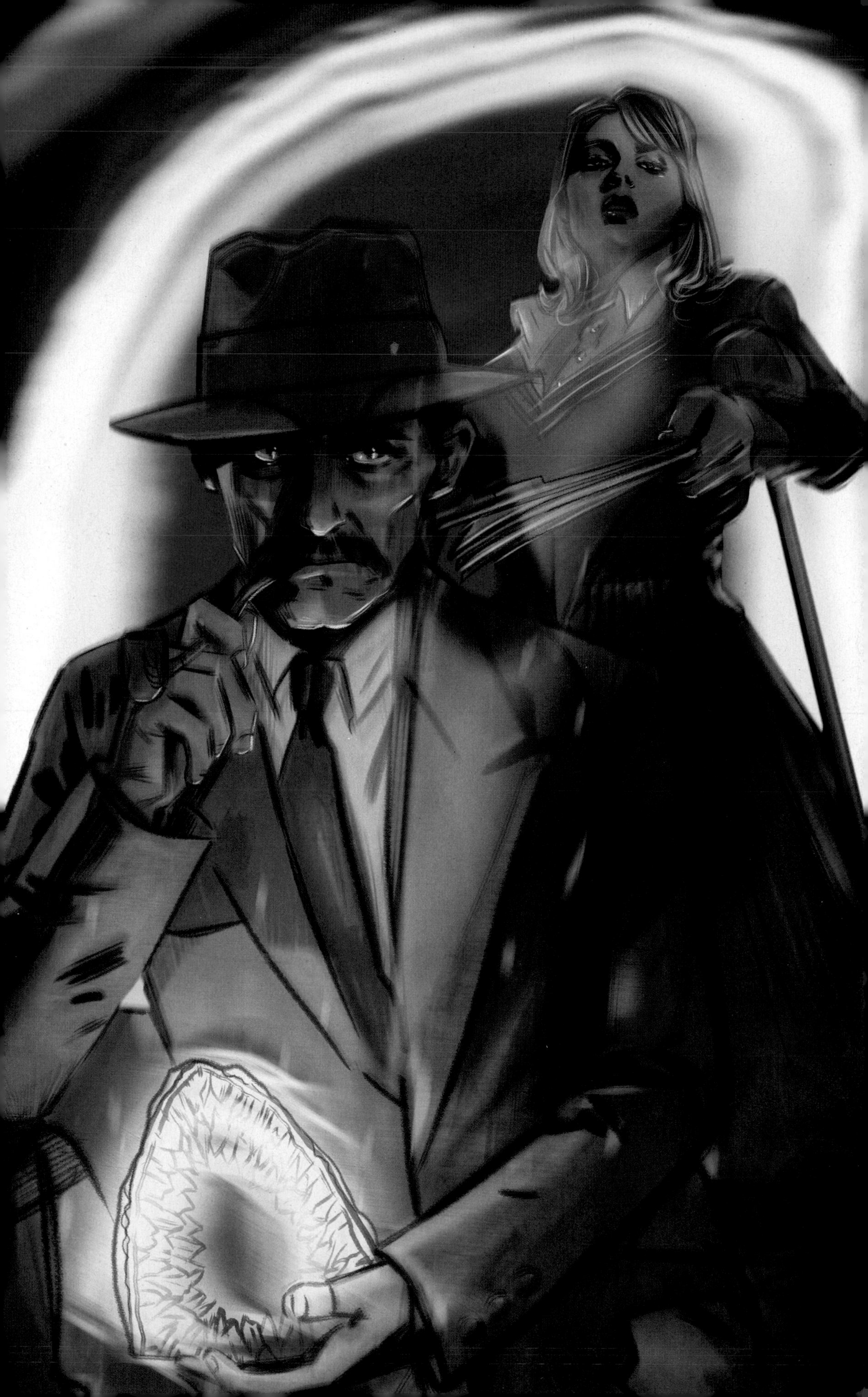

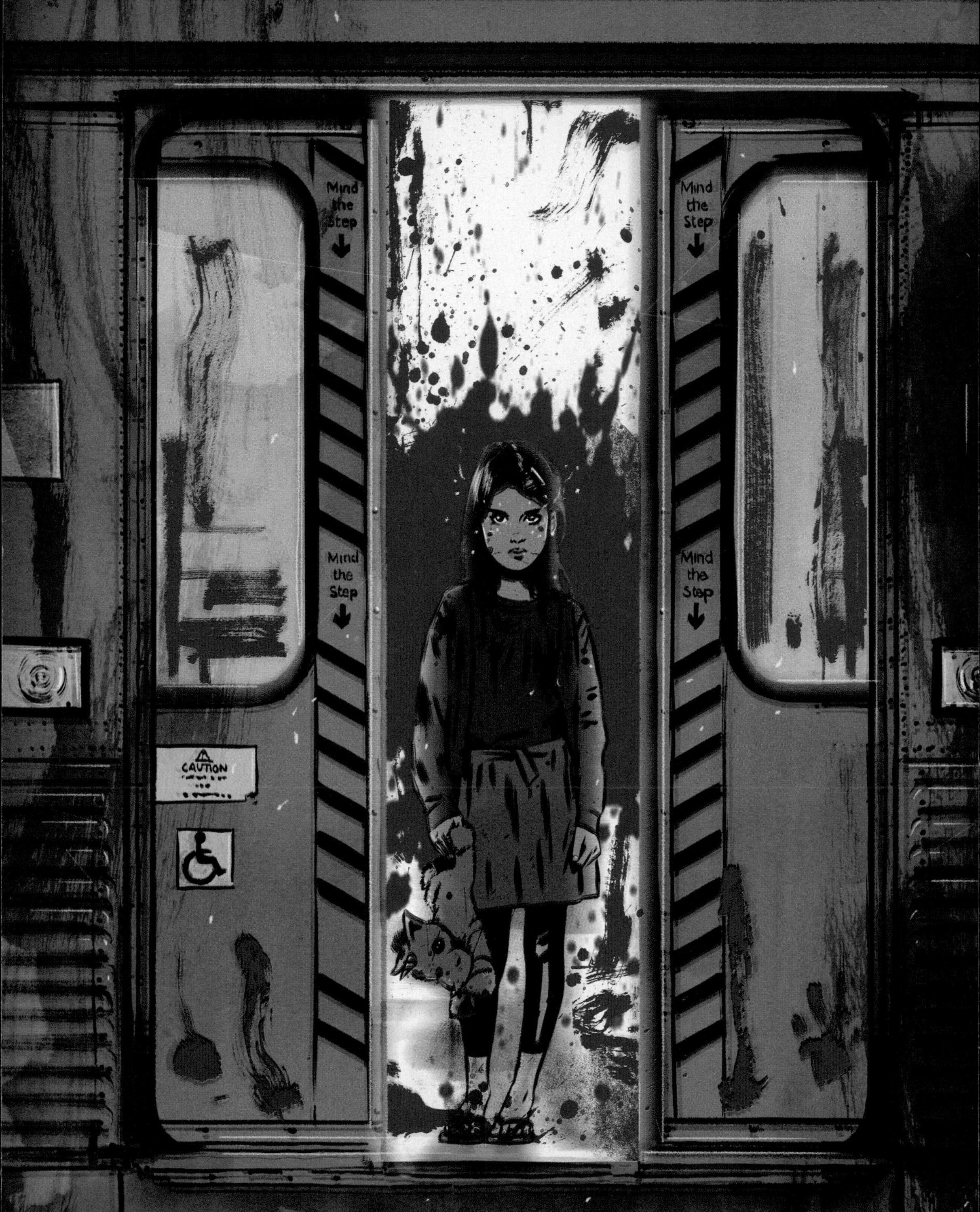
Mind the Step
Mind the Step
Mind the Step
Mind the Step
CAUTION

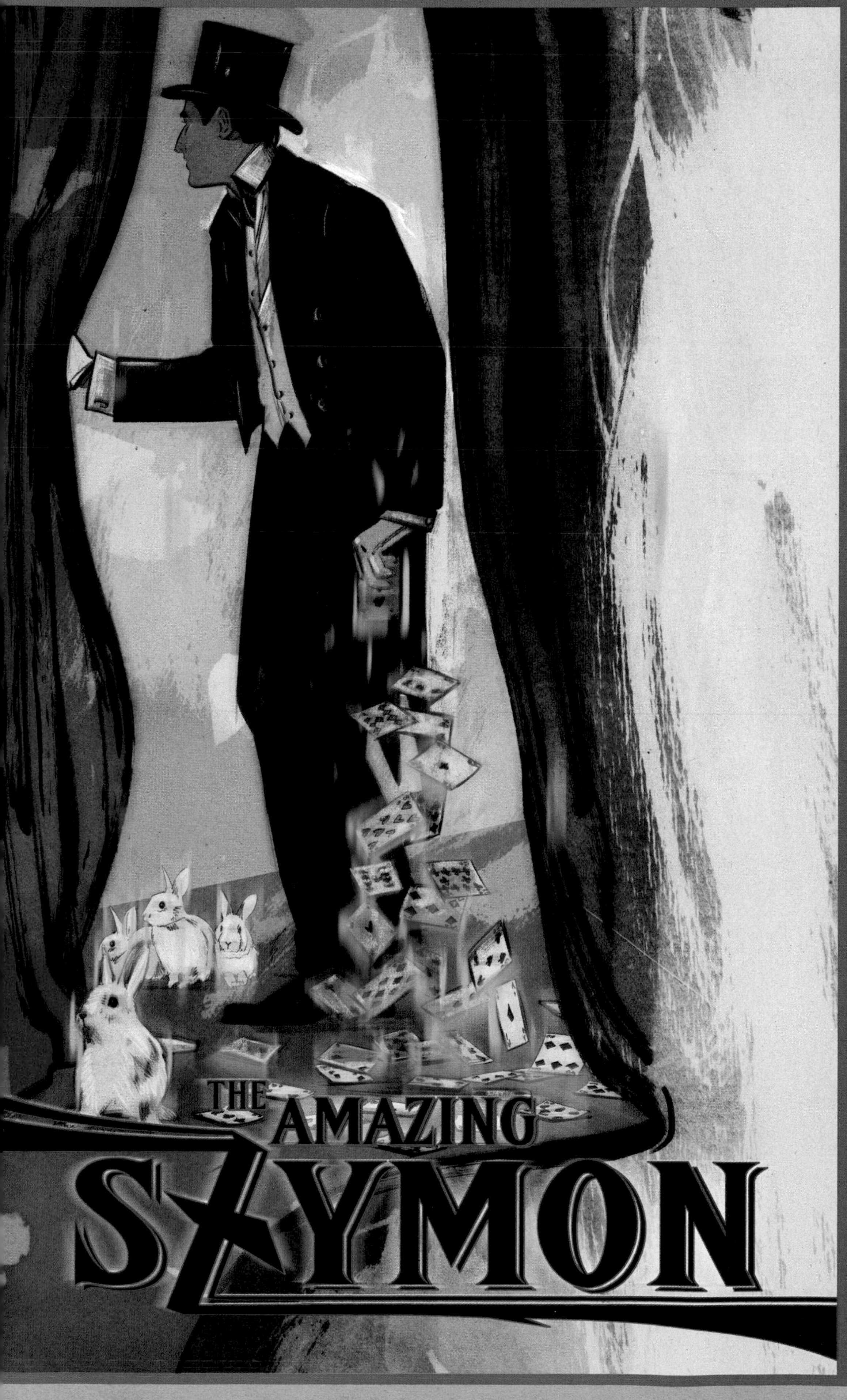
THE AMAZING
SZYMON

"FABLES is an excellent series in the tradition of SANDMAN, one that rewards careful attention and loyalty."
—PUBLISHERS WEEKLY

"[A] wonderfully twisted concept...features fairy tale characters banished to the noirish world of present-day New York."
—WASHINGTON POST

"Great fun." —BOOKLIST

READ THE ENTIRE SERIES!

FABLES VOL. 2:
ANIMAL FARM

FABLES VOL. 3:
STORYBOOK LOVE

FABLES VOL. 4:
MARCH OF THE
WOODEN SOLDIERS

FABLES VOL. 5:
THE MEAN SEASONS

FABLES VOL. 6:
HOMELANDS

FABLES VOL. 7:
ARABIAN NIGHTS
(AND DAYS)

FABLES VOL. 8:
WOLVES

FABLES VOL. 9:
SONS OF EMPIRE

FABLES VOL. 10:
THE GOOD PRINCE

FABLES VOL. 11:
WAR AND PIECES

FABLES VOL. 12:
THE DARK AGES

FABLES VOL. 13: THE
GREAT FABLES CROSS-
OVER

FABLES VOL. 14:
WITCHES

FABLES VOL. 15:
ROSE RED

FABLES VOL. 16:
SUPER TEAM

FABLES VOL. 17:
INHERIT THE WIND

FABLES VOL. 18:
CUBS IN TOYLAND

FABLES VOL. 19:
SNOW WHITE

FABLES: 1001 NIGHTS
OF SNOWFALL

FABLES: WEREWOLVES
OF THE HEARTLAND

PETER & MAX: A
FABLES NOVEL

THE FABLES
ENCYCLOPEDIA

BILL WILLINGHAM
FABLES VOL. 1: LEGENDS IN EXILE

THE #1 NEW YORK TIMES BEST-SELLING SERIES

FABLES
Legends in Exile

"A top-notch fantasy comic that is on a par with SANDMAN."
— *Variety*

DIRECTOR

BULLFINCH STREET

Bill Willingham
Lan Medina
Steve Leialoha
Craig Hamilton